DATE DUE

GAYLORD	PRINTED IN U.S.A.

ZAPOTEC RENAISSANCE

HOWARD CAMPBELL

Zapotec Renaissance

ETHNIC POLITICS

AND CULTURAL REVIVALISM

IN SOUTHERN MEXICO

University of New Mexico · *Albuquerque*

Library of Congress Cataloging-in-Publication Data

Campbell, Howard, 1957–
    Zapotec renaissance : ethnic politics and cultural revivalism in southern
Mexico / Howard Campbell. — 1st ed.
        p.   cm.
    Includes bibliographical references and index.
    Contents: ch. 1. Roots of Isthmus Zapotec ethnic politics, 1350–1750 — ch.
2. The emergence of Juchiteco resistance and rebellion, 1750–1911 — ch. 3.
Capitalist transitions and Isthmus Zapotec society, 1911–1993 — ch. 4.
Isthmus Zapotec intellectuals in the twentieth century: the politics of culture
in Juchitán, 1900–1970 — ch. 5. From caciquismo to grassroots ethnic
populism: the emergence of COCEI, 1964–1981 — ch. 6. ¡Viva Juchitán
libre!: the "people's government," impeachment, and COCEI's return to
power, 1981–1993 — ch. 7. Isthmus intellectuals, Zapotec history and culture,
and COCEI's ethnic ideology — ch. 8. Conclusions.
    ISBN 0–8263–1537–2
    1. Zapotec Indians—Politics and government.   2. Coalición Obrera
Campesina Estudiantil del Istmo (Mexico)   3. Zapotec Indians—Ethnic
identity.   4. Juchitán (Mexico)—Politics and government.
    I. Title.
    F1221.Z3C36   1994
    972'.74—dc20   93–46953
                                                                                          CIP

© 1994 by the University of New Mexico Press.
All rights reserved.
FIRST EDITION

Designed by Stephanie Jurs

For Obdulia, Ruth, and Howard

Contents

Preface

When I arrived in Juchitán, Oaxaca, from Mexico City in the summer of 1981, I noticed several things that were different from the Mexican capital. As I proceeded from the cool highlands to the tropical, lowland Isthmus of Tehuantepec, I also moved from the center of the country to an indigenous community with a distinct regional culture and local political base. Although drained by the steamy Isthmus heat, I spotted the sign over the entrance to Juchitán proclaiming *"Sicarú Guyé"* ("Have a good trip" in the Zapotec language). I also noted the anti-government political graffiti and posters plastered over walls and fences.

Walking downtown, I was engulfed by noisy women vendors dressed in brightly embroidered velvet blouses and long, flowing skirts. The market women harangued the crowds of people who filled the streets around Juchitán City Hall with offers to buy their hammocks and dry tortillas (*totopos*). Looking upward I saw a large red flag, imprinted with a hammer and sickle and the initials COCEI,[1] flying over the building. As I made my way past the stalls of merchants, I realized that most people were speaking a tonal language instead of Spanish. Eventually I learned that I had entered the territory of a radical Zapotec political movement whose "People's Government" then ruled Juchitán.

After several more trips to the Isthmus of Tehuantepec, I decided to do anthropological research on Zapotec political and cultural movements. I conducted fieldwork in the region in 1987 and 1988 and finished my dissertation in 1990. This work and frequent short research trips after my main period of fieldwork are the foundation for the present study.

As I quickly discovered, the people of Juchitán (known as Juchitecos) are

intensely proud of their culture and passionate about local politics. Juchitecos also have a great love for their home region, the Isthmus of Tehuantepec. The Oaxacan section of the Isthmus[2] is located in southeastern
Mexico, bordering the states of Chiapas and Veracruz. Unlike much of
Oaxaca, which is mountainous and rugged, the Isthmus is a flat, broad,
coastal plain adjacent to the Pacific Ocean. Since the Isthmus is barely
above sea level, the Sierra Atravesada mountain range that surrounds it,
though relatively modest in elevation, nevertheless towers impressively
over the plain. The approximate area of the Isthmus region is 3,000 sq km
(Binford 1983:82), and the largest cities are Juchitán, Tehuantepec, and
Salina Cruz.

Until the turn of the twentieth century the Isthmus was isolated to some
degree from the rest of Mexico. With the advent of railroads and highways,
however, transportation and communication to the area from central and
southern Mexico became fairly unproblematic. Despite its recent connections to other Mexican regions, the Isthmus retains its physical and cultural
distinctiveness, and the area remains a land of environmental and social
extremes. Miguel Covarrubias (1946:xxii), the great Mexican painter and
anthropologist, once described these extremes in his characteristic romantic style:

> For many years I have visited the Isthmus of Tehuantepec because
> I was attracted by its violent contrasts—its arid brush, its jungles that
> seemed lifted from a Rousseau canvas; the Oriental color of its mar-
> kets, where chattering Indian women, dressed like tropical birds, speak
> tonal languages reminiscent of China; the majestic bearing and classic
> elegance of the Tehuantepec women walking to market in stately
> grace with enormous loads of fruit and flowers on their heads, or
> dancing the latest "swing" tunes, barefoot but dressed in magnificent
> silks and wearing gold-coin necklaces worth hundreds of dollars.

Stifling hot and humid for half the year, during the dry winter months
(November to April) ferocious winds whip across the Isthmus lowlands,
cooling the air but damaging crops and filling up houses with grit. Lack of
rainfall is also a perennial problem, although occasionally violent storms
wrack the region, flooding poor neighborhoods along the banks of the
Tehuantepec and Perros rivers. More commonly, the summer rains are
sufficient to temporarily brighten up the area's brown, thorny, xerophytic
brush and transform its often desert-like appearance into the *trópico, cálido,
y bello* (tropical, hot, and beautiful) panorama extolled by Isthmus song-

writers. Thus, depending on the season, the region may look arid, gray, and dusty, or moist, green, and luxuriant.

Juchitán, home of COCEI, is a former peasant village that has become a small city without losing the ambience and ethos of rural Zapotec life. Juchitán's current population is about 80,000, of which approximately 80 percent are Zapotecs. The city sprawls out from all sides of the stately City Hall building, which is Juchitán's central landmark and hub of activity. Directly in front of City Hall is a small plaza and large park filled with benches, a kiosk, and palm trees. This area serves as a main locale for casual socializing and is the site of COCEI political demonstrations. At the rear of City Hall is the market, which also spreads out into all adjacent streets, and where hundreds of Zapotec women sell vegetables, tropical fruits, and fish from wooden stalls or simply a spot on the ground. Surrounding the market and City Hall are scores of retail businesses, run primarily by the Zapotec elite, but with some mestizos and other non-Zapotec residents of Juchitán.

Downtown Juchitán is populated by many of the old, rich Zapotec families who now live in huge concrete-and-brick houses. To the south of City Hall lies the Seventh Ward (La Séptima)—the largest and perhaps poorest of Juchitán's neighborhoods, a COCEI stronghold, and a place where Zapotec is the primary language (unlike downtown, where only Spanish is spoken by many store owners and office workers). To the west of City Hall, past the park, San Vicente Church, and the local cultural center, and crossing the Perros River, which runs through town, lies Cheguigo, a dispersed, village-like barrio. This area is composed mostly of pro-COCEI Zapotec peasants and workers. To the north of City Hall, in addition to several working-class and middle-class neighborhoods, are the railroad tracks and the Pan American Highway. Hotels, repair shops, hardware stores, restaurants, bus and gas stations, and other businesses cluster along the highway and the main streets into downtown.

On the northern side of the highway, at a short distance from the main entrance to Juchitán, is a relatively new upper-class subdivision (La Riviera), which looks like suburban Mexico City transplanted to the Isthmus. This is in stark contrast to the two COCEI, land-invasion communities (Colonia Rodrigo Carrasco and Colonia Gustavo Pineda), which resemble shantytowns, that line the Pan American Highway. The highway cuts through the heart of Isthmus agricultural land, and the fields are only a short walk or oxcart ride from town.

Doing research in Juchitán was a rare pleasure because of the friendship and camaraderie extended to me by COCEI leaders and activists and the talented artists, writers, and musicians of the Cultural Center (La Casa de la Cultura). In particular, I want to thank COCEI *compañeros* Oscar Cruz, Daniel López Nelio, Héctor Sánchez, and Polín de Gyves, who shared their knowledge of local politics and allowed me to study sensitive topics. Macario Matus, former director of the Casa de la Cultura, was unflinchingly generous and an endless source of information and good jokes. I owe special thanks to the many Zapotec intellectuals and activists who enlightened me about local history and culture: Víctor de la Cruz, Vicente Marcial, Polo de Gyves Pineda, Oscar Martínez, Manuel López Mateos, Mario López, Heber Rasgado, Felipe Martínez, Omar Luis, Manuel Matus, Julio Bustillo, Enedino Jiménez, Sabino López, Delfino Marcial, Jorge Magariño, Miguel Angel Toledo, Elí Bartolo, Feliciano Marín, Mariano Santana, César Pineda, Javier Charis, Tarú, and César Augusto Carrasco. I also want to thank the following people for their hospitality and support: Dolores Pineda, Maura Matus, Geoff and Edith Hartney, and Peter Hisscock.

In Oaxaca City, a number of fine scholars helped me with my research. They include John Paddock, Isidoro Yescas, Héctor Martínez, Lupe Musalem, Leticia Reina, and Manuel Esparza. While in Mexico City, I enjoyed the gracious assistance of Roger Bartra, Guido Munch, Marie Odile, and Sergio Zermeño.

The members of my thesis committee at the University of Wisconsin deserve recognition for their cogent criticisms and constant backing. They are Frank Salomon, Florencia Mallon, Gary Feinman, Steve Stern, and Herb Lewis. I will never forget Frank Salomon's 11 single-spaced pages of comments on the first draft of my dissertation. Frank's incisive critique transformed my work. I also thank Florencia Mallon for the strong training she gave me in Latin American history and society.

Alejandro Lugo, Pablo Vila, John Peterson, Bill Lockhart, Margaret Schellenberg, and David Stemper read portions of my book manuscript and made helpful suggestions. Francie Chassen and Cheryl Martin, fine historians of Mexico, gave me particularly thorough comments on my writing. Many thanks also to Henry Selby and Ronald Spores for their excellent reviews of the manuscript.

My greatest debt is to four individuals who stood by me from the beginning. My parents, Ruth and Howard Campbell, instilled in me the importance of curiosity and education. Leigh Binford taught me what anthropology was really about and kept me amused with his humor and insight into life in the Isthmus. Obdulia Ruiz Campbell, my spouse, is responsible for much of what I know about Zapotec people, and her love made my research possible.

Finally, I would like to express my gratitude to the following organizations that provided financial support: the University of Wisconsin Graduate School, the Inter-American Foundation, the Organization of American States, the Center for Inter-American and Border Studies of the University of Texas at El Paso, and the National Endowment for the Humanities.

Introduction

Traditions which appear or claim to be old are often quite recent in origin and sometimes invented . . . all invented traditions, so far as possible, use history as a legitimator of action and cement of group cohesion.

ERIC HOBSBAWM

Because discourse in global power systems is elaborated vis-à-vis, a sense of difference or distinctness can never be located solely in the continuity of a culture or tradition. Identity is conjunctural, not essential. . . . If authenticity is relational, there can be no essence except as a political, cultural invention, a local tactic.

JAMES CLIFFORD

This is a book about a group of people who defy many of our stereotypes about Mexican Indians. Indians, as folklore and tourist guides tell us, are picturesque individuals who are set in their ways, exotic, poor, and down-trodden. Anthropologists, while attacking these stereotypes, have replaced them with a new set of assumptions or representations. Indians are exploited peasants, oppressed proletarians, or, from another standpoint, the bearers of rich cultural traditions and languages, but the victims of discrimination by mestizos and bureaucrats.[1] From whatever perspective, indigenous people are invariably viewed as the losers in the social struggle. Even the trendy resistance literature[2] often emphasizes the weakness of native people, who valiantly battle against their oppression, using Scott's "weapons of the weak" (1985) or producing a "vision of the vanquished" (Wachtel 1977). The bottom line is that Indians lose, or, at best, fight back against steep odds.

The Zapotecs of the Isthmus of Tehuantepec, and especially the town of Juchitán, are intensely proud of their history, control local political offices, run most of the local commerce, and have a lively cultural movement that produces fine works of poetry, painting, and music. Moreover, women in Zapotec society are said (by outsiders and local people) to enjoy equality with men, and homosexuality is accepted to an unusual degree.[3] Zapotec people of Juchitán encapsulate their feelings about their positive social status and strong ethnic identity in a millenarian vision of history, which emphasizes military and political victories over the Aztecs, Spanish, French, and mestizo Mexicans. This book is about that history—both past and present—and the way it is remembered, drawn upon, and created by contemporary Zapotec intellectuals and politicians.

Culture and Politics in Juchitán

Juchitán achieved notoriety in Mexico (and, to a degree, internationally) in 1981 when the Zapotec political movement COCEI won Juchitán municipal elections. This made it the first city to be controlled by the political left in Mexico since the Revolution. In 1983 the Mexican government threw COCEI out of office and imprisoned many of its members, prompting the publication of an Amnesty International report (1986) on human rights abuses in the Isthmus. During this time, Juchitán became a cause célèbre of the national left-wing and a key symbol of Indian peasant resistance in modern Mexico for urban intellectuals. Juchitán also became well known as the center of one of Latin America's most active indigenous cultural movements. Additionally, it gained repute as the birthplace of the famous painter Francisco Toledo and as the source of an avant-garde magazine, *Guchachi' Reza*. Juchitán again became front-page news in 1989 and 1992 when COCEI won new municipal elections there, and in 1990 when President Salinas visited the community.

The colorful and controversial events occurring in Juchitán since 1981 have drawn numerous social scientists, journalists, and other curious onlookers to the Isthmus. These observers have attempted to unravel the complex circumstances leading to COCEI's electoral victories and defeats, and to capture the "exotic" flavor of this "Indian town" where (supposedly) women dominate men, people eat iguanas, drunken fiestas never cease, and a kind of primitive communism prevails. Stereotypes and facile conclusions have been bandied about, but serious research into the history and ethnography of Juchitán, COCEI, and the Isthmus has been less common.[4] A review of some of the more-common fallacies about COCEI is instructive. At various times, COCEI has been described as a band of Cuba-inspired totalitarian Communists, a Trotskyist organization whose appeals to ethnicity are a posture, a conjunctural political movement unrelated to Isthmus Zapotec history, and a "united front" of Zapotecs struggling against mestizo outsiders.[5] Although some of these views provide insights into COCEI, none of them combines the necessary elements (historical research, contemporary fieldwork, and an analysis sensitive to class, gender, and ethnicity) that can help us come to grips with the complexities of political and cultural life in Juchitán.

Analyzing Ethnic Politics, Tradition, and Cultural Invention

Given the current skepticism about cultural purity, searches for origins, and "tradition," what should we make of COCEI's claim that it is the lineal descendant of Zapotec struggles for independence dating back hundreds of years? Is COCEI's appeal to ethnic roots really a mobilization strategy for obtaining resources? Or is it an ideological mask for a class-based political program? What theoretical trends in anthropology might help us understand these issues?

One approach, a Marxist perspective represented most eloquently in Oaxacan studies by Cook (1982), emphasizes the class nature of rural politics and downplays ethnicity. From this standpoint, struggles like that of COCEI are primarily a result of class-oriented economic conflicts. Another research agenda that is currently popular, generally referred to as "New Social Movements" research, would stress the newness of current Zapotec political movements. New social movements are the political manifestation of recently formed, non-class forces in society which accrete the multiple and fragmented subjectivities of new actors in the political arena (Laclau and Mouffe 1985; Eckstein 1989; Escobar and Alvarez 1992). A third line of argument sees claims of cultural authenticity and historical continuity as constructive fictions, as forms of indigenous essentialism (Clifford 1988; Linnekin 1991; Warren 1992). This perspective, influenced by or linked to postmodern anthropology, focuses on the ways contemporary political movements represent cultural differences.

All of these approaches are an improvement over the empiricist ethnic populism[6] that has pervaded Oaxaca studies historically (e.g., Bartolomé and Barabas 1986; Diskin 1986; Royce 1975). By themselves, however, none of these approaches can adequately account for what is happening in Juchitán. The Marxist approach of Cook, primarily based on field research in the Oaxaca Valley, not the Isthmus region, too easily dismisses ethnic identity.[7] The intensity of Juchiteco cultural identity and ethnically-based political demands cannot be understood by class analysis alone. Likewise, the New Social Movements literature places too much emphasis on the "newness" of socio-political phenomena. But how can that help us understand communities that are at least 600 years old, and that claim a united (not fragmented) identity and a continuity with those 600 years of life?

Yet, the approach that insists on "invention" and" essentialism" has its weaknesses, also. Despite anthropological claims about sharing ethnographic authority and exposing the researcher's own limitations, the invention/essentialist approach denies the value of indigenous interpretations and insists on the superior authority of anthropological analysis (cf. Hanson 1991, Warren 1992, Jackson 1989). With the labels of invention and essentialism, the political and cultural movements of native people and their views of their own history can be conveniently tamed. Local intellectuals and activists deserve more than to be reduced to essentializers or inventors of tradition (Campbell 1993).

The alternative approach adopted here is derived from the work of William Roseberry. Unlike Cook, Roseberry gives greater room for culture in his political economic analysis. For Roseberry, culture cannot be removed from the analysis of productive processes because culture is itself a productive process (1989). Culture both constitutes political relations and is constituted by politics. Different from the New Social Movements literature, with its focus on emergence and the new, Roseberry argues for intense scrutiny of the long duration of history. If such movements really are new, their newness should be analyzed in terms of deeply-rooted social processes in which both class and non-class elements are mutually determining. Furthermore, the invention/essentialist approach, while illuminating the ambiguous origins of customs and traditions, may not give a full account of the histories of cultural production and political struggle within which such "inventions" are inserted.

Roseberry's work enjoins us to understand the formation of individuals and groups within historical processes of uneven development and structures of unequal power. From this perspective, cultural meanings and knowledge are held differentially, and both shape and are shaped by historically-rooted political processes. Thus, there is little utility in evaluating ethnic movements that invoke tradition and cultural authenticity (such as COCEI) as "new" or "old," "genuine" or "spurious," unless such movements are analyzed within long-term historical developments. "Inventions" of tradition and culture are best understood as part of historical processes of cultural production in which groups generate meaning in situations of unequal power (Roseberry 1989:14). Viewing "tradition," "invention," and ethnic politics as a processual phenomenon provides a more satisfactory analysis than the ahistorical postmodernism of the New Social

Movements literature or the dichotomous thinking associated with invention/essentialist analyses.[8]

The argument developed here is that the tensions between different groups within Isthmus Zapotec society, and their ongoing choices between collaboration and resistance to non-Zapotecs, lead to the (re-)construction of Isthmus Zapotec ethnic identity and culture. From this standpoint, COCEI's cultural revival project is not simply a change in aesthetic styles, but is part of a historically-rooted process of Zapotec ethnic empowerment within Mexican class and ethnic-power structures. At the same time, COCEI's ethnic politics is not only a strategy for defense of the Juchiteco community against outsiders, but the effort of marginal groups within Juchitán to wrest power from local elites through claims to ethnic authenticity. COCEI's politicized cultural revival, then, is not an atavistic return to an ancient cultural tradition, but is a rethinking of the ethnic past and a creation of new cultural forms and meanings in the present situation of conflict and change.

While the strength of current Isthmus Zapotec ethnic identity was forged by political struggles from the colonial period into the twentieth century, COCEI emerged within the context of recent capitalist transformations in the Isthmus. Social and economic changes wrought by capitalist development radicalized the Isthmus peasantry, divided the Juchiteco community along class lines, and politicized an emerging group of Zapotec activists and intellectuals. This leftist intelligentsia conceptualized Isthmus history as a linear process of ethnic resistance culminating in COCEI.

The radical Zapotec intellectual group originated when a lower- and lower-middle class vanguard within the Juchiteco community became more attached to their "ethnic roots" through education and distancing from the community during the 1960s. After returning to Juchitán, the COCEI intellectuals created and embellished upon the histories, myths, symbols, and ideologies that now legitimize and inspire the movement. In so doing, COCEI leaders and intellectuals increased internal solidarity within their organization but precluded broader alliances to other indigenous groups and potential class allies among the mestizo Mexican community.

Chapter 1 examines how the Isthmus Zapotec ethnic group developed historically in the conflictive, multiethnic environment of pre-Hispanic Oaxaca and assesses the impact of colonialism on local society. Chapter 2 analyzes the decline of Tehuantepec and the emergence of Juchitán as a center of Zapotec ethnic resistance during the nineteenth and early twentieth centuries.

Chapter 3 looks at the profound effect twentieth century economic developments have had on Isthmus Zapotec society and how these developments created the conditions in the short-term for the emergence of COCEI. Chapter 4 examines the emergence of an elite Juchiteco intellectual movement in the first half of the twentieth century. Chapter 5 explores recent Juchitán political history, focusing especially on COCEI's rise to power and the radicalization of a new generation of Zapotec intellectuals.

In Chapter 6 COCEI politics and cultural programs from 1981 to 1993 are described, with an emphasis on the movement's crowning achievement—the institution of a "People's Government." Chapter 7 analyzes COCEI's ethnic ideology. Chapter 8 summarizes the main themes, theoretical issues, and conclusions of the book.

ZAPOTEC RENAISSANCE

Roots of Isthmus Zapotec
Ethnic Politics, 1350–1750

Juchitán is a branch of the great tree which is the Zapotec race . . . and as such inherits rebelliousness and detests subjection. . . . That is, the Zapotec race has always been free. . . . The struggle of the COCEI has been congruent with the history of physical and intellectual battles of its predecessors. . . . The victory of the COCEI is the history of a people . . .
MACARIO MATUS 1981

These are the words of Macario Matus, a leftist Juchiteco poet and journalist. They speak of a glorious history of Zapotec rebellion, and the relevance of history to the contemporary COCEI political and cultural movement. But what does that history consist of, and how did it unfold? With whom have the Zapotec struggled, and why? Have they really remained free all these years?

This chapter examines the pre-Hispanic and colonial history of the Isthmus, focusing on the principal events that shaped Isthmus Zapotec ethnic identity and social structure. At the same time, there is a brief discussion of particular, selective aspects of that history, which have been appropriated and emphasized by contemporary Zapotec intellectuals such as Matus. It is this chapter's contention that the frequent political and military conflicts first between Isthmus Zapotecs and other Mesoamerican ethnic groups, and later between Zapotecs and Spaniards, instilled in the Zapotecs a strong sense of ethnic distinctiveness and a hostility towards non-Zapotecs.

Isthmus Zapotec responses to colonialism were not uniform, however. The native elite of Tehuantepec and nobility from other Isthmus towns played an ambivalent role. They initially collaborated with the Spanish colonists, promptly adopting Hispanic customs, but they led and participated in messianic revolts and clandestine religious activities for a brief

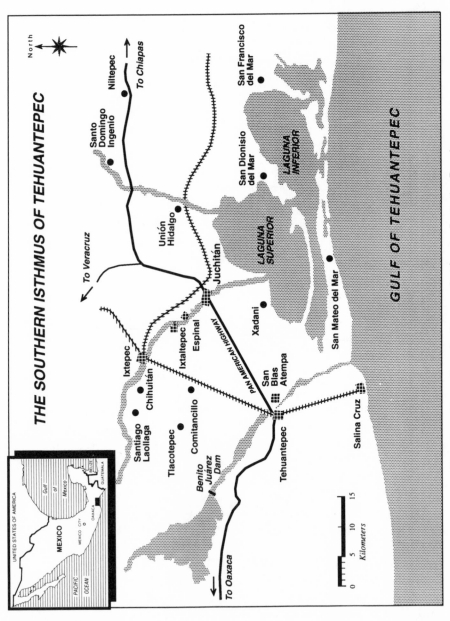

THE SOUTHERN ISTHMUS OF TEHUANTEPEC

North

To Chiapas

Niltepec

Santo
Domingo
Ingenio

San Francisco
del Mar

San Dionisio
del Mar

To Veracruz

LAGUNA
INFERIOR

Unión
Hidalgo

GULF OF TEHUANTEPEC

LAGUNA
SUPERIOR

Juchitán

Ixtepec

Ixtaltepec

Espinal

Xadani

San Mateo del Mar

PAN AMERICAN HIGHWAY

Chihuitán

San
Blas
Atempa

Santiago
Laollaga

Tlacotepec

Comitancillo

Salina Cruz

Benito
Juárez
Dam

Tehuantepec

To Oaxaca

0 5 10 15
Kilometers

UNITED STATES OF AMERICA

Gulf
of
Mexico

MEXICO

MEXICO CITY

OAXACA

BELIZE

GUATEMALA

PACIFIC
OCEAN

(Map, From *Zapotec Struggles*, Courtesy, Smithsonian Institution Press.)

4

period (1545–1563). But they also became the targets of rebellions by lower-class Zapotecs—who were consistently in the vanguard of revolt— as the colonial era continued. Thus, Spanish-Zapotec political conflicts, while strengthening the ethnic identity of the majority of the Isthmus Zapotec population, also served to isolate elite collaborators from the indigenous masses. Likewise, in the economic realm, upper-strata Zapotecs were better situated to take advantage of new economic opportunities under colonialism. Commoners, though, were coerced into working on the Marquesado haciendas and in other Spanish enterprises. Consequently, Spanish rule did not abolish divisions within the Zapotec community, but gave them new forms.

Zapotec Conquest of the Isthmus

According to Isthmus mythology, the ancient Zapotecs, known as *binni gula'sa'*,[1] either descended to earth from clouds in the form of beautiful birds, emerged from the roots of trees, or were born from large rocks or wild beasts (López Chiñas 1982:103–4; Burgoa [1674] 1934:1:412). Regarding the relevance of these myths to contemporary Zapotecs, an Isthmus writer rhetorically stated:

> Researchers may perhaps encounter the scientific truth of our origins, but we the *Binni Za* or Zapotec live, dream, and die bound to the poetic truth of our ancient mythology [López Chiñas 1982:104].

These comments were made by an urbane, expatriate Juchiteco intellectual who lived most of his life in Mexico City, and whose proximity to the everyday life of the Zapotec peasantry can therefore be questioned. They, nonetheless, are indicative of the importance of the *binni gula'sa'* (the Zapotec ancestors), and of a mythical view of their supernatural powers, in the consciousness of Zapotec people. There is still considerable folklore in Isthmus communities about *binni gula'sa'* and *binni guenda* (spirits similar to *nahuals*[2]), and the Zapotecs attribute the ceramic idols and other archaeological objects they find around their homes, in the fields, or along river beds to the *binni gula'sa'* (Chiñas 1983:10). They also consider themselves to be the descendants of the makers of these items (López Chiñas 1974:15). Thus, the COCEI's ideological connection between their current political movement and the "great Zapotec past" is a powerful rhetorical statement, since it appeals to existing notions of antiquity and an ancestor cult in Zapotec culture.

Archaeological findings show that the Zapotecs split off from the Mixtecs around 3700 B.C. (Marcus 1983a:6). For most of the pre-Columbian period the Isthmus was characterized by ethnic discontinuity and change rather than fixed settlements with considerable time-depth (Zeitlin 1978:21). The region was coveted by many different groups because of its economic resources (salt, fish, and good farm land) and its location as a crossroads of commercial and transport activity. By the fourteenth century, Huave and Zoque people had established themselves in the Isthmus. Although contemporary COCEI ideologists describe Zapotec-Huave interactions as harmonious, the Zapotecs have dominated relations with the Huave, Zoque, and other local indigenous groups since they conquered the Isthmus in late pre-Hispanic times.[3] This history is very relevant today because it restricts the Zapotec COCEI political movement from expanding into Huave, Mixe, and other non-Zapotec indigenous towns in the Isthmus.

Zapotec conquest of the region (ca. 1350) occurred during a conflictive era characterized by Marcus and Flannery (1983:217) as the "postclassic Balkanization of Oaxaca." Indigenous historical traditions and archaeological excavations indicate that by the mid-fourteenth century, Zapotecs from Highland Oaxaca (probably Zaachila and the Oaxaca Valley) had occupied the Isthmus, taking the best land, salt pans, and habitation sites from the Huave and Zoque (Burgoa [1674] 1934:2:328; Zeitlin 1989:33).[4] The Zapotec elite and their followers may have left the Highlands in response to pressure from the powerful Mixtecs. Zapotec expansion into the Isthmus also may have been a result of divisions within Zapotec society between groups of Highland Zapotecs and those who settled in Tehuantepec. In any case, by the time of the Spanish conquest, the emigré Zapotecs had established a regional power center in Tehuantepec and were receiving tribute from Highland Zapotecs as well as the other indigenous people of the Isthmus.

Zapotec movement into the Isthmus was prompted, at least in part, by conflict with rival Oaxacan ethnic groups, and was itself an act of expropriation of the land of the previous, non-Zapotec inhabitants of the area. This heightened the colonizing Zapotec group's sense of "otherness" vis-à-vis the peoples left behind in the Highlands as well as the new peoples encountered on the Isthmus coastal plain. Moreover, as recent arrivals to a new territory, the Isthmus Zapotecs may have held tightly to their cultural patterns in the face of the rival traditions, languages, and ways of life they found there (Tutino 1993).

While the Zapotecs were not seriously threatened by the much smaller

Zoque and Huave populations, Aztec interlopers constantly challenged Za-potec control of the Isthmus. Although the Aztecs would conquer the Isth-mus Zapotecs on a number of occasions, each time their power over the region would wane and troops would have to be sent to reassert Aztec authority (Hassig 1988:176–235). The most famous confrontation between the two Mesoamerican powers took place about 1511 at Guiengola, a large Zapotec fortress/ceremonial center located on a rugged mountain near the Tehuantepec River (Hassig 1988:231; Peterson 1990). The Aztec ruler sent many battalions to attack the Zapotecs, and fighting lasted for seven months, yet the intruding army apparently could not defeat the entrenched forces (Burgoa [1674] 1934:2:341–45). Subsequent negotiations reesta-blished Zapotec autonomy but granted free passage across the Isthmus to the Central Mexicans.[5] While Hassig's detailed research concludes that the Aztecs, ultimately, maintained the upper hand in relations with the Za-potecs, Víctor de la Cruz (1981:8), a leading Zapotec intellectual, argues that studies of Aztec-Zapotec relations have been biased by the relatively greater number of documents left by the Aztecs and their chroniclers. De la Cruz prefers to emphasize the Zapotecs' successes on the battlefield. Guiengola, in particular, has remained in the minds of Zapotec intellectuals as a symbol of the ethnic group's military prowess.[6]

Zapotec Society and Ethnicity in the Pre-Hispanic Isthmus

While the Zapotecs shared many cultural traits with the Aztecs, they dif-fered from their rivals in important respects. Unlike the large hegemonic Aztec state, preconquest Zapotec society was composed of a series of loosely connected head towns and tributary villages located primarily in the present-day state of Oaxaca (Blanton et al. 1981:106; Chance 1986:147).[7] Zapotec nobles resided in head towns, and nearby communities were governed by their representatives (*colaabachiña*) (Whitecotton 1984:140). The elite enjoyed tremendous power over their subjects (Chance 1986:169). Tehuantepec was the principal Isthmus Zapotec town and an important regional market center.

Pre-Hispanic Zapotec society was divided both socially and spatially. The Zapotec social hierarchy was composed of four groups: nobles (who were further divided into *caciques* and lesser nobles, which the Spanish called *principales*), commoners, slaves, and serfs (Chance 1986:169). Class endogamy divided commoners from the higher and lower ranks of the hereditary nobility, who controlled political and military affairs. Nobles enjoyed large elegant residences, special foods, and lavish tombs upon their deaths (Zeitlin 1989:32). Zapotec *caciques* wore long braided hair, feather headdresses, luxurious cotton robes, lip plugs, earrings, and jewelry made of gold and precious stones (Whitecotton 1984:143; Torres de Laguna [1580] 1983:15). They held court on thrones covered with jaguar skin and moved about on litters carried by their subordinates, who employed reverential linguistic forms when addressing them (Zeitlin 1984:69; Whitecotton 1984:143). Elites were the recipients of tribute in goods and labor from 31 Isthmus towns and they managed the salt flats, irrigated tropical fruit orchards, and cotton fields of the area. The Zapotec hierarchy also monopolized the works of artists and artisans, as they had in Classic Monte Albán (Winter 1989:59). Female members of the Zapotec nobility, however, still ground corn for their families in the sixteenth century (Marcus and Flannery 1983:222). Additionally, the *Relación Geográfica* recorded that the Isthmus Zapotec male nobility could consort with any women they chose (Torres de Laguna [1580] 1983:13).[8]

Zapotec commoners made up the majority of the population; their humble lives contrasted sharply with the pampered existence of the nobility. Most commoners were farmers, but others worked as curers, weavers, sculptors, or in other crafts (Whitecotton 1984:149). Serfs were tied to the lands of the *caciques* and belonged to their estates (Chance 1986:169). Slaves, who were purchased in markets or captured in warfare, worked as servants and were potential victims of ritual sacrifices (Whitecotton 1984:151).

The extent to which pre-Hispanic Zapotec-speaking peoples formed a single ethnic group or federation appears limited, given existing data. Chance (1986:146) emphasizes the "incredible complexity" of interethnic relations in Oaxaca, as depicted by the *Relaciones Geográficas*. Social relations among the hundreds of Zapotec-speaking city-states and villages scattered throughout the mountains, valleys, and coastal plains of Oaxaca must have been equally complex. In some parts of Oaxaca there was a degree of political unification beyond the level of the city-state or community, but it was fragile in character and of short duration (Chance 1986:147).[9] Zapotec warfare promoted alliances between communities, but not even the threat posed by the Aztecs could unite the diverse Zapotec groups into a single nation (Flannery 1983:318). These divisions persist today in Oaxaca and are germane to the history of COCEI. As I will argue below, Isthmus Zapotec localism, especially in Juchitán, is both the greatest strength and the Achilles' heel of the movement.

Given such sharp ethnic and spatial fragmentation, it appears that by the time of the Conquest, the Zapotec occupants of Tehuantepec and surrounding tributary villages had begun to form a separate micro-ethnic unit, closely related to other Zapotec groups, especially the Valley Zapotecs, but with a distinct identity, territory, and local dialect. Additionally, the existence of numerous communities of non-Zapotec enemies in close proximity (Huave, Zoque, Chontal, and Mixtec) who fought over territory, commercial advantages, and use of natural resources, increased the early Isthmus Zapotecs' sense of separateness and internal solidarity vis-à-vis their ethnic neighbors. Moreover, the Tehuantepec dynasty's privileged social status set it apart from other Zapotec communities in the nearby sierras. The successful battle of the Isthmus Zapotecs against the Aztecs at Guiengola may have also strengthened their in-group identity, since, as Chance (1986:148) notes, war was one of the main factors that "served to create and reinforce ethnic boundaries" in pre-Hispanic Mexico. The next challenge to Zapotec political power and internal social solidarity emerged with the arrival of the Spanish.

The Colonial Encounter and Its Aftermath

Isthmus Zapotec people had begun to branch off politically and linguistically from the Highland Zapotecs prior to the Spanish conquest, and the loose structure of Isthmus villages linked by tribute obligations to Tehuantepec worked against the creation of a tight-knit ethnic community in precolonial times. The Spanish invasion of Mexico in 1519 and its aftermath had a contradictory effect on Zapotec ethnic conceptions. On the one hand, the Spaniards classified "Zapotec" people as just another example of the overgeneralized, new ethnic category *indio*, using the Nahuatl-derived word "Zapotec" (*Zapoteco* in Spanish) to refer to them instead of the indigenous self-classification *binni za*.[10] Thus, in the imposed Spanish system of people-defining, the Zapotecs were reduced from a self-created category (*binni za*), which meant "the type of people we are" to an externally applied label, *Zapotec*, which took on the meaning, "another type of *indio*."[11] On the other hand, by dividing and limiting ties among indigenous Mesoamerican groups, the Spaniards reinforced the growing ethnic differences between Isthmus Zapotec and Highland and Coastal Zapotec-speaking peoples.

Ironically, Zapotec antipathy towards the Aztecs, Mixtecs, and other native groups facilitated their subjugation to the Spanish in the long run. At first, though, the Zapotec ruler of Tehuantepec, Cosijopi, may have seen the Europeans as his chance to do away with the troublesome Mixtecs and Central Mexicans. He quickly promised allegiance and sent fine gifts to

Cortés' envoys when they made their first trip to the Pacific Coast (López de Gómara [1552] 1964:301). As a result, the Isthmus Zapotec never suffered the violence and humiliation of armed conquest. Moreover, the Spanish-Zapotec pact strengthened Zapotec hegemony over other indigenous inhabitants of the region (Zeitlin 1989:34). On the other hand, the native nobility's willingness to ally themselves with the newcomers eliminated any possibility of prolonging Isthmus Zapotec independence.

For Cosijopi personally, the alliance meant a chance to don Spanish clothes, exchange his jaguar throne for a European chair, and ride horseback. Not only did he adopt Spanish habits of consumption (while initially retaining his powers and privileges within indigenous society), but he also dropped his native name, underwent baptism, and took on the name of Don Juan Cortés. His father became Carlos Cosijoeza, and the Princess Donají became Doña Juana Cortés. Gay ([1881] 1986:156) stated that the Zapotec masses were repulsed by this and would have revolted if Cosijopi had not talked them out of it.[12] Cosijopi also favored the Spaniards by building a convent for the Dominican Order in Tehuantepec and supplying it with food (Burgoa [1674] 1934:2:378).

Although Spanish rule provided certain benefits to the nobility, colonialism probably worsened the living conditions of Zapotec commoners. In the sixteenth century, they were forced to labor in Spanish enterprises and provision colonial *encomenderos*, who demanded gold, food, cotton cloth, and other items.[13] A far more serious consequence of early colonialism, however, was the spread of Old World diseases, which assailed members of all classes of indigenous society. Coastal areas of Mesoamerica, such as the Isthmus, may have suffered the worst effects of these plagues (Taylor 1979:14).[14] Catastrophic epidemics hit the region from the 1530s to the end of the century (Taylor 1979:14; Brockington 1982:45). The Isthmus town of Jalapa plummeted from an estimated 16,000 inhabitants in 1550 to 3,714 in 1567 (Brockington 1982:47). Tehuantepec Province fell from a 1529 population of 120,000 to 31,314 in 1563, and less than 10,000 by 1623 (Brockington 1982:47).

Thus, in less than 100 years (1529–1623) the province of Tehuantepec lost 88 percent of its entire population. Entire villages ceased to exist. Although the Isthmus was spared the wars of conquest that ravaged many other indigenous zones, it did not escape the frequent famines that swept through Mexico in the wake of the Spaniards' arrival. In addition to the effects of disease and famine, the Spaniards overworked the Zapotec and took choice pieces of their land. Sixteenth-century Zapotecs complained that forced dietary changes, increased alcohol consumption, declining work habits, and congregation into nucleated towns caused the disease epidemic (Torres de Laguna [1580] 1983:16–17).

Regarding the overall psychic impact of conquest on the Isthmus Zapotec, we can only speculate. However, a recent oral version of the one surviving fragment of pre-Hispanic Zapotec oral narrative (de la Cruz 1983b:16) may provide some clues. Zapotec people may have retained this discourse, which has been preserved in children's rhymes and philosophical wedding sermons (*libana*), because it metaphorically describes the apocalyptic effects of colonization on the Zapotec world:

> Oh! Water jug, water jug,
>   water will fall, stones will fall,
> it will be cold and earth will fall,
>   the *binni gula'sa'* are going away,
> Oh! Water jug, water jug.

Cajígas Langner (1954), a non-Zapotec writer from Tehuantepec, has noted that the Zapotecs believe that the arrival of Spaniards to the Isthmus caused floods to occur for the first time in the region. López Chiñas (1974:16) interprets the rhyme in mythical terms, as the departure of the great Zapotec ancestors (*binni gula'sa'*) with the arrival of the Spaniards (cf. Covarrubias 1946:312). Whether the images of flood and destruction in the verse reflect earlier Isthmus Zapotec people's symbolic association of conquest with deluge and the leaving of the *binni gula'sa'*, or simply the reflections of modern intellectuals is unclear. In any case, contemporary Isthmus intellectuals vilify the colonial era as a period of violence and barbarity, which they say the Zapotecs nonetheless survived without losing the essential elements of their culture.

Colonial Economic Development and Its Impact on Native Society: The Marquesado del Valle

The Spanish settlers sought rapid economic gain in the Tehuantepec area, and the indigenous peasantry bore the brunt of these efforts. From the 1520s onward, Cortés' Marquesado del Valle, an *encomienda* encompassing large sections of the Oaxaca Valley and the Isthmus, was the site of ambitious enterprises including ship-building, mining, and livestock-raising. These projects relied heavily on African and Mexican slave labor, and the work and tribute of Zapotec commoners. In 1529 alone, indigenous residents of Tehuantepec paid Cortés tribute worth more than 31,000 pesos (Brockington 1982:74).

The Tehuantepec shipyard, established by Cortés in 1524, was the first significant Spanish business in the Isthmus, and the largest colonial ship-building facility of its time (Brockington 1982:32). The conquistador used his ships to carry the products of the Marquesado estate (hides, foodstuffs, etc.) to Spanish markets in Peru. Unpaid Zapotec, Mexican, and Huave laborers (many of whom died) built the vessels under the supervision of Spanish technicians (Gardiner 1955:5; Burgoa [1674] 1934:2:400).[15] Although colonial government officials, in a power struggle with Cortés, soon reduced his Indian labor supply for ship construction, the Tehuantepec harbor remained the primary departure point for New Spanish trade goods shipped to Peru until 1537 (Hassig 1985:168). Ship-building continued on the Isthmus until the 1550s, and the Tehuantepec harbor played a significant role in maritime trade until the Crown transferred its official port northward to Huatulco in 1562 (Zeitlin 1989:35; Brockington 1982:33).

Cortés began placer mining for gold in the 1520s in the drainages north of Tehuantepec. By 1538, large-scale operations were under way at the Chichicapa gold mines (Cadenhead 1960:283–87). Hundreds of Zapotec slaves, and a lesser number of African slaves, worked the mines, until their increasing mortality rates and declining production totals forced Chichicapa to close in the late 1540s (Berthe 1958:122–131; Brockington 1982). The Marquesado also ran several other small-scale industries concerned with salt, pitch, and timber (Zeitlin 1989:35).

The main activity of the Marquesado del Valle in Tehuantepec, however, was livestock-raising on Cortés' enormous tracts of land. Whereas Cortés' mining, ship-building, and other early colonial industries soon petered out, Spanish cattle-ranching in the Isthmus had much greater longevity. By 1543 the Tehuantepec ranches were already home to more than 13,000 sheep and 700 cattle (Zeitlin 1989:36). In time, the Marquesado became one of the largest business enterprises in the New World, and it had a profound impact on Isthmus Zapotec society. Brockington's research (1982, 1989) on Cortés' haciendas makes clear that the Isthmus can no longer be considered an economic backwater, inactive and isolated from events in colonial Mexico.[16]

Controlled from central offices in Mexico City, Madrid, and later Naples, the Marquesado was a pragmatic and profitable enterprise based on draft, slave, and wage labor. Spaniards were at the top of the ethnic labor hierarchy, followed by Africans and mulattoes in the middle, and Indians at the bottom. The laborers produced hides, wool, tallow, salted meat, and live animals for sale in markets in Oaxaca, the Valley of Mexico, and Spain.

In addition to imposing new labor and tribute obligations, Cortés' expanding Marquesado estate took sizeable tracts of the best Isthmus land from the Zapotecs. The appropriated lands were used for pasturing thousands of cattle, sheep, horses, burros, and mules raised by the estate on its eight haciendas (Brockington 1982:88).[17] Of these haciendas only one was fenced, which meant that Marquesado animals constantly trampled and devoured Zapotec corn fields. Throughout the colonial period, the Zapotec complained to government officials about crop damage from cattle, violation of land boundaries, and other problems stemming from Marquesado operations (Brockington 1982:274–278). They also took matters into their own hands by stealing and slaughtering cattle, refusing to work, or damaging Marquesado property. Defiance of Spanish rule was possible because Isthmus Zapotecs retained enough land to provide them with some "leverage" vis-à-vis the colonizers (Brockington 1989:167).

Spanish Immigration, the New Political Economic Order, and the Indigenous Elite

In addition to Marquesado administrators and employees, other Spaniards soon arrived at Tehuantepec in a second wave of immigration. Some of these men established commercial businesses or private cattle ranches. Between 1590 and 1599, 122 land grants were made to Spaniards on the Isthmus during a "ranching boom" in the aftermath of Cortés' death and a mid-sixteenth-century economic lull (Zeitlin 1989:38). Thomas Gage, a British traveler, saw mule trains of from 50 to 100 animals loaded with salted fish bound for Oaxaca, Puebla, and Mexico City when he traveled to Tehuantepec in the 1620s ([1648] 1958:115). He also observed wealthy merchants who sent small ships of goods to Peru and the Philippines. Other European arrivals were Dominican missionaries in pursuit of "spiritual conquest" (Ricard 1986:84).

In 1620 Spanish immigrants formed a thriving community of approximately 100 families in Tehuantepec (Burgoa [1674] 1934:2:394).[18] The wealth of the region impressed Gage, who exclaimed, "In this plain and champaign country of Tehuantepec are five rich and pleasant towns full of fruits and provision of victual" ([1648] 1958:115). He considered Nejapa one of the richest towns in Oaxaca, because of the sugar cane, indigo, cacao, and other crops grown there. In 1629 another traveler claimed to have seen 50,000 sheep on the Isthmus coastal plain (Zeitlin 1978:279).[19] By 1634 Spaniards owned more than 4,000 sq km of Isthmus land, i.e., approximately 90 percent of all available land in the Isthmus coastal plain and adjacent piedmont areas (Zeitlin 1989:39). Prior to that time, however, the Spanish had already taken control of many aspects of local society.

Although native elites retained many of their rights and privileges immediately after the conquest (AGN Mercedes, vol. 7, fa. 109), these began to erode as the Spanish asserted themselves in the political, economic, and religious spheres of Isthmus life. In 1555 the Crown reduced the amount of tribute and personal services owed by commoners to native nobles (de la Cruz 1983c:59). But the most dramatic event in this political transformation occurred in 1563, when Cosijopi, by then known as Don Juan Cortés, was caught practicing "idolatry" and was stripped of his powers and tribute income (Burgoa [1674] 1934:2:355–58). This incident suggests that the Zapotec elite's relationship to the Spaniards in the early colonial period was contradictory. On the one hand, they welcomed the Spaniards, collaborated with them, and adopted many of their lifeways. On the other hand, Cosijopi, at least, subverted the evangelizing plans of the Catholic friars in secret native religious ceremonies. Soon after Cosijopi was punished, however, he died, and his sons were not allowed to succeed him as native governor (Zeitlin 1978:276).

From that time onward, Spaniards dominated politics, economics, and religion in Tehuantepec. The Zapotec elite retained patrimonial rights to land, but its power to affect community affairs diminished as the Spaniards instituted a cabildo-type government based on election rather than heredity (Zeitlin 1978:276–77). Additionally, non-Indians and commoners, as well as native nobles, became officeholders (even though non-Indians were legally barred from the cabildos). An even more significant consequence of cabildo government was the decline of regional Zapotec leadership, as towns formerly subject to Tehuantepec elected their own local governments and intervillage ties weakened (Zeitlin 1984:78). The Zapotecs' declining political power was also evident on the Marquesado haciendas, where Africans invariably held higher and better paid positions than the local people. Although many blacks obtained positions of authority in the Marquesado hierarchy, only one Indian ever became a supervisor (Brockington 1982:207).

In the religious domain, indigenous priests were replaced by Dominican friars who could invoke the fate of Cosijopi and the specter of the Inquisition to deter clandestine native religious rites. Throughout Oaxaca, Spanish inquisitors punished "sinful" Indians for committing heretical acts, sacrilege, assault, and other "offenses" (Brockington 1982:61). Some of the Dominicans, especially Córdova ([1578] 1987), were excellent linguists who promptly learned the Zapotec language, which they used to spread their Christian doctrines and weed out "paganism" (Gay [1881] 1986:182, 189). They also accumulated property, such as the four cattle ranches, worth more than 33,000 pesos, which they owned in 1597 (Zeitlin 1978:278). In addition to these assets, Magdalena, daughter of Cosijopi, granted salt flats, orchards, agricultural fields, and the Laollaga Springs to the friars (Martínez Gracida 1883:93).

Finally, the cash economy—which gradually replaced existing economic relations based on goods and tribute obligations—weakened the native elite's direct control over commoners, but provided the nobility with new possibilities for individual economic gain through commerce and cattle ranching (Romero 1988:125; Brockington 1982:188). For example, at least 46 petitions to establish livestock *estancias* were filed by Isthmus native nobles between the mid-1500s and early 1600s (Zeitlin 1989:48). Overall, the reduced political and religious powers of the Zapotec nobility, their rapid adoption of Hispanic clothing and habits, and their entrepreneurial successes in the colonial economy left them susceptible to charges of collaboration and attacks by Zapotec commoners during periods of unrest and revolt.

Isthmus Zapotec Resistance and Rebellion During the Colonial Period

The history of Zapotec resistance and rebellion against Spanish rule began in early colonial times. Isthmus Zapotec rebellions were part of a larger pattern of Mesoamerican rural revolts whose extensiveness distinguishes Mexico from the rest of the hemisphere (Katz 1988:65). As Coatsworth (1988:57) notes, "No other region in the Americas presents the historian with so rich and diverse a historiography of rural struggle."

If Cosijopi welcomed Cortés to Tehuantepec, when and under what conditions did Isthmus Zapotec resistance begin? In 1522 Jalapa Indians killed one of Alvarado's men in retaliation for the gold he had taken from them, but they were quickly subdued by the conquistadors (Martínez Gracida 1883:70–73). Barabas (1986:224) states that Isthmus Zapotec people participated in a multiethnic coalition of Mixe, Zapotec, Zoque, and other groups from Tabasco to Chiapas, which rebelled against the Spaniards from 1524 to 1526.[20] These are the only known incidents of armed resistance by Zapotec people to the Spanish occupation of the Isthmus. Although violent resistance was uncommon during the first decades of Spanish rule over the Isthmus, Tutino (1993) suggests that at this time Zapotec identity solidified as a "cultural defense" against colonialism.

RELIGION AND RESISTANCE.

In 1545, after the Spaniards had established a firm foothold in the Isthmus, a millenarian movement based in Coatlán, Oaxaca, proclaimed the return of ancient indigenous gods who would restore pre-Hispanic religion and return the Indians to power (Barabas 1986:231). Zapotec *caciques* and commoners joined this movement, including Cosijopi, who acted as an oracle for the prophesies of the Zapotec deity, Guiscipoche, in Tehuantepec (Barabas 1986:231). In 1547 these prophesies inspired a widespread insurrection of Chatinos, Mixtecs, and Zapotecs, which nearly succeeded in taking over Oaxaca City (then known as Antequera). The insurrectionists were fueled by the message, revealed in Titiquipa, that three native lords born in Mexico City, the Mixteca, and Tehuantepec had come to take over the world. The new lords were to receive the tribute then given to the Spaniards, and the Indians were instructed to kill the Spanish intruders. Soon, said the oracle, an earth-shaking storm lasting eight days would wipe out the Europeans and restore the old politico-religious order (Barabas 1986:232). Although the messianic rebels killed a Spanish priest and attacked Miahuatlán, eventually they were crushed by a Spanish military detachment (Gay [1881] 1986:202).

A more generalized messianic insurrection, probably linked to previous millenarian activity, broke out in 1550 (Gay [1881] 1986:202). In this case, old *caciques* of several Oaxacan towns identified the messiah as both Quetzalcoatl and a mythicized local chief (Barabas 1986:234). The rebels' grievances included mistreatment of Indians by authorities, destruction of corn fields by Spanish cattle, and *repartimientos* that requisitioned Indian laborers at a time when the labor force had been ravaged by diseases. Rebel leaders exhorted indigenous youth to take up arms against the Spaniards in support of a divine savior who had come to free them from colonial slavery. Viceroy Mendoza quickly sent soldiers to punish the rebels and their leaders, who were finally captured in Tehuantepec (de la Cruz 1983c:60).

These movements appear to have taken on an interregional and pan-ethnic character, contrary to the common assertion that indigenous resistance was primarily isolated, localized, and unrelated (Barabas 1986:234). This is implied by the rebels' invocation of Quetzalcoatl, a generalized Mesoamerican deity, as well as by the participation of *caciques* and *principales* from several ethnic groups. Messianic sentiments were shared by Zapotec people—who kept in contact through the salt trade—from Tehuantepec all the way to Zaachila (de la Cruz 1983c:60). Although colonialism had further fragmented already diverse pre-Hispanic polities by the mid-sixteenth century, there still existed enough interaction and common cultural values among Zapotec pueblos to allow them to unite in a nativistic revitalization movement.

These incidents of revolt also manifested the tension between collaboration and resistance that marked the actions of the Zapotec elite. Although these elites had facilitated the arrival of the first Spaniards to the Isthmus and had copied many Hispanic customs, they had also retained an indigenous religious role, which became the focus of resistance activities in the early years of the colonial period until the Spanish wiped out the Zapotec priesthood. The Isthmus Zapotec resisted the imposition of Catholic dogma and institutions because colonial evangelists attacked many practices and beliefs that were fundamental to indigenous culture. Additionally, colonial religion involved much more than a spiritual conquest; it also entailed the alienation of Indian lands, persecution of practitioners of native religion, exaction of tribute and forced payments to the friars, and obligatory labor to construct and maintain church buildings. Tehuantepec friars even kept slaves as late as 1730 (Brockington 1982:1).

Initially, though, Cosijopi accepted the Dominicans who came to the Isthmus. He helped them establish their operations and ordered San Blas fishermen to supply seafood for eight religionists and their servants (Gay [1881] 1986:182). But this was only the beginning of the priests' requirements. In 1554 and 1555, the Zapotecs were ordered to pay the priests a salary of 150 pesos in gold for teaching the Indians Christian ways (AGN Mercedes, vol. 4, fa. 9; vol. 4, fa. 207). While the priests went about their business of destroying Zapotec temples and stone idols and punishing heretics, they also acquired large cattle ranches at the expense of Isthmus villagers.[21] However, Zapotec people quickly found ways to undermine the missionaries' plans.

Zapotec religious resistance was primarily a clandestine activity, with the exception of the messianic revolts discussed above, and it entailed the continued practice of native spiritual customs such as ritualized animal sacrifices, bloodletting, ceremonial burning of copal incense, chanting, and offering tamales to dead ancestors (Balsalobre [1656] 1988; Marcus 1983b:345–51). The last-named practice expressed the Zapotecs' intense feelings towards their ancestors, beliefs which persist today. Images of deceased local royalty were the subject of especially fervent belief, as evidenced by special temples built above their tombs or in other sacred places (Marcus 1983b:348–51). These structures may have taken on a totemic significance for local communities.

Under colonialism, Zapotecs continued to make pilgrimages to sacred

sites, albeit clandestinely. According to Gay, the Isthmus Zapotec maintained a secret religious site in a cave near the lagoons of San Francisco
del Mar ([1881] 1986:276). Likewise, the anthropomorphous ceramic idols
frequently found by contemporary Isthmus Zapotec buried underneath
their houses or out in the fields may have been hidden there by ancestors
seeking to avoid persecution by colonial priests. Although these icons
avoided detection, numerous Zapotec commoners were discovered by colonial inquisitors (who were astounded by the extensive persistence of native religion) to be engaging in prohibited spiritual activities throughout
the sixteenth and seventeenth centuries (Gillow [1889] 1978; Balsalobre
[1656] 1988). However, few religious heretics had the nerve to do what
Alfonso López did in a Tehuantepec church in 1613, namely, blow the
beard off a statue of St. Peter with a musket (Brockington 1982:61).

The indigenous religious practices, such as those mentioned above, demonstrate the close relationship Zapotec people perceived between living and
deceased humans, and between humans and nature. They also indicated
the semidivine aura associated with dead Zapotec royalty and priests, who
were chosen from the native nobility (Whitecotton 1984:146). Hence, the
continuance of indigenous religious practices, although in seclusion, helped
the Zapotecs to maintain (at least for a short time) an animistic world view
that celebrated the role of the nobility (living and deceased) as the sacred
mediators between local communities and the supernatural. Thus, the
Spanish attacks on Zapotec "idolatry" struck at the heart of Zapotec conceptions of cosmology and community.

The lack of open religious resistance is not unusual, given the consequences of being caught. For example, in 1609 in Jalapa, Indians were
found making flower offerings to an icon of the deceased daughter of Cosijopi (Pinopiaa) in a nearby cave. A local friar captured the culprits and
took them to the town church, where he had them stripped to the waist,
placed crowns of thorns on their heads, put ropes around their necks, and
made them hold black candles. Tehuantepec and Jalapa residents were
summoned to witness the heretics and listen to a Catholic sermon, delivered in Zapotec (Burgoa [1674] 1934:2:329–31).

The key moment in Catholic efforts to eradicate Isthmus Zapotec religion occurred one night in 1563 when Cosijopi was caught in his home
dressed in a long white tunic and feathered miter, sacrificing turkeys and
other creatures to a large, shining stone statue perched on an altar surrounded by candles and burning incense (Burgoa [1674] 1934:2:350–59).
Cosijopi began to engage in covert spiritual activities after being made high
priest of Zapotec religion after the fall of the Mitla priesthood (Whitecot-

ton 1984:214). Although an angry mob of Zapotecs from several Isthmus towns converged on the Tehuantepec convent to protest the subsequent jailing of Cosijopi, the deposed religious/political leader himself calmed down the crowd and a possible uprising was averted (Burgoa [1674] 1934:2:356–57).

"EVERYDAY" RESISTANCE.

From the mid-1500s to the early 1600s, disease decimated the Isthmus population. Yet archival sources document Zapotec participation in numerous judicial actions against the Spaniards, as well as many acts of everyday resistance, despite the impact of maladies brought by the Europeans. Many of these disputes and incidents were related to the Marquesado del Valle and the cattle ranches of other Spaniards, which gobbled up Isthmus land.[22] Indians also requested land to raise sheep and other animals, although native ranches were dwarfed by Cortés' massive haciendas, whose cattle wreaked havoc on Zapotec corn fields and competed with Indian herds for grazing sites (Zeitlin 1989:41; AGN Mercedes, vol. 15, fa. 76; vol. 22, fa. 52 vta.; vol. 23, fa. 224; vol. 23, fa. 224 vta).[23] Expanding Spanish cattle ranches also impinged on existing water sources in the dry Isthmus and interfered with lands used by Indians for hunting, gathering, and other purposes.

Wayward cattle, excessive *repartimiento* and tribute demands, and miscellaneous abuses of villagers by Crown and Marquesado officials are some of the most common grievances registered by Zapotecs in the Spanish courts. Isthmus Zapotecs complained to colonial authorities about the intrusions of Marquesado herds on Indian fields at least eight times between 1590 and 1650 (Zeitlin 1989:41).[24]

Labor abuses and subsequent litigation against the Marquesado increased after 1620, when owners of the estate began leasing it to managers. Under the new system, hacienda managers were far less accountable to Marquesado owners, a situation which led to greater mistreatment of workers (Brockington 1982:14). Indians responded with new complaints to Crown authorities, as in a mid-1600s dispute in which a group of sheep- and goatherders requested that officials fire the Marquesado administrator (Brockington 1982:235–36).[25]

Despite its inherent risks, direct action against Spanish property was often a more appealing form of resistance to Isthmus Zapotecs than lengthy litigation. Livestock poaching was an especially common activity, as the colonial viceroy lamented in a message to the *alcalde mayor* of Tehuantepec: "The Indians are causing very great damages, slaughtering all manner of livestock, chasing them down with dogs" (Brockington 1982:275).[26] Petapa natives even entered corrals and killed calves. Theft, flight to the hills, arson, squatting on land claimed by Spaniards, abandoning the work site, and refusal to work on haciendas were other resistance tactics employed by Zapotecs (Brockington 1982:274–282). Occasionally, however, indigenous grievances went beyond individual or minor acts of subversion and escalated into large-scale uprisings. The most prominent uprising in the Isthmus was the Tehuantepec rebellion of 1660, which became the largest insurrection in Oaxacan colonial history.

"HAREMOS TEHUANTEPEC": THE TEHUANTEPEC REBELLION.

A principal cause for the rebellion, according to Tehuantepec natives and Spanish officials, was the forced purchase of Spanish goods at high prices (*repartimiento de efectos*) and the coerced sale at low prices of indigenous agricultural and handcrafted goods such as vanilla, cochineal, and cotton cloth (Manso de Contreras [1661] 1987:51).[27] [28] Anger over these abuses ignited when the *alcalde* had an Indian *cacique* of Tequisistlán flogged to death and ordered the whipping of a native leader of Mixtequilla for delivering inferior mantles.

In response, a noisy mob of Zapotec men and women (estimated at 6,000) stoned, looted, and burned the Spanish buildings of Tehuantepec and killed the *alcalde mayor*, two of his servants, and one African.[29] They also ousted Hispanicized native officials from their positions (Rojas 1964:27). The rebels took 40 muskets and the royal flag from the *Casas Reales*, as well as fifes and drums, which they played raucously in celebration of the victory. One of the first buildings torched by the Zapotecs (perhaps because of its significance as a symbol of Spanish culture) was a stable with 16 horses in it, all of which perished in the flames. According to a Spanish report on the incident, the boldest and most obstinate stone-throwers were the Zapotec women (Manso de Contreras [1661] 1987:16). Additionally, when Catholic leaders of Tehuantepec attempted to pacify the rebels, women threatened the churchmen with death if they did not return to their refuge in the local convent (Manso de Contreras [1661] 1987:21). The rage of Zapotec women towards Spanish authorities was acute because they had been forced to produce an extraordinary quantity of mantles (Rojas 1964:25–27).[30]

After routing the surviving Spaniards, who fled to safety in the Tehuantepec church, the mutinous Zapotecs elected their own *cabildo* (including a *gobernador*, *alcaldes*, *regidores*, and other officials), set up guards to secure roads in and out of town, sent word of the rebellion to other indigenous communities, and restored land taken by a Spaniard to Petapa villagers (de la Cruz 1987a:5). All of this was accomplished between late morning and mid-afternoon of the first day of the rebellion (Manso de Contreras [1661] 1987:19). For the following year and one month, the Zapotec *cabildo* elected by the populace wielded the *bastón de mando* (staff of justice), which symbolized political power in Tehuantepec. The sophistication of the rebel *cabildo* is reflected in their correspondence with the viceroy after the rebellion, and by the apparent ease by which they administered Tehuantepec until being disarmed by the Spaniards (Manso de Contreras [1661] 1987: 22–23, 36, 38).

The Tehuantepec uprising, despite the limited ends of its initiators, quickly spread to Nejapa, Villa Alta, and Ixtepeji, where it brought in Mixes, Chontals, and Sierra Zapotecs. The more than 20 Mixe towns that joined the rebels were inspired by their mythical culture hero Cong Hoy, who, they believed, would return from a lagoon where he had been hiding along with a legendary Zapotec king of Tehuantepec (Congun) and another indigenous leader (Barabas 1986:239–40).[31] Other Indian towns were emboldened by rebel actions, and the battle cry *"haremos Tehuantepec"* (literally "we will do [or make] Tehuantepec") jumped from pueblo to pueblo, where it was invoked every time the Spaniards dictated policies disliked by the indigenous people (Manso de Contreras [1661] 1987:14).[32] An alarmed Bishop of Oaxaca reported that as many as 10,000 Indians armed with 1,000 crossbows had joined the uprising (Manso de Contreras [1661] 1987:26). Eventually the insurrectionists reached the outskirts of Antequera, proclaiming, "Up to now Indians have been subject to the Spanish, now the Spanish will be subject to the Indians" (González Obregón 1907:29, cited in Barabas 1986:236).

The insurrection finally came to an end when the viceroy's envoy, promising justice and fair treatment, lured the rebel leaders into a trap, where they were captured and jailed. Of the 53 imprisoned rebels, at least seven were women. One of these women, Magdalena María (*la Minera*), was convicted of having sat on the dead Spanish *alcalde mayor* and pounded his corpse with a stone while scornfully reproaching him (Manso de Contreras [1661] 1987:46). Her sentence: to have her hair and one hand cut off, to be flogged 100 times in public, and for the amputated arm to be hung to the gallows near the site of her alleged crime.[33] The severity of the punishment indicates how seriously the revolt shook Oaxacan colonial officials. Minor uprisings normally resulted in limited punishments; the death penalty and long prison terms were seldom applied, except in the few regional insurrections of the eighteenth century (Taylor 1978:192).

Despite the harsh punishments administered to the rebels of 1660, Isthmus Zapotec peasants rose up against the Spaniards once again in 1707. As in 1660, fighting took place not only in Tehuantepec and Ixtepec where the revolt began, but in a wide area that stretched 75 km to the north and 50 km east (Hart 1989:22). Hostilities were touched off by the expansion of the La Marquesana hacienda, formerly part of the Marquesado del Valle estate, onto Indian communal lands. Indian land had again become desirable to Spaniards because of greater traffic on the rough road across the Isthmus and the potential for increased sales of agricultural goods and other products. Whereas several pueblos, including Juchitán, exchanged land for cash payments or tenant farming agreements with the estate managers, the Ixtepecanos chose to defend their lands by force, as did many other Isthmus communities. Although New Spain's so-called "Indian courts" helped reduce tensions through adjudication, the colonial courts did not stop Spaniards from taking Isthmus Zapotec land, and the result was often violence (Hart 1989:23).

In 1715 Tehuantepec again became the center of Zapotec resistance. Tehuano insurgents ousted the *gobernador* and other Hispanicized native officials and replaced them with people to their liking, bypassing the Indian *principales* who normally selected local officeholders (AGN Indios, vol. 39, fas. 256–58 cited in *Guchachi' Reza* 12:12–13, 1982). They also slapped a royal lieutenant governor, cursed, and refused to pay offerings to the Catholic priests. As in the 1660 revolt, Spanish officials and their native allies fled to safety in the Tehuantepec convent, and the residents of Santa María barrio (currently the Tehuantepec barrio with the strongest attachment to the Zapotec language and customs) played a key role in the rebellion (de la Cruz 1983c:62). Spanish officials identified a native leader known as the *Golaba*,[34] his companion, and the "Indian Teresa," as instigators of the uprising. The principal motives for the revolt were territorial invasions and commercial conflicts between Spaniards and Indians (Barabas 1986:243).

Finally, a land conflict broke out in the Zapotec town of Ixtaltepec in 1753, which led to the killing of a Spaniard (Zeitlin 1989:43). While further archival research would be required to ascertain the direct relationships, if any, between the participants of the 1660, 1707, 1715, and 1753 conflicts, contemporary Juchiteco intellectuals of COCEI not only view these events as connected to each other but as links in a historical chain connecting *Coceístas* to the Zapotec heroes and heroines of the past (de la Cruz 1983c; Matus 1981). Isthmus intellectuals have commemorated this history by naming March 22, the first day of the Tehuantepec rebellion, as the Day of Zapotec Dignity, and by founding the Juchitán Cultural Center on this day as well.[35]

Intracommunity Social Tensions, the Native Elite, and Ethnic Definitions

Although Zapotec people resisted Spanish domination, they did not do so as a unified whole. The popular classes of Tehuantepec, including many women,[36] were in the vanguard of rebellion, as were members of other smaller Isthmus communities, while the Tehuano elite sided with their colonial masters (with a few notable exceptions in the early colonial period). In both the 1660 and 1715 uprisings, Tehuantepec townspeople deposed native authorities and replaced them with leaders who attracted more popular support. After the 1660 rebellion, native elites helped the Spaniards capture dissidents (Zeitlin 1978:284). In return, colonial authorities reinstated these men in their former offices in the Tehuantepec *cabildo* (Rojas 1964:115). Likewise, on at least two occasions, Cosijopi sided with Spanish authorities instead of favoring the Zapotec masses who threatened revolt (when he was baptized, and when he was caught practicing idolatry), and his daughter gave prime land to the conquerors. Zapotec *caciques* also served their colonial masters as tribute collectors and foremen for Indian laborers on the Marquesado (Brockington 1982:181). Finally, Zapotec elites demonstrated their acceptance of Spanish culture and colonial status symbols (as opposed to indigenous customs) by their prompt adoption of cattle ranching, European clothing, horseback riding, the wearing of swords, and the use of titles such as Don and Doña (Torres de Laguna [1580] 1983:15; AGN Indios, vol.2, exp. 833, exp. 706).

Isthmus Zapotec society was highly stratified in pre-Hispanic times and remained divided under colonialism,[37] although the difference between nobles and commoners was reduced (cf. Chance 1978). In addition, the system of social stratification instituted by the Spaniards altered many of the forms and meanings of the existing hierarchy within Zapotec society. Prior to the conquest, the Zapotec elite based its authority on heredity and spiritual mediation with native deities. As colonialism consolidated, elite power derived from association with Spanish authorities, participation in the imposed *cabildo* political system, and entrepreneurial activity.[38]

In the economic sphere, Isthmus Zapotec nobles were active in commerce, salt extraction, and cattle ranching. In the latter enterprise, they imitated Spanish ranch administrators and African cowboys of the Marquesado haciendas. Both men and women requested permission to raise livestock (AGN Mercedes, vol. 23, fa. 224). In Tehuantepec, 10 Zapotec nobles petitioned to raise sheep and goats on 23 parcels, and mares for raising mules on another tract (Zeitlin 1989:48). In other Isthmus communities, normally only two or three nobles made petitions for individual ranches. While traveling across the Isthmus in the 1620s, Gage observed the wealth of Tapanatepec: "Here is great plenty of cattle for flesh, and rich Indians which have farms, called there *estancias*, in some a thousand, in some three or four thousand head of cattle" ([1648] 1958:120).

The Zapotec elite also avidly engaged in commerce. In 1580 Torres de Laguna ([1580] 1983:8) observed that Zapotec merchants made trips to Soconusco and other areas to sell fish, shrimp, and salt. He also saw Zapotec women selling cotton cloth ([1580] 1983:21). In the seventeenth century, Burgoa found that Zapotecs of Tehuantepec maintained herds of from 40 to 50 mules, which they used to transport goods for a fee to Mexico City, Veracruz, Chiapas, and Guatemala ([1674] 1934:2:389). Burgoa ([1674] 1934:2:389) described them as well-dressed, punctual, and reliable men who possessed excellent mules and saddles. He called them *"Ladinos,"* indicating their adoption of Spanish clothing, customs, and language, which separated them from the less Hispanicized members of the Zapotec community.

These patterns of differential resistance, acculturation, and political and economic power suggest that Zapotec majority opinion about who was "self" rather than "other" became problematic as the colonial era unfolded. As the Tehuantepec nobility increasingly allied themselves with Spanish political rule and social customs, their ethnic "authenticity" became open to question, and local definitions of Zapotec ethnic identity and culture apparently became more closely associated with the lifeways of the lower classes and the inhabitants of rural villages than with those of the old elite families (Zeitlin 1989:46–47).

Zapotec Commoners and Local Economic Recovery

While the Zapotec elite successfully adapted to the colonial economy, the rest of the population did not simply sink into oblivion but also participated in a bustling local economy centered around the Tehuantepec market. Open daily year-round, the market supplied a local and regional clientele with salt, cotton, dried meat and fish, birds, iguana and turtle eggs, corn, and tropical fruits (Burgoa [1674] 1934:2:389; Torres de Laguna [1580] 1983:21). Salt and cotton were Tehuantepec's most important trade goods and attracted buyers from as far away as 250 km (Brockington 1982:25). Zapotec women specialized in the sale of cotton garments in the Tehuantepec market (Torres de Laguna [1580] 1983:21) In addition to tropical fruits and corn, Zapotec peasants cultivated chile, beans, squash, sweet potatoes, vanilla, achiote, and cacao. These crops were watered by annual rains, supplemented by irrigation canals, which branched off local rivers. Isthmus farmers also raised turkeys, bees, and dogs. Although livestock ranches were run primarily by the Zapotec elite, whole communities also kept flocks of sheep.

All of this was possible because, despite the large size of the Marquesado haciendas, Isthmus communities were able to hold on to a substantial amount of their land (Brockington 1989; cf. Taylor 1972, 1979). Additionally, the diverse Isthmus physical environment allowed for the combination of several different subsistence modes: fishing in Isthmus lagoons, rivers, and ocean bays; salt extraction from sea water (Torres de Laguna [1580] 1983:18–19); farming and ranching on the coastal plain; and hunting, gathering, and wood-collecting in the nearby hills. Among the numerous animal species hunted by the Zapotecs were iguana and other lizards, wild pigs, rabbits, deer, and birds. Wild silk was also collected (Borah 1943:106). Thus, despite Spanish exploitation and the ravages of disease, the Zapotecs had rebuilt a multifaceted local economy, which operated in the midst of the European haciendas.

Summary and Conclusions

Although the conquest of the Isthmus by Zapotec people and the emergence of Isthmus Zapotecs as a distinct ethnic group—separate from Highland Zapotecs—occurred during the late pre-Hispanic era, the consequences of these events continue to have significance today. Since then, the Isthmus Zapotecs have dominated the Huave and Zoque, whose lands they took, and the regional opposition between Isthmus Zapotecs and Oaxaca Valley residents has persisted to the present. Isthmus Zapotec ethnic identity in the pre-Hispanic era was forged in a context of frequent political conflicts with Highland Oaxacan peoples, other Isthmian peoples, and the Aztecs. Spanish conquest of Oaxaca subdued these interethnic hostilities to some degree, but also contributed to the Isthmus Zapotecs' sense of ethnic distinctiveness vis-à-vis a new and more powerful "other." In addition to this, however, the growing acculturation of Zapotec nobles (and some commoners) introduced a tension within the ethnic community.

Carmagnani (1988:13) argues that although native Oaxacan society was affected by the loss of its endogenous political organization in the sixteenth century, the indigenous people retained their kinship networks, territorial organization, and capacity for self-defense of the ethnic community. Thus, he suggests, Oaxacan Indians "reconstituted" themselves ethnically as the colonial period unfolded. Although this study has not focused on the survival of Zapotec kinship organization, the Isthmus Zapotec communities were able to maintain their territorial bases (albeit reduced in size), reconstruct their economic infrastructure, preserve the indigenous language, and sustain a capacity for armed rebellion against colonial rule (even though not all Zapotecs participated equally in these revolts). In this sense, Carmagnani's hypothesis applies to the Isthmus as well.

The relevance of this history to current Isthmus Zapotecs is manifold. Today, as in the past, the Isthmus is an area of rich economic potential and a crossroads for trade and travel. Many different groups have attempted to control the Isthmus for their own benefit, sparking conflicts and struggle. By the time of the conquest, the Zapotecs had already established a dominant position relative to other native peoples of the region. This is undoubtedly one of the reasons that Isthmus Zapotecs have a strongly positive ethnic identity, unlike so many other Mexican indigenous peoples. But it also limits the possibilities for modern Zapotec people to establish multiethnic political alliances.

If the Zapotecs were conquerors, they also suffered the ignominies of colonial domination. The level of Spanish economic penetration into the Isthmus, through cattle ranching and other enterprises, was significant. However, this, in part, may explain the relatively high level of indigenous resistance in the Isthmus. Although the Zapotecs were never able to overcome the Spanish, except on a local basis for a brief period in Tehuantepec, what is perhaps more important is the legacy of rebellion left by colonial Zapotecs to their descendants. Current Zapotec intellectuals celebrate Isthmus history as a glorious period of successful revolts, struggles for self-determination, and cultural survival. While some analysts would question the historical legitimacy of these views, they are firmly rooted in the hearts and minds of today's radical Zapotec political activists in Juchitán.

CHAPTER TWO

The Emergence of Juchiteco
Resistance and Rebellion, 1750–1911

*I should point out that in order to maintain the State's internal peace I
have principally taken care of two things: (1) to respect individual rights
. . . ; and (2) to organize and maintain public forces and prepare the
elements of war. . . .*

*   With the aforementioned measures, public peace has been secured, in
general, in the State. Only the town of Juchitán . . . has scandalously
altered the tranquility enjoyed by the District of Tehuantepec. This was
done neither to carry out a political plan, nor to propose any useful reforms. . . . It was done to evade obedience to all authority and the healthy
burden of the law, and to rob with impunity and engage without obstacles
in excesses which morality condemns.*

EXCERPTS FROM A SPEECH DELIVERED BY
GOVERNOR BENITO JUÁREZ TO INAUGURATE THE
OAXACA STATE CONGRESS, JULY 2, 1850[1]

Tehuantepec was the center of Isthmus Zapotec culture in precolonial and
early colonial times. Juchitán, previously a peripheral community, emerged
as an important new site of Zapotec culture and political resistance in the
late colonial era and nineteenth century. The events of this period helped
form the intense, politicized ethnic identity of contemporary Juchitecos
and established many of the ethnic and regional divisions (and alliances)
that frame current COCEI political struggles.

    Before analyzing Juchitán's emergence as a locus of ethnic resistance, it
is necessary to make a few observations about Isthmus colonial history and
the consequences of that history. For Zeitlin (1989:57–60), the survival of
Isthmus Zapotec society under colonialism and the current strength of
Zapotec ethnic identity are a function of elite mediation of outside incur-

sions and the group's "stratified social structure." In Zeitlin's view, native authorities maintained economic and social boundaries against foreign encroachment, and the Zapotec's complex social hierarchy and centralized political power provided better defenses against Spanish aggression than did the more decentralized, egalitarian polities of the Huave, Zoque, and Mixe.

The historical material that follows challenges aspects of Zeitlin's interpretation. While her hypothesis may help us understand the persistence of the Zapotec community in the sixteenth century, it is less relevant to the latter half of the colonial period and the nineteenth century.[2] Indeed, if we compare the interests of different social strata within the Isthmus community rather than assuming that they are the same, as in Zeitlin's approach, we can shed new light on the issue of indigenous survival historically.

To begin, we may question to what extent Zapotec nobles, who had ordered the sacrifice and ritual consumption of lower strata individuals in precolonial times,[3] indeed became the protectors of commoners under colonialism. We have already examined the native elite's role in allowing Spaniards into Tehuantepec, granting them access to key resources, controlling the labor power of commoners, and rounding up Zapotec rebels. Spanish authorities were thankful for this, a fact that is reflected in their opinion of Don Juan Cortés (Cosijopi), whom they considered "a good Indian" and "a friend of the Spanish" (Paso y Troncoso 1905:313). Additionally, we have seen how the nobility took advantage of the new economic opportunities under colonialism.

It is not clear exactly how these actions shielded the commoners from Spanish encroachment, although it is apparent that the elite benefitted from them.[4] Therefore, rather than emphasizing the indigenous nobility's protection of the masses from colonialism, this study focuses on the new divisions between native elites and commoners created by colonial society and the Tehuantepec elite's growing rapprochement and collaboration with the Spanish.[5] Thus, in order to understand the vitality of contemporary Zapotec culture, we must look away from Tehuantepec, the center of colonialism in the Isthmus, and away from the Europeanized Zapotec hierarchy that resided there. Instead, we must examine peripheral areas of the colonial and postcolonial Isthmus (such as Juchitán), where small indigenous communities were able to maintain a greater degree of solidarity in the face of Spanish intrusions. In these areas, the fortification of Isthmus Zapotec culture and ethnic unity, rather than resulting from elite intervention or a stratified social system, may be better explained as "a practical response to dangerous class forces that had emerged" within the community itself (Stern 1987:48).

Thus, the persistence of indigenous Isthmus society historically is less a result of elite mediation than the ability of the Isthmus Zapotec to overcome internal class divisions and maintain ethnic unity in outlying communities such as Juchitán (although by the twentieth century problematic schisms emerged there also). That this did not happen in Tehuantepec, where colonial institutions predominated and native elites emulated and collaborated with Spaniards, is a major reason why Tehuantepec is today primarily a mestizo town where Zapotec is seldom spoken.[6]

The postcolonial period in the Isthmus was also a time of major political and economic change, as in the rest of Mexico. Wars and large-scale development projects dramatically altered social contours. As Mexicans forged a new nation, liberal reforms, the transformation of tribute-paying Indians into citizens, and changes in the status of municipalities reshaped community life. In the Isthmus, the nineteenth century spawned ambitious money-making schemes and numerous grassroots political movements. Eager developers embarked on colonization projects, built a railroad, and staked out large haciendas. Isthmus Zapotec people worked on the railroads and haciendas but also rebelled when they felt their interests were being infringed upon.

Juchitán was a crucible of change and struggle during this era. As Juchitecos resisted control of their contraband textile trade and fought to protect land and decision-making powers from encroaching outsiders, they also constructed a cultural identity as fiercely independent fighters. Although the conflictive events of the time radically altered Isthmus Zapotec life, they instilled in local people an ideology of toughness and valor which persists in the minds of contemporary *Coceístas*.

The Colonial Economy: Boom and Bust

The colonial Spaniards' plans to develop the Isthmus never panned out. The long distance between Tehuantepec and regional and national colonial centers,[7] and frequent economic downturns, discouraged Spanish settlement in the area. Despite the initial promise of the Isthmus as a center for capital accumulation, it never lived up to the colonizers' lofty economic expectations. Mining went bust in a scant 10 years (Berthe 1958). The Tehuantepec harbor experienced a boom in the first three decades of its operations but also fizzled, as Huatulco and eventually Acapulco took over the Pacific maritime trade. The shipyards likewise closed. Finally, although sericulture became one of Oaxaca's most profitable businesses in the six-teenth century, silkraising was better suited to highland regions than low-land tropical areas such as the Isthmus (Borah 1943:29).

Aside from the region's relative remoteness and disappointing economic performance, the Isthmus had other drawbacks that restricted colonial im-migration. One disincentive was the extreme Isthmus climate, which has since prevented the area from becoming a major tourist attraction, despite its proximity to magnificent beaches. During the so-called "rainy sea-son"—drought years are actually far more common than years of sufficient rainfall—most of the Isthmus is oppressively hot and muggy. In the dry season, northern winds averaging 70 km/hr pound the region (Binford 1983:83). In the aptly named savannah area of La Ventosa, 200-km/hr winds have been recorded, and stories abound of palm trees being up-rooted, mules and horses being thrown to the ground, and vehicles being turned on their sides. Prior to the recent construction of a dam on the Tehuantepec River, damaging floods were also common. Even in years of adequate rainfall, the thin Isthmus soils, intense heat, and battering winds made the area risky and problematic for most would-be Spanish agricul-turalists.

As a result of these difficulties, Spanish immigration to the region was confined to a small contingent of merchants, colonial officials, *hacendados*, ranch hands, and Dominican priests, most of whom resided in Tehuan-tepec or Jalapa. The Isthmus unit of the Marquesado, despite its wide geographical extension, was "a relatively small and simple operation" com-pared to many other colonial enterprises (Brockington 1982:9). Moreover, soon after heirs of Cortés transferred control of the estate from Mexico City to Europe around 1629, the Tehuantepec haciendas experienced a series of problems (graft, mismanagement, declining production) from which they never quite recovered. Thus, the European presence in the Isthmus gradually declined, and by 1742 the Spanish/mestizo population of Tehuantepec had dwindled to only 50 families, whereas native tributar-ies alone numbered 3,831 (Tutino 1978:201). Like the Yucatán peninsula and other outlying parts of New Spain, the Isthmus was less affected by European immigration than were more densely settled areas such as the Valley of Mexico (Farriss 1984). Because of the extensive nature of Isthmus cattle ranching on vast plains, Zapotec communities (aside from the co-lonial center of Tehuantepec) had relatively little contact with the every-day economic activities of the Spaniards, other than during seasonal labor drafts or the occasional invasion of a corn field by stray livestock. Consequently, despite colonial impositions, Zapotec culture remained strong in Juchitán.

A Third Wave of European Interest in the Isthmus: The Cochineal and Indigo Booms

After an approximately 100-year lull (1650–1750) in European economic activity in the Isthmus, interest in the region picked up during the cochineal bonanza and Bourbon Reform era (ca. 1750–1820). Sugar cane was also introduced into the area during this time, as lucrative silver mining injected new life into the overall colonial economy. The Isthmus demographic revival (which began in the mid-1600s) helped attract Spanish investors to the region, since cochineal was a labor-intensive enterprise. Cochineal insects generally did well in the tropical Isthmus climate and had been used for dyeing cloth there since the pre-Hispanic era (Donkin 1976:20). Another type of purple dye was also extracted from shellfish by Isthmus women (Burgoa [1674] 1934:406; Fossey [1844] 1983:22).

Thus, when Tehuantepec *alcalde mayor* and prominent businessman Juan Echarrí introduced cochineal cultivation around 1750, he did so to a community that was quite familiar with dyes (Hamnett 1971:45, 159). The Zapotecs apparently did not resist cochineal production, because it required no structural changes in community life and provided supplemental income in a period of population expansion (by 1793 there were 16,189 Indians in the Isthmus) (Tutino 1978:204).[8] In fact, Isthmus cochineal was so successful—production levels doubled during Echarrí's 18-year tenure—it helped cause dye prices to fall in Oaxaca, Veracruz, and even Spain (Hamnett 1971:45).

Indigo was another source of bright-colored dye, and it became an important Isthmus cash crop for Spaniards in the late eighteenth century. Before the Independence wars broke out, Tehuantepec exported a total of 82,000 pesos worth of indigo dye to Mexico City, Puebla, and Veracruz (Hamnett 1971:141). Like cochineal, indigo did not cause major disruptions in indigenous community life, but instead provided supplemental income to Isthmus peasants (Tutino 1978:203; cf. Chance 1989). Most of the land for indigo cultivation was provided by existing Spanish cattle ranches, and many of the laborers in the industry were blacks and mulattoes. A small number of indigo fields were also controlled by Zapotec elites. Although indigo and cochineal production provided some benefits for

Isthmus communities, the renewed European interest in the region eventually led to conflicts and the emergence of new Zapotec resistance movements.

Juchiteco Resistance

From the mid-eighteenth century onward, the center of Isthmus Zapotec resistance shifted from Hispanicized Tehuantepec, former home of the Zapotec royal family and indigenous "high culture," to the previously insignificant village of Juchitán (Tutino 1993). Although there is little mention of Juchitán in historical sources prior to 1700, after that time the community begins to appear in records of land struggles, commercial conflicts, and, by the 1800s, militant uprisings. Conversely, in the same period Tehuantepec became known for its support of conservative causes.

Juchitecos are very proud of their reputation for feisty behavior and courage, and these cultural motifs are fundamental to the contemporary self-definitions of *Coceístas*. According to local lore, Juchitán was founded by the most aggressive and combative Zapotec warriors (López Gurrión 1976:14; Orozco 1946:14; Henestrosa [1929] 1987:59–60). Although this legend is probably a modern attempt to glorify Juchiteco origins, numerous non-Zapotec, nineteenth century observers also commented on the Juchitecos' toughness and valor (e.g., Brasseur [1861] 1981:145–47; Ratzel [1878] 1981:5). Williams (1852:205) remarked that unlike other Indians of the Isthmus, Juchitecos were unafraid of jaguars and would not hesitate to attack them with nothing but a machete, even if the Juchiteco were alone. This was the case, he said, because Juchitecos were more athletically built and more courageous than other Isthmus residents. Von Tempsky (1858:282) noted that the inhabitants of Juchitán were famous for being "a very unruly set, turbulent politicians, and revolutionists."

Contrasting the colonial status of Juchitán with that of Tehuantepec may help explain why Juchitán became a locus of resistance and Tehuantepec turned conservative. Whereas Tehuantepec was the center of Spanish operations in the Isthmus, Juchitán existed on the periphery of colonial society. Unlike the lush oasis-like ecological setting around Tehuantepec, Juchitán was (and is) located on an arid, windswept plain covered with xerophytic brush that was unattractive to the Spaniards (Dorsett 1975:361). It had but one plain church, no important government or Marquesado offices, and little ecclesiastical or military presence. In 1586 a Spanish priest traveling through the area attempted to hold mass in Juchitán but was unable to because the town had no altar (Ciudad Real [1586] 1980:5). Juchitán may have even been abandoned from 1603 to 1604 when the town was congregated to Ixtepec. Zapotec leftist de la Cruz (1983c:61) asserts the Juchitecos openly rebelled against the change and decided to return to their pueblo, but he provides no data to substantiate this. In any case, the relative isolation of Juchitán from colonial institutions and the minimal Spanish immigration to the town gave it a degree of autonomy unavailable to the Tehuanos. Instead of being ground into submission by colonialism, Juchitecos retained a degree of combativeness nurtured by their adversarial relationship with the *hacendados*.

The Juchitecos showed their capacity for resistance in 1736 by filing a legal claim against usurpation of the town's communal land by a Tehuantepec friar (TPJ [1736–1737] 1987:3–45). The litigants complained that a 1717 fire had destroyed most of the town's houses along with the Juchitecos' "primordial" land titles,[9] leaving them unprotected against colonial interlopers.[10] Members of the Juchitán *cabildo*, the *gobernador* of Ixtaltepec, and 15 other Zapotec witnesses fervently defended their rights in the colonial courts. Speaking through an interpreter (TPJ [1736–1737] 1987:9), Zapotec witnesses lamented that they had previously enjoyed their lands since "time immemorial" without conflict or incident.[11] The Juchitán *gobernador*, an *alcalde*, and several other Zapotec men protested so vigorously that religious authorities had them jailed until the end of the trial. Other dissidents took flight in fear of mistreatment by the friars.

The irate Juchitecos claimed they had used the disputed land (which included five native ranches) to grow cacao, corn, fruit crops, and livestock to meet their tribute burdens and payments to the church. Additionally, the Indians complained that they worked the lands in order to provide for widows and the infirm, and to produce the goods used in indigenous fiestas. Thus, the friar's incursion affected not only the subsistence base of the community and indigenous mechanisms for sharing surplus food, but struck at the heart of Juchiteco cultural life. The Zapotec witnesses described each segment of land with great precision and provided the indigenous names for landmarks that formed their boundaries (TPJ [1736–1737] 1987). Additionally, they called for punishment of the curate and insisted he not harass them with charges of failing to comply with church doctrine.

After a lengthy legal fight that ended indecisively, Juchitán townspeople reclaimed the land themselves and thereafter periodically cleared its boundaries to insure usurpation would never reoccur (López Gurrión 1976:48). This would not be the case, however. Title to these lands remains a hotly disputed issue today, and the Juchiteco's "primordial" land titles are a key symbol for COCEI ideologists and peasants.

Another natural resource that became the focus of controversy was salt,

which was vital to the diet and an excellent preservative of fish and meat.
Prior to the conquest, Isthmus residents were among the principal pur-
veyors of salt to the Oaxaca Valley, Soconusco, and other regions. The
importance of salt increased during the colonial era as commerce expanded
and the Marquesado began producing great quantities of salt-cured hides
(Brockington 1989:49). The abundance of high quality salt along the Isthmus lagoons and coastlines was such that Spaniards, Zapotecs, Huave, and
Chontals were all able to extract as much of the mineral as they wanted
without serious conflict throughout much of the colonial period. This all
changed as a result of the Bourbon Reforms, which in 1779 gave control
of Isthmus salt deposits to the Crown (de la Cruz 1983c:63).

In 1781 a Spanish administrator ordered the expropriation of the Isthmus salt flats from the Zapotecs. Isthmus natives responded in 1796 by
producing an individual who identified himself as a lineal descendant of
Cosijoeza and therefore the legal owner of the *salinas* (AGN Tierras, vol.
2783, cited in *Guchachi' Reza* 14:4, 1983; de la Cruz 1983d).[12] The Zapotec
legal arguments failed to impress colonial officials, who declared them
without foundation and dismissed the case. Despite this setback, the case
is significant, since it demonstrates not only the continuation of Zapotec
legal resistance but the survival, albeit in decadence, of elements of the pre-
Hispanic Zapotec dynasty. As in the case of Juchiteco agricultural land, the
Isthmus salt pans continue to be a coveted prize for COCEI militants, who
link their current claims to the historical struggle for Zapotec natural resources.

Despite government efforts to confiscate the salt beds, the mini-econ-
omy of Juchitán remained solvent due to its successful textile industry (the
only one left in the Isthmus in 1793) and its flourishing export trade, which
was facilitated by the free commerce law adopted in 1765 (Romero
1986:52). These two enterprises went hand in hand as Juchiteco cloth was
sold both locally and in Guatemala, "a rare example of surviving Indian
entrepreneurship" (Tutino 1978:206). The vigor of indigenous economic
activity and the region's low population density may explain why the Isthmus was relatively free from conflict from 1770 until independence (Reina
1988:208–10). However, when outside forces impinged on Isthmus Zapotec economic interests and threatened Juchitán's political autonomy in
the 1800s, the Juchitecos responded forcefully.

The Nineteenth Century: Independence and Rebellion on the Isthmus

The Isthmus of Tehuantepec did not figure prominently in the Independence wars. Except for the flight of Oaxaca Bishop Bergosa to Tehuantepec

in 1812 and Matamoros' victory over a royal army at Niltepec in 1813, the Isthmus seldom appears in accounts of this era (Martínez Gracida 1883:582–83; Gay [1881] 1986:402–508). In one of the few significant incidents, insurgent armies looted Isthmus plantations and production facilities, temporarily crippling the indigo industry (Hamnett 1971:141). Although the rebel leader Morelos captured Oaxaca City, it was retaken by royalist forces in 1814, stalling the independence struggle in Oaxaca. When independence from Spain finally came in 1821, it began an era of rapid change and intense conflicts on the Isthmus.

Although independence removed the yoke of colonial domination from the shoulders of the Zapotecs, it also opened the way to a multinational assortment of ranchers, developers, and merchants who descended on the Isthmus in search of fortune. Colonialism had destroyed indigenous Oaxacan city-states and, in at least one respect, had simplified the Isthmus political environment. Instead of confronting a multiplicity of often-hostile ethnic neighbors, under colonial rule the Zapotecs had confronted only one major nemesis (the Spaniards) in the struggle for self-determination and control of natural resources. Independence complicated matters considerably. During the freewheeling years of the nineteenth century, Isthmus Zapotec communities (whose populations were now steadily expanding) battled North Americans, the French, Italians, mestizo Mexicans, and others for local power. New groups of outsiders appeared on the scene, and divisions within Isthmus society—especially between Tehuanos and Juchitecos—became more pronounced. The rebellions, battles, and secessionist movements that marked this era reflect the efforts of these diverse groups and factions to pursue their interests within the post-Independence political vacuum. These events also are used by COCEI activists to inspire contemporary political struggles.

In 1823 the Isthmus (combined with the Acayucán region) was declared an independent province, but in 1824 this decision was reversed and the area once again belonged to Oaxaca (O'Gorman 1973, cited in *Guchachi' Reza* 5:11, 1980). One aspect of the 1823 decree, which was carried out, was the granting of free land to foreign colonizers and veterans of the Independence wars (Binford 1983:87). In 1825 the state government passed a law which allowed the Tehuantepec salt beds to be monopolized by "an individual who could exploit the salt more economically than the indigenous people" (Reina 1988:255). Government authorities hoped to revive the battered Mexican economy through foreign investment and the exploitation of hitherto sparsely populated regions like the Isthmus. One result of this was an influx to Oaxaca of European merchants and would-be *hacendados*. The newcomers consisted of a tightly knit French commu-

nity, one German, and one Italian (Esteban Maqueo). They soon dominated the cochineal and indigo trade, and also obtained control of the best
Isthmus sugar cane and livestock estates (Tutino 1978:204). By 1842 Maqueo possessed a hacienda that encompassed 61 km of the rough road
across the Isthmus and encroached upon several Zapotec towns including
Ixtepec (Hart 1988:266).

While foreign immigrants considered the Isthmus a promising site for
capital accumulation, native people viewed their post-Independence future
differently. No longer subordinated by the Spaniards, the Isthmus Zapotecs saw an opportunity to fight for community land, pursue new commercial opportunities, and establish local autonomy in a context of reduced
central state power. Additionally, independence meant a change in status
for indigenous people from that of tribute-paying "Indians" to "citizens,"
and from membership in caste-like social strata to participation in a class
system. But independence also posed new risks to indigenous communities,
including changes in the status of municipalities, which facilitated the penetration of mestizos and other non-Indians into local political and economic life (Pastor 1987:495–536). As Mallon (1988:3) has concluded, the
nineteenth century was a period of profound transformations marked by
"social and political conflicts over who should have a say in defining the
character of the Mexican state, and the future of the Mexican nation," and,
I would add, the future of local communities.

On the Isthmus, the town of Juchitán became the center of Zapotec
efforts to achieve political and cultural autonomy in the nineteenth century.
Although Tehuantepec had begun to lose its ethnic distinctiveness and
Tehuanos now offered little resistance to outside dominance, Juchitán survived as a bastion of indigenous culture on the periphery of hacienda and
colonial town life. Unlike Tehuantepec, Juchitán's population was still predominantly Zapotec, townspeople primarily spoke the native language, and
their leaders were Indian (Tutino 1978:206).

One reason the Juchitecos resisted government intentions was that there
was money to be made by doing so. After native cloth production succumbed to the cheaper, machine-made European fabrics that entered the
market after independence, Juchiteco traders, undeterred, began smuggling the new fabrics into Mexico. In violation of Mexican law, Zapotec
merchants sent shipments of Isthmus salt, cochineal, and indigo to nearby
Guatemala in exchange for contraband European textiles (Tutino
1978:206; MA 1831). These actions both broke Mexican law and frustrated
the (mostly European) merchants of Oaxaca City and Tehuantepec, who
had hoped to monopolize the trade themselves.

Another reason the Zapotecs undermined the government's plans was that they considered much of Isthmus territory to be their rightful property, and they took measures to recover it. The need to regain land heightened as the Isthmus native population increased and the new European immigrants staked claims to prime Isthmus soil. Thus, in 1827, peasants of Ixtaltepec (a village near Juchitán) rose up in arms, burning two cattle ranches on land they claimed was their own and repudiating civil authorities who had failed to resolve previous land claims (Reina 1986:231).[13] Local landowners were so alarmed that they asked the military to establish a permanent guard post in the zone to prevent further uprisings.

Additionally, in what would become a nagging problem for Oaxaca authorities, the Juchitecos openly defied the state's power to dictate affairs in Juchitán. In 1829 the Oaxaca government was recruiting local men to serve in the state army. Juchitecas, opposed to the potential loss of their husbands and relatives, incited townspeople into taking over municipal buildings and retrieving the men recruited by the army (Basauri 1940:382–83). This was only one of many such incidents that occurred throughout the middle years of the nineteenth century.

The Meléndez Rebellions: 1834–1853

From 1834 to 1853 the political interests of the Isthmus peasantry crystallized around José Gregorio Meléndez (a.k.a. Che Gorio Melendre), a radical Juchiteco leader, ranch owner, and veteran of the Independence struggle. Assembling a force composed primarily of Isthmus Zapotecs but also including other Indians, Meléndez led a series of rebel mobilizations, including concerted acts of social banditry, efforts to restore communal lands and resources, separatist movements, and (his opponents said) "caste war."[14] Von Tempsky (1858:284), a German traveler who met Meléndez, described him as "a tall, fine-made man, of massive and deeply-marked features, an eagle's eye, dark and flashing from underneath thick eyebrows, and an arched and muscular brow," whose most outstanding character trait was "an inextinguishable hatred of Mexicans in general, and Santa Anna in particular." Brasseur [1861] 1981:145), who feared Meléndez but never met the rebel leader, described him as "sly and daring, like his superstitious compatriots." He lamented that the Juchitecos and their opponents on the Isthmus, "with their cruel discord, had turned this terrestrial paradise into a hell" ([1861] 1981:155).

Meléndez's first uprising (1834–1835) was in defense of communal lands, lagoons, and *salinas* threatened by creole outsiders (de la Cruz 1983c:64).

Militant Juchitecos, claiming the former Marquesado haciendas, nearby lagoons, and coastlines as their own, rejected the property rights of Cortés' heirs and other Europeans and rose up in arms.[15] Although the military eventually "restored order," the Zapotecs resisted local authorities and landowners and worked their ancestral salt pans throughout the 1840s, in defiance of the government's concession of the *salinas* to Echeverría, an outsider.[16] Isthmus salt had become increasingly important as a revenue source because of the declining value of indigo and cochineal dyes (caused by the rise of dye production in Asia, North Africa, and elsewhere) and because of local population growth (Tutino 1978:205). Additionally, salt had become the main item exchanged by Juchiteco smugglers for contraband textiles. In the early 1830s Oaxaca government officials complained that Isthmus salt prices had reached exorbitant levels, whereas most other commodity prices had gone down (MA 1835). In 1844 the government, also hoping to profit from salt, placed a two-*real* tax on each load of the Isthmus raw material, which angered Juchitecos (Exposición 1850:10). Given salt's value, it is no surprise that the people of Juchitán would not relinquish the *salinas* that they had worked since pre-Hispanic times without a fight.

With the end of the U.S.–Mexican War in 1847, Oaxaca Governor Benito Juárez attempted to reassert central control over the Isthmus, where, he complained, residents of Juchitán incessantly killed hacienda cattle and stole salt (de la Cruz 1983e:10). By this time, Meléndez had somehow become regional governor of the Isthmus. Juárez, perhaps thinking that the Zapotec leader could be coopted into restraining the troublesome Juchitecos, removed him as Isthmus governor and appointed him to head the local branch of the national guard instead (Reina and Abardía 1990:463–64).[17] The strategy backfired, since Meléndez considered the change a demotion. Instead of pacifying the region, Meléndez and his followers joined with rebels from San Blas (Juchitán's traditional ally) and called for separation of the Isthmus from the state of Oaxaca.[18] Although the coup attempt was put down, Meléndez had established his credentials as not only a leader of the Juchitecos but a spokesman for other Istmeños as well (Reina 1986:240–42).

In 1848 the Juchitecos defiantly pastured their cattle on hacienda lands owned by Maqueo and Guergue, and Meléndez led numerous raids on salt beds claimed by Echeverría and relied on by the government for tax revenue (Tutino 1978:208; Exposición 1850:11). In a document submitted to Isthmus authorities, Meléndez's band also challenged outsiders' exploitation of salt. The document stated "The Supreme Being put it [salt] on our soil, on our coast. . . . We are Mexicans, we are the nation, we are owners and we have an equal right to take advantage of this resource" (de la Cruz 1983e:29–30). From the Juchitecos' standpoint, they had a "natural right" to the salt—which Zapotec people had mined since pre-Hispanic times—and their "legitimate ownership" granted by God should not be abrogated by non-Istmeño entrepreneurs (de la Cruz 1983e:29). The effect of these varied incursions was to unite practically the entire Juchiteco population[19] against outsiders who sought to exploit their communal resources (de la Cruz 1983e:29).

The dissident's growing strength allowed them to take over the Juchitán jail and free partisans captured during the 1847 uprising. Meléndez's detractors also accused the Juchitecos of sheltering smugglers, looting Tehuantepec stores, and killing 5,000 head of cattle on the ex-Marquesado haciendas (de la Cruz 1983e:50). Public functionaries complained that the Juchitecos held public gatherings to disseminate information about government policies and engaged in illegal actions to the beat of drums (de la Cruz 1983e:30, 33). This is probably what prompted the governor in 1851 to prohibit all unauthorized public meetings promoted by the "sound of drums, conchs, or bells" (de la Cruz 1983e:21). Another official complained that the violence of the rebels had become so notorious that by merely declaring "I am a Juchiteco" they could get whatever they wanted in any nearby town (de la Cruz 1983e:50). Juárez ([1850] 1981:7–8), who began to view his government's conflict with Meléndez as a personal vendetta, attacked the Juchitecos in melodramatic terms:

> It would take a lengthy discourse to describe the state of immorality and disorder in which the residents of Juchitán have lived since ancient times. You know well their great excesses, you are not unaware of their depredations under the colonial regime and the attacks committed against the agents of the Spanish Government. You are not ignorant of the fact that in the time of the Central Government, they made a mockery of the armed force sent by the general power to repress their crimes. . . . You have been witnesses to these scenes of blood and horror. . . . This is not the first time that the State has been so scandalized [by Juchitecos] . . .

The Juchitecos, for their part, held no love for Juárez, even if he was Zapotec by birth. Contemporary COCEI intellectuals refer to Oaxaca Valley power-holders as the *vallistocracia*[20] (valley aristocracy), or simply *vallistos*, indicating a hostility rooted in Isthmus-Valley conflicts like the

Meléndez-Juárez confrontation. Throughout this violent period, Juchitecos engaged in numerous mobilizations—involving virtually all sectors of the community united against bitter enemies in Oaxaca, Tehuantepec, and Mexico City—which strongly shaped their sense of being a people with a distinct ethnic identity and a set of common political interests. A multiclass alliance was possible in Juchitán because, unlike the situation in Tehuantepec, the majority of Juchitecos retained their indigenous ethnic identity. For Juchitecos, ethnicity could serve as the glue that bound them together when their communal lands, salt fields, and fisheries were encroached upon by outsiders.[21] Likewise, Juchiteco leaders were firmly linked to the peasantry, as Tutino (1993:59) observed:

> Zapotec culture compromised the goals of Juchiteco notables focused on profit and local power with the values of a peasant majority insistent on subsistence autonomy. Zapotec peasants joined in commercial production—as long as it built upon subsistence production. And Juchiteco notables understood, at least implicitly, that the price of peasant support for their political agenda of local autonomy was a reciprocal support for the peasants' right to subsistence autonomy.

The mid-nineteenth century was a crucial period in the consolidation of the new Mexican state. But as Mallon (1988:5) has shown, "state formation was not only the product of struggles within and between the dominant classes and foreign powers, but also a process in which the peasants, small farmers, and other folk who made up the bulk of the population in the nineteenth-century were involved." In mid-century Juchitán, the future shape of local society was an open question, as various groups vied for political and economic power. Although the state and national authorities eventually won out, Meléndez and his rebels maintained local autonomy for an extended period and their actions limited the state's ability to unilaterally enforce its will on the populace.

In the spring of 1849, the Oaxaca government prohibited the sale of salt in Juchitán and sent a small contingent of soldiers to put an end to what it considered a series of abuses committed by Juchitecos (Reina and Abardía 1990:465). Preoccupied with the upcoming corn-planting season, Zapotec peasants opted to avoid conflict. However, in 1850, with the imposition of an unpopular new tax on salt, the stage was set for another confrontation with the state government (Brasseur [1861] 1981:145).

In April, Meléndez provoked official wrath to new heights when he and his followers jailed and fined a local official (Manuel Niño) who they caught illegally selling Juchitán communal land and a related map to Maqueo, the Italian hacienda owner (Tutino 1978:208). Unappreciative of this act of "revolutionary justice," the government sent troops from Tehuantepec to free the official and jail members of Meléndez's band. The Meléndez movement responded by routing the Tehuantepec garrison—killing 10 and wounding 22 others—and taking over Juchitán (de la Cruz 1983e:39). By then, the movement had grown to about 1,000 men from Juchitán and the surrounding Zapotec communities of Huilotepec, Ixtaltepec, and San Blas—all of which would later become strongholds of COCEI—as well as Huave and Chontal pueblos (Reina 1986:240–42; Tutino 1978:208).

In a letter to Governor Juárez, Meléndez explained that he was forced to fight the soldiers in order to prevent them from confiscating Juchitán's sacred land titles and map (which his men had recaptured from Manuel Niño):

> ... knowing that I had the map and titles in my possession, said authorities [a military commander and Echeverría, the salt monopolist, who had also become governor of the Juchitán district] sent for them by way of a *regidor*, C. Juan Castillejos; and considering that these documents are very interesting and relevant items because they belong to the commune, I refused due to my obligation to the people ... [de la Cruz 1983e:40].

Emblematic of the collective nature of Juchiteco land tenure (and the significance attributed to the communal land titles), Meléndez stated that the land documents should only be turned over in the presence of traditional community authorities and the populace, who, he said, forbade him from doing so. Thus, local conceptions of land management and political authority conflicted with the central government's liberal economic program, and the result was violence. In this case, at least, the Juchitecos were victorious. Meléndez celebrated the triumph of his peasant band over the hated government forces by composing a *corrido*.[22]

Eventually, Juárez decided things had gone too far and sent more than 400 soldiers and light artillery to Juchitán to crush the Meléndez movement (de la Cruz 1983e:46). Although the troops killed 70 rebels and wounded many others in a 3-hour gunfight in May 1850, Meléndez and the majority of his supporters escaped to Chiapas, pursued by the national guard. During the battle, Juárez's soldiers set fire to several palm huts. The fire spread and eventually wiped out almost a third of Juchitán's dwellings (Tutino 1978:208–9). In the aftermath of this incident, which remains indelibly printed in the minds of COCEI intellectuals, Juárez attempted to avoid responsibility for the fire, claiming high winds had caused it to spread from house to house (Exposición 1851).

At this point, the Meléndez movement turned increasingly to social banditry and outright rebellion against the state. A horrified government observer exclaimed that Meléndez's war cry had become "Death to the state of Oaxaca and long live Juchitán" (de la Cruz 1983e:50). Beware of a caste war, the official warned, because the Juchitecos are indifferent to anything but their lands, their robbery, and their town. The mutual hostility between Juchitán and Oaxaca City was also manifested in a rumor that the government meant not only to punish the rebels, but to exterminate the entire population of Juchitán as well (MA 1852).

Enraged by the burning of Juchitán, Meléndez's forces regrouped in Chiapas and returned to the Isthmus with a vengeance. En route, the rebels sacked Tapanatepec and Niltepec, burned La Venta hacienda and killed its Spanish administrator,[23] and invaded Tehuantepec (Martínez Gracida 1883:587). In all these actions, the insurgents directed their anger against the properties and representatives of the Oaxaca City and local elite, especially Maqueo (Tutino 1978:209; Baltazar 1982:14). Tehuantepec businessmen and politicians were prime targets of the Juchitecos, who longed for freedom from the political and economic domination of that city (Nuñez Ríos 1969:1). Taking advantage of a cholera epidemic that weakened the Oaxaca state army, Meléndez took over Juchitán and killed its subprefect. He also staged another raid on Tehuantepec, burning several barrios and killing Tehuanos who got in his way (Martínez Gracida 1883:588).

The Meléndez uprisings, and the expense of trying to crush them, took their toll on the state government. In their annual "state of the state" reports, Oaxaca officials complained that the rebellion interrupted the flow of commerce, impeded tax collection, absorbed almost all of the funds of the treasury, and paralyzed public works projects (MA 1851, 1852).

Between October 1850 and January 1851, the rebels released two manifestos calling for an end to "9 months of revolution between Juchitán and Tehuantepec," the elimination of customs offices that restricted Juchiteco trade to Guatemala, and (once again) the secession of the Isthmus from the state of Oaxaca (Martínez Gracida 1883:209). Soon thereafter Juárez sent a large enough army to finally quell the Meléndez movement. Though Meléndez escaped to the hills with other rebel leaders, the majority of his followers laid down their arms and returned to their pueblos. Meléndez resumed his politico-military activities in 1852 with yet another attack on Tehuantepec, the exaction of "loans" from local merchants, and a separatist plan for the Isthmus (Martínez Gracida 1883:270; Brioso y Candiani 1941:133). Finally, Meléndez died of poisoning (presumably administered by his enemies) in 1853, but not without first negotiating with Santa Anna to obtain Isthmus independence from Oaxaca (Tutino 1993).[24]

The Meléndez rebellions represented, above all, Juchiteco struggles against postcolonial exploitation by European land usurpers, foreign merchants, and a government bent on sacrificing Indian communal lands and autonomy to the altar of centralized state power and incipient capitalist development.[25] The nature of this challenge—the intrusion of ethnically distinct outsiders onto indigenous communal territory—was such that nearly the entire Juchiteco population (indigenous merchants, ranchers, artisans, and peasants alike) united against their common enemies. Moreover, intrusion onto lands and *salinas* affected the Zapotecs, Huave, and Chontals relatively equally, allowing for a multiethnic front. As the former center of colonial power, the site of the mestizo elite in the post-Independence Isthmus, and a regional opponent, Tehuantepec was the prime focus of the Meléndez movement's hatred. In addition to the properties of European *hacendados* and businessmen, the other main target of the Meléndez rebels was the Oaxaca government, which hoped to control the Isthmus for its own political and economic ends. Thus, the Meléndez revolts were not only a form of ethnic resistance but also expressed regional rivalries and the Juchitecos' separatist intentions. But for a leading COCEI intellectual, the Meléndez rebellions are important because they provide lessons for contemporary Zapotecs—"to win in the struggle for a more just society" (de la Cruz 1983e:23).

Nineteenth-Century Development Schemes: Foreign Exploration, Hegemonic Intentions, and "the Other"

By mid-century, the Isthmus had become a hotbed of development schemes and transportation projects that sparked another series of Juchiteco rebellions. Because of its strategic location, the slender Isthmus has long figured in European plans for communication between the Atlantic and Pacific oceans. Cortés first suggested the advantages of a passage across the region's 120-mile breadth in 1525. Viceroy Bucareli renewed calls for a road or canal through the Isthmus in 1774, and Von Humboldt echoed these sentiments in 1808 (Covarrubias 1946:164). But it was not until the post-Independence era that foreign firms obtained concessions to the area and sent survey teams to explore possibilities for constructing a transcontinental road, canal, or railway. The reports of these early explorers provide a window onto mid-nineteenth century Isthmus life and the region's role in the hegemonic designs of powerful nations.

The first of these expeditions was funded by a shrewd entrepreneur, José de Garay (Moro 1844). Though based on extensive surveying and measurements, the expedition's report was obviously designed to present a favorable picture of the Isthmus, in addition to any scientific pretensions it may have had. The images of future profit to be reaped from a rich and exotic land depicted in the report helped Garay sell his rights to the region to a British firm. This scenario was repeated again and again until completion of the railway in 1907. For Europeans and North Americans, the Isthmus was a promised land (or at least it could be described as such for the sake of raising stock values) that would provide personal profit, corporate gains, and "national security" to those brave developers or governments able to conquer it. Its residents were an industrious and intelligent lot, who would be a willing and able labor force in the construction of a canal or railroad (Moro 1844:19, 88, 94). Cayetano Moro (1844:137), the director of Garay's survey, exclaimed: "The inhabitants of that territory [the Isthmus] evinced the greatest desire for the realization of this great undertaking."

Gushings about friendly Indians aside, the Isthmus Zapotecs surely saw through the pretensions of this new breed of foreign developer. Indeed, the U.S. consul in Tehuantepec observed that "the country is full of rumors of the designs and intentions of the Americans to possess themselves of the Isthmus of Tehuantepec" (Consul 5/8/1852). Any doubts the Zapotecs had would have been confirmed by seeing Garay's commission reconnoitering the area accompanied by Esteban Maqueo, hacienda owner and archenemy of Juchitán peasants (Moro 1844:37).[26] As Von Tempsky (1858:282) noted in 1853, the Juchitecos were very wary of European intruders: "This village [Juchitán] was . . . reputed for its hostility against white strangers, or strangers of any kind." Similar sentiments were echoed two years later by the American consular agent in Tehuantepec: "Among the villages most notorious for the propensity to strife is Juchitán. . . . The inhabitants have acquired a character for courage and fierceness. . . ." (Consul 2/24/1855). According to current COCEI leader Daniel López Nelio, Juchitecos are taught at an early age to love Zapotec culture and hate dxu' (foreigners). Not a gratuitous ethnocentrism, Juchiteco hostility towards foreigners developed precisely because of constant incursions by Europeans during the colonial era and continuing into the 19th century.

The motives of outsiders who coveted Isthmus lands became starkly apparent in 1847–1848, when the United States insisted the Treaty of Guadalupe Hidalgo contain a clause conferring free transit for North American citizens, soldiers, and merchandise across the region (F. Campbell 1988). The North American government planned to establish military and naval bases on the Isthmus (Fernández MacGregor 1954:28). U.S. negotiators declared their willingness to pay Mexico as much as $25 million for New Mexico and California, provided the Tehuantepec clause was included in the treaty (Fernández MacGregor 1954:12–13). In 1853 Santa Anna granted free passage across the Isthmus to North Americans as part of the La Mesilla Treaty; this privilege remained intact until it was revoked by the nationalistic Cárdenas regime in 1938. Although the U.S. government was unable to advance its claims beyond obtaining transit rights, British and North American private interests' attempts to build an Isthmus railroad continued throughout the nineteenth century and eventually succeeded.

In 1850–1851, U.S. engineers conducted their own survey of the "boundless riches" of the Isthmus, and a road was opened from Coatzacoalcos to Tehuantepec (Williams 1852). Williams notes that the majority of workers on the road project were from Juchitán. The new route attracted numerous European travelers, some of whom wrote colorful travelogues of their experiences and misadventures in the region. Although these accounts, and the surveyor's reports, are laden with Eurocentric racial opinions and the political and economic agendas of their authors or benefactors,[27] they also provide insights into Isthmus life in the mid-nineteenth century and the region's importance to world powers.

Although Garay's surveyors made exaggerated claims about the fine health of Isthmus residents and the region's beautiful climate, they were superb engineers with a fine eye for natural resources. During their 9-month study, the Spanish and Italian crew produced excellent maps, detailed descriptions, and thorough statistical data about the exploitable animals, agricultural products, and minerals of the Isthmus. Make no mistake about it: these were plans for development and colonization on a large scale. In the early 1850s the Louisiana Tehuantepec Company posted advertisements of the sale of Isthmus land in major cities throughout the United States (Meier 1854:42). According to the developers' plans, North Americans and Europeans would take control of the "treasures of incalculable value" (Moro 1844:89) and the local population would do the drudge work necessary to make it all happen. Indigo, cane, tropical hardwoods, ixtle, corn, brasilwood for extracting red dyes, cacao, wild game, gum, salt, fish, shrimp, and excellent pasture lands were just waiting for the white man to benefit from them. And even if cochineal had largely been abandoned, in Tehuantepec there were

> bakers, carpenters, smiths, tinkers, silversmiths, tanners, shoemak-ers, saddlers, and . . . every family, whatever may be their circum-stances, manufactures the soap necessary for home consumption. The clothes woven by the women from wild silk and cotton are really ad-mirable . . . [Moro 1844:95].

Engineer Williams' results, "foreshadowing as they do an enterprise cal-culated to effect a commercial revolution," embellished many of the same themes taken up by Moro, but with even finer maps and drawings. Williams (1852:250–51) was especially impressed by Juchitán:

> The inhabitants of Juchitán are characterized by habits of industry, and their numerous manufactures of hats, shoes, cotton cloth, hides, buckskins, mats, hammocks, etc. bear ample testimony to their mental superiority over the other settlements of the Isthmus. Among the ar-ticles raised are maize, indigo, and fruits. In addition, considerable valuable wood is annually gathered, and the inhabitants export large quantities of tallow and gum-arabic. Altogether, and in spite of many severe obstacles imposed by the government, Juchitán is the most in-dustrious and thrifty town on the Pacific plains. Its appearance is en-livened by bustling shops, and the streets are more or less filled with ponderous carts drawn by oxen, and laden either with salt from the lagoons, or goods brought from Guatemala.

Whereas the engineers painted an idyllic picture of the Isthmus, two French travelers attracted to the area by these accounts around 1860, de-scribed the aftereffects of a U.S. company's (the Louisiana-Tehuantepec Railroad Co.) activities there. Instead of the bountiful profits prophesied by Garay and Williams, the company "left Tehuantepec in ruins, as well as the peasants, who still await the salary for their labor, payment for the rental of their animals, and for the work implements they provided" (Char-nay [1863] 1982:7). Charnay observed that the route built by the "Yankees" had been invaded by vegetation and washed out by floods. Moreover, Meier (1954:177) found that large numbers of workers on the railroad, the ma-jority of whom were Indian (Consul 9/30/1858), died of yellow fever.

Brasseur, upon arrival in the Isthmus in 1859, encountered a band of

Juchitecos on their way to confront gringo patrons who had failed to pay them for their services. If the gringos refused to pay, the Juchitecos were threatening to boycott the company and burn down its main building (Brasseur [1861] 1981:118). Although Brasseur ([1861] 1981:150) was horrified by seminude Juchiteco soldiers lying on their *petates* in "obscene promiscuity" with their concubines, wives, and children, he was fascinated by the Zapotec women. In his romantic account of the Isthmus, Brasseur ([1861] 1981:159) described a colorful Zapotec woman he met (presumably Juana C. Romero):

> She was a Zapotec Indian with bronze-colored skin, young, slender, elegant, and so beautiful that she enchanted the hearts of the whites, as Cortés' mistress had in an earlier time. . . . She wore a wrapped skirt of a sea-green, striped material, a bodice of red silk gauze, and a great necklace of gold coins, hung closely from a gold chain. Her hair was done in two splendid braids tied with blue silk ribbons, and a headdress of white muslin framed her face, with exactly the same pleats and in the same manner as the Egyptian *calantica*. . . . I never saw a more striking image of Isis or of Cleopatra.[28]

European observers were particularly impressed by the dynamic Isthmus markets and the fiery, elegantly dressed Zapotec women who ran them.[29] For Europeans and North Americans, the Isthmus was a tropical paradise with untapped riches waiting to be plundered, a promising transoceanic communication link, and an essential site for military maneuvers. For the Isthmus Zapotecs, it was a homeland, occupied first by Spaniards and now many others, but theirs to defend at all costs.

"Reform" and Resistance

While foreigners' hegemonic schemings were a growing threat to Isthmus Zapotec autonomy throughout the nineteenth century, a more immediate attack on indigenous communities in the mid-1800s came from within Mexico, in the form of the so-called Reform Laws. Between 1849 and 1851, Governor Juárez passed laws allowing public auction of Oaxaca "land, ranches, bodies of water, hills, houses, and other things" belonging to the municipalities (Esparza 1990:393). In 1856 Juárez decreed disamortization laws, which were designed to streamline the Mexican economy by breaking up indigenous communal land holdings and the properties of the Catholic church. In some areas of the Isthmus, such as Ixtepec and Ixtaltepec, the laws took their toll, reducing Zapotec pueblo lands to a bare minimum (Hart 1988:266). Nonetheless, the objectives of pure liberalism were not always implemented in Oaxaca. In that region, and perhaps much of Mexico, another important element of the reform era resided in the political battles that ensued as the government attempted to force capitalist institutions and values onto an often reluctant population (Berry 1981).

This was evident on the Isthmus, where Juchiteco liberals and Tehuano conservatives engaged in constant conflicts and violence. Although the events of this period are enmeshed in murky accounts of vendettas, banditry, and intervillage hatred, we can also read in these reports references to continued struggles for ethnic independence and control of natural resources. Thus, the internecine conflicts of the reform era on the Isthmus contained elements of both individual and collective struggle. In the end, the outcomes of these struggles were just as significant to local history as legal changes imposed from above. Today COCEI leaders see them as the foundation of their own political movement.

After the death of Meléndez, groups of Juchitecos, allied with Blaseños, continued to denounce and rise up against local authorities. Despite the establishment of an Isthmus Territory separate from the state of Oaxaca, the Juchitán-Tehuantepec rivalry persisted. In 1855 Juchiteco liberals (who wore green colors to distinguish themselves from the conservatives, who wore red colors,[30] pronounced for the Plan de Ayutla and defeated conservatives in several local skirmishes (López Gurrión 1976:79–80). In 1856 Tehuanos killed the Juchiteco leader Miguel López, further inciting intervillage hostilities (Iturribarría 1939:46). The following year, the Isthmus was reincorporated into the state of Oaxaca and Juchitán was raised to the status of *villa*, but it remained subject to mestizo authorities in Tehuantepec, which rankled the Juchitecos. The conflict between Juchitán and Tehuantepec had cultural as well as political dimensions, one of which was a competition between the women of both towns, who tried to outdress each other (Terrones 1990:154).

Although Tehuantepec and Juchitán declared a truce, peace lasted only until 1858, when a conservative Spanish general, backed by Tehuantepec *patricios* ("traitors" to the liberal cause), invaded the Isthmus. As in the past, the Juchitecos fought against the Tehuanos and their allies, although in this case the Juchitecos were in the rare position of defending the government and its local representative, Captain Porfirio Díaz. When the young Díaz was named *gobernador* of the Isthmus, his only supporters were the Juchitecos, a group from Guevea, and the Blaseños; the rest of Tehuantepec's barrio inhabitants opposed him (Iturribarría 1939:167). Brasseur ([1861] 1981:147) observed that while Díaz controlled Tehuantepec, Juchitecos occupied the major offices of municipal government. Presumably because of Juchitán's loyalty to the national government which was faced with a conservative counterrevolution, in 1858 the town was finally granted administrative and judicial independence from rival Tehuantepec, which had dominated it since pre-Hispanic times (López Gurrión 1976:86).

In his memoirs, however, Díaz (1947:86–88) recalled that the Juchitecos almost killed him in 1859 because they feared that the government's new civil registration law[31] was a threat to popular religion.[32] Additionally, despite the Juchitecos' temporary support of established authority, in 1861 the state government reported it had been unable to eradicate Juchitán's contraband trade (MA 1861). Moreover, in an important battle with the conservatives in 1860, a group of Juchitecos deserted Díaz's army and returned to their hometown (Orozco 1946:31). Juchitecos, it seems, were ultimately loyal only to Juchitán or themselves. Or, as a Oaxaca Valley establishment newspaper bitterly put it, "Juchitán is a war camp, each citizen, with a gun on his shoulder, recognizes no God nor law other than his own will" (Iturribarría 1939:2:73).

There was also an anti-imperialist element in Juchiteco resistance to outside authority. In 1858 a Juchiteco soldier attacked the U.S. consul in Tehuantepec with a machete or flat sword (Consul 9/3/1858, 9/30/1858). Additionally, a group of Juchiteco rebels tore down and stole the flag of the Consulate (Consul 9/30/1859), which prompted the following comments:

It would have been very easy for Col. Salinas and his Juchitecos, who by the downfall of Santa Anna became the governing party, to have at least offered some apology in saluting the flag on some special occasion. Nothing of the kind was however done, and the insult remains to this time unaccounted for [Consul 9/30/1858].

An antiforeign element may also have been a feature of the frequent assaults on the coaches and passengers of the Louisiana Tehuantepec Company during this period. Noted the U.S. consul: "I have made out a list of about 40 foreigners principally Americans, who have been robbed, assaulted with intent to kill" (Consul 9/30/1858).

Although residents of Juchitán participated in several minor uprisings in the first half of the 1860s, the next important battle involving the community occurred in 1866 during the French Intervention. True to form, the liberal, primarily indigenous Juchitecos (and their Blaseño allies) opposed the European invaders, while the Hispanicized Tehuanos sided with them. Inhabitants of San Blas were especially fervent allies of the Juchitecos because of their shared hostility towards the Tehuanos and because San Blas, like Juchitán, remained predominantly a community of Zapotec peasants and fishermen.[33]

In 1864 the Tehuantepec military captain Remigio Toledo pronounced for Maximilian, earning for himself the pejorative nickname *gubizi* (rattlesnake) from Juchitecos and Blaseños who opposed French rule. Liberal anger towards the Tehuano captain increased after he attacked and burned San Blas, forcing its inhabitants to flee and leaving the town in smoking ruins (Molina 1911:15). From November 1865 until a decisive battle on September 5, 1866, the Blaseños survived on rotten tree roots and slept in the bush or relied on their Juchiteco allies to provide them with lodging and a daily ration of *rancho* (a meager quantity of broken *totopos*, a type of dried meat called *tasajo*, and one medium-sized fish), or bits of cheese (Molina 1911:35). Forming a ramshackle army, the Juchitecos and Blaseños waged a guerrilla war against Toledo and his Tehuano followers until the French sent a large detachment to quell the resistance.[34] The rebels were so poor that their Juchiteco leader could only buy them machetes without handles. Instead of uniforms, the men wore loose cotton shirts, *calzoncillos*, cheap black hats, and huaraches (Molina 1911:32).

Given the humble condition of this peasant army, it should come as no surprise that their subsequent victory over the "finest soldiers in the world," as a Blaseño historian (Molina 1911:38) described the French battalion, had a profound effect on Isthmus Zapotec consciousness. The rebels' strategy was to abandon Juchitán, which they had first burned and emptied of all food and potential weapons, to the invading army (A. Martínez López 1966:74). Prior to the fighting, the oldest of the Juchiteco *principales* (according to local accounts) invoked the help of Juchitán's patron saint, *San Vicente Ferrer*, and urged his fellow townspeople on with the following words: "Now is the time, Father Vicente, let's jump on them, it's either them or us, but they will not pass through here!" (A. Martínez López 1966:72).[35]

Once the 2,500-strong imperialist troops occupied the town, the poorly armed men, women, and children of Juchitán and San Blas laid siege to it, exploiting their mobility and familiarity with local geography to the fullest. According to a Juchiteco version of the battle, a Zapotec woman—"aware of the psychology of the men of her race"—rang the church bells and goaded the male combatants into action by shouting, "If you cannot get them [the French] out of the center of our town, Speak up!, and give us, the women, your weapons and you will see if we get them out or not" (A. Martínez López 1966:82).[36]

Women figure prominently in local accounts of the 5 de Septiembre battle and the considerable folklore surrounding it. Molina (1911:41), a Blaseño intellectual who Covarrubias (1946: 228) describes as an "eyewitness," mentions the participation of four Juchiteca "heroines" in the battle, as well as a fifth Juchiteca who alerted her comrades to the retreat of the French army. Rueda Sáynez and Rueda Jiménez (1981:102–3) note that Zapotec women, in addition to urging on the rebel soldiers, took up arms, prepared food for the combatants, and nursed the injured. Other versions of events claim that Zapotec women from Espinal came to the aid of injured French soldiers, who they took to their homes and married. According to contemporary Istmeños, Espinal is populated by numerous tall, blue-eyed, light-skinned women who are the attractive products of these unions. Some Juchitecas, less impressed with these beauties, occasionally refer to the women of rival Espinal as *Espinalgas*.[37]

A favorite legend involving women during this period has General Porfirio Díaz hiding under the petticoats (*enaguas*) of Juana C. Romero during combat with the French (Krauze 1987:18). The empirical veracity of this account is questionable, because such imagery—of men seeking refuge in the skirts of matriarchal Zapotec women—appears in many different versions of conflicts past and present on the Isthmus. The author encountered it several times during fieldwork, sometimes in accounts of relatively minor events. The image has more to do with local gender discourses and mythology about powerful Zapotec women than with specific historical incidents.

Though neither side was able to gain an advantage in the initial 5 de Septiembre battle, the French were finally forced to retreat due to the lack of available foodstuffs, but their escape was spotted by a Juchiteca who enjoined the rest of her Zapotec allies to pursue the fleeing Europeans (A. Martínez López 1966:86). The French, opted for the most direct route back to Tehuantepec, which sent them through a swampy area (*Laguna Igú*) made treacherous by the September rains (A. Martínez López 1966:86). There, the Zapotec slaughtered the water-logged imperial troops and carted off their two cannons, which have since become part of a prominent monument to the battle located near the entrance to Juchitán.[38]

Ever since this time, on September 5 Juchiteco politicians stand in front of the cannons and commemorate the battle with windy speeches, pomp, and ceremony followed by a *vela* (fiesta) celebration in the evening. The

participation of Juchiteca heroines in the conflict receives special com-
mendation, which reflects the Juchitecos' own conceptions about the power
and combativeness of Zapotec women. While a wide gap exists between
the interpretations of the event made by local and national historians (who
have paid little attention to it), the 5 de Septiembre battle did effectively
end French attempts to control the Isthmus, and prevented the imperial
army from invading Chiapas (A. Martínez López 1966:96). For Juchitecos,
however, this incident meant much more than a slight advance in the
French-Mexican War. For the Zapotecs it was an ethnic victory, a vindi-
cation of Juchiteco and Juchiteca integrity and bravery, and a demonstration of Juchitán's equality, if not superiority, vis-à-vis other peoples of the
world. It also demonstrated their "patriotism," as opposed to the "treach-
ery" of the "*Tehuanos traidores*," an epithet invoked even today by Blaseños
and Juchitecos against their village rivals.[39] The 5 de Septiembre battle is
now a cornerstone of Juchiteco pride and a politicized version of local
history espoused by COCEI leadership.

As a result of the San Blaseño's solidarity with the Republican cause and
their personal support of Díaz, the powerful general made San Blas a free
municipality, separate from Tehuantepec, in 1868. He rewarded Juchitán
by sponsoring the education of a group of young Juchitecos in Oaxaca and
Mexico City, and including one of them (Rosendo Pineda) in his innercir-
cle of allies and advisors (known as *científicos*) when he became dictator
(López Gurrión 1976:105–6). According to Chassen (1986:272), Pineda
was the most powerful member of the *científicos*.[40] Pineda's position gave
Juchitán access to valuable favors from the highest tier of Mexican politicians and prompted a migration of Juchitecos to Mexico City for education,
which eventually produced a fertile Juchiteco literary movement.

Ironically, one of the first Juchitecos supported by Díaz, Juvencio Robles, later made a name for himself as a ruthless general who ravaged Morelos while in pursuit of Zapata (Womack 1969). Another Díaz protégé
from Juchitán, Rosalino Martínez, became Undersecretary of War and
gained notoriety for killing dozens of striking workers at Rio Blanco, Veracruz, in 1906, in an incident that helped provoke the Mexican Revolution
(López Gurrión 1976:106). These "reactionary" Juchitecos are seldom
mentioned by COCEI intellectuals.

Binu Gada and Félix Díaz:
Juchiteco Rebellion in the 1870s and 1880s

As the Juchiteco disciples of President Díaz would demonstrate, not all of
Juchitán's children were bound to become rebels and revolutionaries. Still,

the majority of townspeople did maintain their political independence. In either case, Juchitecos displayed an uncanny knack for thrusting themselves into national political events, the small size and relative poverty of their home community notwithstanding. Indeed, the state of Oaxaca enjoyed its political zenith between the 1860s and the 1910 Revolution, during which time the country was governed first by Juárez and then by Díaz, both of whom were required on numerous occasions to deal with dissident Juchiteco movements.

While these mobilizations each had its particular etiology, in general the uprisings of this period, and the earlier nineteenth-century rebellions discussed previously, roughly corresponded with what Knight (1986:115–27, 301–9) has described as "*serrano*" rebellion. For Knight (1986:122), *serrano* movements (as opposed to "*agrarista*" rebellions, as typified by *Zapatismo*) consisted of "rebellion against an external political agency (of which the cacique and his *camarilla* might figure as local representatives) . . . often capable of mobilising very nearly the entire community."

Struggles over land could play a role in *serrano* rebellions, but agrarian demands were only one aspect of the complex set of motivations that inspired such movements, whose paramount goals were village autonomy. Rather than being fundamentally class struggles within local rural society, as in *agrarista* rebellions, *serrano* revolts typically pitted one village against another, or the home village against the state, in struggles that united local people across class lines against their external enemies.

While nineteenth century Juchiteco political movements (and the Che Gómez movement discussed below) meet many of the criteria that define Knight's *serrano* movements, they differ in one fundamental respect. For Knight (1986:116), the archetypal *serrano* rebels were the mestizo villagers of the northern sierras, and he notes that *serrano* rebellion was sparked by political and economic factors rather than ethnic identity: "Ethnicity affected the character of the [*serrano*] protest, but it did not determine who the protesters would be." Such a neat distinction, while appropriate for many parts of northern Mexico, is less applicable to Juchitán (although Knight considers Juchitán a classic site of *serrano* activity also), where political economy and ethnicity cannot be so easily separated.

For Juchitecos, the defense of village autonomy meant not only a fight to defend a piece of land and the right to be governed by local individuals, it touched on their very existence as a people with a distinct language, set of customs, and identity rooted in a particular centuries-old ecological and social adaptation. Indeed, in Juchitán, land, political autonomy, and ethnic identity were indissolubly linked. Only people who had been born in the community and had their placenta [*doo yoo*] buried there could qualify as

Juchitecos (Royce 1975:194). Juchitán rebels fought for control of particular places with Zapotec names (e.g., *Guelabigo, Quieguichachi, Guelayaga-*
siga) and local histories associated with them, and they believed that they
were protected in battle by *San Vicente*, their patron saint (TPJ [1736–
1737] 1987).⁴¹ Moreover, the Juchitecos viewed their political enemies
(French soldiers, Oaxaca Valley and Mexico City politicians, and the mestizo or European merchants of Tehuantepec) in oppositional ethnic terms,
as *dxu'* (foreigners) rather than *binni za* (Isthmus Zapotecs). The Juchitecos'
attachment to their hometown was more than just "parochial sentiment,"
but cut to the very core of their being and definition of self. Thus, ethnicity
was tightly interwoven with political and economic motivations that cod-
etermined "who the protesters would be" and who their opponents would
be also (cf. Knight 1986:116).

In 1872, just 6 years after the 5 de Septiembre battle, Juchitán once again
became involved in a conflict that aroused local ethnic sentiments and stimulated internal community solidarity vis-à-vis outsiders. In this case the
Juchitecos' adversary was Félix Díaz, brother of the country's future dictator. Like Porfirio, Félix was a soldier and prominent politician, and in
1867 he became governor of Oaxaca. Hoping to reinforce Oaxaca Valley
control over Juchitán—which continued to reclaim its communal lands and
salt beds, engage in illegal commerce, and evade state sales taxes⁴²—Díaz
named an outsider *jefe político* of the town (an ill-conceived maneuver that
Oaxaca authorities would also try at a future date—with the same unfortunate result) (Berry 1981:123). The localistic Juchitecos ran out the *"dxu'*
yuudxu' " (rotten foreigner) and set up their own government led by Albino
Jiménez (a.k.a. Binu Gada), who had directed them in battle against the
French (Covarrubias 1946:230). They also plotted separation from Oaxaca
once again. Díaz responded by attacking Juchitán. After defeating Binu
Gada's forces, Díaz and his troops killed any prisoners they could capture,
burned down most of the town's houses, and looted its treasury (Martínez
Gracida 1883:596). Falcone (1990:508) notes that Díaz's men mercilessly
killed numerous Juchitecos. Finally, Díaz stole Juchitán's patron saint, San
Vicente, dragged the statue behind the back of a horse, and burned it
(López Gurrión 1976:105).

The seriousness of this offense, in the minds of Juchitecos, derived from
the fact that San Vicente or (Xabizende, as they called him in Zapotecized
Spanish) was more than just a wooden idol. Juchitecos viewed the statue
as a guardian who looked after the well-being of the community and
granted favors to its residents.⁴³ The Juchitecos' rallying cry in their many
battles was *Viva Xabizende!* Moreover, Juchitecos even called their com-

munity Xabizende. Thus, the statue of San Vicente was the physical embodiment of group identity, and its desecration was viewed as a serious insult by all Juchitecos. Once again, a nearly all-sectoral mobilization of townspeople was possible.

After Díaz and his army left Juchitán, Binu Gada, who had escaped to the hills, returned and took control of the town (Martínez Gracida 1883:596). While the survivors rebuilt their shattered community, they also begged Díaz to return the stolen saint, and when these efforts failed, they appealed directly to President Juárez. Díaz finally yielded to the President's entreaties and sent what remained of the statue in a box to Juchitán. When the Juchitecos received San Vicente, however, they were horrified to find that his feet had been cut off to accommodate the statue to the size of the box (Cosío Villegas 1980).

In the meantime, Binu Gada and his followers chose to support Juárez over Porfirio Díaz for the presidency. When the Díaz brothers rose up in arms and Porfirio pronounced the La Noria Plan, Binu Gada defeated Díaz supporters on the Isthmus (López Gurrión 1976:105). Elsewhere, the Díaz movement also failed, and Félix Díaz was forced to flee. While attempting to escape by boat from the southern Oaxaca coast, Díaz was captured by Binu Gada and his supporters (Covarrubias 1946:230).

Numerous versions exist as to what happened next, but all concur that Díaz was brutally tortured before being killed by the Juchitecos. According to Henestrosa de Webster (1985:71), the Juchitecos sliced the skin off the bottom of Díaz's feet, then forced him to walk on burning hot sand, before castrating and shooting him. Díaz's testicles were then placed in his mouth and his body was mounted on a horse and sent into Pochutla, where he was buried. *Xabizende* had taken its revenge, and whatever the veracity of these accounts, Juchitán's ferocious image (which is both cultivated by Juchitecos and held by many non-Juchitecos) continued to grow. Likewise, Juchitecos' enmity towards Oaxaca government officials was hardened by Félix Díaz's treatment of their town. Contemporary Juchitecos revel in this incident, which they view as one episode in their long history of valiant struggle against oppressive outsiders.

Juchitecos rebelled again in 1876 as part of an attack on Tehuantepec in support of Porfirio Díaz's Plan de Tuxtepec. The rebellion led to the death of Binu Gada and 34 of his men, however (López Gurrión 1976:106). Unrest resumed in 1879 when a group of Juchitecos threatened revolt in protest of despoliation of their communal lands and salt flats (Terrones López 1990:159–60). In 1880 the dissidents ran the *jefe político* of Juchitán out of town and declared the community independent (López Gurrión

1976:108). In 1881 they engaged in banditry throughout the Isthmus and protested new head taxes imposed by local authorities (Terrones López 1990:165–67).

Although the 1881 rebels were crushed by the army, which also burned several towns in the San Miguel Chimalapa area, in 1882 they rose up yet again under the leadership of Ignacio Nicolás (Mexu Chele), a former *gobernador*, who called for independence of the Isthmus from Oaxaca. According to one account (López Trujillo 1984:17), Mexu Chele also opposed construction of the Tehuantepec railroad. Mexu Chele's movement also fought to regain communal land which the Maqueo family had annexed to their hacienda (López Gurrión 1976:70).[44] This time the Juchiteco dissidents killed the *jefe político* imposed from the Oaxaca Valley, and took over the town until a military battalion from Oaxaca suppressed them (Martínez Gracida 1883:274). Mexu Chele escaped but his supporters surrendered and were either forced to labor on construction of the massive Juchitán City Hall building (which still stands today), or were exiled to the prison work camps of Valle Nacional and Quintana Roo (de la Cruz 1983c:68). Zapotec women associated with the rebels were sent to San Miguel Chimalapa (*Neza* 12:3, 1936). Eventually, however, the government granted amnesty to the participants in the rebellion, a precedent which COCEI leaders would later invoke after their own conflicts with governmental authorities (Arellanes 1982:12). The Mexu Chele movement was the last major Juchiteco revolt until the Mexican Revolution.

The Porfiriato, Colonization, and Railroad Construction

The nineteenth-century Juchiteco rebellions occurred within the framework of attempts by the newly formed state of Oaxaca and the Mexican national government to assert their authority over outlying areas like the Isthmus. This was the beginning of a gradual political transition—which gained momentum during the Porfiriato—in which the authoritarian but distant colonial state gave way to a federalist system, in which power over Juchitán was wielded more directly, proximately, and efficiently from the Oaxaca Valley and Mexico City. Although this process began in the early to mid-nineteenth century, it did not reach fruition until after the Revolution.

Thus, during the Porfiriato, local communities like Juchitán were increasingly drawn under the political umbrella of the state. In Juchitán, the Porfiriato also marked the emergence of a small but powerful group of Juchitecos whose interests were not served by rebellion against Mexico

City and Oaxaca authorities (Nuñez Ríos 1969:14; Matus 1985:92). Whereas the nature of the 5 de Septiembre battle of 1866 was such that all Juchitecos could unite against the naked aggression of a clear-cut ethnic enemy, the economic changes wrought by the Porfiriato had more equivocal effects. Economic development produced social differentiation, which gradually began to diminish the Juchiteco unity that had previously been so strong. Nonetheless, the majority of the Juchiteco population retained a common set of political interests, which, if challenged, as they would be at the end of the Porfiriato, could still lead to *serrano* rebellion.

Juchiteco peasant uprisings of the 1800s sought independence from encroaching regional elites and preservation of indigenous control of communal land and natural resources. But these struggles also took place within a larger political and economic context. Soon after independence, international interests attempted to take over much of the Isthmus for the purposes of raw material extraction, large-scale agriculture, construction of transportation systems,[45] and establishment of military outposts. After many fits and starts, dubious business deals, and other failures throughout the first three quarters of the nineteenth century, foreign developers began to have success in the Isthmus as Porfirio Díaz consolidated his rule over Mexico. Díaz was very familiar with the region, and his personal power and partnership with developers were instrumental in the construction of the Tehuantepec railroad which began in 1880 (Meier 1954).

The Tehuantepec railway was eventually completed in 1907 by the quintessential British engineer/businessman, Weetman Pearson (a.k.a. Lord Cowdray), amidst tremendous fanfare and expectations of profit. In the meantime, however, the Isthmus—with Díaz's assurances of enforced law and order—had already become fertile ground for colonization projects and land speculation. The Porfirian and Oaxaca State governments promoted colonization in order to raise population levels (which had been reduced by epidemics, famine, and the nineteenth-century wars), stimulate economic growth, and "bring civilization" to sparsely settled, indigenous zones like the Isthmus.

Colonization attempts had already begun as early as 1823, with Tadeo Ortíz's exploratory mission and eventual settlement of 6 French and 15 Mexican families near Guichicovi by 1830 (Esparza 1990:392; Barrios and López 1987:89–154). Covarrubias (1946:165) reports that the French colonists were decimated by tropical diseases and suicides, and by 1831 only one French family remained, along with the original Mexican settlers (Esparza 1990:392). In the 1850s, North American companies advertised Isthmus colonization schemes to U.S. citizens. Colonizing plans resumed in an 1879 project designed to bring 200 families from the Canary Islands to the Isthmus, each of which was to be granted 50 ha of land in the Juchitán district (Esparza 1988:320). In 1883–1884, the Mexican government passed the Colonization Laws, and companies formed to survey land boundaries in the so-called vacant lands (*tierras baldías*) of the country. In return, the companies were granted segments of the surveyed lands, and other parcels were sold at low cost (Spores 1984:166).

The extent of actual physical settlement of the Isthmus during this era was not overwhelming. Oaxaca government records for 1871 indicate that only nine foreigners (several North Americans and various Europeans) resided in the Juchitán district, including Alejandro de Gyves, a prominent French businessman and landowner, whose descendants have played prominent roles in the COCEI (MA 1871). Nonetheless, right-of-way and other concessions granted to the railroad and survey companies allowed them to alienate large tracts of Isthmus terrain which later ended up in the hands of foreign individuals and companies such as Illinois Coffee & Rubber, Mexican Land and Coffee, the Mexican Tropical Planters, the Isthmus Plantation Association, the Brown State Company, Rock Island Tropical Plantation, and United States Mexico Sugar, among others (Esparza 1990:404–5; Ruiz Cervantes and Arellanes 1986:48; Meier 1954). The Tehuantepec Ship Railroad Company alone obtained 1.5 million acres (Hart 1989:132, 400).[46]

The building of the railroad also had dramatic consequences for agricultural practices. During the Porfiriato, haciendas, plantations, and cattle ranches grew at a rapid rate alongside the Tehuantepec rail line (Chassen 1986:55). Construction of the railway not only opened up hitherto virgin land and permitted its sales to outsiders, it also provided a transportation route for Isthmus agricultural products to urban markets. Hacienda growth was especially marked in the Juchitán district. By the turn of the century, two of the largest properties in the state were located in the Isthmus— Ingenio Santo Domingo and La Venta hacienda. Both of these properties were owned by Matilde Castellanos, the widow of the Italian entrepreneur Maqueo, and both were remnants of Cortés' Marquesado lands. They were used to grow sugar cane, cotton, and indigo.[47] Another large estate owned by the Tehuantepec Mutual Planters Company contained the largest orange groves in the country and was used to grow tomatoes for export to the United States (Chassen 1986:113, 120). Stockraising also boomed in the Juchitán district during this time (Esparza 1988:294–311). Chassen (1986:124–25) lists 15 cattle ranches larger than 1,000 ha in the Juchitán district as of 1901 and notes the existence of many others as well. Much of the work on these lands was done by Zapotec peasants who were paid a mere 75 centavos a day for their efforts (Chassen and Martínez 1990:66).

Hacienda expansion had a profound impact on many native communities in the Isthmus, such as Zanatepec, which did not have enough land in 1894 to support all of its indigenous inhabitants (Esparza 1990:409, 1988:294–95). Juchitán, however, had more success in preserving its land, perhaps because of the town's amply demonstrated capacity for resistance. In 1845, for example, one José D. Carballo complained that the boundaries of his land had been unfairly altered, and noted that he would have protested earlier but "for fear of the Juchitecos because of their armed attacks and other turbulences" (Esparza 1990:427). Maqueo and Guergue, owners of the Marquesana haciendas, noting that the Juchitecos had taken over some of their land, whined about the "insatiable greed of a barbarous town [Juchitán] which possessed no other title but brute force" (Esparza 1990:427). In 1890 Juchitán controlled 35 square leagues of communal land, which bordered the Maqueo hacienda and the town of Ixtaltepec to the north, Laguna Superior to the south, Niltepec and San Dionisio del Mar to the east, and Tehuantepec to the west (Esparza 1990:430–31). In 1894, however, the Díaz government by fiat granted 13,000 sq m of Juchitán land to the Tehuantepec railroad company for the construction of a station, and another chunk of land to the local parish to build a school next to the church (Esparza 1990:433). Still, Juchitán entered the twentieth century "in relative peace with respect to its lands" (Esparza 1990:433).

Sir Weetman Pearson, the powerful engineer and entrepreneur who completed the Tehuantepec Railroad, owned the largest British company in Mexico prior to the Revolution (Katz 1981:465). Pearson's vast resources and political connections permitted him to overcome finally the natural and financial obstacles that (in addition to corruption and profiteering) had prevented previous firms from finishing the job. Accompanied by Porfirio Díaz himself and the U.S. ambassador, Pearson inaugurated the railroad and sophisticated port facilities he had built at Salina Cruz on New Year's Day, 1907 (Covarrubias 1946:171). Though terribly costly, the new cargo transportation system seemed at the time to be a marvel of modern technology, which promised a bright and profitable future. It was generally considered to be the best railroad in Mexico (Meier 1954:198). With as many as 20 cars of sugar cane and other commodities traversing the Isthmus daily in some of the first oil-powered locomotives in Mexico, business was brisk (Chassen 1986:52). Between 1908 and 1909, 96 ships from many international ports arrived at the Salina Cruz harbor, which boasted the best dry docks on the Pacific Coast from San Diego to Panama (Young

1966; Chassen 1986:53). In 1910 the Isthmus was home to the consulates of the United States, Great Britain, Germany, and six other European and Latin American countries.

Yet in a familiar Isthmus pattern, the development scenarios of wealth and progress generated by the railway ended in disillusion and despair. In 1914 the United States completed the Panama Canal, which almost over-night destroyed the Tehuantepec route's monopoly on rapid transconti-nental shipping. Moreover, the fighting and destruction of the Mexican Revolution took a drastic toll on the railroad's facilities (Meier 1954:262–63). From 1917 onward, the railroad companies lost increasingly larger sums of money, and the railway itself decayed from neglect and underuse. By the 1980s, emblematic of this decline, one of the old, majestic consulate buildings in Tehuantepec had been turned into *"La Embajada"* ("The Em-bassy"), a notorious brothel. Nonetheless, the Istmeños' fears of foreign intrusion sparked by nineteenth century colonization, surveying, and con-struction projects persist and are frequently invoked by COCEI to oppose contemporary Isthmus development plans, such as the ill-fated Alpha-Omega project.

Juchiteco Revolution:
Adolfo C. Gurrión and the Che Gómez Rebellion

Whether because of favors granted to the town by the Juchiteco *científico* Rosendo Pineda, economic growth related to railway construction and the location of a train station and military barracks in the community, or other factors, by the turn of the century Juchitán had begun to surpass its rival Tehuantepec in many areas.[48] In 1895 Juchitán became the second most populous Oaxacan city, and the Juchitán district was the largest in the state and possessed the most ranches (Chassen 1986:Appendix). Juchitán was an important regional market center, and many native sons began to have success in the Mexican educational system.

But all was not well in Juchitán. Throughout the Porfiriato, Juchitán was controlled by hand-picked Díaz supporters, such as the authoritarian Fran-cisco León, who stifled political opponents by sending them to the faraway work camps of Quintana Roo, from which few internees returned. While Juchitán experienced considerable economic growth and peasants main-tained most of their land during the Díaz regime, Juchiteco politics were dominated by outside appointees and a small clique of Porfiristas who in-curred the wrath of a majority of local people (de la Cruz, ed. 1989:31; *Guchachi' Reza* 16:21, 1983). Thus, Juchiteco protest during and immediately following the Porfiriato did not assume a primarily agrarian character (even though land struggles continued in the Isthmus) as in Morelos, but rather was centered around the issue of self-government (Reina 1990:483; Knight 1986:378).

For Juchitecos, self-rule meant that the community should be governed by men who had been born in the pueblo, spoke the Zapotec language, were versed in local customs, and enjoyed popular support.[49] Ironically, these criteria allowed for the inclusion of mixed-race individuals, such as the offspring of unions between European males and Zapotec females. Prominent Juchitecos of mixed-race ancestry at the turn of the century included Enrique Liekens (whose mother was Zapotec and father was Flemish), the mestizo descendants of the French merchant Alejandro de Gyves, and Rosendo Pineda (son of a French engineer and a Zapotec woman). Unlike in Tehuantepec, where mestizos and even members of notable Zapotec families identified primarily with the Hispanic elements of Mexican society, in Juchitán it was possible for mixed-race and indigenous elites to participate equally in Zapotec and national culture (Royce 1975).[50] Moreover, as Knight (1986:304) has pointed out, the "polyclassist" nature of *serrano* political rebellion was such that it was "often led by men of property and status" (p. 122). Thus, the fact that Juchiteco movements for self-determination might be led by an acculturated elite individual such as Che Gómez did not detract from their strongly ethnic and populist character.[51] Nonetheless, not all Juchitecos viewed self-determination in the same way, and a small minority of wealthy Juchitecos opposed the *serrano* movements.

The hopes of early-twentieth-century Juchiteco dissidents centered initially around a young intellectual, Adolfo C. Gurrión. Along with the Flores Magón brothers (also from the state of Oaxaca), Gurrión was one of the principal intellectual precursors of the Revolution in southern Mexico. In addition to writing articles for the Mexican Liberal Party's (PLM) newspaper, *Regeneración*, Gurrión started his own local opposition paper, *La Semecracia*, and was a member of a Oaxacan pro-reform group called the Juárez Association (Zarauz 1988). In and out of jail throughout the early 1900s, Gurrión called for an end to rubber-stamp reelection of Porfirian Oaxaca governors, and attacked the corruption and inefficiency of the *científico* administration (Zarauz 1988). Although he was exiled from the Isthmus for many years, Gurrión returned to the region in 1912—after Madero's liberal revolution ousted Díaz—and he was promptly elected Oaxaca state deputy. Instead of conforming to the new political circumstances, Gurrión called for Isthmus independence from Oaxaca and his supporters espoused the motto "the Isthmus for the Istmeños" (Gurrión [1935] 1983; Bustillo 1968:37). A year later, during the Huerta counter-revolution, Gurrión was murdered on the orders of the Mexican Interior Minister for alleged involvement in an Isthmus rebel movement centered in Tehuantepec (Zarauz 1988).

While Gurrión's political influence was primarily intellectual and leg-islative, the most famous Juchiteco revolutionary, Che Gómez, made his mark on the battlefield in open rebellion against the state. Although Oaxaca has earned a reputation among some scholars (e.g., Waterbury 1975) as a passive, "non-revolutionary" region, this stereotype could hardly be ap-plied to the Oaxacan Isthmus. In the winter of 1911, Gómez's mobilization became, after *Zapatismo*, the largest armed rebellion in Mexico (Knight 1986:376).

Students of the rebellion are fascinated by the figure of Che Gómez who, according to Knight (1986:375), appears in the Casasola photographic archives as a "squat, fat mestizo, standing in a dusty Isthmian street a re-volver stuck in his bulging waistband, his eyes askance, avoiding the cam-era."[52] De la Cruz notes that in this classic photograph Gómez is well-dressed, although he is surrounded by several palm thatch huts and a filthy pig (images of the poor barrios of Juchitán), which raises the issue, men-tioned earlier, of how a well-to-do landowner could become the leader of a Zapotec revolutionary movement (1987b:57).

To begin with, Gómez was not the first member of the Juchiteco elite to lead Zapotec peasants in armed rebellion against Oaxaca and national authorities, as was seen earlier in the case of Meléndez. Born and raised in Juchitán, Gómez almost certainly spoke Zapotec and shared the provincial sentiments of his peers. Moreover, for Juchitecos, being born in Juchitán (symbolized by the burial of the baby's placenta[53] underneath the home), can under certain circumstances override other ethnic markers such as skin color, clothing, Zapotec language ability, etc., in defining an individual as an insider rather than as an outsider (Royce 1975:193–202). Thus, to in-terpret Gómez's Western clothing, his marriage to a white woman, and worldliness as a sign that he was not a member of the Juchiteco community would be a mistake. The key point is that in the early revolutionary period, the Juchiteco indigenous peasantry's needs were best met by supporting a popular local elite figure (Gómez) rather than an unpopular individual (En-rique León) imposed from outside by the federal government.

Without romanticizing Gómez any more than he has been already, we can safely state that like Zapata and his followers (cf. Womack 1969), Gó-mez and his followers were primarily concerned with local autonomy as opposed to national political causes.[54] As one Juchiteco participant explained: "The people from the government wanted an outsider to occupy the position and 'Ché Gómez' asked that it be one of our people, so that they would be of our blood" (Matus 1985:85).[55] That Juchiteco autarky might also entail socioeconomic inequalities (in this case, the wealth of Gómez compared to that of his peasant supporters), does not negate the central issue, namely, that Juchitecos, above all, wanted to control their own affairs (cf. de la Cruz 1987b:69; Knight 1986:375–78). Ruiz Cervantes (1988:368–69) also notes that Gómez "went beyond being a simple political *cacique* to whom his grassroots supporters only owed favors and loyalty, he was interested in the recovery for his people of the salt fields . . . and the restitution of communal lands."

Gómez's concern for Juchiteco rights had been heightened when he was a young law student in Oaxaca City who defended the cases of his *paisanos* jailed in the state capital by Oaxaca authorities (Nuñez Ríos 1969). This experience may have been one of the factors that later led him to coin the phrase, "While we depend on Oaxaca we are lost" (Ramírez 1970:40). For many years, however, President Díaz and his Istmeño advisor Rosendo Pineda posted Gómez to bureaucratic positions in northern Mexico, allowing conservative Juchitecos of the Red Party and outsiders appointed from Mexico City to dominate local affairs (Justo Pineda 1986). This prevented Gómez from carrying out his promise that if elected mayor, he would return local salt pans (granted by Juárez to a non-Istmeño) to Zapotec peasants—a promise that caused Gómez's local opponents to brand him a socialist (de la Cruz 1987b:58; *El Eco del Istmo* 1/1/1894, cited in *Guchachi' Reza* 16:11, 1983). However, at the end of the Díaz dictatorship, Gómez was able to return to Juchitán, and in 1911, backed by Madero and liberal Juchitecos of the Green Party (including elderly veterans of the 1882 revolt), he became mayor (Matus 1985:77).[56]

Subsequently, when Oaxaca Governor Benito Juárez Maza attempted to replace Gómez, the Juchitecos revolted, as they had done before to protest previous intrusions into local affairs by Félix Díaz and by the then governor, Benito Juárez, Sr. For Juchitecos, Juárez Maza's maneuver was typical of the impositions and injustices that had sparked Juchitán–Oaxaca confrontations in the past. Recalling these events, Gómez's niece—who observed the 1911 rebellion—explained that "*Xavisende* has always been in conflict with Oaxaca" ("*Toda la vida Xavisende ha tenido pugna con Oaxaca*") (Matus 1985:103).

Che Gómez's replacement was to be Enrique León, who, though not a relative, was associated by the Juchitecos with a previous local despot, the

Porfirista Francisco León, who had crushed the Mexu Chele uprising and exiled dissident Juchitecos to die in Quintana Roo. León rode into Juchitán backed by 200 government soldiers. A survivor of the encounter eloquently recalled that Léon was met by a large crowd of *Chegomistas*:

> Never in the political history of Juchitán, neither before or now, have so many people assembled to receive a dignitary. It can be affirmed that gathered there in the vicinity and gates of the [railroad] station were 90% of the population, crowded together in an expanse of one kilometer bounded by the town cemetery and the two sides of the train tracks. But I should clarify that this reception was not of affection but of protest, and with the intention of lynching the intruder [Matus 1985:88].

León's military escort sought refuge in the local barracks, where they were promptly besieged by thousands of Juchitecos and pro-Gómez residents of more than a dozen nearby villages armed with machetes, sticks, slingshots, spears, and a few rifles (Ramírez 1970:39; Matus 1985:78). After battling the *federales* and their small group of Zapotec supporters in Juchitán for four days and killing a judge, a tax collector, and many soldiers, some 5,000 *Chegomistas* retreated to allied villages to the east of town.[57] Then, as in the Meléndez rebellion, government troops burned down Juchitán. The U.S. consul in Salina Cruz noted that this was done not only to prevent the spread of disease but to warn the population against further acts of dissent and to punish the rebels (consul letter reproduced in *Guchachi' Reza* 16:14, 1983). The consul also observed that hundreds of people died in the fighting.

Meanwhile, from his rural outpost, Gómez called for independence from Oaxaca and the establishment of a sovereign Isthmus Territory (Ramírez 1970:40). The Juchiteco insurgents remained in rebellion against the Mexican military for another month, until Gómez was tricked into traveling to Mexico City to negotiate with Madero, only to be captured and killed en route by Oaxaca government agents at the behest of Governor Juárez Maza (Henderson 1983:9). Approximately 2,500 Juchiteco peasants continued the uprising for another eight months, until the arrival of a new governor, offers of amnesty, and the need to return home and plant their fields convinced them to end the last large-scale rebellion in Juchitán history (Knight 1986:378). Nonetheless, though Governor Juárez Maza's men had riddled Che Gómez with gunfire—an autopsy found 52 bullet holes in his cadaver (Ramírez 1970:108)—and though the *Chegomista* revolt was eventually dissolved, memories of the movement and its colorful leader persisted as a potent stimulus for future generations of Juchiteco dissidents.

Summary and Conclusions

By the end of the colonial period, Tehuantepec, the former capital of Isthmus Zapotec society, which had become the center of local Spanish operations, was no longer a site of ethnic rebellion. While the Tehuano elite became conservative and Hispanicized, Juchitán, a peripheral town, remained a united indigenous community that resisted outside incursions. The Juchitecos' survival and collective self-image were linked to illicit business practices, opposition to the Marquesado hacienda, and defense of local salt flats and agricultural lands.

These emerging cultural differences between the two main Isthmus towns sharpened during the nineteenth century, as the Zapotec identity of Tehuanos was diluted further by in-migration of European foreigners and by the Tehuantepec elite's identification with these newcomers. Juchitán received fewer foreign immigrants, and the mixed-race progeny of immigrants and Zapotec women identified as Juchitecos. Political rivalries further hardened cultural oppositions as the Juchitecos fought Tehuanos repeatedly throughout the nineteenth century.

The political vacuum created by independence allowed the Juchitecos to free themselves once and for all from rule by Tehuantepec. Allied with Blaseños, the Juchitecos not only rebelled against local elites, but also sought autonomy from the new Oaxaca authorities, defeated French intruders, and fought to regain communal lands and marine resources. The large number of conflicts in the Isthmus was a result of major economic and political changes that were imposed on Isthmus Zapotec people by the Mexican government and private developers. Indeed, Hart (1989:23) describes the Isthmus as "one of Mexico's most capitalistically advanced commercial and agricultural zones."

The recurring political and military clashes, which pitted a majority of the Zapotec population of Juchitán against ethnic "others" and regional enemies, were the crucible from which the politicized ethnic identity of twentieth-century Juchitecos emerged. Although by the Che Gómez rebellion fissures were evident within the Juchiteco community itself, the nineteenth- and early-twentieth-century conflicts between Juchitán and Tehuantepec, Oaxaca City, and Mexico City demarcated the ethnic and regional battle lines (and many of the political issues) later seized upon by COCEI to inspire the most recent Isthmus Zapotec resistance movement.

CHAPTER THREE

Capitalist Transitions and Isthmus Zapotec Society, 1911–1993

Irrigation district No. 19 [in the Isthmus of Tehuantepec] was not built to benefit the peasants; they were the pretext, the facade, the social reason brandished in order to attend to problems emanating from another sector: industrial society, modern Mexico.

ARTURO WARMAN 1972:25

This chapter examines twentieth-century Isthmus history with emphasis on the recent economic processes that have profoundly changed local society. It begins with a discussion of principal features of Isthmus Zapotec economy, social structure, and polity in the post-Revolution era prior to the advent of large-scale development projects in the 1950s. Although during the Porfiriato the Isthmus experienced a marked increase in capitalist activity, by the middle of the twentieth century Juchitán was still primarily a peasant community with a localized economy, rich indigenous culture, and strong ethnic identification. Reproduction of a distinctive Juchiteco way of life occurred despite the social divisions and political rivalries that separated a small merchant elite and their followers from the artisans, agriculturalists, and petty market vendors who made up the majority of the population. From the 1930s to the 1950s, General Heliodoro Charis established a system of boss rule that maintained a degree of social peace despite occasional electoral conflicts. Political dissidence was sometimes violently repressed, and many lingering social demands remained unresolved.

From the 1950s onward, government development projects—made possible in part by the political stability of *Charismo*—transformed economic, political, and cultural life in Juchitán. The chapter also explores how economic development challenged indigenous subsistence practices, in-

67

creased proletarianization, and strengthened the Mexican state's formerly tenuous hold over the Isthmus. Political and economic transformation from the 1960s to the present has been accompanied by population growth, urbanization, ecological crisis, and multiple social problems. These changes—which both intensified class differences within the Zapotec community and once again put Juchitecos in conflict with Oaxaca and Mexico City authorities—formed the social matrix from which COCEI emerged. COCEI's political and cultural response to these developments is the subject of Chapters 5, 6, and 7.

SOCIAL REPRODUCTION OF ISTHMUS ZAPOTEC SOCIETY, 1911–1950

Before examining the impact of recent government development programs on the Isthmus, it is first necessary to discuss the endogenous socioeconomic practices that reproduced Zapotec society prior to the 1950s, and still do, to some extent, today. Following Gailey (1985) and Parrish (1982), the term social reproduction is used here to refer to: (1) maintenance and replication of the labor force, division of labor, and internal class relations;(2) biological and demographic reproduction; and (3) the reproduction of cultural beliefs and practices, ethnic identity, and gender relations.

Although the chapter focuses on local processes of social reproduction in the first half of the twentieth century, global political and economic processes also had a profound impact on the Isthmus during this time. In spite of these processes, however, the Isthmus remained an essentially non-industrial, agricultural society. For our purpose, the chapter provides an overview of Zapotec society in the pre-1950s period, with an emphasis on Juchitán, rather than detailing the many local variations of society among and within Isthmus towns.[1]

In the early twentieth century, the Zapotecs lived in endogamous villages with diversified and vigorous local economies that provided for most basic needs, although there were also recurrent periods of drought and scarcity. The mainstays of indigenous livelihood were agriculture, fishing, salt collecting, hunting, artisanry and petty commodity production, and commercial trade (MA 1900, 1901). Zapotec men grew corn, beans, sesame, flowers, tomatoes, and other vegetables in small plots often ringed by bananas, coconut palms, mango, lime, plum, and *chico zapote* trees (MA 1902). Peasants cleared their fields with machetes and axes, and plowed them with ox teams. Prior to construction of the Benito Juárez dam, some peasants irrigated land with water from natural springs, primitive canals constructed in the pre-Hispanic era, and a small dam and canal system built during the Cárdenas regime (1934–1940) (Ybarra 1949:48). Most farming, however, relied on the fickle Isthmus rains. Therefore, it was not a year-round activity for many peasants. Because of Juchitán's aridity and generally less favorable environment for farming, Juchitecos mainly grew corn or produced meat and dairy products, and to a lesser degree grew other vegetables and fruits (Dorsett 1975:118–152).

Until 1930, when it was replaced by sesame, some Isthmus peasants raised indigo and then processed it into blue dye for sale to local merchants (Binford 1989). In addition to raising livestock, many peasants kept a few pigs and chickens. Peasants also obtained income by cutting wood for the production of ties for the Tehuantepec Railroad and charcoal for domestic firewood, and weaving palm into hats and baskets (Segura 1988:222). In general, Isthmus males engaged in multiple occupations, although maize cultivation was their primary task (Dorsett 1975).

Intermediaries, who controlled financing and sale of the few marketable crops, skimmed off surplus product from the peasantry (Binford 1989). This stimulated social differentiation, but most peasant producers maintained control of their land and tools of production. Consequently, capitalist relations in agriculture developed only gradually during the 1900–1950 period. A few haciendas existed, but they did not dominate the landscape as in parts of northern Mexico (MA 1902).[2] The largest landed estate was the 77,000-ha Santo Domingo hacienda, which provided sugar cane to the mill of the same name (Chassen 1985:40).[3]

In the Isthmus, fishing has traditionally been controlled by the coastal Huave, although some Zapotecs of Juchitán and several smaller communities fished on a small scale (Covarrubias 1946:58–66). Zapotec fishermen, like their Huave counterparts, used simple instruments, such as the dugout canoe (*cayuco*), poles for leverage, small nets (*atarraya*), large seines (*chinchorro*), palm baskets for carrying the catch, and other items (Gadow 1908:166). Though a dangerous activity because of the ferocious Isthmus winds that constantly threatened to overturn the wobbly canoes, fishing was potentially quite productive, albeit sporadic. Even today, the polluted and overfished Isthmus lagoons, rivers, and ocean waters produce significant amounts of shrimp, fish, abalone, lobster, and other crustaceans. Another productive marine activity was salt collecting in hotly disputed, manmade salt beds adjacent to lagoons and the sea (Ybarra 1949:103).

Hunting also provided supplementary foodstuffs. Hunting was an activity in which most farmers engaged as opportunities presented themselves, although there were hunting specialists as well. Government records from the 1899–1902 period list large numbers of animals killed in the Tehuantepec area: 1,531 deer, 277 wild pigs, 14,988 rabbits, and 8,623 *chachalacas* (a native bird) (MA 1899–1902). Numerous other game animals are listed for the Juchitán area also.

In many Isthmus communities, petty commodity producers made pottery, bricks, sugar, fireworks, leather, hats and other palm items, and hammocks (MA 1901; Stirling 1941; Ruiz Santos 1991; Binford 1992). Other craftsmen and skilled tradesmen included the following: jewelers, cobblers, butchers, carpenters, barbers, leather-workers, bone-menders, masons, masseurs, clothing dyers, wheelwrights, mechanics, musicians, horse-cart operators, and many others (MA 1901; Olsson–Seffer 1910; Covarrubias 1946:282–83). Juchitán, in particular, had a well-developed division of labor (Dorsett 1975:142–49).

Isthmus towns were divided into sections, or barrios, each of which often had its own occupational specialties. In Espinal and other areas lacking significant petty commodity production or demand for craft products, men migrated to Chiapas cotton and coffee plantations or to the sugar cane mills of Veracruz and elsewhere during the dry season (Binford 1989). Men also performed most local political and administrative tasks, unskilled jobs for the municipality (e.g., policemen, watchmen, street sweepers), and miscellaneous other activities.

Muxe', male transvestites similar to the North American berdache, were bakers, hairdressers, healers, tailors, and designers of dresses, floral arrangements, and other wedding accouterments (Chiñas 1983). *Muxe'* did not take part in agriculture and occupied a third gender category with its own social roles and expectations apart from those of heterosexual men and women (Chiñas 1985).

Women made and sold tortillas and *totopos*, processed and sold men's agricultural products, prepared and sold various types of foods, and sold numerous other items in the market or out of their homes. As Chiñas (1983:31) put it: "The traditional and still prevalent basic division of labor between the sexes . . . is simply this: Men are the producers and women are the processors and vendors of the men's production." Other female occupations included the following: midwife, weaver, clothes dyer, embroiderer, candlemaker, seamstress, clothes washer, healer, servant, masseuse, and prostitute (Covarrubias 1946:283; Chiñas 1983). Women took care of the children and were responsible for most domestic chores (Covarrubias 1946:275–83).

The female-controlled Isthmus markets were a primary hub of village social and economic life. Unlike the rotating markets in many other parts of Oaxaca, the large Tehuantepec and Juchitán markets were permanent, daily institutions. They served not only local needs, but provisioned regional and interregional buyers as well. The naturalist Hans Gadow (1908:150) was particularly impressed with the way Zapotec women (or "tiger-beauties," as he called them) managed the well-stocked Tehuantepec market he visited in 1902:

> At the market-place all the vendors are women, most of them sitting on low, peculiarly-shaped chairs, called "butacas," which are covered with the skin of a jaguar, or a cow, or with red-stained leather. The goods are brought and deposited by the men, who then withdraw. There are "huipiles" and other forms of clothing of many colors and patterns; heaps of fruit and flowers; turkeys, fowls, fish, and meat, and—a curious sight—rows of "tilcampos," or black iguanas. . . . Another corner is given up to pottery, notably the hard-baked black Juchitán ware . . .

In Juchitán, storefront businesses were controlled by the native elite and a small group of European, Japanese, Middle Eastern (known as *Turcos*), and mestizo immigrants, most of whom arrived in the late nineteenth and early twentieth-centuries (Sánchez Silva 1985:22; Covarrubias 1946:283). Most *Turcos* eventually became permanent Isthmus residents, married indigenous women, adopted local customs, and learned the Zapotec language.[4] In any case, none of the immigrant groups was sufficiently large or powerful enough to establish economic or cultural dominance over the Zapotecs. Miscegenation, likewise, did not weaken the Zapotec ethnic community, because the offspring of these relationships usually identified as Juchitecos, spoke Zapotec, and remained in the community. While living in Juchitán in 1909, Vasconcelos ([1935] 1963, cited in *Guchachi' Reza* 2:11, n.d.) commented on this phenomenon:

> One of the agents of our bank concerned with local land transactions was a native Juchiteco, but of European origin. The name of his family, which was very influential in the area, gave away his French origins. Both he and his cousins had bronze-colored skin [*tenían la piel tostada*] and blue eyes. For women, the indigenous mix gave them a statuesque and languid bearing. No other mestizos of America are more sculpturally beautiful.
>
> The French-descended Juchiteco spoke Spanish, English, and Za-

potec. His friendship opened up doors normally closed to the foreigner, even if he were Mexican, which in this case was the same as being a Yankee, you see the women only spoke the language of the region [Zapotec].

While this somewhat Orientalist observation by Vasconcelos reflected his utopian theories about "the Cosmic Race" (*la raza cósmica;* i.e., the fusion of Amerindians and Europeans to form a great future race), it nonetheless captures an important element of Juchiteco society at the turn of the century, namely, the physical and cultural mixing of Zapotecs and Europeans. Unlike some other parts of Mexico, however, such mixing did not lead to the decline of the indigenous ethnic community. Instead, the new social influences brought by these unions were incorporated into new facets of Juchiteco identity and culture. In this respect, Juchitán stood out among Mexican indigenous communities for its "celebration of an Indian identity and its ability to impose that definition on the rest of its inhabitants" (Royce 1982:169).[5] A key factor in the survival of Zapotec ethnic identity was the political and economic independence Juchitecos were able to maintain during the nineteenth century and the maintenance of an ideology of resistance that celebrated Zapotec culture and success in military conflicts with ethnic outsiders. COCEI claims to be the standardbearer of this tradition in contemporary Juchitán.

Social Reproduction and Intracommunity Relations

According to Royce (1981), the Zapotecs have created an elastic system of subsistence strategies and productive activities, which they have used to respond successfully to changing ecological, economic, and political conditions. The system is based on extended households that engage in multiple occupations—farming, fishing, animal husbandry, market vending, artisanry, etc.—and form flexible and resilient "domestic/economic units" interconnected by kinship (1981:269–274). The Zapotecs combined multiple occupations with short-term and long-term investment practices (especially in gold), and extensive social relationships of cooperation and ritualized reciprocity with kinsmen, fictive kin, and others. In addition to kinship, occupational groups were focal points of extra-household social and economic interaction (Dorsett 1975).

A diversified local economy was made possible by the complex Isthmus ecological niche, which contains ocean and riverine fisheries, salt sources, extensive flat farming and pasture lands, and tropical forests, all within close proximity of the main Zapotec communities. Juchitán, in particular, was also conveniently situated vis-à-vis north-south (Central Mexico-Southern Mexico) and east-west (Veracruz-Oaxaca) trading routes, which took on greater importance after the construction of the railroad and later the Pan American Highway. These particularities of Isthmus ecology and geography, and the Zapotec's diversified adaptation to them, provided the Isthmus Zapotecs with economic possibilities unavailable to many other Oaxacan indigenous groups who have been confined to poorer regions with less ecological diversity and fewer commercial opportunities. Finally, another crucial factor in the Isthmus Zapotec's relative prosperity historically is their political and economic dominance of their "ethnic neighbors" (the Huave, Mixe, Zoque, and Chontal).

The Zapotec's amalgam of subsistence strategies gave them a degree of self-sufficiency which, combined with the region's remoteness from metropolitan Mexico, allowed them to devote energy to conserving local traditions and customs, while leaving less room for the impingement of influential outside traditions (Santana 1988:15; UNAM 1986:9–10). Thus, the Isthmus was home to a distinctive, somewhat insular, regional culture, as was also the case in the Yucatán, the Tarascan area, and several other parts of rural Mexico (cf. Benjamin and Wasserman 1990). The complex of economic strategies discussed above, coupled with indigenous social arrangements of reciprocity and cooperation, community rituals and customs, local ethnic identity, and internal class and gender relations were the central elements of Isthmus Zapotec social reproduction prior to the 1950s.

While Royce's subsistence strategies are critical to understanding Juchiteco social reproduction, several qualifications must first be made. Royce (1982:169–74) argues that the Zapotecs have been able to dominate Juchitán because of their local political autonomy, early economic prosperity, and the successful wielding of Zapotec ethnic identity against opponents. The latter factor is possible, she asserts (1982:181–82), because:

> In any threat from without, the outsiders are frozen out because they are not Zapotec. That can only be effective if the Zapotec have a united front backed by material resources and the outsiders are unable to mount a unified opposition. This, in fact, is the case in Juchitán.

According to Royce, the cornerstone of Zapotec dominance of Juchitán is the family and the economic strategies it developed. She notes that Juchitán families operate according to the Isthmus Zapotec concept of *guendalizaa*, which means kinship or reciprocal cooperation, and also refers to kin-based work groups. For Royce, the notion of *guendalizaa* applies to multifaceted cooperative relationships among Zapotec people, starting with the family and eventually connecting all of the Zapotecs of Juchitán (1981:284).

Although Royce's descriptions of Isthmus Zapotec identity and recip-rocal social relations provide insight into the strength and resiliency of indigenous life in the face of external threats, they obscure tensions within "traditional" Zapotec society. Her use of family and "united front" met-aphors to characterize Juchitán may lead us to accept facilely the notion that the Isthmus Zapotecs, even into the 1980s, were a thoroughly unified entity based on sharing and social solidarity. This conceptualization min-imizes the extent to which social stratification, or at least incipient class differences, had already taken root in Juchitán by the early twentieth cen-tury.

Although nineteenth- and early-twentieth-century conflicts involving Juchitán frequently mobilized large segments of the Zapotec population against intruders and regional enemies, as the Porfiriato unfolded eco-nomic development of the Isthmus set in motion processes of social dif-ferentiation within the community. The growing divisions within Juchitán in the early twentieth century were expressed politically through the "lib-eral" Green Party, whose partisans put green leaves on their hats, and the "conservative" Red Party, whose partisans wore red ribbons.[6]

While neither of these parties was guided strictly by ideological tenets, nonetheless, they represented the contending social interests in the Za-potec community. The Green Party consisted of the majority peasant pop-ulation, many of whom lived in the southern part of Juchitán. In the 1920s the Red Party was composed of the clergy and a minority of well-to-do Juchitecos (and some peasants also), many of whom had been Porfiristas, who resided on the northern side of town (Henestrosa de Webster 1985:76; Matus 1985:77). Thus, according to a survivor of the Che Gómez era:

> The members of the Red Party hated the people of the lower side
> of town, of the south. The majority of the people of the north be-
> longed to the Red Party and they always ran the judicial system, always
> them. That is why the people hated that party. The *licenciado* [Gómez],
> as he was from our town, said: "I will not let them walk all over my
> people." . . . That is why "Ché Gómez" founded the Green Party
> [Matus 1985:92].

Violent conflicts between the "Reds" and "Greens" during the Revolution became so bloody that in 1912 the Juchitán *jefe político* passed a resolution outlawing the use of red and green clothing or adornments:

> All persons, whatever their sex or age, are completely prohibited from wearing in public places red flowers or green branches, whether in a hairdo or on their clothing. Likewise, the use of green or red colored *huipiles, enaguas,* and bows is prohibited [*Guchachi' Reza* 16:24, 1983].

Despite this order, which was protested against by a large group of Juchitecas (see *Guchachi' Reza* 16:23–24, 1983), the social antagonisms represented by the struggle between Reds and Greens continued after the Revolution. Such tensions are quite evident in Covarrubias (1946:159), who found that in the 1930s:

> Socially, . . . the people [of Juchitán] observe four divisions. Those who live in the center of town (*bini galawi gizi*) are merchants and storekeepers, the "better" families. The section to the north of the municipal hall is called "uptown" and its inhabitants (*bini neza gia'*) are mainly embroiderers and makers of palm-leaf artifacts, an industry introduced and controlled by the Syrian merchants. The people who live to the south of the municipal hall, "downtown" (*bini neza ge'te*), are the poorer peasants and pottery-makers, a section contemptuously nicknamed by the upper class Juchitecos *Barrio zu* ("Loincloth Ward") because of the naked children that play in the streets and because it is whispered that its grown-ups like to go half-naked at home. Those who live across the river (*bini cegigo*) constitute the fourth group, peasants, flower-growers, and hunters of iguana and wild boar. They are looked upon as wild people by those in the center of town.

Moreover,

> Juchitán . . . has . . . the sprinkling of a peculiar aristocracy of white, mestizo, and Indian well-to-do families that ape the ways and prejudices of the big cities and go out of their way to look down upon the simple and direct behavior of the peasants. This pseudo-aristocracy of merchants and property-owners is the only obstacle that stands in the

way of making Juchitán the most authentic, nearest approach to a true democratic community [1946:162].

Covarrubias observed that segregation and hostility divided members of different Juchitán neighborhoods and social classes, and he noted that local politicians controlled large landholdings at the expense of the peasantry. These conditions belie notions of a "united front" or a big, happy Zapotec family. Economic and political divisions were reinforced by attitudes of social superiority/inferiority linked to differential levels of education, occupational prestige, and sumptuary options (especially in relation to women's ability to obtain gold jewelry and wear elaborate fiesta costumes) (Covarrubias 1946; Velma Pickett, personal communication, 1992).[7] In sum, while Juchitán remained predominantly a Zapotec town in the first half of the twentieth century, significant divisions existed within the community along gender, economic, and political lines.

Post-Revolution Politics: The Charis Cacicazgo

After Che Gómez's death in 1911, Juchiteco participation in the Mexican Revolution was far less spectacular, if no less bloody. During this time Juchitecos took part in numerous local battles between Reds and Greens and engaged in sporadic rebellions. Two of the best-known revolts were those associated with Efraín R. Gómez in 1916 and Che Gómez, Jr., in 1924. In 1917, Che Gómez, Jr. continued in his father's independent tradition by proposing that the Isthmus of Tehuantepec be named a separate state (Ruiz Cervantes 1985:286).[8] Also like his father, Gómez, Jr. was an archenemy of Oaxaca Valley authorities, such as Governor García Vigil, who Gómez is reputed to have tried to kill in 1923 (Parmenter 1984:xxiii). In 1924, Che Gómez, Jr., in alliance with the de la Huertistas, revolted against the Oaxaca state government. Government soldiers crushed his movement and killed the younger Gómez a mere 3-km from where his father had been killed (Bravo Izquierda 1948:51–61). These circumstances were duly noted by Juchitán residents and only deepened their hostility toward Oaxaca government officials.

Outside of the Isthmus four battalions of Juchiteco soldiers, recruited through the local barracks, fought all over Mexico, primarily in support of Obregón and Carranza (Bravo Izquierda 1948:60; de la Cruz 1989). Many Juchiteca *soldaderas* also went on these campaigns, performing vital tasks such as cooking and smuggling messages in their *huipiles*, and sometimes engaging in the fighting, although they were seldom rewarded for their efforts (Matus 1985:146–59; Salas 1990:68–81).[9] Their proud testimonies are an important part of Isthmus oral history.[10]

Revolutionary general, and later President, Alvaro Obregón was very impressed by the bravery of the Juchiteco warriors about whom he once commented there was no cemetery in Mexico that did not contain the remains of a Juchiteco killed in the Revolution (Chopitea 1961:94–95). Juchitán produced at least ten generals during the war, but the most famous of these was Heliodoro Charis, the key symbol of modern Isthmus Zapotec identity and the quintessential Juchiteco in local lore.

Charis' colorful legacy is recalled in *corridos*, public ceremonies, books and essays by local authors, a statue in Juchitán, and schools and streets bearing his name. Isthmus Zapotecs also remember Charis in an infinite number of folk tales, oral histories, and jokes concerned with his military triumphs, social faux pas, and difficulties with the Spanish language (Altamirano Conde 1985; Jiménez 1989). During my fieldwork I frequently heard versions of this typical Charis joke:

> General Charis was waiting at the Juchitán railroad station for a train that was long overdue. All of a sudden the director of the station came up to Charis and informed him: "My general, the train is delayed." ["*Mi general, el tren viene demorado.*"] And Charis [confusing the word *demorado* (delayed) with *de morado* (purple-colored)] replied: "I don't care if it comes painted green, I'm going in it." ["*Aunque venga pintado de verde, yo me voy en él.*"]

When Zapotec people discussed Charis' life with me, they invariably began with statements such as "Charis was an illiterate *indio* who never spent a single day in school," "Charis was a poor iguana hunter," or "Charis was a common bandit until he joined the Revolution." One of Charis' *pistoleros* described him to me in these terms:

> I want to tell you something about my general, you know, General Heliodoro Charis Castro, an Indian, that's for sure [*un indio, pero deveras*]! He became a general of his division and without knowing anything. He was a senator of the Republic, a federal deputy. He occupied these positions and without knowing anything. The only thing he had was his bravery.[11]

In such accounts, Istmeños describe how, despite his humble origins, Charis' native intelligence, understanding of human nature, and toughness allowed him to become a successful general and, later, politician. For Isthmus Zapotecs, Charis is now a reflexive icon, a repository of myth and history about being Zapotec in the twentieth century. By admiring tales of the general's war exploits or laughing at Charis jokes (which especially emphasize the general's confused Spanish and social blunders in "civilized society"), Istmeños both celebrate their ethnic and regional pride and comment on the bittersweet process of becoming a bilingual, bicultural (i.e., Zapotec-Mexican) people.

While uniquely Zapotec in character and style, Charis was typical of *cacique* leaders who consolidated their power in the Mexican countryside after the Revolution. Through a mixture of military and economic power, kinship and patron-client relations, and local and national political connections, *caciques* were mediators par excellence who used their multiple linkages and networks to maintain local power bases. *Caciques* were particularly strong in regions like the Isthmus, Tarascan Michoacán (see Friedrich 1986), and elsewhere where geographical and cultural differences separated local communities from state and national capitals. *Caciques* played a double game. To local constituents they provided favors and services derived from their links to national authorities (often a result of military service, as in Charis' case) in exchange for community political backing. And they smoothed over local disputes or implemented national political policies at the regional level in return for support from the power structure in Mexico City.[12]

According to Isthmus oral history, Charis began his military/political career at an early age as a member of a small group of Juchitecos who rebelled against the local government. He eventually participated in many of the major military campaigns of his day, though not always on the side of factions today considered progressive. For example, he fought against Zapata (de la Cruz 1989; Justo Pineda 1986). In 1920, Charis and his rebel band of Juchitecos defeated the local *Carrancista* forces in Xadani and then took over Juchitán (López Marín 1985). Charis' aggressiveness, strategic talents, timely opposition to Carranza, and friendship with President Obregón allowed him to become a general in the Mexican Army in 1921. Charis' 13th Battalion, composed primarily of poorly armed Juchitecos, was a troubleshooting force sent to squelch unrest all over the Mexican republic. Among the general's most important military victories were the 1924 Battle of Ocotlán, Jalisco against the *de la Huertista* uprising, the defeat of the Sonora Yaquis in 1926, and many lesser-known triumphs over the *Cristeros* in the late 1920s (ESF 1976; Jiménez 1989).[13]

In addition to being the consummate Juchiteco soldier, Charis was a classic postrevolutionary boss with firm ties to national political and military luminaries. Retiring to Juchitán in 1930, Charis used his influence to temporarily subdue the Red vs. Green conflict (Arellanes et al. 1988:24), and to establish an agricultural colony (the Alvaro Obregón Colony), supposedly for the benefit of his former Zapotec soldiers.[14] Here, the darker side of Charis emerged. Instead of expropriating ex-hacienda lands and granting them without cost to his soldiers as an *ejido*, Charis had the soldiers pay him for the lands in loads of corn, cash, and cattle, and gave no title documents.[15] In addition to these flagrant violations of Mexican law, Charis, in collusion with a large landowner, had a leader of a dissident group murdered.[16] Eventually, Charis became the de facto authority of an approximately 7,000-ha area, although he did allow the soldiers to live on the land and farm it.

In 1931 two Juchitán doctors (Carrasco and Robles) led an uprising against the state governor's imposition of an unpopular candidate for mayor (López Nelio 1981:7–12). Charis initially supported the doctors' movement for municipal autonomy because of his own power struggle with Governor Francisco López, who Charis had challenged for the governorship in 1928 (AGN, Abelardo Rodríguez, exp. 524/52). However, when fighting broke out, Charis did not come forward to help the rebels. Consequently, government troops crushed the movement and killed its leaders (de la Cruz 1983c). Opposition to López, and calls for Isthmus independence, resumed in 1932 after the murder of the Juchitán mayor (AGN, Abelardo Rodríguez, exp. 524/52). Once again government troops subdued the dissidents.

Eventually, calm returned to Juchitán, aided by a deal struck between Charis and the state governor (Rubin 1990:252). By this time, Charis had used his ties with President Obregón and other national figures and his control over the Alvaro Obregón Colony to set himself up as the man behind the throne of the Juchitán mayor's office. For the next three decades Charis had a tremendous influence on local political life.[17] He also used his national connections to become a federal deputy and senator (as well as mayor, or de facto mayor, of Juchitán), although Charis spent most of this period in Juchitán and let his alternate attend sessions in the Mexican Congress. Like so many other Mexican revolutionaries, Charis, the former rebel, became a PRI politician, an "institutionalized revolutionary" allied with elements of the local bourgeoisie.[18] Charis' power in Juchitán discouraged local rebellions such as those of the nineteenth century, and his national connections facilitated economic development of the Isthmus.

From his compound in the Alvaro Obregón Colony or his majestic two-story home in downtown Juchitán, Charis was a shrewd mediator between national politicians and local leaders, and did numerous favors for common Istmeños in return for their political loyalty. Opponents of *Charismo*, however, often were given an ultimatum to leave town within 24 hours or suffer harsh consequences. Charis stole elections when necessary and intimidated his enemies (Arellanes et al. 1988:21–25). Likewise, thieves and other criminals were sometimes summarily shot. Nonetheless, local opposition to Charis grew to the extent that a regional alliance, the Frente para Renovación Democrática (FRD), formed in the 1940s to protest the general's boss rule (Rubin 1990:253). This organization of merchants and professionals was strong enough to gain minority representation on Juchitán city councils, but could not uproot the Charis *cacicazgo*.

During the Charis era, economic development took place in a climate of relative social tranquility and order. However, this occurred at the expense of civil liberties, fair elections, and free political expression. Yet, Charis was to some degree a popular leader with a social vision, unlike many of his *cacique* peers. In the Revolution, he led the Green Party, composed primarily of lower-class Juchitecos against their social rivals in the Red Party. In 1919 his San Vicente Plan called for secession of the Isthmus from the state of Oaxaca and formation of an independent federal territory, a position passionately supported by ethnically proud Juchitecos (de la Cruz 1983c:71). During the *Cristero* rebellion, General Charis closed Juchitán's San Vicente Church and confiscated church lands. As Juchitán political boss from the 1930s to the late 1950s, he brought numerous public works projects to the Isthmus. These included the first schools, roads, a library, a hospital, electricity, irrigation facilities, etc. (ESF 1976; de la Cruz 1992a).

Charis also threw elaborate, popular fiestas at his ranch and loaned young ox teams to peasants in exchange for two days of *tequio* labor annually. At his home in Juchitán, Charis kept a large bottle of mescal, from which his friends could drink whenever they wanted, and Charis regularly socialized and imbibed with the peasants of Xadani, Alvaro Obregón, San Blas, and Juchitán. Instead of wearing suits and expensive clothing, Charis favored huaraches, cowboy hats, and rough peasant attire, and he seldom spoke Spanish, preferring the Zapotec language.[19] His lively jokes, told in Zapotec, and hedonistic lifestyle are now the stuff of local legend.

In addition to his earthiness and political savvy, Charis possessed many of the other attributes of postrevolutionary Mexican *caciques*. He was a swashbuckling character who charmed people with his audacity, while also using dramatic gestures and a powerful image to bolster his power. On one occasion in Comitancillo (Oaxaca), Charis proclaimed: "Although the Revolution never reached this town, today it arrives with me, I am the Revolution (*El Satélite* 7/8/1973)." Other Charis oral accounts describe how he killed his own son for stealing a horse, to set an example for would-be thieves. Charis' harshness is also reflected in his treatment of an illegitimate son, now (ironically) a prominent Juchitán COCEI politician, who he called "*amigo*" rather than recognizing him as his progeny.

Charis' relationships to women paralleled those of many of his *cacique* peers. During the Revolution, Charis took numerous Zapotec *soldaderas* as his concubines, only to abandon them as he moved from one battlefield to the next (Matus 1985). Back in Juchitán after the fighting ended, Charis continued his sexual exploits, leaving a trail of offspring in and out of wedlock throughout the Isthmus. He was especially fond of young peasant girls, who he bought from their parents if they would not go with him willingly. Finally, like many Mexican *caciques*, Charis died of cirrhosis in 1964 after years of carousing and hard living. According to some of my informants, Charis "dried up" from having too much sex. The day of his death, Juchitán school children were taken from their classes and marched past the open tomb of their dead general.

During the Charis era, reformist factions from the professional and business community frequently presented alternative Juchitán mayoral candidates to the hand-picked proxies of Charis (Rubin 1990, 1991).[20] These individuals and their movements were stifled by the general, with the exception of the 1944, 1946, and 1956 elections, when Charis accepted the victory of non-*Charista* candidates (Arellanes et al. 1988:26; de la Cruz 1992b:66).[21] Thus, Charis,[22] who abandoned the secessionist cause after he became a general, helped keep the Isthmus in check and amenable to national government policy in return for federally funded development programs, public works, and a degree of regional autonomy (Rubin 1990).[23]

CAPITALIST TRANSFORMATION OF THE ISTHMUS, 1950–1993

Although the Isthmus was a stage for international capitalist development at the turn of the century, the impact of development was not as substantial as originally projected, since North American plans to build a canal through the region were dropped in favor of a site in Panama. The most lasting effect of this period was the construction of the Tehuantepec railroad.[24] In its brief heyday, the Tehuantepec line was heavily used. Although volume rapidly declined with the advent of the Panama Canal, the railroad was instrumental in linking the Isthmus to Veracruz, Mexico City, and elsewhere and opened up the area to many outside influences. However, transportation between these regions, which are divided by jungle and mountainous terrain, remained a slow and cumbersome process even with the railway. This situation worsened as the rail system deteriorated.

When Covarrubias explored the Isthmus in the 1930s and 40s, he traveled in "a picturesque assortment of boxcars, oil-cars, and second- and first-class coaches surviving from the boom days of the railway, but now rickety and overcrowded, threatening to come apart at every curve" (1946:145). The North American linguist Velma Pickett first arrived in Juchitán in 1943; she described the prevailing systems of transportation to me as follows:

> When I first went, there was no road, you either—if you had the money—went by plane . . . to Ixtepec or by second-class train. Second-class because the first-class . . . seats were plush and the little biting animals could hide in them very easily. . . . After two nights and a day, at least, on the train we got there. . . . We got an oxcart taxi to take us to where we were going.

Until the completion of the Pan American Highway in 1948, commercial trade with Oaxaca was undertaken with mule teams, which took 12 days to reach the Isthmus from the Valley (Martínez Vázquez 1986). Contemporary Blaseño informants still remember the large stable where mule trains were received in the Santa María barrio of Tehuantepec. Indeed, after the "golden era" of the end of the century, Isthmus economic growth stalled, and despite previous colonial and postcolonial incursions, the Isthmus remained physically and culturally isolated, to some extent, from urban Mexico.[25] This scenario gradually changed after the building of the highways.

The inauguration in Tehuantepec of the Pan American Highway by President Miguel Alemán in 1951 opened up a new chapter in Isthmus history. It not only connected the Isthmus to Chiapas, Oaxaca City, and Mexico City, but it incorporated this rebellious region, far more firmly than ever before, into the economic development plans of the expanding Mexican state. Isthmus mercantile trade picked up markedly after the building of the Pan American Highway through Tehuantepec and along the outskirts of Juchitán. Whereas in the 1940s Covarrubias (1946:283) described local retail stores as "dingy shops" which sold "pennyworths of flour, coffee, or nails," by the 1960s both Zapotec and foreign merchants engaged in a growing Isthmus commerce, whose total sales for 1960 were a respectable 129 million pesos (Ortíz Wadgymar 1971:97).[26] Local construction companies also profited from road construction, and many Istmeños obtained jobs on road-building crews.

Major economic changes in the region, however, did not take full effect until the completion of the Trans-Isthmic Highway (from Coatzacoalcos, Veracruz, to Salina Cruz) and the Benito Juárez Dam and canal system in 1958 and 1961, respectively.[27] By then, land prices were climbing rapidly and land was becoming scarce because of population pressures and expectations of high profits from the application of irrigation to Isthmus lands (Binford 1985). These problems were especially acute in Juchitán, which has grown by approximately 5 percent per annum since 1950, when it had 13,814 inhabitants, to its present population of about 80,000 (SEDUE 1988; Díaz 1984:19).[28] Rising prices set off a bitter struggle within the Juchiteco community for control over land, a struggle that continues to the present day.

Land Tenure and Politics

Prior to the building of the Benito Juárez Dam at Jalapa del Marqués (25 miles from Juchitán) and creation of Irrigation District 19, Isthmus land tenure was a relatively simple matter. Although Chiñas Flores (1955:84) notes that 12 percent of peasants in the Juchitán district did not have land in 1950, landless individuals could usually obtain access to land by mobilizing kin ties or negotiating with community authorities. Among landholders, property was divided as follows: 20 percent had below 1 ha, 40 percent had from 1 to 3 ha, 30 percent had from 3 to 5 ha, and 10 percent had more than 5 ha. Of the latter group, six very large properties (including that of Charis), located mostly in the richer northern Isthmus land, stood out from the rest (Ybarra 1949:58).[29] Around Juchitán city there were few large cattle ranches or sugar cane plantations. These were mostly located near Matías Romero, the Chimalapas area, or Chahuites.

Unlike what occurred in many other regions of the country, agrarian reform was not carried out in the Isthmus to any significant extent after the Mexican Revolution. Land distribution was unequal, but most peasants at least had some access to it. In fact, most Isthmus land was neither fenced nor cultivated, but was used for cattle pasture or hunting and gathering (Binford 1989). In 1946 Orozco (1946:54), a local intellectual, remarked that there were no agrarian problems in Juchitán.[30] Juchiteco agriculturalists used traditional methods involving little mechanization, and production was primarily oriented toward the local market (de la Cerda 1980:46).

Land titles were not a major concern, since control of land was based upon de facto occupation, common consent, or, occasionally, old documents. The eldest son normally inherited his father's land. Legally, most of the land in the municipality of Juchitán was classified as communal[31] based on "primordial titles" granted by the Spanish colonial administration to the community (TPJ [1736–1737] 1987). In fact, land was treated like private property and was relatively cheap and available, although tradition discouraged sale to outsiders and municipal authorities had formal power to effect land transactions (Binford 1985).

Thus, in 1949, when Juchitán residents requested government confirmation of communal lands to resolve a boundary dispute with neighboring municipalities, there was no response (Binford 1985:185). As they had done in several previous Isthmus land controversies, federal bureaucrats dragged their feet and temporized. Agrarian conflicts provoked by construction of the dam, however, were more complicated and had more serious consequences than those of the past. The Mexican government's way of handling Isthmus agrarian problems also changed; it abandoned its laissez-faire approach in favor of an interventionist policy that has made matters worse (de la Cerda 1980:60).

In 1959 the Department of Agrarian Affairs and Colonization gave orders to expedite communal land confirmation for Juchitán and other communities in connection with legal actions allowing work on the dam and canal system to proceed (Binford 1985:185). In 1962, President López Mateos expropriated 47,000 ha of prime Isthmus land (much of it within the immediate vicinity of Juchitán) for the creation of an *ejido* instead of communal lands.[32] This land is in the heart of the area that would later be irrigated by the dam and its network of canals. López Mateos' measure, rather than clarifying issues, touched off a morass of legal and political battles over Isthmus land tenure that has alternately paralyzed regional agriculture and led to violent confrontations. A second decree in 1964 expanded the *ejido* area to 68,000 ha and unilaterally declared that there was no private property within this area, despite the fact that private *pequeñas propiedades* in Juchitán had been guaranteed legal protection under national laws passed in 1942 (Binford 1985). To this day, the status of these lands remains ambiguous, and control over their use is one of the main issues that has fueled the struggle of COCEI.

The 1964 decree evoked a powerful response from Juchitán landowners of all classes, who feared that government intrusion would cause them to lose control of their lands.[33] Large landowners, many of whom had acquired sizable tracts through pre-dam construction speculation, organized Committees in Defense of Small Property to combat the resolutions (Santana 1988:5; de la Cerda 1980:53).[34] The committees were joined by Juchiteco peasants. This latter group stood to lose proportionally fewer hectares than the upper classes, but land loss to the peasantry meant not only material hardship but damage to an entire way of life.

These legitimate concerns were aggravated by rumors, cultivated by the elite, to the effect that the peasants' lands would be given to politicians and residents of Veracruz and the Valley of Oaxaca.[35] Furthermore, the entire indigenous town of Jalapa del Marqués was displaced by backwater from the dam's reservoir, setting an ominous precedent. Anxieties and tensions sparked by the government's actions were vented in rallies and protest meetings attended by groups of from 3,000 to 5,000 protestors. In these gatherings there was mention of the 1882 Mexu Chele revolt against usurpers of Juchitán lands and talk of armed rebellion (López Gurrión 1976:151). Political demonstrations were accompanied by the filing of petitions and legal claims challenging the *ejido* resolution.

The government's initial response to growing grassroots opposition was to conduct land surveys and censuses in order to determine which Juchitán residents were entitled to usufruct rights and how large their lands would be in the *ejido* area. However, in 1966, President Díaz Ordaz, in a politically motivated gesture (he had promised resolution of the Juchitán land problem during his election campaign), reversed the 1964 decree and put in its place a resolution declaring approximately 4,000 private land titles (Binford 1985). Díaz Ordaz earned political points for the move, and the *vela laayu*, or land fiesta, was created in his honor (Santana 1988). Nevertheless, land tenure problems remained unresolved because of the ambiguity of title language that only confirmed possession of originally communal lands rather than granting ownership. The new resolution and its haphazard execution created additional irregularities, including overlapping and contradiction with previous decrees, improper filing of title documentation, granting titles to the same piece of land to two different individuals, etc. (Binford 1985). In 1976 even the director of the Ministry of Agrarian Reform called the 1966 titles illegal (López Gurrión 1976:162).[36] As a consequence of legal ambiguities, land titles were subject to multiple interpretations, which each interest group in Juchitán interpreted to their own advantage (Binford 1985; de la Cerda 1980:118). From COCEI's standpoint, all of the land should be declared communal and given to poor Juchiteco peasants. But the national government has been unable to resolve the status of the disputed lands, and, until they do, bitter agrarian struggles will continue in Juchitán.

Bureaucratic inefficiency is only half the story. Economic development of the Isthmus has led to an increase in corruption and intense class warfare over land, local political power, and the benefits of government projects. For Zapotec peasants, who were never consulted regarding construction of the dam and irrigation system, development resulted in land loss or decreased decision-making power over the use of their lands (Warman 1972). Mestizo civil servants, engineers, and politicians assumed these powers, as the Mexican state integrated the Isthmus into its politico-economic domain to a much greater degree than in the past (Binford 1983).[37] The new authorities often used their powerful positions to obtain land illegally or to engage in corrupt deals at the expense of the government budget. For example, several informants who ran a tractor rental business told me how agricultural bureaucrats accepted kickbacks in exchange for the purchase of obviously impractical Belgian and Russian tractors. These machines worked satisfactorily for a short time, but when they began to need repairs and spare parts, the expensive European tractors had to be abandoned because of the prohibitive cost of obtaining parts and service from abroad.

Local merchants, white-collar professionals, money-lenders, and land barons also fared better than the peasants, since they were able to exploit the new economic possibilities provided by the highways, dam, and later the refinery, in ethical and unethical ways (Binford 1985:197). The names of the Juchitán Zapotec elite appear repeatedly in local newspapers (e.g., *El Satélite, La Voz del Istmo*) of the 1960s and 1970s and SRA records (SRA 1971) in accusations of illegal land transactions, possession of enormous tracts, intimidation of peasants, and various acts of corruption.[38] Yet at the same time that they were engaged in illicit actions to the detriment of the peasantry, these same elite figures controlled local peasant organizations, private property defense committees, and related agricultural associations (as well as local government and business), which they used to defend their interests (Santana 1988:7; de la Cerda 1980:62–63).

According to the needs of the moment, the bourgeoisie claimed that its disproportionately large lands were either communal, *ejido*, or private property, and masqueraded as average peasants in order to avoid redistribution by the government.[39] This strategy paid off. Hence, the elite solidified its control over local agrarian affairs and the authentic peasantry became increasingly marginalized from land ownership and agricultural decision making. Dorsett (1975:135) notes that the irrigation project was directly linked to the emergence of a landless rural proletariat. Consequently, the percentage of the economically active population of Juchitán engaged in agriculture declined from approximately 66 percent in 1960 to just 29 percent in 1980 (Segura 1988:196; SPP–INEGI 1984:471). The percentage of land in the irrigation district held communally declined from 88 percent in 1962 to just 9 percent in 1980 (de la Cerda 1980:43).[40]

Green Revolution Debacle (ca. 1970–1993)

Even though the land tenure issue was not satisfactorily resolved and peasant insecurity over titles continued, the government went ahead with plans to recoup the 450 million pesos incurred in building the dam (Warman 1972:25). Two main strategies it pursued were promoting new commercial crops and lending money against the harvest. Ironically, corn-farming peasants, the supposed beneficiaries of the Benito Juárez Dam,[41] did not use its irrigation waters for four years during the 1960s as a tacit protest against the government's intrusion into their affairs (SRA 1971). Zapotec peasants saw water as a "God-given" natural resource, which they should not have to pay mestizo agricultural bureaucrats to use (Warman 1972). Nor did peasants—fearing involvement with a government they did not trust—take quickly to the use of fertilizers, tractors, new cultivation techniques, and credit (*Neza Cubi* 4:13, 1968).[42]

Irrigation per se was not a panacea for the peasantry's problems. Sesame, a cash crop already sown by Zapotecs, not only failed to benefit from irrigation, but was damaged by diseases (e.g., fungi) which proliferated as a result of increased moisture (Warman 1972:16). Additional water did not substantially augment low-yielding (800 kg./ha) native corn production either in years of normal rainfall.[43] In essence, the Zapotec peasantry continued to operate their time-honored, rain-fed subsistence agriculture inside a modern irrigation district.[44] Ironically, the expensive dam and canal system was underused, its valuable waters flowing past dry fields into the ocean.

If this sounds like a worst-case scenario, it unfortunately is. As in other Third World development failures of this era, developers considered indigenous culture an obstacle and applied their supposed expertise to the task of "modernizing" the peasantry (Ortíz Wadgymar 1971; *Neza Cubi* 3:10, 1968). Consequently, they lost a potentially rich source of local knowledge about soils, climate, salinity problems, infestations, and other information vital to Isthmus agriculture. Witness, for example, these comments of engineer del Conde and Licenciado Piedra (n.d.:50–51):

It would be redundant to mention the figures revealing the cultural
backwardness of the Isthmus people which appear in all of the studies
done in the region, therefore in the following we will describe only
the gravest and most apparent consequences related to possible agricultural development in the Tehuantepec, Oaxaca Irrigation District. . . . It can be said that in 500 years there has been no innovation
in agricultural practices or in the customary crops. . . . The type of
dwelling and the clothing have not been modified and have only been
impoverished through time, the same as religious traditions, fiestas,
and forms of government, that after apparently constituting an adequate social structure, have degenerated in customs that contain very
little of what originally was essential and, instead, generate wastage of
money, laziness, and conflicts with grave consequences for the impoverished economies of the region's inhabitants. . . . It is evident that
there is a wide gap between the culture they [i.e., the Zapotecs] possess
and that necessary for their development . . .[45]

I was confronted with equally ethnocentric attitudes when I interviewed
the assistant director of the SARH office in Tehuantepec, who blamed "*las
costumbres*" (local customs) and "*el factor humano*" (the human factor) for
Isthmus agricultural problems. When I asked him to explain what he meant
by this, he stated that Zapotec peasants are savage and spend too much
time boozing at fiestas instead of tending their crops. Moreover, he insisted
that Isthmus peasants do not learn new agricultural methods, regardless of
how many times they are explained to them by extension agents, because
the new ideas just go "in one ear and out another."
According to the state's development plan, Isthmus farmers were supposed to grow inexpensive food for urban residents and thereby subsidize
industrial development. Dissatisfied with local corn production, agrono-
mists attempted to replace the disease- and wind-resistant *zapalote* corn
with new cultigens. Efforts to replace subsistence production with commodity production generally failed, partly because many peasants were un-
willing to exchange a proven crop for an untried, and potentially inferior,
one. As a COCEI leader observed, "From the capitalist viewpoint, *zapalote*
is no good, but for the peasant it has been his *raison d'etre*, that is why he
has not abandoned it" (Santana 1988:13).
Government-initiated crop substitution failed, in other cases, because of
the introduced plants' unsuitability for Isthmus conditions. Technicians
might have recognized this had they asked local agriculturalists. Isthmus
peasants continue to use indigenous corn because few other crops, aside

from tropical fruits and certain vegetables, thrive in the weak soils and extreme climatological conditions of the region without large amounts of fertilizer and water (Martínez Vásquez 1986:45). Furthermore, unlike introduced cash crops, corn can always be consumed directly by the peasant, if necessary, as well as sold if there is sufficient surplus.

One of the most absurd episodes in this agricultural nightmare was an attempt by Mexico City-based technicians to promote cotton production in the Isthmus.[46] Unlike the sturdy, low-growing *zapalote*, cotton simply cannot stand the tremendous gale winds that sweep the Isthmus between October and March of each year (Warman 1972:16). Although cotton-growing efforts were short-lived, even greater time and federal money was invested in promoting rice, yet another catastrophe.

Rice cultivation failed for a host of reasons, including high production costs, low prices, mismanagement, and corruption on the part of the Ejido Bank and the agricultural bureaucracy (Binford 1983, 1989; de la Cerda 1980:36). From the beginning (mid-1960s), government officials promoted, directed, and funded rice planting. Peasants were allowed no input into planting decisions and essentially became wage laborers on their own lands or the lands of others. Perhaps this lack of concern for peasant opinion is why technicians made errors in regard to planting times and the choice of seed varieties. Nonetheless, peasants were saddled with the debts left over from unprofitably low yields. They were also left with lands ruined by salinity, which resulted from rice monocropping, inadequate drainage, and other factors (Binford 1983:117)—all of which could have been prevented. In the end, the Benito Juárez rice processing plant had to be closed and rice growing abandoned.

Next, the state promoted a cattle-fattening scheme and sorghum cultivation, both of which also failed. A program to increase dairy production (the *Ganado Oaxaca* plan) was also unsuccessful (*El Imparcial* 3/15/1988).[47] In a study of Oaxacan agriculture, de la Cerda (1980:39) found that livestock production and productivity were very low in the Isthmus irrigation district.

Sugar cane—which replaced rice as a major cash crop—is a key factor in the government's most recent, and largest-scale, adventure in Isthmus agricultural development (de la Cerda 1980:82–89). The modern history of cane monocropping in the Juchitán area is a volatile mixture of bureaucratic bumbling, outright corruption,[48] and *caciquismo*.[49] As if this were not enough, the region experienced drought conditions during much of the 1980s, causing severe damage to cane.[50]

Sugar cane has been grown and processed in the Isthmus since at least the mid-nineteenth century (Ybarra 1949). Until the turn of the twentieth century, when the Santo Domingo cane factory was built, cane was milled exclusively in small, animal-powered operations known as *trapiches* (Binford 1983; 1992). Large-scale, industrial sugar production did not occur in the immediate vicinity of Juchitán until the Mexican government built the Jose López Portillo factory near Espinal in 1980.

Several observers suggest that the government constructed the mill to quell peasant politicization over the land question, legitimize private property, and solidify its political and economic hegemony over the Isthmus (Santana 1988:11). Prévot-Schapira and Riviere d'Arc (1984) note that originally Juchitán was chosen for the mill site because of its more expansive terrain and higher degree of mechanization. Mill construction was shifted to Espinal, they assert, in order to avoid direct clashes with militant peasants allied with COCEI. According to these researchers, Espinal was a more docile community that would more easily accept the capitalistic relations of production promoted by the mill bureaucracy. While these assertions remain unverified, the mill until recently played an important role in local economic life and has been a politicized arena of struggle for competing individual and class interests (Binford 1983:188–284).[51]

The mill bureaucracy controlled the scheduling of many tasks and activities involved in cane production, a job which it often botched. As in the case of rice, direct producers were excluded by agricultural officials from decisions affecting the cultivation of their own land. Nonetheless, the cane bureaucracy saddled producers with most of the risks involved in growing cane. The danger of the cane crop failing stems from drought conditions, labor shortages for harvesting cane, bad planning by sugar mill administrators, and other factors. However, not all producers are affected equally by the hazards and potential rewards (which, under the right conditions, may be considerable).

Isthmus cane growers, in order to have access to credit, equipment, and milling of their product, must belong to the official cane-growers' organization, the CNC, which has two branches: the CNC–CNC and the CNC–CNPP.[52] Each of these branches is controlled by the PRI, which excludes all but clandestine *Coceístas* from gaining access to the occasionally lucrative cane industry. Moreover, in the CNC, as in PRI organizations generally, power is highly centralized. The Isthmus CNC–CNPP and CNC–CNC are dominated by two charismatic Zapotec leaders. In addition to their institutional power, the two cane leaders have the unofficial authority of traditional *caciques*. They have personal followings beholden only to them, the capacity and willingness to use violence against their opponents, and the ability to serve as brokers with regional and national political actors. Both *caciques* made their way to the top of the cane organizations by killing or intimidating their enemies, practices in which they continue to engage.

The current cane leaders used their powers to set up empires consisting of large tracts of land and personal control of CNC property, such as the heavy equipment vital to cane cultivation, harvesting, and hauling the crop to local mills. They also directly control the distribution of agricultural credit, fertilizer, and crop insurance settlements. The wealth of these *caciques* and their closest associates has little to do with effective agricultural techniques, or even with whether they grow sugar cane at all. Rather, it is a result of corrupt management of government funds and materials allocated to cane growers. The rest of the growers, be they big or small, have to depend on proper farming methods and good weather for a successful harvest.[53] However, the large growers, who are a 20 percent minority of all cane farmers but control 40 percent of total cane land, are more likely than the small producers to use political clout to obtain sizable insurance settlements in the event of a bad crop year (Binford 1983:209).

On the whole, the government's foray into Isthmus sugar production has been a failure. The Espinal mill, until its recent closure, was riddled with corruption, run inefficiently, and able to survive only through massive subsidies. The sporadic output of local cane farmers was insufficient to employ fully the inflated mill labor force and its expensive equipment. Thus, the mill only ground one third the amount of cane it was capable of processing (Piñon Jiménez 1988:331). Furthermore, in contrast to the verdant, towering cane of the lush neighboring state of Veracruz, Isthmus cane has frequently been dry and sickly, especially during the crop failures of the 1980/1981 and 1987/1988 seasons.

Additionally, COCEI leaders complain that sugar cane's large water consumption has diverted scarce irrigation water from subsistence corn to market-oriented cane. They argue that cane now occupies a large proportion of the irrigated zone, to the detriment of poor corn farmers (Toledo and de la Cruz 1983:25).[54] They also criticize low corn prices fixed by the government, and the credit bank's preferential treatment of cash crops over subsistence ones, which further discourages corn cultivation.[55] Maize production's decline is reflected in the fact that the Isthmus now must import corn from Chiapas and elsewhere, whereas formerly it was self-sufficient.

Although, to date, sugar cane has been a market failure, it did provide an avenue for the Mexican state's further incursion into Isthmus agriculture and the PRI's mediation of segments of the peasantry. Still, the efforts of the PRI and the government to expand their influence are marred by the violent and arbitrary way in which cane-grower organizations are run, and peasant dissatisfaction with cane's often dismal performance. Rather than pacifying peasants or bringing them under the wing of the PRI/government, the government-run sugar-cane project increased socioeconomic divisions, produced competing cane mafias that further divide the Isthmus PRI, politicized or alienated many peasants, and provided ammunition for COCEI's critique of PRI politics and top-down capitalist development programs.[56]

Overall, state intervention in the Isthmus dramatically changed agricultural practices and favored capitalistic relations of production over noncapitalistic relations (de la Cerda 1980:43, 99).[57] Yet the new system of production did not eliminate the peasantry, indigenous social arrangements, or nonmechanized farming methods. Government involvement, therefore, produced contradictory results. On the one hand, the dam and irrigation system encouraged private sector investment in farming and led to land concentration. On the other hand, many small peasants survived precisely because of new credit opportunities and access to technical goods and services, which, in some respects, began to resemble a welfare system.[58]

Irrigation District 19 is one of the least successful irrigation projects in Mexico (Binford 1989; de la Cerda 1980:35–42; Segura 1988:283–290). After 30 years of operation, only about half of the district is under cultivation. Much of this area is devoted to cattle grazing or sugar cane, leaving only about a quarter of the surface area for corn, which is the key staple of the Isthmus diet (SARH 1985). Production levels are low and peasant unrest high. Meanwhile, rural roads and irrigation canals languish in disrepair because of reduced government budgets, a result of Mexico's economic crisis. Allegations of corruption and mismanagement of the Isthmus agricultural bureaucracy surface repeatedly, but higher authorities have shown no interest in investigating them. At present, no solution to the district's agricultural problems appears on the Isthmus horizon.

Industrial Development of the Isthmus:
PEMEX, Population Growth, and Related Problems, 1970–1993

The government's large investment in modernizing Isthmus agriculture is only a fraction of the amount it spent on the PEMEX oil refinery in Salina Cruz. Almost 10 billion pesos were expended on the first stage alone, making it the largest investment in Isthmus history (Prévot–Schapira and Riviere d'Arc 1984:150). Construction of this huge petrochemical plant began in 1974 on lands wrested from the indigenous inhabitants, and the first of three proposed stages was inaugurated in 1979. Continued expansion of the facility is likely, because of its important role in petroleum sales to the growing Japanese market. Japanese tankers anchor in the Salina Cruz harbor approximately every 3 weeks to load up with refined oil.

Despite the large size of the plant, it has less economic impact on the region than would be expected because of the centralized way in which the Mexican national oil company and its closed-shop unions are run. The number of local workers benefitting from the project is small compared to the large number of laborers who flooded in from northeastern Mexico, former home of the PEMEX oil worker's union.[59] Thus, Salina Cruz became a mestizo enclave in the otherwise rural, indigenous Isthmus, and an oil boomtown whose population exploded from 25,000 to 180,000 over a 10-year period (*Proceso* 3/7/1988). Salina Cruz is also the home of numerous shrimp fishing cooperatives, which sell their product to the North American market. As in the case of PEMEX, the local beneficiaries of the ocean fishing industry are few in number. The average Istmeño gains little from it.[60]

Ironically, many Isthmus Zapotec laborers have had to migrate to the Minatitlán area to seek work, because of the vagaries of Mexican labor contracting.[61] Moreover, the Isthmus has few specialized or skilled laborers with the training to perform many of the new tasks required at the Salina Cruz refinery, which uses relatively few unskilled laborers. The Zapotec workers who have obtained employment in the facility perform the most menial, dangerous, and low-paying temporary jobs, obtaining little training that might help them secure future jobs. Permanent and higher-paid positions (*de planta*) are controlled, in typical PEMEX fashion, by corrupt labor bosses who reserve them for their relatives and friends, or sell them to the highest bidder at astronomical sums by local standards (e.g., $150 at the time of my fieldwork). Even poorly paid, short-term jobs have not been readily obtainable unless a prospective worker engaged in degrading, unpaid tasks at the whim of local leaders (often on their personal homes or ranches) as part of a quasi-official, pre-employment service period (*militancia*).

COCEI's initial attempt to organize construction workers at the plant was immediately repressed (Prévot–Schapira and Riviere d'Arc 1984:160). Moreover, PEMEX recruits workers from far away from the Isthmus, who are unlikely to be attracted to COCEI and are under heavy pressure to join PRI.

Salina Cruz's greater relevance to the national economy than to the local economy is also reflected in the fact that very few of the materials consumed by the plant are provided by local merchants.[62] However, some local business people prospered as a consequence of the influx of population, heightened business activity generated by sales to PEMEX employees and their families, and expanded government spending on agriculture.[63] Whereas Royce (1975:43) counted 103 retail businesses in the center of Juchitán in the early 1970s, by 1987, 460 businesses were members of the local chamber of commerce. A survey I did of Juchitán economic activity revealed an extraordinarily large number of small businesses for a town of about 80,000 people. For example, in 1988 the community had 31 auto parts stores, 39 restaurants, 14 pharmacies, 86 small food stores, and 51 auto repair shops. Clearly, many local merchants prospered as a result of the development projects. Segura discovered that Juchitán had become the principal commercial center of the Isthmus in the 1960s (1988:278).

Isthmus Zapotec market women were also affected by economic changes. The increased size and vigor of the regional and national economy, as well as better transportation systems, increased sales volume at the new Juchitán market, constructed in the early 1970s. Thus, women continued their traditional vending roles in a more competitive, but potentially more lucrative, market. But economic development also brought chain stores to the Isthmus and greatly increased retail store activity, which cut into the business of female market vendors. A few Isthmus women, especially in Juchitán, cashed in on the boom of retail shops and set up hardware stores, fabric stores, and other businesses. Finally, many *viajeras* took advantage of improved transportation facilities and a more vigorous economic climate by traveling to sell their wares in "foreign" markets. In these instances, Isthmus women "commodified" indigenous cultural elements (native foods, local crafts, women's regional costume, and gold jewelry) and sold them to mestizo and gringo tourist markets in Oaxaca City, Mexico City, Veracruz, and elsewhere.

Nonetheless, the new sources of profit for a limited number of individuals are offset by the rapid inflation of the oil boom economy, as a French social scientist discovered in Salina Cruz:

Salina Cruz is considered to be the most expensive locality in Mexico. . . . Price increases are painfully endured by the poorer classes; the agriculturalists and fishermen of the small communities surrounding Salina Cruz have very scarce resources and if they are able to survive at all, they are unable to keep up with the rise in prices. Consequently, the abandonment of the countryside is observed. . . . The rise in the cost of living is revealed as the determining factor in this exodus (to Veracruz, Puebla, Chiapas, and Mexico City) [Fauverge 1982:266].

Indigenous Istmeños harbor considerable hostility towards PEMEX. They blame the Salina Cruz refinery for polluting the ocean and air with oil spills and toxic fumes, for the loss of their land, for hogging limited fresh water supplies, for spurring price inflation, and for causing a dramatic rise in the number of brothels in the region. Moreover, the lack of maintenance of refinery equipment presents the frightening specter of a Bhopal-like accident (*Proceso* 3/7/1988). For the majority of Isthmus Zapotecs, excluding those who have secured employment, the PEMEX plant brought more disadvantages than advantages. The lucky ones, who have obtained decent-paying jobs at PEMEX, construct large homes and purchase conspicuous consumer items, such as cars, pickup trucks, and televisions. This provokes jealousy and envy of the oilworkers (*petroleros*) among poor Zapotecs. Overall, Salina Cruz represents a classic example of the social ills associated with industrialization and urbanization in an "enclave economy" (Wolf and Hansen 1972:160–85).

Apart from the Salina Cruz industrial complex there are few large factories of note in the largely agricultural Isthmus. According to Soto (1984:41), the Juchitán district has but 11 major industries. In the vicinity of Juchitán city, aside from the defunct sugar mill, the only significant industries are a mineral lime factory, an electric power plant, the defunct rice mill, and a facility for soaking railroad ties in tar. Despite its lack of industry, Juchitán is closely linked to the Salina Cruz complex because of the many Juchitecos who commute daily to the PEMEX plant. Indeed, Juchitán and Tehuantepec are quickly becoming bedroom communities for the PEMEX labor force.

Housing has become particularly scarce because of the influx of *petroleros*, general population growth, and inflation. Additionally, municipal services, which were very limited prior to construction of the refinery, had no chance of meeting the needs of a burgeoning population. Housing shortages prompted COCEI land invasions and creation of shantytowns around Juchitán, a strategy promptly copied by PRI. Shantytowns also cover the hills adjacent to Salina Cruz. Indeed, the chaotic urban sprawl of Salina Cruz, Tehuantepec, and Juchitán are case studies of bad urban planning.

Of course, these problems do not affect all Istmeños equally. Members of the bourgeoisie live where they desire and their *nouveau riche* mansions are an affront to traditional architectural practices. Moreover, the Zapotec middle and upper classes can afford to obtain the goods and services they require with private capital, if necessary, or by influencing the distribution of municipal resources. In contrast, poor, illiterate peasants, who live in *carrizo* cane shacks and adobe huts on the outskirts of Isthmus cities, have no way of bringing water, drainage, electricity, or other facilities to their homes. Their problems have increased considerably since 1981, when a prolonged economic crisis hit Mexico and decreased rural wages in parts of the Isthmus by as much as 50 percent (Binford personal communication, 1990).

Environmental pollution is another major problem that PEMEX brought to the Isthmus. The worst examples of this are the refinery's acrid emissions of smoke and chemicals into the atmosphere, and oil tanker spills that severely damaged lagoons fished by Huave and Zapotecs, and that left a permanent, greasy film in the water of once-pristine Salina Cruz beaches. Air and water pollution caused by PEMEX exacerbate growing environmental damage to the Isthmus landscape inflicted by haphazard disposal of garbage and sewage. This was not a major problem in 1966, when Chiñas (1983) undertook her research, since population size and density of Isthmus communities were then unproblematic, and consumption of water and consumer goods maintained low levels. However, with sharp demographic growth, high population density in the major Isthmus towns, and increased consumption levels, the output of solid and liquid wastes has overwhelmed municipal disposal systems. Furthermore, greatly increased water usage has outstripped well capacity, leaving many Istmeños without access to running water for weeks and months at a time.

On the ground, increased population and consumption of all types of goods means that streets are littered with plastic bags and candy wrappers, broken glass, and miscellaneous other debris, including human and animal feces (most peasants keep their oxen and pigs, who roam the streets, in town at their homes). The lack of toilet facilities causes many Istmeños, especially children, in the poorer sections of local communities, to continue the age-old, and much decried, practice of defecating in the streets (*fecalismo al aire libre*).[64] Because of inadequate garbage disposal services, most Istmeños haul their garbage to the nearest river bed or impromptu dump site on the outskirts of town, sullying rivers and fields. The intense heat and gusty winds of the region lead to rapid putrefaction and spreading of such germ-carrying materials into homes and water supplies, where they cause serious gastrointestinal problems.[65]

As a result of the torrid Isthmus climate and quick decomposition of organic substances, visitors to the region's large, female-run markets remember them as much for their strong, often putrid, odors as for the vivacity of market vendors and their colorful vegetables and food products. A prominent image that once attracted tourists to the region was that of nude Tehuanas, bathing leisurely and unashamedly in the Tehuantepec River. Today, Isthmus rivers are cesspools that only the poorest people, of necessity, bathe or wash their clothes in. The innocence and pristine naturalism represented in bygone Isthmus folk images is replaced in current tourist guide descriptions by exhortations to bypass or leave the "sultry" and "dirty" region as soon as possible.

The Istmeños themselves also contribute to the region's environmental woes by purchasing noisy, contaminating, old cars and trucks that clog the narrow, mostly unpaved streets of local towns and endanger townspeople, who are accustomed to whiling away leisure hours on their front porches. This is an especially serious problem in San Blas, where street traffic is dominated by a remarkable, homegrown contraption known as the *moto*, a three-wheeled, scooterlike vehicle with a small flatbed in the rear for carrying passengers and goods. Unfortunately, in addition to their many uses, the *motos'* little two-stroke motors produce a high-pitched wail and clouds of blue smoke at all hours of the day and night. Another common site in contemporary Juchitán or San Blas streets, reflecting class and cultural contradictions, is the showdown between a peasant's creaky wooden oxcart, pulled by a pair of hulking Zebu cattle, and a Ford car or truck, each vying for a space only sufficient to allow one to pass at a time.

Additionally, the current building mania—employing enormous quantities of sand and cement—which obsessed Istmeños as a result of population growth and oil money contributes to the region's already serious problem of blowing dust. This becomes intolerable during the dry, windy winter months and in times of acute drought, when swirling grit causes innumerable cases of conjunctivitis and other ailments.

Finally, another unfortunate aspect of population expansion and economic development is the virtual extinction of indigenous Isthmus fauna: armadillo, alligator, jaguar, iguana, wild pig, and deer. Local people especially lament the near disappearance of the once abundant, and highly prized, iguana—totem of the Isthmus Zapotecs. In earlier times, Istmeños ate iguana with great regularity, and hunting contributed to indigenous subsistence. Today, most iguana in Isthmus markets are brought in from Veracruz and command hefty prices.[66] Fish and shellfish from Isthmus lagoons, trapped for centuries by the Huave and Zapotecs, are also in acute danger of extinction and contamination because of oil spills, riverine pollution, low water levels caused by drought, and intensive fishing. Indigenous salt flats are another victim of PEMEX pollution and construction projects. Firewood is also becoming scarce.

Sociological Problems Related to Development and Change: Alcoholism and Violence

As if the aforementioned problems were not sufficient, the Isthmus is now beset with serious problems of alcoholism and violent crime linked to the profound socioeconomic changes sweeping the area. The federal government's consumer affairs director for the Isthmus told me that Istmeños drink 1 million cartons of beer on average each month, with higher rates during the May and December fiesta seasons. Many Isthmus residents claim, with a mixture of pride and sarcasm, that the region consumes more beer than does any other part of Mexico. While this assertion is difficult to prove, it is noteworthy that both Isthmus residents and visitors to the region such as Fauverge (1982:274), who noted that weekends in Salina Cruz "offer an impressive spectacle of drunken people lying in the streets," are equally amazed at the prodigious drinking habits of the Istmeños. In 1986, Juchitán alone had 166 official beer-drinking establishments, in addition to many clandestine drinking halls, and 160 businesses that sold beer for consumption off the premises (*Proceso* 8/28/1989).

This is in sharp contrast to Isthmus life during the formative years (the 1910s and 1920s) of some of my older informants, who noted that in earlier times people only drank mescal—a drink they characterized as healthier and more natural than bottled beer—and only *horchata* was drunk at many fiestas. One elderly Juchiteco even described to me how impressed he was when the first bottled drinks such as Coca-Cola and beer appeared in the Isthmus. The Juchiteco said he and his friends would share a bottle of the new and expensive beverages, splitting it up into shot glasses so that everyone could try it. Today, however, beer and liquor consumption threaten to become the central feature of many Isthmus *velas*, and *Alcohólicos Anónimos* branches have sprung up in all of the major towns of the region.[67]

Although a mestizo judge in Tehuantepec told me that high Isthmus alcoholism rates are caused by the passionate and decadent tropical mentality of Isthmus Zapotecs, there are better explanations. Alcoholism is a complex problem linked to poverty, malnutrition, limited social and career possibilities, lack of recreational opportunities, and local beer companies' ceaseless advertising. In regard to these factors, the Isthmus is not markedly different from other impoverished areas of Mexico, although the level of beer advertising is probably somewhat higher in the region than elsewhere. The Isthmus clearly stands out from many other parts of Mexico, however, in the extent of its ubiquitous round of *velas* and miscellaneous fiestas, where alcohol is consumed in huge quantities. The Isthmus Zapotec's *joie de vivre* philosophy may also play a limited, but not determining, role in the alcohol problem.[68] In fact, the fundamental causes of Isthmus alcoholism are social, political, and economic inequalities rather than a Zapotec "culture of poverty."

Violent crime has also become a serious problem in the Isthmus (Chiñas 1983:116). According to Tehuantepec civil records, 16 murders were reported in the town in 1986, and local authorities told me that many killings go unreported.[69] The most spectacular incidences of violence during my fieldwork included the robbery and murder of two German tourists at the Juchitán train station, the rape of a Dutch woman in the Juchitán cemetery, and the killing of COCEI poet and activist Alejandro Cruz by *Priístas* in Tehuantepec. Yet many other less-publicized homicides also occurred.

While I was in the field, the dominant San Blas *pistolero* killed at least seven people.[70] *Pistoleros* are hired gunmen who will kill and intimidate one's enemies in exchange for money. They are essentially nonideological, though they are often in league with municipal and state judicial police.[71] Isthmus *pistoleros* perform a vigilante function of rounding up petty criminals for local police authorities, keeping a watch on "*marijuanitos*" (gangs of vagrant youth), and generally "keeping order" in communities without a police force or court system. Their primary function, however, is to kill or injure upon request and, of course, payment. In the case of San Blas, a town of approximately 15,000 people that has no formal police body, the aforementioned *pistolero* not only engaged in contract killings but applied "justice" directly to people accused of murder, robbery, sexual assault, or other offenses. According to my most reliable informants, his predecessor killed a minimum of 18 people before succumbing himself.[72]

In addition to homicides, robbery is becoming a major menace to the public safety of Istmeños. When I first arrived in the Isthmus in 1981, Zapotec women still frequently wore their extravagant gold necklaces around town, to fiestas, and in other public settings. Today, women often use artificial gold necklaces (*fantasía*) outside the home because of their fears of being mugged. These fears are quite legitimate since, for example, 6 to 10 robberies daily were reported to the Juchitán *agente del ministerio público* during September 1988 (*Noticias* 10/23/1988). An earlier local newspaper story (*Noticias* 11/18/1987) called the Isthmus crime wave "alarming," and quoted the following statistics from the Salina Cruz dis-

trict attorney on crime in that city: a 37 percent increase in criminal investigations in 1987 compared to 1986, including three to five burglaries
per day, and 33 reported injuries from knife or gunshot wounds during
September 1987. In November 1987 in Juchitán, a Public Safety Council
was convened to combat rising crime rates, but soon thereafter seemingly
unconcerned highway bandits robbed five different buses on the Trans-
Isthmian Highway during a five-day period. Moreover, on February 15,
1988, the president of the Juchitán Chamber of Commerce complained
that 10 local businesses were robbed during the preceding two-week period.

Although apolitical crimes such as these are now commonplace, members of dissident Isthmus political movements have also been the victims
of ideologically motivated attacks. Political violence in rural Mexico, as
Friedrich (1986) illustrates, has been an all too common feature of life since
the Revolution, and tends to revolve around agrarian struggles. Today's
high violent crime rates in the Isthmus are closely linked to intensified
struggles over land, acute population growth, economic crisis, and the social dislocations of the oil boom. In Juchitán alone, political violence related to peasant land struggles has claimed the lives of approximately 30
COCEI supporters (see AI 1986). While detailed studies of crime in the
Isthmus have yet to be carried out, the harsh reality of violence and insecurity is painfully clear to Isthmus residents and recent fieldworkers.

Economic Development and the Velas

Perhaps no single Isthmus social activity better epitomizes the effects of
recent capitalist transitions on local culture than the *vela* (fiesta) system.
(The cultural content of "traditional" Isthmus *velas* will be discussed in
greater detail. See pp. 131–132.) As Binford (1990:86) observed in Espinal,
the character of Isthmus *velas* is gradually shifting, as their previous emphasis on social reciprocity, religious ceremony, and the reproduction of
community ritual is being supplanted to some extent by the articulation of
"a single discourse of 'modernization,' 'development,' and materialism."
Thus, at the same time that *vela* customs such as the *tirada de frutas* (fruit
throw), collective construction of a palm-and-wood *enramada* to shelter
the fiesta, and the role of the *guzana gola* (a woman in charge of fiesta
etiquette) fall by the wayside, many *vela mayordomos* have adopted a profit-
oriented attitude in which their main objective is to sell as much beer as
possible rather than fulfill ritual obligations. In San Blas, for example, a
woman complained to me that the dues for entering a particular fiesta had

become so inflated that she refused to attend. She said that the fiesta was now nothing more than a business (*"ya es puro negocio, nada más"*). Beer companies are particularly to blame for the commercialization of the fiestas, since they obligate the *mayordomos* to sell large beer quotas in order to obtain discounts, and have encouraged the use of manufactured items instead of customary objects. They provide canvas and metal structures in place of the *enramadas*, metal tables and chairs instead of wooden benches (*bangu'*), electric bands who play mostly popular music instead of *sones*, and innumerable truckloads of ice and beer.

Additionally, contrary to the claims of the Juchiteco elite, poor people are systematically marginalized from the more opulent *velas*. I observed this at the Vela López in 1987, where soldiers stood guard at the gate to prevent entrance to other than invited guests. Indeed, as kinship[73] becomes less significant in the working of the *vela* organizations, and monetary values become paramount, the *velas* are increasingly becoming "orgies of conspicuous consumption, in which the beneficiaries of state-promoted capitalist development commune with one another while the 'losers' in the regional drama enviously peruse the scene through the cracks in the palisade" (Binford 1990:85).

CONCLUSION: THE IMPACT OF CAPITALIST DEVELOPMENT ON ISTHMUS ZAPOTEC SOCIETY

The Mexican government's construction of roads through the Isthmus, "modernization" of local agriculture, and promotion of the petrochemical industry have resulted in uneven development, acute social problems, and environmental pollution. Economic transformations threatened indigenous subsistence practices and sharpened social differences within Isthmus society. On the one hand, business interests, white-collar professionals, large landowners, and the political elite generally benefitted from infrastructural development, government investment, and a more dynamic economic environment. Juchitán became an important regional commercial center, and Salina Cruz, an oil-based growth pole. On the other hand, rural development had unsatisfactory consequences for large numbers of Isthmus Zapotec peasants, artisans, and fishermen.

Rural development programs established a modern irrigation system and introduced new crops and technologies, but also led to land concentration and the proletarianization of many peasants. While a degree of internal differentiation existed in the Zapotec community prior to the 1950s, recent transformations of Isthmus productive capacity turned these strata into full-blown class divisions, which separated an expanding landless proletariat from a land-owning agrarian bourgeoisie. By the mid-1970s, Juchitán was definitely not composed of a "united front" of Zapotecs (*pace* Royce 1982:181).

Economic change had cultural consequences also, since it increasingly exposed Juchitecos to urban, mestizo Mexico via the highways, expansion of government bureaucracy, industrialization, mass media, and tourism. This cultural confrontation had contradictory effects, since even though many indigenous customs such as the *velas* changed markedly and consumer goods flooded into the Isthmus, Juchitecos retained a strong ethnic identity.[74] Indeed, the ethnic opposition between Zapotecs and *dxu'* that had motivated Juchitán movements of the past could still be invoked to mobilize Juchitecos against their political enemies. Thus, when Isthmus Zapotec people who were hurt by the economic developments began to blame the government and the PRI for their misfortunes, the stage was set for the emergence of a new radical Juchiteco movement.

Overall, capitalist penetration of the Isthmus has juxtaposed and interwoven two different economic models: (1) a primarily subsistence-oriented economy based on rain-fed maize cultivation, indigenous artisanry, simple fishing methods, and networks of social reciprocity, and (2) oil-based industrial expansion combined with irrigated, capital-intensive farming oriented towards the market and individual accumulation. Supporters of the latter project, such as many government bureaucrats and PRI politicians, call for changes in, or the eradication of, Zapotec culture, whereas COCEI has championed that culture. The rise of COCEI is the subject of Chapter Five.

THE PLAZA IN JUCHITÁN, OAXACA, 1988.
(Photograph by Howard Campbell.)

EL RÍO DE LOS PERROS, THE RIVER OF THE DOGS,
WHICH RUNS THROUGH JUCHITÁN, 1988.
(Photograph by Howard Campbell.)

Isthmus Farmers Preparing a Field for Spring Corn Planting, 1987.
(Photograph by Leigh Binford.)

A COCEI Flag Flying over Juchitán City Hall, 1988.
(Photograph by Howard Campbell.)

THE ENTRANCE TO THE JUCHITÁN CULTURAL CENTER, 1988.
(Photograph by Howard Campbell.)

THE PATIO OF THE JUCHITÁN CULTURAL CENTER, 1988.
(Photograph by Howard Campbell.)

OIL PAINTING BY MIGUEL ANGEL SALINAS, 1993.
(Reproduced courtesy of Miguel Angel Salinas.)

COCEI Leaders at a Rally in Juchitán in 1988.
*Left to right: Leopoldo de Gyves Pineda (hand on flag pole),
Leopoldo de Gyves de la Cruz (raised arm), unidentified political activist,
Oscar Cruz (at microphone). (Photograph by Howard Campbell.)*

OSCAR CRUZ, COCEI MAYOR OF JUCHITÁN, JANUARY 1993.
(Photograph by Howard Campbell.)

A COCEI Rally, 1988.
(Photograph by Howard Campbell.)

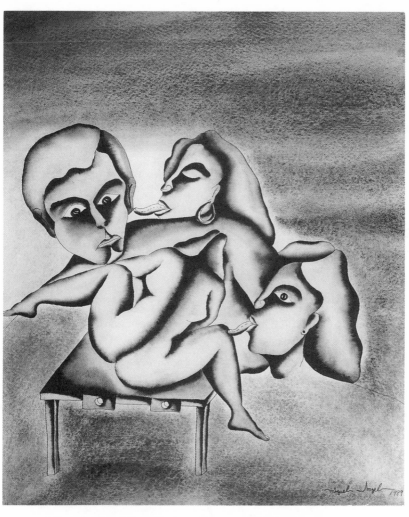

WATERCOLOR PAINTING BY MIGUEL ANGEL TOLEDO, 1989.
(Reproduced courtesy of Miguel Angel Toledo.)

At the center of the photograph wearing a cowboy hat and bandanna is the noted Zapotec intellectual Víctor de la Cruz. (Photograph courtesy of Oscar Cruz.)

A COCEI Partisan, 1989.
(Photograph by Howard Campbell.)

OIL PAINTING ON STONE BY ISRAEL VICENTE, 1992.
(Reproduced courtesy of Israel Vicente.)

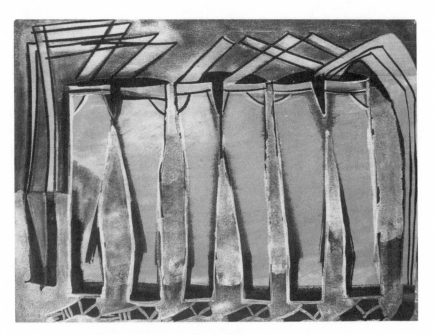

WATERCOLOR PAINTING BY OSCAR MARTÍNEZ, 1987.
(Reproduced courtesy of Oscar Martínez.)

A Zapotec Child Resting in a Hammock,
Ready for the Twenty-first Century.
(Photograph by Obdulia Ruiz Campbell.)

CHAPTER FOUR

Isthmus Zapotec Intellectuals in the Twentieth Century

The Politics of Culture in Juchitán, 1900–1970

Young juchitecos have a strong inner urge to study and to become prominent, following the example of many of their fellow townsmen who have gone to Mexico City and become leading professional men and politicians. Their parents often scrape up savings or obtain scholarships to send their boys to the university in Mexico City. There they join the rabidly sectarian, melancholy colony of émigré juchitecos who speak Zapotec among themselves, meet in cafés, and give full vent to their homesickness. They all chip in to procure help from their prominent countrymen to form societies, give dances, hold literary evenings, and publish a little paper, Neza (The Road), written partly in Zapotec and dedicated to praises of Juchitán, discussion of Zapotec etymology, poetry, and amateur ethnology.

MIGUEL COVARRUBIAS 1946:161

Although economic development has profoundly changed life in the Isthmus, the Zapotec people remain fiercely proud of their culture. A vanguard of Zapotec intellectuals has led the fight to defend and preserve the indigenous language and customs. In the late nineteenth century, young Juchiteco students began to travel to Mexico City and Oaxaca City to continue their studies and seek their fortunes. Their experiences in the state and national capitals broadened their horizons and also heightened their appreciation of the beauty and idiosyncrasies of Isthmus Zapotec culture. These intellectuals created a multifaceted cultural journal, which became the model for the publications of future Juchiteco writers. It was also the focus of a wide variety of artistic creations by the Juchiteco intellectuals in which they glorified their ethnic roots.

The first group of intellectuals came primarily from the middle and upper classes of Juchitán society. Many of them moved permanently to Mexico City. They were not a strongly politicized group and viewed their cultural productions in primarily artistic terms. This would change as economic developments transformed Isthmus society and a less privileged group of Zapotec students gained access to urban higher education, a group that later formed COCEI. This chapter traces the origins of the modern Isthmus Zapotec intellectual movement and its creation of a discourse of ethnic affirmation that is a central element of COCEI ideology today. It also discusses the cultural productions that are an important part of everyday life in Juchitán.

The Beginnings of a Modern Isthmus Zapotec Intellectual Tradition

The Isthmus Zapotecs have a long intellectual history that predates COCEI. Although colonialism wiped out much of Mesoamerican "high culture," the Isthmus Zapotecs retained an artistic tradition, autochthonous language, and local customs which, despite drastic modifications and syncretisms, they viewed as their own. In this respect, Juchitán resembled innumerable other indigenous towns that had distinct habits and subcultural styles. However, around the turn of the twentieth century the Juchitecos began to stand out from the majority of rural, native villagers because of their active involvement and success in Mexican literary circles.

As noted in Chapter 2, the Juchitán intellectual tradition developed partially as a result of Porfirio Díaz's gratitude to the Juchitecos for their support during the 5 de Septiembre battle and numerous other armed conflicts during the 1850s and 1860s. Díaz selected six young Juchitecos to study either at the prestigious Oaxacan Institute of Sciences and Arts or at a military college in Mexico City (Orozco 1946:49). These six eventually became trusted associates of Díaz during his four-decade dominion over Mexico. Other Juchitecos took advantage of these connections at the highest levels of Mexican political power to obtain educational, political, and business opportunities that otherwise would have been beyond their reach.

The key figure in the early Juchiteco migration to the capital was Rosendo Pineda, who became a prominent Mexican politician between the 1870s and the Revolution. After enjoying the opportunity provided by Porfirio Díaz to study in Oaxaca, Pineda earned a law degree at the National

School of Jurisprudence in Mexico City and then went into politics (Henestrosa 1989:176). Although Pineda left his mark primarily in the political
realm as an advisor to President Díaz and Secretary of the Interior, he was
also a noted writer and bank president. His verbal abilities as leader of the
Mexican Chamber of Deputies earned him the nickname "the Volcano of
Juchitán" (Henestrosa 1989:176). In addition to aiding other Juchiteco
immigrants to the capital, Pineda's example gave hope to aspiring young
Zapotecs who strove to better their social standing through higher education. Another prominent Juchiteco who supported aspiring Zapotec
youth was revolutionary General Román López Yu, who obtained scholarships and jobs for his countrymen (Rueda Sáynez 1990:7).

After Pineda, the next significant Zapotec intellectual figure is Arcadio
G. Molina of San Blas, Juchitán's perennial ally in armed struggles against
the Tehuanos and other groups. In the 1890s and early twentieth century,
Molina (1894, 1899, 1911) published a chronicle of the Juchiteco/Blaseño
victory over the French, and wrote numerous manuals for teaching math-
ematics and other subjects in his native language. In 1899 Molina also
helped anthropologist Frederick Starr collect Zapotec songs in the Tehuantepec area (de la Cruz 1984a:20). In Starr's account of his travels
(1908:164–65), he observed,

> [Molina]is one of the few indians of the district who has taken an
> interest in the study of his native tongue. He has already published a
> grammar of the Zapotec, as spoken in his village. He has also printed
> a little tract for lovers, in which high-sounding phrases are translated
> from the Spanish into Zapotec. He has also prepared, and holds in
> manuscript, a dictionary of the dialect containing some 4,000 words.

Following Molina's lead, the generation of Juchitecos who participated
in the Mexican Revolution produced several intellectuals, the best known
of whom was Enrique Liekens (1882–1978), who later became a diplomat
and wrote an etymological study of the Zapotec language (1952) and many
poems. Liekens led a fascinating life. The son of a Flemish immigrant to
Juchitán and a Zapotec mother, Liekens spoke not only Zapotec, but at
least five other languages (Carlock 1990; Velma Pickett, personal communication, 1992). Carlock (1990:11), in a description of an episode that
took place in the Revolution, described the colorful Liekens as follows:

> Very early that morning the telegraph operator was taking some
> messages from Mexico City, while in the bedroom young Captain

Enrique Liekens was writing poetry. Liekens was the egghead among Gen. Calles' soldiers. He was a tall, athletic, fair-complexioned, light-haired boy of Flemish descent. He spoke English, German, and French. And Spanish of course. And Zapotec to boot. He was a regular reader of Shakespeare, Goethe, Molière and Mistral. He was about to round out a sonnet when he heard voices in the telegraph area.

During the Revolution, Liekens served for a time as Mexican consul in San Antonio, Texas. He also assumed consular posts in Europe and Honduras (Rueda Sáynez 1990:7). Liekens later became the director of the Mexican government office of civil pensions and retirement, where he hired many Juchitecos as his employees (Bustillo 1968:151). Pickett, who knew Liekens personally, remembers that he was intensely proud of his Zapotec identity, despite his light skin, multilingualism, and the fact that he lived outside the Isthmus most of his life.

Other Zapotec revolutionary soldiers, besides Liekens, composed *corridos* celebrating the Juchiteco military experiences in the ranks of Carranza and Obregón (de la Cruz 1983b). The events of the Revolution, in which Zapotec soldiers traveled all over the Mexican republic, brought numerous Juchitecos into contact with the Spanish language and national culture more intensely and for a more prolonged period than previously. This heightened their ethnic consciousness and forced them to learn more Spanish.[1] The Zapotecs' ambivalent response to wider contacts with the Mexican nation is reflected in their first *corridos*: "Their reaction was hesitant, they tried to use the Zapotec language [in the *corridos*] but their compositions were infested with all kinds of words borrowed from Spanish" (de la Cruz 1984a:21).[2]

The Neza *Generation*

Rapidly, however, the Juchitecos adapted themselves to national institutions, and a steady stream of Zapotec students migrated to Mexico City.[3] This was necessary because in Juchitán in the early twentieth century there were no schools beyond the elementary level (Velma Pickett, personal communication, 1992). Indeed, educational opportunities were so limited in the Isthmus that a sixth-grade education was viewed as a major accomplishment. Pickett remembered that in the 1940s when Juchiteco children finished elementary school, "It was an emotional thing like graduating from college. . . . [At that point] they were either through with school or going to Mexico City or Oaxaca" for higher education.

In 1923 a group of Isthmus youth in Mexico City formed the Society of Juchiteco Students, which published a monthly periodical, held cultural events, and organized the first Isthmus *vela* ever held in the capital (Henestrosa 1987). Henestrosa described the formation of the Society:

> In 1923 . . . thanks to the enthusiasm of Benigno Jiménez, the Society of Juchiteco Students was founded. In that year, which was when more Isthmus students arrived in Mexico City (the majority from Juchitán), in addition to those who had started to come in 1920, there was a sufficient number of students to create a society. . . . Love for the native land, its traditions, and its history, and the pride of being from a particular place, were the bond that united its members. To proclaim these traditions, history, and legends; to make them known, were the purposes of the society [Henestrosa 1987].

The Juchiteco intellectuals maintained an active social life in Mexico City, focused primarily on the celebration of Zapotec culture. Among the activities at their first formal meeting were musical presentations, a fencing match, a speech, and a discussion of national and local history (Henestrosa 1987). The students also created the small monthly newspapers, *La Raza* and *El Zapoteco*, in 1924 and 1928 respectively (Henestrosa 1987).

In 1929, Andrés Henestrosa published his first book, *Los hombres que dispersó la danza* ([1929] 1987) which became a hit in Mexican literary circles. Like Rosendo Pineda, Henestrosa's intellectual career was made possible in part by his relationship with a powerful patron, José Vasconselos, and by his opportunity to study in North American academic institutions (the universities of Illinois, California, and Tulane) on a Guggenheim fellowship.[4] Henestrosa's literary strength, however, was less his cosmopolitanism than his recording of and embellishments on Isthmus Zapotec folklore and oral narratives. When I interviewed him in 1988, Henestrosa described his first book as a collection of literary inventions, creations, and explanations of "legends, myths, and fables that I heard [as a boy] in the indigenous language." He claimed these myths were at least 200 years old, since they were told to him by his nearly 100-year-old mother, who had heard them as a child from her equally old mother (an obvious exaggeration, but nonetheless an indication of their antiquity).

In the 1930s Henestrosa was one of the prime movers behind an Isthmus Zapotec writer's group that created the periodical *Neza*[5] ([1935–1939] 1987) and an essentially symbolic Zapotec Language Academy. Although the academy was short-lived, it expressed the Juchitecos' passion for their culture. Henestrosa (1987) described the founding of *Neza* in 1935:

> I was the only member of the Society of Juchiteco Students who remained. I was still enthusiastic about things from the land where I was born. In conjunction with the youngest Isthmus students I formed the New Society of Juchiteco Students. Its home was this time the room that I had in an apartment building [*vecindad*] on Ecuador street. . . . The black poet Langston Hughes has told part of this story in his book, *I Wonder as I Wander*. . . . At this time I came into some centavos: the enormous quantity of 1000 pesos. They were enough to pay the rent and to think of the publication of a paper about Isthmus things.

This activity went on in Mexico City instead of Juchitán (Neza no.s 1–20, 1935–1937; Pickett, personal communication, 1992). Pancho Nácar, who wrote the first significant poems in Zapotec, did so while working in an office of the federal bureaucracy (de la Cruz 1982:7). Other members of the Juchiteco intelligentsia in the capital city included students, teachers, doctors, and so forth. Indeed, the first generation of Juchiteco intellectuals were predominantly from the upper classes of Isthmus society. As elite Juchitecos became more involved in the larger Mexican society, their appreciation of their own culture increased and led them to glorify the Isthmus, albeit from a distance, in their writings. Henestrosa told me that as a young boy reading Ortega y Gasset and Greek and Roman history, he realized that he too was heir to a great tradition, the Zapotec civilization, which he dedicated his life to writing about.

Although from a national perspective, *Neza*, Henestrosa's writings, and the other works of the Juchiteco intellectuals may be considered part of a larger process of postrevolutionary *indigenismo*—in which the Mexican state attempted to assimilate Indian traditions and communities into "the nation"[6]—for Juchitecos, they were emblematic of Juchitán's independent cultural vitality.[7] A popular local adage symbolizes the Juchitecos' intense localism: *"Juchitán es el ombligo del mundo"* ("Juchitán is the center of the world").[8] The Juchiteco intellectuals remained chauvinistically proud of their culture even though they made their homes in Mexico City. They frequently made pilgrimages to their beloved pueblo bringing with them friends from the urban bohemian artist scene, such as Langston Hughes, French photographer Henri Cartier Bresson, poet Alfredo Cardona Peña,

Covarrubias, and others (Henestrosa 1987).⁹ Painters and photographers were especially attracted to Juchitán (Matus 1987). Back in Mexico City, the Juchiteco intellectuals elaborated on their experiences and Zapotec culture in books, poems, and especially *Neza*.

The Juchiteco intellectuals developed a distinctive aesthetic focused on romance, eroticism, Isthmus animals and plants, Zapotec customs, and the heroes of local political struggles. They devoted hundreds of verses and lines to the beauty and sensuality of Zapotec women (most, if not all, of the important Juchiteco writers of this era were male). For example, the Juchiteco writer Carlos Filio (*Neza* 6:1, 1935), in a discussion of the Isthmus woman, exalted "the overwhelming protuberance of her creole beauty" and "the voluptuous whole of her gracile body that is emphasized with the rhythm of her step," and "the unanimously coastal simplicity and the bewitchment, finally, of her warm voice that sings when it speaks the sweet native tongue." Natural metaphors played a key role in these creations, especially the metaphor of women as flowers, which is the subject of an entire doctoral thesis by Everts (1990). The Zapotecs' writings also celebrate the joys of life and the intense pleasures of sexuality, usually through a series of vegetative metaphors and allusions to animals and nature.

As in American country western songs, passion, broken hearts and unrequited love abound in the Zapotecs' poetry. A good example of this is a short poem by Nazario Chacón Pineda, a member of the first generation of Juchiteco intellectuals who was still active in the early 1990s:

> In the heavens
> a star
> in the fields
> a melon
> in your eyes
> gladness
> In my soul
> sadness
> of one day
> of two
> of three
> of days without end.¹⁰

The thematic range of the Juchiteco's journal *Neza* was broad for such a small publication. Among the topics frequently discussed or presented in its pages were Isthmus geography, poetry, music, mythology, folklore, Juchitán civic issues and social life, biographies of famous Istmeños, and photography. But its overriding concerns were the Zapotec language and culture and the history of the Isthmus. One issue of *Neza* (no. 6, 1935), for example, contained articles entitled "Songs of the Isthmus," "Zapotec Mutualism," "The Poetry of Pancho Nácar," "Juchitán and its Personages," and so forth. Another issue (no. 3, 1935) includes this romantic description of Juchitán, typical of the fervent ethnic nationalism of the Zapotec intellectuals:

> From this moment onward the traveler experiences a strange sensation. He glimpses a primitive community, suddenly separated from those he is accustomed to seeing. He discovers an inexhaustible wellspring of emotions. Juchitán, that mysterious land, as if suspended in time and space, begins to overwhelm him with its vigor, with the force of its reality . . .
>
> But the unique and marvelous aspect of Juchitán, which is impossible to find in any other region of the Republic is the sculpted richness enclosed in all of its manifestations. Life has a definite, perfect rhythm. No brusque contractions break the harmonious unity of the environment. The people, the houses, and the geographic conditions are made to produce an artistic impression. The beauty of the women of the Isthmus, of Juchitán, and of adjacent pueblos like Ixtaltepec is proverbial.

The Juchiteco writers created a rich body of local ethnography and self-commentary in which Juchitán invariably figured as a kind of indigenous promised land, the mecca of Zapotec civilization. One Zapotec intellectual, Bernabe Morales, even wrote of the process of "*Zapotequización*," in which foreigners, charmed by the Juchiteco way of life, were assimilated into Zapotec culture (*Neza* 2:1–5, 1935). Morales stated, "there is not a single Juchiteco . . . in whom does not palpitate the sense of a superior position in front of any person who is not of his race." The Zapotec savants were especially proud of the Zapotec language, which they described as naturally melodious. Gabriel López Chiñas, the noted Juchiteco poet, spoke for all of the Isthmus intellectuals when he wrote of his love for the native tongue:

Ah, Zapotec, Zapotec!
language that gives me life,
I know you'll die away
on the day of the death of the sun.[11]

The *Neza* generation[12] collected and analyzed the gamut of Zapotec customs—everything from burial etiquette to the precise pronunciation of Zapotec words—and created original poems and short stories in the native language. While these activities and productions were primarily for consumption by Zapotec people, they also were directed to the society at large, as a statement that a thriving regional/indigenous culture persisted on the Isthmus within the confines of mestizo Mexico. In this sense, the *Neza* cultural movement not only created works of intrinsic aesthetic value but engaged in a discourse of ethnic self-affirmation. However, the *Neza* experience also represents the Juchiteco intelligentsia's coming to grips with its own growing assimilation into Mexican society. Thus, faced with the choice of leaving their Zapotec identities behind, the urbanized Juchitecos opted to celebrate and objectify Isthmus life, while simultaneously ceasing to participate in the everyday culture of their people.[13]

Although *Neza* no longer appeared in the 1940s, Henestrosa and López Chiñas, in particular, continued to write prolifically. López Chiñas gained prominence both in the professional world of Mexico City—where he was a professor at the national university and for a time the director of the school's radio station—and in the literary milieu. His best-known works were *Vinnigulasa* (1974), a collection of myths and folklore similar to Henestrosa's magnum opus (*Los hombres . . .*), and a volume of bilingual (Zapotec-Spanish) poems (1975), richly illustrated with color photographs, personally authorized for publication by President Echeverría. López Chiñas (1982) also published approximately eight other books of prose and poetry, and had his work translated into English, French, and Polish. The jacket of one of his books (López Chiñas 1971) proclaims that his writings "project the regional spirit of his homeland; many belong to the Zapotec tradition, with a strong dose of ancestral, pre-Hispanic advice which enriches the 'language of the whites' and offers new dimensions and reference points to the concept of the provinces."

Andrés Henestrosa, who in his mid-80s was still a politician and active intellectual, was even better connected in the nation's capital than López Chiñas. Confidant of presidents and the super rich, former senator and aspirant for the governorship of Oaxaca, and editor and columnist of major

Mexican newspapers, Henestrosa has had the opportunity to present his observations on Isthmus Zapotec life and culture in the most prestigious intellectual forums of the country for the last 50 years. While Henestrosa and López Chiñas are the best-known Juchiteco authors, dozens of other poets and writers—in particular, Wilfrido Cruz, Nazario Chacón, and Gilberto Orozco—participated in the halcyon years of the Isthmus cultural movement. Not surprisingly, several younger generations of Juchitecos have also sought to emulate the intellectual creativity of the *Neza* group, a subject explored later in this chapter. First, however, our focus shifts away from Mexico City, the main venue of the *Neza* generation, and back to Juchitán to take a closer look at the everyday Juchiteco cultural scene of the first half of the twentieth century.

Artistic and Intellectual Life in the Community

Though a few members of the *Neza* literati became famous in Mexico City, most were unknown outside the Isthmus. Moreover, many local poets, musical composers, and orators were either monolingual with little formal education or native Zapotec speakers who spoke Spanish with some difficulty and seldom left the Isthmus. Since at least the late nineteenth century, Juchitán and Tehuantepec have maintained a rich ceremonial calendar revolving around dozens of annual fiestas, or *velas*, in which music and verbal performances play an integral role. Unlike many other Oaxacan towns that are known for the creativity of their popular arts and crafts, the Isthmus Zapotec villages have specialized in the production of songs and romantic poetry. Although until recently few Istmeños had become accomplished sculptors or potters, Covarrubias observed that "the literary and musical arts play an extremely important part in their lives" and the Isthmus Zapotecs "cultivate language with an unusual intensity" (1946:310).[14]

Professional orators (*chagoola'*) play an essential role in traditional Zapotec weddings, funerals, wakes, and so on, and in the sixteenth century Córdova referred to this genre of public speaking (de la Cruz 1983b:21). Though this custom is declining to some extent today, each Isthmus community used to have a number of respected, elderly men who presided over religious and secular occasions and who gave prayers and sermons (*libana*) in Zapotec and Spanish. Juchitán political and civic functions were, and continue to be, showcases for eloquent verbal performances, often including lively jokes in the Zapotec language, an art mastered by the COCEI leadership. Singing was (and remains) highly valued, and each local band usually had one or two individuals with strong vocal chords.

Isthmus brass bands typically featured 7 or 8 musicians playing drums, trombone, trumpet, tuba, saxophones, and clarinets. Their trademark was the *son*, which is a style of music derived from nineteenth-century Spanish waltzes played "with a colorful, barbaric orchestration that gives [it] a strong and individual character" (Covarrubias 1946:323). Yurchenco (1976:7) made these observations about the history of the Isthmus *son*:

> By 1870, the playing of local Isthmus *sones* had begun to supplant the European dances. In that year Cándido Jiménez made the first arrangement of *La Sandunga* [a song considered characteristic of the Isthmus] for his band. Many arrangements followed, and other Mexican songs also became part of the band repertory in the Isthmus and elsewhere.

Although *sones* are common in other parts of Mexico and Latin America, the honking cacophony and jazzy adlibs featured in the Isthmus *son*, and the repetitive, circular Zapotec dancestep punctuated with occasional hops or skips that accompany it are inimitable. A number of these *sones* (*La Llorona, La Martiniana, La Petrona, Son Yaa*), composed primarily by Istmeños such as Eustaquio Jiménez Girón, Juan Stubi, Saúl Martínez, and Rey Baxa, have become regional/ethnic anthems that elicit strong feelings of solidarity among Istmeños. The verses to these songs, and their myriad variations, are sung with emotion and panache by Zapotec performers at the major Isthmus fiestas. In 1901 Starr (1908:330) described the Isthmus *son* as follows:

> The words are largely Zapotec; Spanish words are scattered throughout the song, and the sentiment is largely borrowed. Most of the songs are love-songs, and they abound in metaphorical expressions.

The countless Juchitán bars and cantinas have become a main stage for the Zapotec troubadours, who sing their own compositions (often in Zapotec) or popular tunes accompanied by guitars, marimbas (rare today), and other instruments, interspersed with spicy jokes and *mentiras* (*didxax-hiihui'*), a genre of Zapotec storytelling that emphasizes fantasy and imagination.[15] Included in the traditional repertory of the bohemian minstrels are *sones*, mazurkas, polkas, waltzes, *colombianas*, tangos, and *corridos* (Torres Medina n.d.:10). Zapotec guitarists also perform for the endless rounds of *velas*, weddings, birthdays, *quinceaños*, and funerals, but there they are overshadowed by the brass bands that are an indispensable part of all Isthmus ritual occasions.

Another traditional form of music in Zapotec communities are the songs played on a cane flute with the accompaniment of a small wooden drum (known in the Isthmus as *pito y caja*). The flute and drum duo play their high-pitched, monotonous songs to announce the coming of a fiesta or other important social event, and participate in a variety of civic functions. Yurchenco (1976:8) found that "in general pipe and drum music is associated with religious rather than secular functions." Marimba music is also popular in the Isthmus, and the marimba is considered to be an instrument typical of the region. Many *sones* are played on the marimba during fiestas and at the marketplace, political rallies, and on other occasions.

The most original Juchiteco musician, and the one current Zapotec musicians credit as a major influence on their work, was the legendary blind flute player Cenobio. Yurchenko (1976) first observed Cenobio in 1942 and described him as "a blind octogenarian bent almost double" who "played his *sones* . . . accompanied by drum and a turtle-shell, an ancient pre-Hispanic instrument struck with deer antlers." Covarrubias (1946:321) depicted Cenobio as "famous throughout the region, not only as an extraordinary virtuoso of the flute, but also as a fine composer of *sones*, many with animal names that imitate the songs of birds, the screeching of a flock of parrots, and the mysterious call of the nocturnal aquatic bird they call *bere le:le*" [bittern]. Mario López, a talented contemporary guitarist in Juchitán described Cenobio's music to me as "the closest thing we have to pre-Hispanic [Zapotec] music" in the twentieth century. López recalled that the Juchiteco intellectuals based in Mexico City arranged to have Cenobio play a concert in the capital city's Fine Arts Palace, which was a big success.

Another talented Zapotec musician at mid-century was Eustaquio Jiménez Girón, a guitar player, songwriter, and composer. He was especially well-known for his love songs in the Zapotec language, such as "Badudxaapa' huinni' sicarú" ("Beautiful Young Girl"). Whereas Jiménez Girón was known principally in the Isthmus of Tehuantepec, the gifted troubadour Saúl Martínez also made a name for himself in other parts of Mexico with his romantic ballads, some of which were recorded and sold as records. Perhaps the most popular of all Zapotec musicians was the bohemian balladeer Jesús (Chú) Rasgado (1907–1948). Rasgado, who died at a young age from alcoholism, composed beautiful romantic *boleros* about love, sadness, and deception which reflect Zapotec philosophy about the richness and sorrow of life.

Cultural Content of the Velas

The annual fiestas (*velas*),[16] attended by hundreds or even thousands of people, and the fiesta societies that run them, are the heart of formal cultural life in Isthmus Zapotec communities.[17] They are a forum for musical and verbal performances, ritualized dancing, stylized religious processions, and displays of women's aesthetic clothing (*trajes*). The origin of the *velas*, however, remains somewhat obscure. It seems likely that they have pre-Hispanic antecedents in rites celebrating the changing of the seasons, the agricultural cycle, and so forth, similar to the indigenous ceremonies that underlie the famous Oaxacan *Guelaguetza* festival. In any case, the current form of the Isthmus *velas*, which vary enormously from town to town, is heavily shaped by Catholic religious beliefs and European musical, clothing, and dance styles.

In this sense, the *velas* are just another variation on or offshoot of what is known elsewhere in Mesoamerica as the fiesta system, cargo system, *cofradías*, or the civil-religious hierarchy (Cancian 1965; Smith 1977). If Isthmus *velas* share similarities with other Middle American fiesta complexes, they stand out as some of the most opulent and elaborate of these festivals and are perhaps developed with greater intensity in the region than anywhere else in contemporary Mexico. In the 1940s, Covarrubias (1946:335) noted that "Nowhere else in Mexico does a rural people display such an intense social activity as in the Tehuantepec area." The luxuriance and sensuality, as well as many of the forms of contemporary *vela* customs, may have originated during the Porfiriato, when Díaz himself attended the fiestas held by his Tehuana lover Juana C. Romero.

> Great balls were given in his honor, and Díaz seldom missed the yearly *vela bini* given by Doña Juana in a specially built "ballroom," an enclosure of white and gold wooden columns, roofed by a great canvas canopy and hung with crystal chandeliers. It was compulsory to dress for the *vela bini*—the women in the ceremonial Tehuantepec costume of lace, spangles, and fringe of gold, which Porfirio preferred; the men in black serge suits and stiff collars despite the unbearable heat. . . . Doña Juana gave out little *carnets* with pencils attached for the guests to write beforehand the partners with whom they would dance lancers, polkas, and waltzes. A great supper was served, with rows of roast turkeys, platters of cold cuts, and rivers of imported wine [Covarrubias 1946:234].

While the Juchiteco elite claims that none are excluded from the *velas*, and that all can enter and have something to eat or dance, since the turn of the century at least, the wealthier, often-mixed European/Zapotec families of Juchitán have held their own private *velas* such as the Vela Pineda, the Vela López, and the Vela Sáynez and Vela Gómez (the latter two *velas* no longer exist). Humbler *velas* are organized by neighborhoods and organizations of artisans or people with a particular occupation, such as the Vela Angélica Pipi, Vela Guzebenda, and the *vela* of the fireworks-makers. Still others such as the Vela San Vicente Gola, Vela San Jacinto, and Vela San Francisco are focused around a saint's cult (for more details, see Munch 1985). The *velas* were the main focus of Zapotec artistic and intellectual life in Juchitán during the middle of the twentieth century. The commercialization of the *velas* discussed previously (see pp. 100–101) had not occurred to a great extent as of the early 1950s.

The Juchiteco Cultural Movement in the 1950s and 1960s: From Neza to Neza Cubi

After the initial effervescence of the *Neza* generation wore off, the Juchiteco literary movement continued to produce little books and pamphlets of poetry and amateur ethnography but without the national attention it had attracted previously. In the early 1950s there was an attempt to revive the journalistic tradition of *Neza*. Unfortunately, *Didcha*, its successor, disappeared after only four issues. In Tehuantepec, the cultural/literary publication *Guiengola* emerged in the late 1950s and continued until at least 1969. However—probably due to the two communities' "ancestral" rivalry—the Juchitecos did not contribute to it. Although *Guiengola* had several virtues (e.g., good ethnographic photography and historical documentation), it lacked the ethnic intensity of *Neza*. Reflecting the ethnic differences between the two towns, the Tehuanos' cultural magazine tended to emphasize the glories of the ancient Zapotec past, whereas the Juchiteco's writings focused more attention on the evolving "indigenous" traditions of the present and recent past. *Guiengola* also contained something never found in the publications of the militantly nationalistic Juchitecos—specifically, defensive attempts to deny or rationalize away the Tehuanos' historical identification with conservative political movements such as the French Intervention in the 1860s. *Guiengola* appeared very infrequently in the 1960s and eventually disappeared entirely after the death of its founder, Carlos Iribarren Sierra.

The most important event for Zapotec intellectuals during the mid-twentieth century was a conference of writers and scholars (known as the

"Mesa Redonda") in which a common Zapotec alphabet was agreed upon. Juchiteco intellectuals have always been fascinated with the Zapotec language, which they "cultivate . . . with an unusual intensity" (Covarrubias 1946:310). The need for systematic research on the Zapotec language had been emphasized as early as 1935 by Henestrosa in *Neza*:

> The immediate task of the [Zapotec Language] Academy lies in the study of Zapotec phonetics and morphology, and surely this should conclude with the formation of a dictionary. This enterprise has become necessary. It is necessary to do away with the anarchy that is observable in the graphic representation of the Zapotec language, especially when our language not only has esteemed historical value, but is also full of life. It is not a dead language that has its gravestone in the memory of the righteous. It is a language that lives as long as the heart of an entire race keeps beating [*Neza* 4:1, 1935].

Participants in the Mesa Redonda on the Zapotec language in 1956 included the Juchiteco intellectuals Henestrosa, López Chiñas, and Liekens, as well as prominent anthropologists such as Gonzalo Aguirre Beltrán and Wigberto Jiménez Moreno, and the North American linguist Morris Swadesh. Velma Pickett of the Summer Institute of Linguistics (SIL), who took part in the Mesa Redonda, told me that each of the various participants in the conference brought with him his own version of how to properly write the Zapotec language, but all compromised to create a single alphabet that was acceptable to all.

Neza Cubi *(The New Road)*

The emergence of the *Neza* intellectual generation in the 1920s and 1930s can be explained broadly as a resurgence of Zapotec culture in response to the pressures and opportunities created by economic modernization (construction of the Isthmus railroad, installation of electricity, increased commercial ties between the Isthmus and other regions, etc.), migration, acculturation, university education, and political patronage in the early postrevolutionary period. Although Juchitán was never completely isolated from the Valley of Mexico and urban society generally, it was, until the Revolution and the construction of the railroad, a very inward-focused community located in a hot, inhospitable region where travelers seldom tarried and the local people rarely left. The Juchitecos who took advantage of the greater opportunities available in the 1920s and 1930s (during the early Charis years) were primarily from the middle and upper classes. Their objectives in *Neza* were literary and cultural: to write good poetry and celebrate their ethnic roots. Only an occasional article referred to the diseases (e.g., malaria and typhoid) afflicting the Isthmus, the bad hygiene of school children, and the other social problems of the area.

If the Juchiteco elite were the first to react artistically to the mixed blessing of modernization, they did so in a mostly nonpolemical way.[18] Their writings were not overtly political although their invocation of ethnic identity was part of a phenomenon Royce (1975:203) has described as the manipulation of Zapotec style by the upper and middle classes to preserve their dominance in Juchitán. In this respect, the cultural production of the *Neza* generation shared the conservative politics of the Mexican cultural nationalist movement studied by Vaughan (1982). As Vaughan (1982:265–66) observed: "In the final analysis, within the context of Revolution as a whole, the cultural nationalist movement provided the national bourgeoisie with an ideology affirmative of Mexico and the Mexican which was both an impetus and channel for their own self-expression and self-actuation as well as a mechanism of social control over the working class." The *Neza* intellectuals served a similar function, on a smaller scale, in Juchitán.

From the 1960s to the present, the increasing divisions within Isthmus society have caused Zapotec cultural revivalism to become a more polemical and divisive issue than it was during the *Neza* years. The next generation of Juchiteco intellectuals, unlike their cultural mentors, adopted a radical political stance. In 1968 they created a new Zapotec journal called *Neza Cubi*. *Neza Cubi* means the new, or reopened, road. In its first issue the magazine's founders declared their desire to put Istmeños back in touch with the spirit of their ancestors and to expand on the cultural projects of the *Neza* generation.[19] The creators of *Neza Cubi* were two young Juchiteco college students, Macario Matus and Víctor de la Cruz. Matus, the prime mover behind the magazine, attended the national teacher's college—a prime site of student radicalism—and was heavily influenced by exiled Central American intellectuals and the 1968 Mexican student movement. He was also a writer for the Mexican Communist Party newspaper.

From *Neza Cubi*'s outset it was clear that its cultural mission had become politicized. The first issue of the magazine spoke of "disputes that are dividing us," the poverty, filth, and diseases of Juchitán, and the need to unite divergent factions. Another issue bitterly attacked the Isthmus professionals who claimed to love Juchitán although they lived in Mexico City and never did anything to support their impoverished town. The editor growled about these mediocre bourgeois individuals' requests to have their remains returned with honor to the Isthmus upon their deaths, and suggested instead that they should be incinerated and the residue thrown into a sewage drain!

Other articles complained that unscrupulous composers and musicians were plagiarizing and profiteering from Juchitán's folk tunes, that upper-class intellectuals (the *Neza* group) were not supporting the younger generation, and that the rich had celebrated a *vela* during a time when the poor of the southern part of town were inundated by severe flooding. Moreover, a round table discussion on Isthmus agricultural problems sponsored by *Neza Cubi* found evidence of "sinister control of economic and political affairs by a small caste" which "obstructs the economic development of the region." Finally, de la Cruz lamented that the system of kinship organization that formerly united all the Zapotec as *bichi* (brothers) had disappeared. The current social system has degenerated so much that it would be ridiculous to use this term today, he complained.

One reason for the greater politicization of this generation was their social-class background and contact with the 1968 student movement. Unlike the Zapotec elite who wrote in *Neza*, many of the *Neza Cubi* intellectuals came from working-class, peasant, or lower-middle-class families. Matus' father, for example, was a bricklayer, de la Cruz's father raises cattle on a small scale, and Francisco Toledo was brought up by his grandfather, a shoemaker. Also unlike the *Neza* intellectuals, the younger generation brought their movement back to Juchitán. In this, they were part of a broader process of "returning to the pueblos" by rural Mexican intellectuals and activists in the aftermath of the 1968 movement. Realizing that the political struggle in Mexico City had been truncated by the Tlatelolco massacre, these individuals sought cultural authenticity in the villages and pursued the new possibilities for rural grassroots change offered by the populist Echeverría regime (Zermeño 1987:69).

The New Oaxacan Protest Song

Another Isthmus cultural form that became a vehicle for political protest was the *son*. Its innovator was Mario López, a Juchiteco law student who took part in the 1968 student movement in Mexico City. Influenced in the 1960s by the protest songs of South American folk singers such as Atahualpa and others, López decided to write his own political verses to the rhythms of the Isthmus *son*. He also revived the use of the cane flute, turtle shell, and wooden drum in his group, but with modern songs that denounced the poverty of Zapotec peasants. López returned to Juchitán in 1980, and his protest songs were used as political anthems by COCEI, although López himself never joined the movement.[20] López described to me his musical and political evolution in these terms:

> With the musical ability I had . . . I dedicated myself to composing *sones*. In the era of the 1960s, a style from South American invaded us . . . that songs, in addition to dealing with romantic themes, could also be a vehicle . . . for denunciations, inconformity, to say that things were not going well . . . in the social sense . . .
>
> [At that time] there was no reflection in our songs of the social situation of our towns. . . . And with these [South American] songs I realized that for Oaxaca there was no song which spoke of what was happening in Oaxaca in the social sense. . . . And I began to compose songs with this theme. . . . I was the first person to do Oaxacan social protest songs . . .
>
> And when I was composing songs . . . I said . . . I have to give this now the sense that it is Zapotec music. . . . So then I seized on and incorporated the *carrizo* cane flute, the turtle shell, the small drum, and the guitars. . . . I formed my group and with this group . . . I put out a second record . . . now with social themes and with the Zapotec sound I wanted to give it. And this was a success . . .
>
> I tried to project the social problematic of Juchitán and Oaxaca in my songs. And so I spoke of the peasant . . . of what he lacked . . . of the fisherman, full of children, who is still limited by the use of nets [*chinchorro*] . . . Of a generational struggle of the Zapotecs . . . from the Juárez epoch when they fought alongside Juárez against the [French empire], in the Revolution . . . on the side of the *caudillos* . . . [to] . . . the current generations, the great grandchildren of those who fought in these battles, who continue to not have land, continue to be exploited, and continue to live in misery.

As this quote indicates, the 1960s generation of Juchiteco intellectuals considered Zapotec culture an important weapon in local political struggles. The ways in which Zapotec culture became politicized by these intellectuals and COCEI will be discussed in Chapter 5.

Conclusions

A Juchiteco intellectual group emerged in the early to mid-twentieth century as a result of new educational opportunities in the Mexican capital. This group formed a cultural movement that emphasized the beauty and richness of Isthmus Zapotec culture in books, poems, and songs. Yet these intellectuals mostly stayed in Mexico City and glorified the customs of their people from a distance. The urban Juchiteco intellectuals also distanced themselves from the political issues affecting their community. In the 1960s a younger, more radical group of Juchiteco writers and artists began a new phase of Isthmus Zapotec intellectual production. For this group, it was important to return to their native community and directly confront local political problems. The younger generation of Zapotec intellectuals played a key role in the founding of COCEI.

∎∎∎∎∎∎∎∎∎∎∎∎

CHAPTER FIVE

From Caciquismo to Grassroots Ethnic Populism

The Emergence of COCEI, 1964–1981

At the beginning of the struggle we were young students with no money to buy paint, so we wrote our first political graffiti with tar.

OSCAR CRUZ LÓPEZ, COCEI LEADER

The negative impact of economic development on Isthmus Zapotec society, as discussed in Chapter 3, is a familiar story in anthropological literature. What is not so common is sustained and *successful* resistance to inequitable development by indigenous groups, as in the case of COCEI (cf. Scott 1985, 1986).[1] This chapter examines the origins and history of COCEI, analyzes the movement's composition, structure and tactics, and addresses the following questions: Under what conditions have class tensions, indigenous culture, and Isthmus Zapotec ethnic identity become the foundation for solidarity, political action, and change?

I will argue that COCEI (or the Coalition, as the movement is often referred to locally) differs from major Juchiteco ethnic political movements of the past because it has taken on a markedly *agrarista* character, unlike the predominantly *serrano* nature of the movements discussed previously (cf. Knight 1986:115–22). As capitalist economic changes divided the Juchiteco community internally, the all-sectoral (*serrano*) alliances of former times (which mobilized nearly the entire community against external agents) were replaced by more limited coalitions, which pitted distinct sectors of the Zapotec population against each other in struggles for land and political power. During the Charis *cacicazgo*, these struggles were confined

primarily to electoral battles between the reform-minded business and professional establishment and the *Charista* machine. With the advent of
COCEI, open class warfare set workers, peasants, and students in direct
opposition to middle- and upper-class Juchitecos.

Yet, while class conflict has escalated in Juchitán, the regional and ethnic
oppositions that previously placed Juchitecos in opposition to Oaxaca and
Mexico City authorities (*binni za* vs. *dxu'*) took on new intensity as a result
of government repression. Consequently, COCEI has become a channel
for both class-based agrarian grievances and struggles for local autonomy.
Thus, in a sense, the Coalition combines elements of both *agrarista* and
serrano movements.

In addition to COCEI's accentuated agrarian character as compared to
previous Juchiteco movements, COCEI also represents a change[2] in Juchitán in respect to the Isthmus Zapotec cultural movement. Whereas the
Neza generation was made up primarily of members of the Juchiteco elite
who engaged in an apolitical discourse of ethnic affirmation from their
base of operations in Mexico City, *Coceístas* both politicized their cultural
projects and brought them home to the community. In the process, Zapotec culture itself became a weapon wielded by one Juchiteco class alliance
against their local class opponents as well as against outsiders (cf. Royce
1982:169–83).

The Juchiteco Political Tradition: Past and Present

As we have seen, COCEI was not the first radical political movement to
emerge from the Isthmus Zapotec community. Covarrubias (1946:159–60)
once described the Juchiteco political tradition in these romantic terms:

> The Juchitecos are renowned as the most ferocious, untamable
> fighters in Mexico when it comes to the defense of their own rights
> against petty tyrants. They are proud of their unbroken record of
> loyalty to the causes of democracy, equality, and justice throughout
> the turbulent history of Mexico.

The Juchiteco spirit of resistance was constituted historically and is now
part of a cultural ethos.[3] Contemporary Juchitecos view themselves as audacious, proud, and tough.[4] A concise description of the collective self-
image held by many Juchitecos is contained in a document (see *Guchachi'
Reza* 6:3, 1981) presented by Che Gómez, Jr. at the Mexican Constitutional
Congress of 1917:

The Isthmus Zapotec has conserved throughout all the stages of his History, his essential characteristics: . . . dark skin, . . . a robust physique, strength, health, virility, intelligence, tenacity, abnegation, activeness, enterprise, progressiveness, charity, and liberalism.

This same document refers to "the beautiful qualities that adorn the [Isthmus Zapotec] race, especially its notable intelligence which with astonishing facility assimilates cultural advances; its virility, tenacity and its inextinguishable love for progress and its freedoms."

Despite these comments about the Zapotecs' progressive character, however, Juchitecos have participated in many different political struggles, not all of which were democratic or egalitarian. This is exemplified by the political histories of Rosendo Pineda, Rosalino Martínez, and, of course, Heliodoro Charis. The Charis *cacicazgo* brought a long period of relative calm to the Isthmus after the agitated times of the nineteenth century and the Revolution. With Charis' death, the classic period of Juchitán *caciquismo* was over, and dissident Isthmus Zapotecs began to organize popular movements with renewed vigor.

The Post-Charis Era: A Blaseño Precursor to COCEI

In 1964, the same year Charis died, another charismatic Isthmus Zapotec politician, Facundo Génico, was killed by Tehuantepec police. Like Charis, Génico was an ethnic leader who called for Isthmus independence and had designs on the governorship. Unlike Charis, he was a highly educated, articulate individual who functioned equally well in indigenous and national society. Born in the poor Zapotec town of San Blas, Génico became an expert surgeon whose talents attracted patients from all over southern Mexico. He was also publisher of a local muckraking newspaper (*La Voz del Istmo*) that defended Zapotec language and culture during an era (1950s–1960s) of assimilationist policies, criticized local authorities, and supported popular San Blas struggles. One struggle supported by Génico was a strike by Blaseña vendors who refused to sell their wares in the Tehuantepec market to protest the high cost of market permits.

Also similar to Charis, Génico was an authoritarian leader, at times elitist, even though he attracted significant support from Blaseño townspeople. His father was a politician too and left him land and a degree of wealth by local standards. Génico protected his property and person with a gang of *pistoleros*, who he occasionally turned on his enemies. A megalomaniacal personality and legendary philanderer, Génico tolerated nothing but praise and obeisance. Thus, his collision with local politicians in the 1960s was almost inevitable, given his domineering character and dissenting political views.

Although Génico was not from Juchitán, he is important for our purposes (and for contemporary *Coceístas*) because he was a torchbearer for Isthmus separatist sentiments, promotion of Zapotec culture, and emerging opposition to the PRI. Génico was once a *Priísta* himself, but when his political ambitions were blocked by local power-holders, he went outside the official party machine, joining the opposition Popular Socialist Party (PPS) in the early 1960s. Génico presented a threat to existing powers in other ways as well. Before his death, he had plans to distribute his provocative newspaper daily all over the state of Oaxaca. Finally, his public criticism of the PRI state governor, publication of a separatist manifesto, and desire to become governor himself were simply too much for the Oaxacan authorities.

Istmeños have long rankled at the dominance of the region by Oaxaca Valley politicians (*"la vallistocracia"*). From the perspective of the Isthmus plain, the Oaxaca Valley is the source of high taxes, oppressive policies, political impositions, and the hated *azules* (blue-uniformed state police, often used to put down political protests). Only two Istmeños have governed the state, although many have competed for the position. Génico's dream of becoming governor, however, was doomed by his aggressive confrontation with the PRI government at a time (the early 1960s) when it brooked little dissent. Allegedly, Génico ordered his *pistoleros* to shoot the *Priísta* mayor of Tehuantepec. In turn, local police tortured and killed the doctor, and then dismantled his printing apparatus and medical practice. Despite Génico's untimely death in 1964, his unrelenting criticisms of local and state authorities, and his advocacy of Zapotec culture, were a first step towards more enduring attacks on PRI dominance of the Isthmus.

Subsequently, the story of Génico's medical achievements, political goals, and the manner in which he was killed became a controversial secret kept under wraps by Tehuanos. To this day, little has been written about this talented surgeon and dynamic political figure, although Génico's memory is revered by residents of San Blas, where his spirit is said to appear at spiritual curing sessions. Ironically, Génico may have taken on greater political significance in San Blas after his death than he did during his life. For some time afterward, Blaseños physically attacked any Tehuano caught venturing into their town, as the Tehuano–Blaseño quasi-ethnic feud of the nineteenth century was revived once again. For Blaseños, the murder of Génico by Tehuanos symbolized Tehuantepec's economic and political domination of (and cultural discrimination against) San Blas. Thus, Génico has become a potent symbol of Blaseño defiance and martyrdom.[5]

Ethnic Politics and the Zapotec Cult of the Dead

The cult of dead ethnic politicians, and their role in political memories and ideologies, is deeply rooted in Isthmus Zapotec religious beliefs. Zapotec families maintain altars upon which they place photos of deceased relatives along with items of sacred significance such as flowers, incense, candles, and images of different saints that they worship. Relatives are also remembered and venerated by adorning entire house walls with their photographs. During the Day of the Dead and All Souls' Day festivities (Oct. 31–Nov. 2), Zapotec women set out a special altar upon which they construct a pyramid of sugar cane leaves, marigold flowers, and other objects that surround the photographs of dead family members. Coconuts are placed around the base of the altar, and bread, beverages, chocolate, oranges, and other fruits are set on the table so that the dead souls can consume them when they make their annual return to commune with the living. Also during this time, Zapotec families make a pilgrimage to the cemetery to clean relatives' graves and decorate them with fresh flowers, as well as to drink beer, eat special foods, and sing songs on the tombs in celebration of the deceased. Additionally, a whole series of masses (*mixa guétu*) are celebrated for family members who have recently died. Overall, there is a sense in the Isthmus that the dead are not so very distant. Indeed, Zapotec people maintain a much closer spiritual connection to their deceased relatives, in general, than do Euroamericans.[6]

The Juchitán cemetery is particularly large and is dotted with expensive mausoleums, some of which—especially the one which contains Charis— are almost as big as small houses. The cemetery has often been the site of massive festivities held to mourn the passing of Juchiteco political leaders such as Meléndez, Gurrión, Che Gómez, Sr., and Charis. When prominent leaders are killed away from Juchitán, as in the cases of Gurrión and Che Gómez, Sr. and Jr., the return of their remains for a proper burial takes on great importance to the population, who turn out in large numbers to receive the body (López Gurrión 1976:134–35). The intensity with which these deceased personages are worshiped impressed a retired Mexican military officer who observed the delivery of Che Gómez, Jr.'s body to Juchitán in 1924:

The death of "Ché" caused a tremendous commotion among the rebels of the Isthmus region, especially in Juchitán. . . . The cadaver was received by the people en masse, especially by his supporters. Ninety percent of them had taken up arms in revolt. I kept silent before this gathering of mourners which began a procession with the body toward the home of the relatives of the deceased; the majority of the mourners were of the female gender [Bravo Izquierdo 1948:60].

According to another account, Efraín R. Gómez, a Juchiteco rebel leader who died during the Revolution, was treated like a saint after his death (Matus 1985:133). Likewise, Brasseur ([1861] 1981:148) noted that after his death the indigenous friar Mauricio López's portrait was hung in San Vicente Church and venerated by the Juchitecos side-by-side with their saints. Thus, dead ethnic leaders and political martyrs such as Génico take on an aura of sacredness and become powerful symbols of inspiration for living Isthmus Zapotecs in their ongoing political struggles, as we will see in the case of COCEI.

From Caciquismo to Grassroots Organization: Polo, Tarú, and the Origins of COCEI

In the 1960s local Mexican politics were heavily influenced by authoritarian leaders such as Charis and Génico (Kern 1973). Charis, the former "indio" general-turned-politico, mediated, negotiated, or repressed Juchiteco popular demands. Protests by the FRD and other groups occurred during municipal electoral battles, but usually Charis' candidates ultimately "won" the elections (Hora Cero 12/2/1981). Normally, tussles over the Juchitán mayoralty were resolved without much violence and the losing faction would accept the outcome. However, on occasion, obnoxious challengers to PRI rule (such as Génico was in Tehuantepec), were dealt with more forcefully. While he lived, Charis defended the status quo in Juchitán with the strength of his personality, pistoleros, and political connections. After his death, it was a new political ballgame.

The immediate aftermath of Charismo coincided with a reform movement within the national PRI spearheaded by Carlos Madrazo. This led to open primary elections within the Juchitán PRI in 1965 which—after a ballot-burning incident—produced a mayor with a degree of popular support (Rubin 1990:254). These elections did not result in significant democratic changes in the PRI, however, due to the untimely death of Madrazo in an airplane accident and the subsequent scrapping of his reform measures. Consequently, dissident Juchitecos began to look outside the PRI for political alternatives.[7]

THE MOVEMENTS OF POLO AND TARÚ.

A contemporary and friend of Génico and Charis, Leopoldo de Gyves Pineda (Polo)[8] became the focus of the first major challenge to PRI control of Juchitán during the post-Charis era. Son of an accountant who dabbled in politics, Polo enrolled in a socialist-oriented military school, formed by leftist President Cárdenas in 1939 (*Hora Cero* 3/21/1982). In 1966, Polo retired to Juchitán after 27 years of military service and thereafter directed his energies towards local politics. A ruggedly handsome, dark-skinned man who customarily wears a felt cowboy hat, khaki suit, and huaraches, Polo is a popular figure around Juchitán, and is renowned for his sense of humor. By nature an aggressive individual, Polo became angered by the corruption of Isthmus authorities, economic inequalities provoked by rural development programs, and the barriers erected by the PRI to his own political ambitions within that party. He quickly established a following due to his popularity and prestige.

Polo wrote essays criticizing local officials in Génico's and other regional newspapers. In 1967 he also formed a popular opposition movement to the local PRI, known as the Juchitán Civic Committee-Heroes of September 5 (CCJ). Polo's organization named him their independent mayoral candidate in 1968 (Calvo Zapata 1981). The resultant elections were marred by accusations of fraud, although as usual PRI was declared the winner. This time, however, the populace protested vigorously and federal soldiers were needed to protect the Juchitán PRI candidate from the wrath of the CCJ during his inauguration (*Hora Cero* 3/21/1982).

To the increasing ire of the opposition, the new PRI mayor engaged in unprecedented levels of graft and neglect of municipal services. Currently the owner of a downtown mansion crowned by a satellite television dish, valuable urban property, and considerable farmland, this politician was criticized repeatedly for outright acts of corruption. Charges raised against him included buying the mayor's post with a bribe, stealing from the municipal treasury, pocketing government funds destined for public works, and illegally acquiring prime agricultural lands (*El Satélite* 1970).

Annoyed by these abuses and mounting agrarian conflicts, Juchitán townspeople became increasingly politicized, and with Charis gone, it was much harder to control them. Moreover, under new President Echeverría, rural movements and political organizations outside the PRI began to receive better treatment. The early 1970s also saw the rise of independent unions, revived agrarian protest, political reforms, and increased social conflict in Mexico. This national and local context set the stage for the Juchitán PRI's first electoral defeat.

Ironically, the next colorful Juchiteco to lead the Zapotec population in political combat was a half-Lebanese pilot and small businessman named Manuel Musalem (a.k.a. Tarú). Despite his seemingly foreign background, Tarú's success can be attributed, in large part, to the support he received from the Juchiteco poor, and his ability to mobilize Juchiteco regional sentiments and "Zapotec style"[9] during the 1971 municipal elections (Royce 1975).

In this case, Tarú painted the PRI candidate as a non-Juchiteco because he had been born a few miles outside of Juchitán, even though he had lived most of his life in the town. According to Zapotec tradition, an indigenous person's placenta (doo yoo) must be buried in Juchitán for them to be considered a Juchiteco. Tarú, unlike the PRI candidate, could claim this distinction, even though his father was a Turco and he himself had spent many years away from Juchitán (Royce 1975:191–202). Additionally, Tarú was linked to numerous Juchitán townspeople through his influential family, which had already established fictive kin ties and social bonds via the fiesta system, as well as extensive employer-employee relations through the family's hammock-making business.[10] Thus, Tarú claimed to be the "true" defender of Juchitán (Prévot–Schapira and Riviere d'Arc 1984).

That Tarú could become the leader of an ethnic movement is indicative of the volatility and plasticity of Juchiteco ethnicity in the political sphere. In other words, whether one is or is not a Juchiteco, or whether one is considered "more" Zapotec than another, is not a fixed matter but is rather relational and contingent. That is, the side a given leader is on politically may color other's interpretations of whether that person is characterized as *more* or *less* ethnic.

An illegitimate son of a wealthy Lebanese merchant and a poor Zapotec woman, Tarú sold *empanadas* at local fiestas (a relatively humble activity) to earn money as a child, and he thus communed amply with poor Zapotec youth who were his peers and playmates (*El Satélite* 7/1977; interviews). Despite his later academic and business successes, made possible by his father's connections, it was this aspect of his background that allowed Tarú to identify with, and speak the language of, the Zapotec lower classes. Turning to politics after studying aviation in Mexico City and Guadalajara and establishing a profitable local fishing business, Tarú could not have begun his civic career at a more opportune time (Royce 1975).

In 1971 the PRI imposed yet another unpopular candidate on Juchitán, despite the fact that the previous mayor had infuriated townspeople with his arbitrariness and dishonesty. This time, PRI's heavy-handedness offended even the Zapotec upper classes, who turned to the PPS and chose Tarú as their leader (although he was not the party's official candidate). Tarú was also backed by Polo's CCJ and other groups that merged to form the United Juchiteco Democratic Front (FUDJ). As Royce (1975:198–99) described the situation:

> Zapotec of the upper classes knew they had to find a candidate sufficiently strong to obtain a popular victory, one who could capture the imagination of the masses and appeal to their pride as Juchitecos. Tarú was available and willing, constituting the ideal candidate. Lower-class Zapotec identified with him as one of their own class who elevated himself above his background simply by his will power and racial capacities. Members of the Zapotec middle and upper classes had been his schoolmates. Some of the powerful Arab and Mexican families had authentic and fictive kinship ties with him through the Musalem family. All thought he would promote their interests. His strong and compelling personality inspired confidence and his discourses, equally in Zapotec and Spanish, moved great multitudes of followers . . .

Tarú's defense of the rights of Juchitecos against outsiders, his appeal to Zapotec identity, and his picaresque humor in the Zapotec language helped him establish a strong rapport with the populace. Such tactics were especially effective in the early 1970s, when capitalist expansion challenged indigenous livelihoods and sharpened ethnic differences between Isthmus Zapotecs and mestizo newcomers. Foreshadowing COCEI demonstrations of the 1980s, Tarú's large rallies became showcases for ethnic symbolism and regional pride (Royce 1975:191–202). At these rallies, Zapotec women displayed the pink colors of the PPS (called "Tarú's colors" by his followers) in their *huipiles*, skirts, and braids (Henestrosa de Webster 1985:88). Likewise, the ribbons adorning oxcarts in pre-fiesta processions (*convites*), and the decorations for *velas* and weddings, bore Tarú's colors. Supposedly, PPS loyalists, upon greeting each other, even uttered "Tarú" while shaking hands, and Tarú's mere presence would turn a fiesta into a political meeting (Henestrosa de Webster 1985). The poorer segments of Juchitán and its surrounding villages expressed their fervor for his candidacy in raucous, torch-lit marches and by scrawling graffiti on house walls with pencils and crayons (Martínez López 1985:28). Peasants, senior citizens, women, and children supported Tarú in droves (Martínez López 1985).

Controversy surrounding the election outcome led to negotiations between the PPS, PRI, and the state government. The talks resulted in Tarú being declared head of a coalition government, a triumph his supporters celebrated in grand style. Five bands played only regional tunes (*sones*), women wore traditional dress, and *horchata* was served instead of beer in a lively display of local ethnic pride (Royce 1975:80). Tarú had become the undisputed leader of Juchitán.

When I interviewed him, Tarú claimed his popularity in the 1970s was based on the following: (1) he spoke Zapotec to his followers at a time when the language was under attack by school teachers and those advocating "modernization"; (2) people admired his ability to fly a plane, which he used to distribute political propaganda; (3) he was a model of the self-made Juchiteco man—as he put it, he was successful on land (as a sugar cane grower), in the air (as a pilot), and on sea (his fishing business); and (4) he promised democracy. Tarú also said he introduced political innovations that were later copied by COCEI: forming neighborhood committees, holding festive "lightning meetings" in the poor sections of Juchitán, and uniting the lower classes. However, Tarú's meteoric rise and thorough hold over the popular imagination ended just as rapidly as it began. In 1973, after a shooting incident, he left office and subsequently was accused of graft, illegal land transactions, and selling out his former supporters by joining the PRI and the local bourgeoisie (Prévot–Schapira et al. 1984:19). During this same period, the movement that would become COCEI was formed by poor and lower-middle-class students of Juchitán.

ORIGINS AND EVOLUTION OF COCEI.

The Juchiteco students who eventually created COCEI were first exposed to opposition politics in the Juchitán vocational school, and in the movements of Polo and Tarú. They also gained political experience at Oaxaca preparatory schools and the state university, the militant University of Guerrero, and in the colleges of the nation's capital.[11] In migrating to urban educational centers, future *Coceístas* followed in the footsteps of previous generations of upwardly mobile Juchitecos. Like their forerunners, this group of Zapotec youths experienced an educational rite of passage outside the Isthmus that had a profound impact on their sense of identity. Unlike their predecessors, however, who joined PRI, the late-1960s/early-1970s crop of students (especially those of peasant and lower-middle-class families) were radicalized by the Mexican student movement (Monsiváis 1983).

In Oaxaca City, COCEI students participated in violent struggles for control of the Benito Juárez University and in the movement that caused the downfall of Governor Zárate Aquino (Santibañez Orozco 1982; Martínez López 1985). In Mexico City the Juchiteco student experience had two important dimensions: (1) engagement in national activist movements of the 1968 era and internal struggles for control of the Juchiteco Students Association (AEJ), and (2) the formation of a strongly self-conscious ethnic sensibility through collective interactions with ethnic peers and urban Mexicans.

Traditionally, the Juchiteco Students Association was controlled by wealthier youths who used it as a "trampoline" to political posts within PRI and business careers (Gutiérrez 1981). But in 1973 this organization was taken over by the less-affluent students, who pursued a markedly different agenda. Splitting off from the richer students, the working- and lower-middle-class Juchiteco youths formed the *Casa del Estudiante Istmeño*, which has become the political training ground and dormitory for COCEI students in Mexico City. There, in addition to spending long hours drinking beer and discussing political philosophy, the leftist students began analyzing the Juchitán political situation and making plans to change it.

The late 1960s and early 1970s were a prime period for radical political consciousness-raising in Mexico. This had an important impact on the founders of COCEI. Yet, there was another equally important influence on the Zapotec students—that is, their heightened sense of ethnic "otherness," which results from the process of separation and reattachment associated with schooling outside the native community. Oscar Cruz and other COCEI members have described to me the heady years they spent in the capital—sharing *totopos*, dry cheese, shrimp, and other Isthmus foods they brought back with them from their most recent trips to Juchitán, singing Zapotec songs, and engaging in intense discussions about their town's history and what it meant to be a Juchiteco.

In some cases these students even reproduced Isthmus social patterns in Mexico City. For example, among Cruz's group was a Juchiteco *muxe'* who, as in the Isthmus, adopted a feminine role at the *Casa del Estudiante*—he became the house cook. Juchiteca students, likewise, might wear their *huipiles* and *enaguas* to accentuate their ethnic distinctiveness among the *chilangas*. Similarly, Istmeños from different communities held annual *velas* in the capital. In sum, the Juchiteco student experience in Mexico City not only radicalized them politically, it was a crucible for their growing appreciation of their own ethnic roots and sense of otherness vis-à-vis mestizos.

Back in Juchitán, the new student leaders applied the lessons they learned in campus politics to the task of changing their hometown. For example, as a student Daniel López Nelio became a member of the national hunger strike committee that protested the 1968 Tlatelolco massacre. He also engaged in demonstrations, marches, bus-hijackings, and building takeovers while enrolled in schools in Oaxaca and Mexico City. Influenced by the Marxist teachings of his UNAM sociology professors, López Nelio returned to Juchitán with the intention of establishing, as he put it, "red communes."[12]

Many critics of COCEI claim the movement is a creation of the Mexican governmental system itself (Santana 1988:39). They argue that the Juchitán student movement was funded by PRI politicians who, for example, helped establish the *Casa del Estudiante* (*Ovaciones* 8/5/1983). Supposedly, Luis Echeverría supported COCEI leaders politically and economically while he was Secretary of the Interior and later President of Mexico. Oaxaca state government officials are also reputed to have promoted COCEI (Martínez López 1985).

Because these views come from enemies of COCEI, they cannot simply be accepted at face value. However, those who could shed light on these subjects do not discuss them openly. Hence, this shadowy question concerning COCEI's origins remains a mystery. Nonetheless, it is clear that COCEI was able to develop, in part, because of the so-called democratic opening of the Echeverría years and the tacit backing of high government officials (Rubin 1987a). In the mid-1970s the government even tried to make COCEI's two principal founders (López Nelio and Sánchez) the government's Agrarian Reform representatives in the Juchitán. COCEI leaders rejected the offer as an attempt to co-opt and manipulate the movement (Santana 1988:8).[13] In any case, COCEI is a relatively autonomous organization today.

The Juchiteco Students Association's first major political success resulted from the takeover of a Juchitán health clinic—a direct action tactic that later became a trademark of COCEI strategy. The director of the clinic had been charging Juchitán students for health checkups that should have been free (Gutiérrez 1981). After a series of demonstrations in 1973, the AEJ stormed the clinic and forced the ouster of its director, a move that brought acclaim from townspeople. Soon thereafter, radical students led by López Nelio and Sánchez allied with a group of peasants to found the Juchitán Peasant–Student Coalition (CCEJ), the organization that would eventually become COCEI (Gutiérrez 1981). The Coalition focused on the demands of Zapotec peasants, who had become politicized as a result of lost lands (Santana 1988). Their major concerns included regaining land, reinstating the 1964 ejido decree,[14] and wresting control of the communal lands governing body (*Comisariado de Bienes Comunales*) from large land-owners and elite power brokers—which they did in 1974, although PRI quickly regained control. The Coalition also pushed (successfully) for the elimination of taxes on the peasantry and for greater credit opportunities (Gutiérrez 1981).

Accomplishments of the Coalition during this period of intense activism included freeing political prisoners, obtaining indemnification for families of bus accident victims, securing wage increases for local workers, and forcing the rehiring or indemnification of fired workers (*El Satélite*, various issues during 1973–1975).[15] With each political victory, the movement grew stronger and its plans became more ambitious. The Coalition's grow-ing emphasis on labor issues led to name changes, as CCEJ became COCEJ (Juchitán Worker–Peasant–Student Coalition) in 1974, and finally COCEI (*Coalición Obrera Campesina Estudiantil del Istmo*) in 1975. Coalition mem-bers also participated in the budding Juchiteco cultural movement of the late 1960s and early 1970s.

Francisco Toledo and the Casa de la Cultura

Although the Zapotec cultural magazine *Neza Cubi* disappeared after 1970, the new focus of the Juchiteco intellectuals' energies was the creation of the Casa de la Cultura, which opened in 1972. The Casa is housed in a picturesque old school building with whitewashed walls and a high-pitched tile roof supported by large wooden beams.[16] The spacious facility covers about one quarter of a city block in downtown Juchitán and has a wide, inner patio with a small garden, a stage for theater performances, and sev-eral native shade trees. The patio is surrounded on three sides by the Casa's modern art gallery, print-making shop, library, archaeology museum, local art exhibition room, several classrooms, a small children's library, and the main office. The Casa de la Cultura is the headquarters of the contem-porary Juchiteco intellectual circle, whose predecessors Covarrubias (1946:161) described in the 1940s as "a peculiar intelligentsia that cultivates poetry" and hangs out in bars "engaging in deep philosophical discussions over iced beers."

On an average morning during the school year, the Casa is relatively quiet, except for the laughter and chatter of the bohemian Juchiteco poets and painters criticizing each other's work, discussing local politics, or play-ing chess. Occasionally, the rapid gait of an earnest-looking COCEI activ-ist trying to locate someone will interrupt the languid atmosphere of the place. In the afternoon, when school gets out, the Casa fills up with noisy Zapotec schoolchildren, who use the library or just play with their friends. By this time, however, the Juchiteco art crowd has already moved on to a nearby cantina to continue the day's gossiping, sell a few paintings to local businessmen, recite poetry, or arrange the publication of a pamphlet of poetry or local history. After listening to the Zapotec ballads of a local guitar player, and having consumed numerous *caguamas* (liter bottles) of Corona beer, or just a few shots of mescal if no one has any money, the Juchiteco intellectuals disband until their next meeting. Somehow, in between this regular routine of socializing and drinking (in addition to the almost weekly *velas* or wedding fiestas), the Juchiteco artists and writers find time to produce a richly adorned cultural magazine (*Guchachi' Reza*), publish numerous books and pamphlets, and paint a diverse portfolio of colorful, avant-garde paintings.

A key figure behind the Casa and the emerging Juchitán cultural movement was Francisco Toledo, who by the 1970s was already a famous artist residing in Mexico City. As a child in Juchitán, Toledo had demonstrated a gift for drawing and painting on the walls of his family's house. After secondary school in Oaxaca, Toledo went to Mexico City, where he obtained his initial formal training in the *Taller Libre de Grabado* (Sparks 1989:1). While still a teenager, Toledo displayed his genius in solo shows in Mexico City and Fort Worth, Texas. In 1960, at the age of 20, he went to Europe, where he studied under William Hayter in Paris. There, as in the case of Andrés Henestrosa, Toledo's contact with the great cultural traditions of the West reinforced his appreciation of his own culture. Although Toledo is said to have wandered through Europe wearing, even in winter, Isthmus huaraches and peasant garb, he took some time along the way to steep himself in the work of Paul Klee, Jean Lucat, and Salvador Dali (Everson 1978). By 1965 his works had appeared in major galleries in Paris, London, and New York. Today, Toledo is one of Mexico's most famous painters. Riding (1985:305) notes that Toledo's works routinely fetch five-figure prices.

Having such a wealthy and influential patron (as well as the direct aid of President Echeverría) gave the Casa a tremendous boost.[17] Its small modern art gallery housed not only the valuable works of Toledo, but prints and original paintings by Mexican and foreign masters which he had obtained in his travels. In addition to approximately 200 artworks, Toledo also gave the Casa expensive art books, Zapotec archaeological treasures, and photographs (*Unomásuno* 4/21/1989). These items were kept in the Casa's exposition halls, museum, and library (the largest in the Isthmus).

Other Casa facilities included a stage and classrooms in which instruction was given in art, indigenous music, the Zapotec language, theater, dance, and literature. Additionally, on several occasions, Toledo has auctioned off some of his own expensive artwork to raise funds for the Casa and COCEI (an interesting example of art subsidizing politics). With such impressive cultural resources for a rural Mexican community, the Casa was well equipped to carry out its mission to revive and promote Isthmus Zapotec culture.

Despite the Casa's overtly cultural agenda, its activities have been influenced by political considerations from its inception. Against Toledo's wishes the Casa was granted a subsidy by the National Fine Arts Institute and Oaxaca state government (*Unomásuno* 4/21/1989). This gave the national and state governments political leverage over the Casa, which they subsequently used (COCEI would say abused). Moreover, with economic development projects transforming the Isthmus landscape and challenging indigenous traditions, the young Juchiteco intellectuals (nearly all of whom were *Coceístas*) began to see cultural revivalism as not merely a literary pastime or dilettantish hobby but a political imperative. Whereas the relatively affluent and privileged *Neza* generation of the 1930s faced the choice/pressure of individual assimilation into a mestizo urban lifestyle, the intellectuals linked to the Casa de la Cultura felt that the very foundations of their indigenous, agrarian society were being undermined, and they sought to defend it. Consequently, young Zapotec poets and painters became fervent ideological supporters of COCEI.

The 1974 Mayoral Elections and Beyond: Growth and Expansion of COCEI

As COCEI's reputation grew, it attracted many former supporters of Polo and Tarú. Tensions between the Coalition and other local political organizations (PRI, PPS, FUDJ) intensified as a result of the 1974 mayoral campaign, in which COCEI, represented by Héctor Sánchez, competed for office for the first time (COCEI 1988:36). Electoral conflicts led to violence when PRI gunmen killed Lorenza Santiago, a pregnant Coalition militant, and her unborn baby during a protest march near the home of the PRI candidate (*El Satélite* 10/10/1974). This killing sparked anger and resentment towards local PRI authorities, which has fueled COCEI ever since.

Another important moment in the evolution of COCEI was its joint takeover with the PPS of Juchitán City Hall to protest PRI vote fraud in the 1974 elections. Negotiations between the contending parties and the government led to confirmation of a PRI electoral victory. In response, the Coalition charged the PPS with selling out to PRI and condemned the decision. This watershed experience permanently separated COCEI from the PPS and FUDJ, both of which declined as political forces in Juchitán as COCEI expanded and absorbed many of their members. By mid-1975, COCEI was the dominant Juchiteco opposition movement, and in 1976 the PPS formally aligned itself with the Juchitán PRI (*El Satélite*, various issues from January 1976). Moreover, unlike the PPS, which had been mainly a way for men to gain political power without having to put in long years of service in PRI, COCEI presented a clear ideological alternative to the ruling party. In place of Tarú's amorphous majority movement that did not directly address most social problems, COCEI's program crystallized around the concrete interests of local peasants and workers. Whereas Tarú had appealed to Juchiteco ethnic and regional identity in forging a multiclass movement, COCEI linked Zapotec identity to the struggles of the poor versus the local bourgeoisie, be they Zapotecs or outsiders.

After the unsuccessful 1974 elections, COCEI returned to the agrarian, student, and labor struggles that are the organization's *raison d'etre*. A hot spot for peasant activity was the Alvaro Obregón Colony (population 5,000) established by Charis. When Charis died, confusion reigned, because he had refused to grant title documents to his ex-soldiers. Hence, most of the land was under Charis' name. According to the General, his colonists needed only "six hectares and a bullet" to protect the land, not legal papers. After his death, a vicious struggle broke out between Charis' heirs and allies and the Alvaro Obregón colonists and their offspring for control of the approximately 7,000 ha left by Charis. COCEI intervened on the side of the colonists and the battle raged.[18]

A critical issue in the dispute was the sale by Charis' widow and daughter of rich salt flats and lands occupied by peasants to Federico Rasgado, a powerful landowner and former Charis ally. Rasgado lacked the political power and popular appeal that had allowed Charis to dominate the Alvaro Obregón area; the possibilities for peasant organizing improved. The prime years of Isthmus *caciquismo* were indeed over.

The disfranchised peasantry allied themselves with COCEI and began to invade Rasgado's land. Rasgado responded by sending *pistoleros* and the military to suppress the land invaders, which resulted in several deaths. COCEI, in turn, led 400 peasants in the takeover of the offices of the Agrarian Reform Ministry in Mexico City (COCEI 1988:38). Coalition leaders also met with President Echeverría in Mexico City and Cancún to resolve land problems (*El Satélite* 12/21/1975). Eventually, COCEI pressure brought results and the government granted titles for 1,000 ha to Alvaro Obregón peasants, who became a bulwark of the movement (Martínez López 1985:54).[19]

When I interviewed peasants in the rural Alvaro Obregón area bordering the salty Isthmus lagoons, they described to me the difficult situation they had been in, and how COCEI activists from Juchitán came and held meetings to organize people and plan strategy. As we sat in hammocks in their large, open yards surrounded by *carrizo* fences, spiny brush, and pig pens, the residents of the Colony—who, for the most part, call themselves Juchitecos[20]—recounted the bloody battles they fought with Rasgado's gunmen. The Alvaro Obregón peasants described how in exchange for the COCEI leaders' organizational assistance, they participated in exhausting hunger strikes, protest vigils, land invasions, demonstrations, and marches to Oaxaca City. One informant remembered that in one particular assembly a corrupt local leader punched a poor, familyless peasant who had dared to register a complaint about the handling of agricultural credit. In turn, *Coceísta* Héctor Sánchez beat up the leader to the satisfaction of all present. In general, the Alvaro Obregón peasants expressed gratitude to COCEI for helping them obtain *ejido* land, but they lamented the many sacrifices they had to endure in the process.

The Alvaro Obregón land issue flared up again in 1983, when Charis' son-in-law (*"el Rojo"*) ran for local deputy (with PRI), invoking his affinal connection to Charis to legitimize his political aspirations (López Monjardin 1983). However, this tactic backfired on him when one of his COCEI rivals for the position, Javier Charis,[21] son of the General, claimed Rojo and his wife had fraudulently altered Charis' will and forged his signature in order to obtain control of the General's lands (López Monjardin 1983). Thus, the heritage of Charis remains contested terrain at the same time that his *cacique* politics are being replaced with the grassroots populism of COCEI.

Another victory for COCEI peasants in the mid-1970s was the recouping of a 250-ha cattle ranch from the Juchitán Rural Credit Bank. Although Credit Bank officials tried to force Zapotec peasants to pay a 20-million-peso debt left by the ranch's previous owners, they refused to pay and pastured their cattle on the ranch (COCEI 1983:4). In addition to participating in numerous land struggles of the 1970s,[22] COCEI gave classes in political ideology, organized more than 40 peasant groups to obtain credit, and fought to control local agricultural associations (*El Satélite* 4/10/1977). Between 1975 and 1977, COCEI regained control over the Juchitán communal land board[23] and took over the Alvaro Obregón land board for the first time. The Coalition also had one of its leaders named to the Juchitán office of the Agrarian Reform Ministry.

Additionally, COCEI candidates won seats on the local cattlemen's association, which eventually split into two separate groups, one run by COCEI and the other by PRI. COCEI also established or participated in regional and national peasant and student organizations, although these tentative liaisons seldom endured (Santana 1988).[24] Perhaps in response to COCEI's growing strength among the peasantry, *pistoleros* and PRI leaders attacked a 1976 meeting between *ejido* authorities and COCEI leaders, forcing the agrarian activists to seek refuge in a house for 10 hours to avoid repeated machine gun fire (COCEI 1988:37).

Polo's decision to join COCEI, which he said worked year-round instead of only at election time like the other Juchitán political groups, was another important development of the mid-1970s (*El Satélite* 9/18/1977). Polo had opposed COCEI at first, because he thought COCEI students were opportunists who lacked his tradition of struggle. However, viewing COCEI's gains and the decline of his own movement, Polo put aside differences with the Coalition and assumed a leadership role in the movement. Adding this prestigious leader of the Juchitán peasantry and middle-class boosted the Coalition, as did the addition of Javier Charis and Desiderio de Gyves of the PPS, and Enedino Jiménez from PRI—all of whom now play key roles in COCEI.

At the same time, *Coceísta* activists were actively recruiting students at the Juchitán technical school and at various other Isthmus secondary schools. In addition to giving speeches about Isthmus agrarian and political issues, *Coceístas* provided manpower to dissident students in their own school-oriented political demonstrations, and in return received the students' assistance in COCEI protests and rallies. Several Juchiteco student activists described to me how they helped organize the students of San Blas. The Blaseños then became so combative that they engaged in militant marches through the streets of Tehuantepec punctuated by bursts of rock-throwing at the houses of wealthy Tehuano families. Other former student activists told me about their urban political propagandizing in Oaxaca and Mexico City, while residing at the pro-COCEI student houses. Finally, during this same period, the Mosquito Squadron (*Escuadrón Mosquito*), made up of the children of COCEI activists, was formed.

Unfortunately for the movement, this era of fervent political activity and concrete accomplishments was also marked by intense government and paramilitary repression. Exactly one year after pro-PRI gunmen killed a pregnant COCEI woman, 7 COCEI peasants and a popular student leader were murdered and more than 20 people injured at a COCEI rally (COCEI 1988:37). The killers were members of a mysterious ultra-left guerrilla group (*Liga 23 de Septiembre*), which had engaged in bombings and kidnappings in other parts of Mexico. In 1977 state police fired on a pro-COCEI demonstration (protesting the detention of 37 students who had participated in several school strikes and bus takeovers) outside a jail, killing three men and two children (Rubin 1987a:139).

During this time, COCEI demonstrations were broken up and numerous COCEI members (including Polo) were kidnapped, jailed, and tortured (Rubin 1987a:139). Several more *Coceístas* were also killed, and the three principal leaders of the mid-1970s (López Nelio, Sánchez, and César Pineda) were "exiled" from Juchitán after a shootout with an opponent (Martínez López 1985:38). In many of these cases, armed civilians linked to the local PRI, large landowners, and commercial groups were blamed for the violence (AI 1986). In March 1977 military platoons took control of Juchitán, occupying City Hall and stationing troops near the Coalition's headquarters (COCEI 1988:39).

Violence and repression were unsuccessful in breaking COCEI. Use of such methods only angered Juchitán townspeople, turned victim's relatives into passionate COCEI supporters, and tarnished the reputations of the government and PRI. Martínez López (1985:62) notes the martyrdom of numerous COCEI members was a rallying point for the movement "in a society [i.e., Zapotec society] where the cult of the dead has primordial importance." Indeed, as government repression against COCEI intensified, the organization began to develop a new pantheon of victimized heroes to take their place alongside the martyred rebel leaders of the past (such as Meléndez, Gómez, and Binu Gada) and whose legacy is appealed to by movement ideologists.

Thus, *Coceístas* painted demonstration placards and banners with the images of their dead *compañeros*. Female relatives of "disappeared" *Coceístas* wore pictures of them around their necks, Juchiteco intellectuals wrote hagiographic essays, and the leadership began to talk of fighting on behalf of the deceased. In a booklet of poetry dedicated to several of his dead *compañeros*, a COCEI poet invoked a line from Roque Dalton that epitomized the radicalizing effects of political killings on the Juchiteco community: "Each day the dead become more unruly" ("*Los muertos son cada día más indóciles*").[25] Rather than crushing the organization, violence directed against COCEI boomeranged against its perpetrators as the Coalition grew stronger.[26]

COCEI responded to repression by stepping up its own political mobilizations and carrying out daring protest actions. From 1975 onward, COCEI engaged in strikes, meetings, press conferences, and campus activism. The Coalition also held frequent demonstrations in which it called for the impeachment of Oaxaca Governor Zárate Aquino and the local mayor (COCEI 1988:36–40). Additionally, COCEI seized offices of the state agrarian delegation and the national Ministry of Agrarian Reform,[27] invaded land, took over buses, and participated in hunger strikes. The efficacy of COCEI's militant protests (combined with mobilizations by several other Oaxacan political groups) is demonstrated by the resignation of Governor Zárate Aquino, at that time a relatively rare occurrence in Mexican politics (Santibañez 1980).

COCEI was hurt, however, by the exile of three of its principal leaders (Sánchez, López Nelio, and César Pineda) in 1976. Fortunately for the Coalition, the addition of Polo to their cause gave them an experienced and popular leader, who was able to attract followers and voters of the middle class as well as the peasantry when he became COCEI's mayoral candidate in 1977. The absence of the three leaders also provided opportunities for a new cadre of *Coceístas*, including Polo's son Polín, to gain leadership experience. Thus, COCEI was able to continue its political activities despite the loss of three key members (Gutiérrez 1981).

The 1977 Election

The 1977 Juchitán mayoral elections took place in an atmosphere of tension. In March, COCEI leaders complained that their supporters had been denied voting credentials and that government soldiers had occupied the organization's office, establishing a state of siege in Juchitán (TIS 1984:310, 314–16). Soldiers also patrolled the countryside to prevent COCEI land invasions. The soldiers were part of the Eleventh Battalion from Sinaloa—brought to the Isthmus in 1976—which had been hardened by the antinarcotics campaign and which was unsympathetic to COCEI. The Eleventh replaced the Eighth Battalion, which had been made up of Istmeños with a degree of empathy for the Coalition (Alfaro Sánchez 1984:130).

Although COCEI was still not legally registered as a political party and hence could not elect a mayor from its organization regardless of the vote outcome, it entered the 1977 election with gusto. Polo repeatedly attacked the PRI and the local bourgeoisie in newspaper stories, and COCEI held lively rallies attended by old people, women with babies in their arms, and children, as well as peasants, students, workers, and middle-class Juchitecos. Despite COCEI's wide popular support, PRI was declared the victor (*El Satélite* 12/4/1977). Moreover, as in several previous elections, PRI's candidate, a naval officer residing outside the Isthmus, was an unpopular member of the Juchiteco elite whose candidacy had been imposed by the PRI national and regional hierarchy.

Opposition to the elections mounted and the Juchitán merchant's union participated in a taxpaying moratorium (TIS 1984:318). On January 1, 1978, a large COCEI crowd protested the inauguration of the PRI mayor at City Hall. Soldiers and police fired on the gathering, killing a COCEI supporter and wounding many others (*El Satélite* 1/8/1978). In response, angry *Coceístas* looted nearby businesses, including a restaurant, bank, a Sears store, and several other shops. In a scene reminiscent of 1960s urban riots in the United States, *Coceístas* broke into stores and carried away type-writers, adding machines, calculators, and whatever else they could get their hands on (*El Satélite* 1/8/1978). In total, property worth 20 million pesos was taken. The PRI blamed Polo for the incident, and he was later arrested and sentenced to a 3 1/2-year jail term.

COCEI Regroups: 1978–1980

COCEI's large following notwithstanding, PRI had once again forced Juchitecos to accept an undesirable mayor. Therefore, the Coalition adopted a new strategy. Since the government would not accept its voters at the polls, COCEI set up its own parallel government to simply bypass the PRI regime (TIS 1984:320). *Coceístas* called the new arrangement the *ayuntamiento popular* (People's Government), which they distinguished from the imposed government (*ayuntamiento impuesto*). At the heart of COCEI's alternative government was its newly formed system of neigh-borhood committees which, in addition to organizing political affairs, judged and resolved marital disputes, personal quarrels, labor conflicts, legal battles, and other matters normally handled by municipal authorities. The neighborhood committees were especially popular in *la séptima* and Cheguigo, neighborhoods with large, impoverished peasant populations.

The COCEI committees drew on a history of such neighborhood or-ganizations in Juchitán that goes back to at least the 1940s. In nearby Tehuantepec, barrio headmen (*xuanas*) have served as moral authorities and multipurpose neighborhood arbitrators since perhaps as early as the sixteenth century when the Spaniards instituted the barrio system, if not earlier (Dorsett 1975:102). In Juchitán, neighborhoods have been led by *jefes de sección* (section bosses, or chiefs) with a mandate—invested in them by neighborhood residents—to decide on matters of concern to individuals and groups. The *jefes de sección*, however, always played second fiddle to municipal politicians. By the 1970s these men were known more for their corruption and the high fees they charged to resolve disputes than for responsiveness to the public.

COCEI's new section chiefs performed the same functions as the old neighborhood bosses without charging for their services, which gave them credibility with poor Juchitecos.[28] Coalition section bosses also counseled or represented neighborhood members when they had to appear in front of local or state officials. If necessary, entire section committees would accompany a neighborhood resident in protests against arbitrary decisions by municipal authorities. Additionally, COCEI refunctionalized the committees to serve as open forums for citizens' complaints and staging areas for grassroots public works projects and political mobilizations. Consequently, poor villagers began to view COCEI as the de facto political leader of Juchitán, and the organization gained experience in grassroots government.

Another major venue of COCEI activity in Juchitán was the large, female-dominated central market, where hundreds of Zapotec women sell their wares on a daily basis. COCEI is especially popular among the generally poorer fish-sellers, flower-hawkers, and vegetable, fruit, and prepared-food vendors who set up shop in the streets around the market building. The Coalition also enjoys the support of many of the grocery vendors and other market women on the first floor of the building. (The generally more affluent and conservative gold merchants and clothing retailers who control the second floor of the marketplace tend to side with PRI.) COCEI activists frequently give speeches in Zapotec at the market and solicit donations and political support from the vendors. Market vendors have been, for the most part, loyal *Coceístas* because the organization is responsive to their demands for low tax rates and permission to sell their wares in the street. A fiery female COCEI activist, Idalia Linares, has played a key role in organizing these women.

From 1978 to 1980 the Isthmus experienced cycles of violence and protest. In January 1978 police beat and jailed COCEI labor leader Carlos Sánchez (COCEI 1988:40). One month later, a gang of Zapotec women attacked Governor Jiménez and knocked him to the ground in Ixtepec, where he had gone to resolve a political dispute (TIS 1984:321). Also in February, COCEI held a hunger strike in front of the United Nations building in Mexico City, calling for Polo's release from prison. Soon after that, market women threw vegetables and fish at police who tried to detain

COCEI youth near the Juchitán market (*El Satélite* 2/12/1978). During the spring and early summer, *pistoleros* and police broke up attempted COCEI land invasions, wounded and jailed peasants, and tried to throw COCEI peasants off lands they had recaptured in Alvaro Obregón (TIS 1984; COCEI 1988:40). June was marked by the killing of a COCEI student by Juchitán municipal police. Finally, in July armed individuals (four of them wearing military uniforms) kidnapped Víctor Pineda Henestrosa (a.k.a. Víctor Yodo), a popular COCEI founder and leader, in broad daylight from the streets of Juchitán (AI 1986).

At the time of his kidnapping, Víctor Yodo was an official of the Agrarian Reform Ministry in Juchitán and an advisor to the communal lands board. The kidnapping occurred shortly before scheduled elections for a new president of the lands board, a hotly contested issue between COCEI and the Juchitán bourgeoisie. COCEI accused the Eleventh Battalion of having kidnapped Víctor Yodo in order to stifle COCEI agrarian struggles he had led. In spite of hunger strikes by his female relatives in Juchitán, Oaxaca, and Mexico City, numerous meetings with government officials, endless demonstrations and building takeovers, and international pressure via Amnesty International, Víctor's whereabouts remain unknown.[29] Presumably he was murdered by the military, as were numerous other dissidents during this period, as part of an intense campaign of repression against the left in Oaxaca and Guerrero (*Proceso* 4/18/1988). Nonetheless, Víctor Yodo has become the most famous COCEI martyr and a symbol of government repression. No Coalition demonstration is complete without calls (¡*Víctor Yodo Libertad!*) for his release.

The loss of Víctor Yodo, Polo, López Nelio, Sánchez, and César Pineda left COCEI without its founders and principal leaders. The fact that the movement was able to regroup and maintain its strength and purpose is indicative of a shift in Juchiteco politics from *caciquismo* to grassroots ethnic populism. Although the young crop of activists who assumed control of the organization were also charismatic figures like their predecessors, COCEI had become more than just a vehicle for the aspirations of a few persuasive individuals. By the late 1970s, COCEI had become a broadly based, well-organized movement, seasoned by years of struggle and driven by anger and resentment towards the Mexican government and the Juchitán bourgeoisie.[30] Not only was the movement popular in the countryside, it also enjoyed support in the marketplace, in poor neighborhoods, in the secondary schools and the Casa del Estudiante, at the Casa de la Cultura, and in the few large workplaces such as the beer and soft drink companies.[31]

Despite COCEI's strength, cohesion, and militancy, the movement still lacked government approval to run candidates for public office. That finally changed in 1977 when a new law (LOPPE)[32] instituted political reforms that legalized leftist parties (Rubin 1987b). As a consequence, COCEI was able to establish an alliance with a now-legal national left party and gain the right to register candidates for future municipal elections. However, COCEI's initial response to the political reform was to reject it as another "trap" set by the government to justify its political system. Instead, the Coalition called for "real democracy of the base community" and independent organization of workers and peasants (*El Satélite* 4/22/1979, 5/20/1979). As had been the case previously, *Coceístas* viewed elections as forums for consciousness-raising about agrarian and labor issues rather than opportunities to take power.

Nonetheless, by 1980 Coalition leaders determined that it was in the movement's best interests to run a candidate for mayor and thus accepted an alliance with the Mexican Communist Party (PCM). This alliance gave COCEI access to municipal electoral committees, representation at voting booths, and the right to appeal controversial election outcomes (Gutiérrez 1981:261). COCEI's legal status also increased its appeal to the Juchitán middle class, which previously had been reluctant to support independent Coalition candidates. The COCEI–PCM alliance formulated an administrative plan (written by COCEI) that offered specific planks for the three key sectors of the Juchitán population—peasants, workers, and market sellers. Peasants were offered support for efforts to regain lost lands, better prices for farm products, and increased credit. Higher wages, increased benefits, and the institution of the 8-hour workday and 6-day work week was COCEI's appeal to urban and rural workers. The plan also called for improved maintenance and hygiene at the Juchitán market, and protection of the rights of market vendors and small merchants (Gutiérrez 1981:262–63).

Other provisions of COCEI–PCM's political program included ending illegal detentions and torture by police and the military and respecting the right of public assembly. Additionally, the COCEI–PCM alliance advocated controlling prices on food, consumer goods, and transportation; constructing clinics in poor neighborhoods and outlying villages; expanding access to public utilities; combatting illiteracy; and supporting the Casa de la Cultura. In sum, COCEI offered something for most sectors of the Juchitán population with the exception of big businessmen and large landowners. The bulk of COCEI's following, however, came from poor landed peasants, artisans, landless rural workers, fishermen, students, urban laborers, female market vendors, small merchants, and intellectuals. The main leaders of the movement were predominantly of working class or lower-middle-class origins, although they have all risen today to, at least, solid middle-class socioeconomic standing.

Rubin (1987a) notes the difficulty in determining precisely what percentage of Juchitán's population backs COCEI. There are no reliable statistics on this controversial subject. For that matter, one cannot rely on government census figures for the population of Juchitán either, since, according to knowledgeable informants, census-takers often simply invent numbers rather than undertake the painstaking house-to-house labor necessary to obtain solid demographic data.

Coceístas and some PRI members told Rubin that COCEI has a definite majority. Rubin concluded that COCEI does have a clear majority, which he suggests is 60 to 70 percent of the population. According to Bucuvalas (1986:48), the lower classes make up 86 percent of Juchitán's population. Since COCEI is extremely popular among this segment of the population, Rubin's estimate seems reasonable. My fieldwork in 1987–1988 also corroborated Rubin's findings. In any case, COCEI is the most dynamic and visible political entity in Juchitán and routinely attracts thousands of enthusiastic supporters to its rallies, dwarfing the turnouts for PRI events. Since the late 1970s, newspaper accounts of COCEI demonstrations have reported estimates of between 10,000 and 20,000 people in attendance. One source (*El Universal*, 3/21/1988) states that COCEI can mobilize 30,000 people in the state of Oaxaca. Finally, a COCEI leader claimed the movement has supporters in more than 60 Oaxacan communities (*Unomásuno* 4/1/1988). These figures seem fairly accurate, although the attendance at COCEI demonstrations is probably slightly exaggerated.

As previously noted, COCEI's political agenda was not revolutionary, although it did criticize the bourgeoisie and promote the causes of peasants and workers. Therefore, COCEI's program frightened only the most right-wing elements in Juchitán. Nor was its connection with PCM a major liability, since the majority of townspeople thought mainly in terms of local politics; hence, they were not easily swayed by red-baiting rhetoric. Furthermore, COCEI's link to the PCM was tenuous (the two groups had squabbled over student politics in 1977 and 1981) and primarily strategic (for electoral purposes) rather than ideological. The Coalition maintained local autonomy free from PCM intervention in the movement's functioning.

COCEI's turbulent relations with the PCM and (later) other national leftist organizations stemmed from conflicts between the Juchitecos' local interests (and outlook) and the more-centralized, top-down approach of these other organizations. Despite Prévot–Schapira et al.'s assertion (1984:16) that ethnicity is a secondary dimension of COCEI and that the movement's attempts to unite ethnic revivalism and class politics are a "posture," ethnicity and regionalism are fundamental to the way COCEI defines its interests, goals, and policies (as well as a key feature of the movement's ideology, style, and to some extent its structure). That is, the members of COCEI, despite their use of Marxist rhetoric and their solidarity with Central American revolutionary causes, are ultimately interested in the well-being of Juchitán and the Isthmus Zapotec community, and are not particularly impressed by grandiose global ideologies or pie-in-the-sky plans for the Mexican left to take over the country.

Furthermore, *Coceístas* do not trust the national left's state-focused and authoritarian way of doing things. Local autonomy has been a primary goal of Juchiteco movements for the last 150 years, and it continues to be strongly supported today. Therefore, Juchitecos react negatively to outside groups dictating policies or imposing their plans on the community, whether the groups in question are central government authorities or socialist political parties. One can accuse *Coceístas* of opportunism or unwillingness to compromise, but to deny the legitimacy of COCEI's concern for regional autonomy and ethnic self-determination would be a mistake.[33]

Nonetheless, COCEI is also a movement made up primarily of peasants, workers, and lower-middle-class elements whose interests are well-served by land invasions and land redistribution, plant takeovers, and strikes for higher wages. In this respect, *Coceístas* are very receptive to class-oriented projects that can provide them with the things they need—namely land, jobs, and better wages. But they see no reason why this should entail the loss of their native language, their customs, and the right to local self-determination. Thus, to the extent that the national left is respectful of the Juchitecos' way of life and does not try to impose on local politics, *Coceístas* see no major contradiction between the movement's ethnic ideology and socialist theory.

Unfortunately, national left parties have not always understood Juchiteco cultural idiosyncrasies or the Zapotecs' desire for autonomy (e.g., in 1981). On other occasions, the left has taken advantage of Juchitán's value as a symbol of leftist insurgency and has been very supportive of COCEI (as in 1983 and 1988). Likewise, at times COCEI has needed the backing of the urban left and has been grateful for such assistance (e.g., in 1980). In other instances, however, the Coalition has taken an independent path and angered the national left. For example, in 1990 COCEI received President Salinas in Juchitán against the wishes of Cuauthémoc Cárdenas, leader of the Party of the Democratic Revolution (PRD). Additionally in 1991, COCEI mayor Héctor Sánchez spoke before 1,000 other mayors (primarily PRI members) at a meeting for Solidarity, the president's much-acclaimed "social development" program, also to the displeasure of the PRD leadership. Thus, COCEI's relations with major leftist parties remain tentative and subject to change.

COCEI Electoral Victory in Juchitán

Whereas COCEI strengthened its position in Juchitán during the 1970s, PRI lost standing. After the death of Charis, the party repeatedly chose corrupt, incompetent mayors who accomplished few public works and offended the populace with their open graft and elitism. The reputation of the Juchitán PRI hit bottom during the tenure (1978–1980) of Javier López Chente, who gained power through dubious clandestine negotiations (Ornelas 1983). Discontent with his administration was so widespread that even PRI compatriots accused López Chente of defrauding the municipal treasury and called for an audit (TIS 1984:329; Martínez 1985:46). Such accusations are common in the fractious world of Isthmus politics. Indeed, Istmeños assume that all politicians will steal, but they expect graft to be discreet and that at least some public improvements will be made. A popular saying sums up this attitude: *"Esta bien que roben, pero que hagan algo"* (It's okay if they steal, as long as they accomplish something). According to local lore, López Chente was the worst Juchitán mayor of the twentieth century because "he did not even deign to pick up a rock from one place and move it to another" (Martínez López 1985:46).

One Juchitán paper (*El Satélite*) reported a litany of unethical acts and ugly incidents involving the mayor and his collaborators. In one of the worst incidents, López Chente's son was set free after killing a local youth (TIS 1984:333). In another case, COCEI peasants were jailed and tortured by Juchitán police (TIS 1984:331). However, police violence did not stop COCEI from carrying on strikes, protests, building takeovers, and other actions during this time.

The extent of PRI ineptitude, brutality, and graft reached such high levels that many Juchitecos, even some rich merchant families, began to think "why not give COCEI a chance to govern, they could not be any worse than PRI." Indeed, during the 1980 elections, some Juchitecos who cast ballots were not so much voting for COCEI as they were voting against the PRI. Internal divisions within PRI were another factor in COCEI's victory. These were a manifestation of the PRI's "historical conflict between machine politicians and reformist challengers" (Rubin 1987a:141), which further weakened the party. PRI's candidate in 1980 was the leader of the weak peasant sector (the CNC)[34] and did not obtain adequate backing from the professional and commercial branches of the party.

However, it would be insufficient to explain Juchitán intra-PRI conflict entirely in terms of competition between the old-guard and reformers (cf. Rubin 1987a). Despite PRI rhetoric about "transparent democracy" in the election of party candidates, personal rivalries and hostilities, raw ambition, factional loyalties, back-room conniving, and the *dedazo* (the naming of electoral candidates by political higher-ups, such as the president or governor) are what drive the innerworkings of the Isthmus PRI (Ornelas Esquinca 1983:84–90).

This was particularly the case prior to the 1980 election. In December 1979 a Juchitán PRI faction printed an article in a national magazine criticizing the mayor (*El Satélite* 12/23/1979). Likewise, the head of the PRI municipal committee carried on a personal feud with López Chente. In 1980 when the PRI local deputy candidate was chosen, members of the PRI youth organization announced that they would not support the candidate since his selection "was one of the ugliest and most shameful things we can remember" (Martínez López 1985:44). In July 1980 only 1,278 Juchitán voters (unofficially) out of a possible 20,000 supported the PRI's gubernatorial candidate, a clear indication of local discontent (Ornelas Esquinca 1983:43).[35] What was unusual about these circumstances was not that conflict within PRI existed, but that it was openly and belligerently expressed rather than being covered up with "subtle disguises" (Ornelas Esquinca 1983). Whereas PRI protocol calls for losers in internal squabbles to "discipline themselves" and support the winners at election time, in 1980 the three Juchitán PRI factions attacked one another more vigorously than they attacked their opponent, the COCEI candidate. The eventual PRI candidate even pledged to conduct an audit of the López Chente regime as his first act should he be elected mayor (Martínez López 1985:46).

Although the four previous municipal elections in Juchitán had been marred by violence, the 1980 elections occurred in a state of relative calm. In the absence of Polo and several other exiled COCEI leaders, Polo's son (Polín) ran for mayor. Unlike his father, who was something of an old-style politician, Polín was a dashing young (age 29) figure with new ideas and a brilliant oratorical style in both Zapotec and Spanish. A spellbinding speaker and a master of dramatic hand gestures, he captivated audiences in all sections of Juchitán. The Coalition finished its election campaign strongly with a large rally. With PRI in disarray, COCEI's big moment had seemingly finally arrived. First, however, they had to overcome the PRI's extensive repertoire of electoral maneuvers.

PRI vote fraud during the November 1980 elections took many forms, but this time COCEI was better equipped to combat PRI tricks. Using its national political connection (the PCM) to full advantage, COCEI publicized PRI electoral wrongdoings throughout the country and attracted considerable support from urban leftists and intellectuals. COCEI also engaged in its patented mass mobilization tactics. Movement supporters occupied the Guatemalan and Indian embassies in Mexico City,[36] took over Juchitán City Hall for 34 days, and conducted a sit-in at the Oaxaca cathedral (TIS 1984). Eventually, PRI was forced by these actions, and national publicity of the situation, to negotiate with COCEI. Talks between the two groups produced the following accord: (1) the original election was annulled, (2) a new election was scheduled, (3) amnesty was granted to several exiled COCEI leaders, and (4) measures were designed to ensure honest elections in the future (Gutiérrez 1981:266–67).[37]

In the interim between elections, a coalition government of COCEI and PRI members ran Juchitán, giving the left its first taste of power. PRI's new candidate—appointed by the governor—for the special election in March 1981 was a well-known member of a prestigious Zapotec family who resided in Mexico City. He was also considered a liberal within the official party (Gutiérrez 1981:267). Nonetheless, the Juchitán PRI viewed the candidate as another imposition by Oaxaca Valley politicians (who took control of the 1981 election campaign) and were offended by his candidacy (Rubin 1987a:141). COCEI sympathizers, likewise, viewed this local-boy-made-good-in-the-city with suspicion:

> The PRI . . . for the 1980 elections ran a modernizing candidate who was obliged to practice Zapotec, which he had stopped speaking, because the COCEI speaks in Zapotec to its militants, to its brothers. Stumblingly, the candidate used the radio daily to expound on the values of the bourgeoisie in the language spoken by the peasantry. Political propaganda, with a photograph of the candidate seated on the sofa in the living room of his house surrounded by his family, was placed on the exterior walls of the houses of Juchitán. How many Juchitecos have a sofa in their living room? The image is also part of the modernizing discourse . . . [de la Cruz 1984a:22–23].[38]

This is just one in an series of examples of PRI mishandling of political campaigns and candidate selection in Juchitán. Because of the heavy-handed way PRI has chosen candidates and conducted its campaigns, issues of local culture are often ignored or dealt with in a clumsy fashion. Hence, in Tarú's time the PRI ran a mayoral candidate who the opposition branded as an outsider. Similarly, in 1989 the PRI chose for their mayoral ticket an elite, non-Zapotec-speaking *norteño* who had no chance of acceptance by the majority of Juchitecos. Furthermore, PRI's emphasis on national political matters and its rhetoric and the stereotypical style of its rallies lack the appeal to Istmeños of the festive, overtly ethnic style of COCEI. While the Juchitán PRI is well-funded, it could learn a few things from COCEI about how to connect with the Juchiteco populace through lively speeches in Zapotec, culturally oriented activities, and, above all, addressing the needs of the Zapotec majority.

Despite a desperate campaign, involving public works projects and gifts to potential voters, apathy and antipathy towards the 1980 PRI candidate led many *Priístas* to abstain or even vote for COCEI (Rubin 1987a:141). Coalition voters, however, remained loyal to the movement and to their charismatic candidate, who also led urban improvement projects in the election interim. To the surprise of many, COCEI won the election—that is, the government respected COCEI's majority vote rather than disallowing it, as is normally done with non-PRI political entities—with 51 percent of the vote (3,538 to 3,330). The 1980 election ushered in a new and highly controversial period in Isthmus history (Bailón 1987:57).

The exact reasons why the government decided to allow COCEI's electoral triumph remain shrouded in mystery. One factor was undoubtedly the relative weakness of the newly elected Oaxaca state governor, Pedro Vázquez Colmenares, who wished to avoid a messy, politically dangerous, confrontation at all costs (Bailón 1987:55). Vázquez had just been installed as governor, after a lengthy residence in Mexico City, when the Juchitán situation erupted. Without a firm base among Oaxaca's commercial bourgeoisie or political elite, Vázquez was in no position to engage in a violent conflict, as the Juchitán case threatened to become should the government attempt to repress COCEI. Having used the national political opening as one of his campaign planks, Vázquez chose to invoke it at this time of crisis, declaring that "in Juchitán there were neither winners nor losers, the triumph belongs to the people of Juchitán and the Political Reform" (Bailón 1987:57). In another quirk of fate, the Oaxaca business establishment had been distracted by internal squabbles over control of the statewide Chambers of Commerce during the time of the Juchitán elections (Bailón 1987:55–56). Thus, at the time they were indisposed to pressure the governor into a repressive solution to the "Juchitán problem." Later, many conservatives would espouse just such an approach, because of their intense hatred and fear of the Marxist alternative represented by COCEI.

To summarize, because of COCEI's strength and capacity for agitation, the national left's support of the movement, divisions and weaknesses within PRI at the local and state level, and national government reforms, COCEI's electoral victory was allowed to stand (Bailón 1987:57). Thus, Juchitán became the first and only major municipality in Mexico controlled by the left. In the resultant fiesta at City Hall, *Coceístas* danced to the *zandunga* and *fandango tehuano* [regional tunes considered anthems of the Isthmus Zapotec] in front of television cameras and the national press. The scene was reminiscent of the Sandinista takeover of Managua, Nicaragua, in 1979 (*Hora Cero* 3/8/1981).[39] Despite many setbacks and against high odds, the left had finally triumphed. This is how Mariano Santana (1988:50), a COCEI leader, described the scene as the movement assumed control of the government of Juchitán:

> The people took possession of City Hall with great joy on March 10 [1981]. The streets of Juchitán were adorned with red flowers, and in the Municipal Palace the red flag of the COCEI flew at full mast. After a long road with many sacrifices and obstacles we had realized a Zapotec dream: to be the government [*ser gobierno*]. But this also represented a twofold historical challenge: (1) to meet the political aspirations of the Zapotec people with respect to their autonomy, traditions, cultural patterns, and so on within a context of class struggle and (2) to carry out this project . . . [while] immersed in a capitalist society which has only manipulated ethnic groups for its own benefit.

The Coalition called its fledgling administration the *Ayuntamiento Popular*, or People's Government[40] (as it had referred to its former parallel government) which, according to Santana (1988:46), "put into practice a form of municipal government with deep roots in Zapotec culture." COCEI leaders viewed their regime as more than simply an exercise in leftist politics; for *Coceísta* politicians and intellectuals, the *Ayuntamiento Popular* symbolized indigenous self-government, an ethnic millennium. For COCEI militants, it was as if the Zapotecs had regained control of the Isthmus for the first time since the Spanish Conquest.

Summary and Conclusions

For the past 150 years, Juchitán and the Isthmus Zapotec population have produced movements for regional and municipal autonomy, of which

COCEI is only the most recent manifestation. Historically, indigenous radical politics have been expressed in an idiom of ethnic and regional conflict that pits the Isthmus Zapotecs against the national government, Oaxaca Valley politicians, and non-Zapotec immigrants to the Isthmus. The key exponents of such ideas (Meléndez, Gurrión, Gómez, Génico, Tarú, Polo, and Polín) have been charismatic Zapotec leaders who articulated popular demands and directed opposition movements.

After the state government put down the Robles and Carrasco uprising in 1931, Juchiteco dissidents of the FRD were, for the most part, restrained by Charis, himself a former rebel. During the Charis *cacicazgo* (1932–1964), the national government laid down the infrastructure for far-reaching economic development and began to establish the PRI's power in the Isthmus. After Charis' death, Génico, Polo, and Tarú forged movements that challenged the status quo, though only Tarú was successful in taking office. Although his influence was short lived, Tarú's popularity among the poor and the peasantry, as well as with many upper-class Zapotecs, united townspeople behind a populist program and the sentiment, "Juchitán for the Juchitecos." Tarú's demise prepared the way for the emergence of a young radical group which absorbed the momentum and membership of Tarú's and Polo's movements and shaped them into a new organization, COCEI.

Inspired by revolutionaries in Cuba and Central America and toughened by the 1968 student movement, López Nelio, Sánchez, and Polín organized a close-knit coalition of peasants, workers, market women, students, and local intellectuals. Although COCEI leaders continued the tradition of charismatic Isthmus Zapotec politicians, the Coalition transcended many features of the *caciquismo* of the past and evolved into a large but well-run organization capable of mobilizing more than 10,000 people at a time.

Like previous Juchiteco ethnic movements, COCEI mobilized against external political agents, but the circumstances under which it operated were markedly different from the conditions that had prevailed during the nineteenth and early twentieth centuries—the era of the *serrano* movements. By the 1970s the Zapotec community was sharply divided by class, and a significant portion of the peasantry was in danger of losing its agricultural livelihood. Thus, COCEI's agrarianism was (and is) far more pronounced than that of earlier local movements. Also different from their predecessors, the founders of COCEI directed the popular struggle, with equal intensity, against the Zapotec elite as well as against mestizo "intruders" and government officials. This included taking control of the Juchitán cultural scene, formerly a privileged domain of upper-class Zapotecs. Overall, COCEI's political task is more complex than that of earlier movements. Today, it is not only necessary to maintain ethnic unity against outsiders, but COCEI must also combat powerful class enemies within the ethnic community. The political and cultural strategy adopted by COCEI at the time it first came to power in 1981, and still in use today, is the subject of the following chapter.

CHAPTER SIX

■■■■■■■■■■■

¡Viva Juchitán Libre!

The *"People's Government," Impeachment, and COCEI's Return to Power, 1981–1993*

On Polín's desk there is a small white bust of Lenin. The police wear
khaki-colored pants, shirt, and caps, and red bandannas around their
necks. In front of the police office there are several photos hanging from
the wall, one of them is a march with the "mosquito battalion" (a
COCEI children's group) in the lead. To one side there are several posters
demanding the presentation of people "disappeared" for political reasons.
Marx appears everywhere in memory of the 100th anniversary of his
death. In the medical dispensary . . . there is a picture of Che Guevara
[Unomásuno 5/8/1982, cited in TIS 1984:354].

A MEXICAN REPORTER DESCRIBING THE RADICAL CHIC
ENVIRONMENT OF COCEI'S PEOPLE'S GOVERNMENT

Chapter 5 analyzed COCEI's roots in previous Isthmus Zapotec movements and its difficult rise to power during the 1970s and early 1980s.
COCEI control of Juchitán City Hall did not mean that the local political
struggle was over. Indeed, the entire period (1981–1983) of COCEI's People's Government (*Ayuntamiento Popular*) was marked by violent agrarian
and labor conflicts and bloody street-fighting between *Priístas* and *Coceístas*.
This chapter examines these conflicts, as well as COCEI's ambitious Zapotec cultural program. After a discussion of the political dynamics that
led to COCEI's removal from office in 1983, the chapter focuses on how
the Coalition regrouped and returned to power in a bipartisan government
with PRI in 1986. This is followed by a discussion of COCEI's second
victory in Juchitán municipal elections in 1989, and the new conditions
under which the movement took control of City Hall.

Since the advent of the People's Government, the class divisions within Juchiteco society have been especially pronounced. At the same time that internal divisions wrack the Zapotec community, a flourishing local cultural movement has reinforced existing Juchiteco customs and created new cultural forms and meanings as well. These cultural changes are directly connected to the political transformation of Juchitán. Since COCEI took power in 1981, City Hall has no longer been the sole domain of the Zapotec elite, and the left's strength has empowered a group of bohemian Juchiteco writers and painters who have redefined the Isthmus Zapotec intellectual scene. While the future of the Isthmus cultural movement, as well as that of COCEI itself, remain an open question, it is clear that Juchitecos will continue to defend their culture and fight for local autonomy.

The Style of COCEI's People's Government

From the beginning of their administration, COCEI leaders and intellectuals linked the movement's project to the "glorious" rebellions of the Isthmus Zapotec past, while also invoking Marxist symbols and rhetoric. In his inaugural speech on March 10, 1981, Polín traced the recent Juchiteco struggle from its beginnings with Che Gómez in 1911, through the Carrasco and Robles uprising, to the victory of COCEI (de Gyves de la Cruz 1981:10–11). He described this struggle in millenarian terms as a long road traveled by the Juchitecos and fertilized with the blood of Juchitán's most worthy sons and daughters until it bore fruit with COCEI's victory. Thus, he said, the Coalition had written the most brilliant pages of Juchitán's history. After giving his talk in Spanish, Polín gave a shorter one in Zapotec.

In the Zapotec speech, he spoke of the need for *Coceístas* to stay vigilant and united. Yet Polín also said that COCEI must cooperate with Oaxaca authorities to obtain funds for improving Juchitán. This would allow the Coalition's new government to attend to the demands of poor Juchitecos.[1]

COCEI's use of Zapotec was not confined to this speech, however. Indeed, Zapotec became the language of the leftist administration, and a symbol of it, from the mayor on down to the police force. Previous PRI governments had forced the populace to speak Spanish at City Hall, thereby increasing distance between politicians and the masses, and control over them. As a COCEI intellectual put it:

> The young [COCEI] administrators begin to feel that the pressure of Zapotec is much stronger when they have municipal power. Up in City Hall, they yell, tell jokes, collect taxes, and administer justice in

Zapotec. Those who cannot speak Zapotec are unsuitable for public office [de la Cruz 1984a:23].

During the *Ayuntamiento Popular*, COCEI put up a sign in Zapotec over the entrance to Juchitán bidding travelers a safe trip (*Sicarú Guyé*). COCEI altered the urban landscape in other ways: city walls were plastered with pro-COCEI graffiti in Zapotec and Spanish, colorful murals adorned buildings, and a huge red banner with a hammer-and-sickle insignia flew over City Hall. In the streets, male *Coceístas* were identifiable by their hua-raches, long hair, and red bandannas. Female *Coceístas* wore red *huipiles* and ribbons. Horse cart drivers painted the COCEI red star on their vehicles, political street theater performances took place in front of City Hall, and beat-up pickup trucks with loudspeakers cruised through town announcing COCEI events (Zermeño 1987:69). Radios tuned to COCEI's under-ground station broadcast impassioned speeches in Zapotec by COCEI ac-tivists. COCEI neighborhood committees held weekly meetings and the movement regularly convoked festive rallies filled with ethnic symbolism at which the leadership delivered emotional discourses in the Zapotec lan-guage. These talks contained frequent references to local heroes and battles of the past. Juchitán had become the most politicized town in Mexico, and almost every aspect of local life was transformed into a battlefield for the COCEI-PRI conflict (Bailón 1987:36).[2]

Cultural Programs of the Ayuntamiento Popular

The most noteworthy accomplishments of the COCEI administration, re-flecting its overt ethnic orientation, occurred in the cultural realm. In just two years the *Ayuntamiento Popular* supported the following projects con-cerned with Zapotec culture: a public library, a bookstore, a literacy cam-paign, a radio station, schools, a publication series, and the multifaceted activities of the Casa de la Cultura. For COCEI, Isthmus Zapotec culture was both the historical foundation of Juchitán radical politics and a com-munity resource to be nurtured in the present. Likewise, Zapotec culture became a weapon utilized by left-wing painters, writers, and musicians against the PRI. This is how a Mexican intellectual described the setting for the People's Government's promotion of local culture in 1983:

> In front of City Hall, on the plaza, was a solid construction that housed the Municipal Bookstore. There one could find for sale *Guch-achi' Reza* (Sliced Iguana), a trimestral publication of the *Ayuntamiento Popular*. . . . In another format, there were about 15 publications—

reports, legends, folklore, poems, etc.—concerned with the customs, heroes, legends, wars, mythology, and history of the Juchitecos and the Zapotec people. Another editorial design, [was] . . . exclusively in Zapotec . . . near the back of the store, the poster area, many of them evoking also a romantic fundamentalism, the return to the soil, but others with contemporary themes such as one dedicated to Víctor Yodo, a popular COCEI leader kidnapped by the army since 1978 [Zermeño 1987:70].

The People's Government and the Isthmus Zapotec Renaissance

While COCEI governed between 1981 and 1983, the Zapotec language became the preferred mode of communication in all political and social activities in Juchitán. Before this time, most Juchitecos spoke the language at home and in the street, but Spanish predominated in government offices and schools. Under the COCEI regime, the public use of Zapotec became a very conscious, symbolic act of ethnic affirmation.

Felipe Martínez López, PRI mayor of Juchitán from 1986 to 1989, told me that prior to the advent of Tarú, the peasants' use of the Zapotec language was viewed by a growing number of educated Juchitecos as *muy indio* (very Indian) and a sign of the poor's inability to speak Spanish, hence a stigma. Indeed, many status-minded Isthmus parents discouraged their children from speaking the native "dialect."[3] Middle- and upper-class Juchitecos viewed Zapotec monolingualism as a symbol of backwardness and lack of formal education (Royce 1975:78; Velma Pickett interview).

Ironically, most middle- and upper-class Juchitecos also knew Zapotec, but they claimed to speak a pure form of the language superior to that of the peasants, in addition to speaking Spanish.[4] Royce (1975:78) notes that the Juchitán upper classes based their claims to cultural superiority on the fact that they could choose when to use the Zapotec language, which they generally did to emphasize selectively and embellish upon ethnic symbolism (since they could also speak Spanish, and they employed Mexican national symbols with equal facility), whereas the lower classes had no other option but the native language and customs. For example, poor Zapotec women could only afford to wear simple, inexpensive *huipiles* and *enaguas*, with no gold jewelry, while rich Zapotec women could wear either expensive regional costumes loaded with gold or fancy, new, Western-style dresses. Thus, according to Martínez, it was only the upper classes who glorified Zapotec culture with the conscious elaboration of the Zapotec language, indigenous clothing, and local customs in certain ceremonial contexts.[5] They were the ones who wrote passionate Zapotec poems, founded *Neza*, and threw the lavish *velas* in which mountains of fried fish and stewed iguana were washed down with beer and liquor, and it was their women who wore the extravagant *huipiles, enaguas*, and gold necklaces worth a small fortune.

COCEI, whose leaders and rank-and-file came from the peasantry, working class, and lower middle class, reversed this trend. While COCEI governed, the Zapotec language became the most important symbol of grassroots political radicalism and the ethnic pride of the lower and middle classes. Style-conscious *Coceístas* gave their babies names like *guie'xhuuba'* (jasmine) and *sicabi* (like the wind), which had formerly been mostly an upper-class habit.[6] COCEI members who were not fluent in the language clandestinely studied it in order to save face. COCEI demonstrations became showcases for Zapotec ethnic style and oratory. These elaborate events became a kind of ethnopolitical performance providing an outlet for the *Coceístas'* ethnic fervor and the expression of a ritual elegance that had previously been available only to the rich through their *velas*. Now, however, it was the Zapotec poor and middle sectors who celebrated their ethnic identity in the Juchitán streets, park, and plaza in front of City Hall.

Zapotec Style in COCEI Demonstrations

Well-organized yet uninhibited, COCEI demonstrations would begin at the approximately 17 neighborhood committee headquarters where COCEI supporters met. There, COCEI representatives, adopting the roles of the *mayordomos* of Isthmus fiestas, would distribute flags, red confetti, and beverages. When the neighborhood *Coceístas* would arrive, the large, rowdy groups would march through Juchitán's dusty streets chanting political slogans and waving COCEI banners until they reached the Coalition's main office. These marches were patterned after the funeral, wedding, and religious processions that punctuated everyday Isthmus life.

COCEI-style demonstrations continue to be an important vehicle for Zapotec cultural expression. *Coceístas* of all ages participate. As in processions, men and women are segregated, and women wear their elegant regional costumes in bright red COCEI colors, complemented by gleaming gold jewelry and red flowers in their hair. Young boys wearing masks (*mbiooxho*) dance in the streets, while the women's committee raises its banner, followed by the smaller banner of the Mosquito Squadron composed of COCEI children. Local brass bands or teenagers playing the traditional bamboo flute, small drum, and turtle shell animate the marchers with lively tunes during their march through town.

On special occasions, such as the closing of an election campaign, ox-drawn carts decorated with banana leaves, sugar cane, palm stalks, and flowers have been used to carry COCEI supporters in imitation of the *convite de flores* processions that initiate *velas*. During these raucous rallies, *Coceístas* laugh at Zapotec jokes and shout "¡*Viva la COCEI!*" (Long live COCEI!) or "¡*Muera PRIhuela!*" (Death to the old, worn-out PRI!).[7] The Juchitán neighborhood committees and contingents from other Isthmus towns arrive one-by-one to the COCEI headquarters in the center of town. Cattle trucks loaded with Coalition peasants also push their way through the crowded streets. Each arriving group is greeted by ¡*vivas!*, applause, firecrackers, and bottle rockets as at the end of weddings or mass. Loud-speaker announcements drone and the bands play *dianas*. As the different contingents blend into the communitas of the red-clad COCEI crowd, a speaker warms up the audience with stories of local history. Zapotec women work their way through the crowd, pouring red confetti on people's hair, as in fiestas, to indicate attendance.

After another spirited march through town, the large COCEI following reassembles in front of City Hall. The COCEI leaders and visiting dignitaries emerge with long *guie'chaachi* wreaths and red bandannas around their necks. They mount the improvised stage to a rousing ovation. Invariably, the first words of their speech will be *paisanuca* (my fellow countrymen), *binni laanu* (our people), or *binni xquidxinu* (people of our town),[8] which instantly identifies them with the crowd. COCEI leaders are charismatic figures who specialize in rousing Zapotec oratory interspersed with elegant hand gestures, pumping fists, and bravado. For example, in 1981 at the *Ayuntamiento Popular's* first "state of the union" address in front of the Juchitán municipal building, Enedino Jiménez spoke passionately in Zapotec about how at the beginning of their struggle the *Coceístas* had dreamed of occupying City Hall, and "Now we are here!," he exulted, to roars of applause from the COCEI crowd.[9]

Ribald humor is also a key element of Coalition political speeches. For instance, at the final COCEI rally of the 1989 mayoral campaign, a Coalition leader joked that the divided local PRI resembled the (supposedly) sparse pubic hair of Mixe women: one going this way, one going that way.[10] During the 1986 campaign, Polín cracked that if City Hall were a person it would let loose a big sneeze, sending the *Priístas* who occupied it straight to hell![11] The names of PRI politicians are also the brunt of derisive wordplay, such as the 1989 PRI mayoral candidate Ramón Caraveo who became "*Carafeo*" (ugly face), or Carlos Salinas de Gortari, who in 1988 was labeled Salinas de "*Gueutari*" ("*gueu*" is Zapotec slang for homosexual).[12] Additionally, in a reversal of the epithet traditionally hurled at Juchitecos by other Istmeños (*Teco gubaana'buey*, Juchiteco cattle thief), COCEI orators sometimes refer to local PRI administrations or the Oaxaca state government as *ti gobiernu gubaana'* (a thieving government). Finally, the gay PRI mayor who took over Juchitán City Hall after the ouster of COCEI in 1983 is still trying to shake off the unwanted nickname, "the Caramel Princess", given him by *Coceístas*.

COCEI crowds respond enthusiastically to these picaresque jokes, which unite movement supporters against their enemies. Jokes also relieve the tension that builds to a crescendo as the Coalition leadership expounds on their current political objectives, which they invariably link to Binu Gada, Che Gómez, and other dead Zapotec heroes. The speeches explicitly frame COCEI politics as an ethnic and regional struggle against Oaxaca Valley politicians and the national government, and recall the illustrious battles of the past. The microspecific local references and Isthmus Zapotec idioms contained in the speeches are incomprehensible to outsiders, who are excluded de facto from the COCEI discourse.

The contrast between the flamboyant, provincial COCEI speakers and the serious, philosophical leaders of the national left, such as Heberto Castillo and Cuauthémoc Cárdenas, is instructive. Whereas the latter politicians bore COCEI crowds—already tired from the obligatory predemonstration march through town and hours of standing in the scorching Isthmus sun, the COCEI leaders are well attuned to the pulse of the Juchitecos. They keep their followers amused with humor, audacious comments, and culturally specific anecdotes. Because of all the pageantry, COCEI rallies assume the atmosphere of a popular fiesta at which the political agenda of the movement is ritually celebrated. Moreover, COCEI demonstrations often end with the participants convening en masse to a local fiesta.[13]

The Casa de la Cultura and COCEI

Since its founding in 1972, the Casa de la Cultura has been the center of an Isthmus Zapotec cultural revival led by the Juchiteco intellectuals. Building on the efforts of the earlier *Neza* generation, the Casa intellectuals study, promote, and disseminate Isthmus Zapotec culture and history. The Casa has also been a bastion of COCEI ideological support and pro-COCEI cultural productions.

Prior to the People's Government, the Casa de la Cultura published a few booklets of poetry and encouraged local artists, but when COCEI took control of City Hall, the movement had unprecedented access to resources and funding, which it exploited to the fullest. Moreover, the volatile political atmosphere of Juchitán between 1981 and 1983, and the COCEI administrations' ties to national leftists and urban intellectuals injected new life into the local cultural movement. During this period, the Casa conducted classes on Zapotec poetry, autochthonous music, and Zapotec language; and held workshops devoted to drawing, painting, dance, photography, and piano. In addition to these activities, the Casa was the site of political lectures, poetry conferences, films, photography expositions, and art exhibitions, often with a marked anti-PRI bent. The Casa's photography salon displayed pictures of COCEI marches and ethnographic photos of Isthmus life by famous Mexican and foreign photographers as well as local camera aficionados. Its modern art gallery displayed a permanent collection of paintings by Tamayo, Toledo, Cuevas, and Posada, and pieces by Max Ernst and other European artists.

An indication of the quality of the Casa de la Cultura's art collection is the fact that, in a rare turnabout, the artwork was loaned for an exposition in Mexico City. Normally, "high culture" in Mexico emanates out from the capital to the provinces. Of course, none of this would have been possible without Francisco Toledo's connections with world-famous artists in Mexico City, Europe, and the United States.

The remarkable range and sophistication of the Casa's programs, for an institution located in an impoverished rural region, are possible, in large part, because of the financial largess[14] of Toledo and the constant backing of COCEI. These efforts are highly politicized because PRI has tried to wrest control of this key cultural institution from the largely pro-COCEI artistic community. The Casa's role in Juchitán political combat emerged in the mid-1970s, as COCEI grew in strength. In 1975, Amira Musalem, a PRI sympathizer, was deposed as director of the Casa by Toledo for allowing government soldiers to use the building for a staging ground in anti-COCEI repression.[15] Víctor de la Cruz subsequently replaced Musalem as the director of the Casa and founded the journal *Guchachi' Reza*.

Juchitán political struggles continued to affect the Casa in 1976, when the building was vandalized and de la Cruz was harassed by *Priístas*. In 1977, de la Cruz resigned as director, and in 1979 Macario Matus took charge of the institution. In 1980, during the political campaign of governor Pedro Vázquez C., *Priístas* attacked the Casa as a "bunker" of COCEI. When voter registration took place there in 1981, the PRI cried foul and charged Matus with vote fraud and threatened his life. *Priístas* also attempted to have Matus replaced as director of the Casa, but this move was squelched by timely support from Toledo and his gang of artistic friends, who occupied the Casa de la Cultura until Matus was reinstated. Finally, with COCEI in control of Juchitán from 1981–1983, the Casa indeed became a Coalition stronghold as well as a bohemian hang-out. It was at this time that the politics and programs of COCEI and the Casa began to overlap.[16]

Zapotec Art, Literature, and Historiography
During the Ayuntamiento Popular

With the support of the *Ayuntamiento Popular*, the Juchiteco intellectual movement produced significant works of art, poetry, and local history. Toledo led the way with his wide repertoire of paintings, drawings, and sculptures. Toledo's *oeuvre* is saturated with Isthmus flora and fauna, imbued with key imagery and symbolism of rural Zapotec life, and nurtured by the imagination and fantasy of Zapotec folklore and mythology.[17] One of his biggest artistic successes—inspired by COCEI's People's Government—consisted of a 49-piece show demystifying Mexican national hero Benito Juárez and juxtaposing the official history of Juárez with a Juchitán-based view (Toledo 1986). This perspective, linked to COCEI's version of Isthmus history, emphasizes the burning of Juchitán by Juárez's soldiers. The pro-COCEI cadre of young Isthmus artists who follow Toledo also paint political themes, such as key moments in COCEI history or Coalition symbolism. In addition, many of them utilized their skills to promote the Coalition directly during the *Ayuntamiento Popular*, in wall murals, multi-colored street graffiti, and political banners. More recently, Zapotec artists have painted pro-COCEI murals with ethnic imagery (such as red COCEI flags in the form of Juchiteca *huipiles*) on the houses of the movement's two land-invasion communities.

The contemporary literary movement in Juchitán was also fueled by COCEI struggles, and the new generation of Isthmus Zapotec writers are key Coalition supporters.[18] The poetry of Matus, de la Cruz, Alejandro Cruz, and Enedino Jiménez focuses on the rise of COCEI, Isthmus Zapotec culture, and the martyrdom of *Coceístas* (de la Cruz 1983b). In addition to the four major poets, a young crop of Juchiteco bards emerged during the *Ayuntamiento Popular*. Being a radical poet or artist has its risks, however. Right-wing thugs constantly hassled Matus when he was director of the Casa, a PRI mob assaulted de la Cruz and Toledo in 1983, and PRI members murdered Cruz in 1987. PRI members have also tried to discredit Matus with homophobic attacks and Toledo with charges that the graphic sexuality displayed in his paintings (e.g., sex between different animal species or between humans and animals) is immoral (Santana 1988:65).

Key elements in the *Ayuntamiento Popular's* cultural program were recuperation of local oral, musical, and written traditions, research on history and mythology, the translation of famous poems and literature into Zapotec, and the production of original Zapotec or Spanish-language works focused on regional themes. During the COCEI administration, local writers published dozens of books and pamphlets. These included a collection of Isthmus *corridos*, an anthology of writings by Isthmus Zapotec intellectuals, several volumes of poetry, a Zapotec-Spanish dictionary, and a collection of vintage portraits by an early-twentieth-century Juchiteco photographer.

Another major editorial accomplishment of the first COCEI administration was the publication of *H. Ayuntamiento Popular* (Doniz 1983), which consists of a chronicle of COCEI political events by Carlos Monsiváis (one of Mexico's best-known modern authors) and ethnographic photography by Rafael Doniz. Doniz's striking photographs deal with significant occurrences during the *Ayuntamiento Popular*, characteristic Zapotec social activities, and panoramas of the Isthmus. This book and *Guchachi' Reza* disseminated information about COCEI to intellectual circles in urban Mexico and abroad. Several albums of Isthmus music, recorded with the help of the Casa de la Cultura, also attracted attention to the Zapotec cultural/political movement.

Guchachi' Reza:
Juchiteco Localism and the International Art and Literary World

The best-known publication of the People's Government was *Guchachi' Reza*, published earlier by de la Cruz but without city government funding. Heir to the traditions of *Neza* and *Neza Cubi, Guchachi' Reza* takes its name from a popular song. It was an appropriate choice, since the *guchachi'* (iguana) is a prized delicacy in the Isthmus, a kind of totem for the Zapotecs, and a symbol of resistance to harsh conditions.[19] While COCEI governed Juchitán, this remarkable multigenre magazine was designed by Mexico's best graphic artists, and adorned with Toledo's art, the works of young Juchiteco painters, and colorful photographs of Zapotec life. In addition, each issue of *Guchachi' Reza* included a rich mix of poetry in Zapotec and Spanish, folklore, historical documents relevant to Juchitán, COCEI political statements, social science analyses, and other material concerned with Isthmus Zapotec culture.

The pastiche format of *Guchachi' Reza* resembles that of *Neza* and *Neza Cubi*. However, it is far more heterogeneous (including many items by non-Zapotec intellectuals and artists), emphatically avant garde, and polemically anti-PRI. Examples of avant garde material in *Guchachi' Reza* include drawings by José Luis Cuevas of stylized bourgeois men masturbating and urinating, drawings and paintings of inter-species erotica, and surrealistic poems. Both reflective and self-reflective, the magazine often publishes articles, essays, and historical documents about the Zapotecs written by non-Istmeños, then critiques these representations of Zapotec life or incorporates more favorable outside perspectives into its internal discourse. In the process, the Zapotec intellectuals subvert the external discourse about Juchitán, while enriching their own self-representations.

Guchachi' Reza, like the paintings of Toledo, is fashionable despite its relatively humble origins. The translation of Brecht and Neruda into Zapotec reflects the Juchiteco writers' awareness of trends in radical literature (see, e.g., *Guchachi' Reza* no. 13, 1982; *Guchachi' Reza* no. 24, 1985). In fact, *Guchachi' Reza's* readers are more likely to be gringo anthropologists or urban Mexicans than Zapotec peasants. Nonetheless, COCEI's opponents were so convinced of the magazine's subversive potential that they burned it and parts of the COCEI-created library of Juchitán after they crushed the *Ayuntamiento Popular* (de la Cruz 1984a).

Guchachi' Reza's juxtaposition of drawings and paintings by famous Mexican artists with poetry and artwork by Juchiteco intellectuals is indicative of the eclectic nature of the Zapotec cultural movement. In addition to presenting Zapotec translations of works by famous European poets, the magazine has also published Spanish versions of writings about the Zapotecs by foreign intellectuals (e.g., Edward Weston, D. H. Lawrence, Paul Radin, Desiré Charnay). Although the magazine's overriding concern is local cultural expression and history, its form and content make clear that the COCEI intellectuals consider Zapotec culture on a par with that of European societies. Moreover, they see no inherent contradiction between the Juchitecos' intense localism and global trends in the art and literary worlds, which they appropriate for their own purposes.

The excellent technical quality of *Guchachi' Reza* (to my knowledge there is no comparable publication in rural Mesoamerica) was made possible by the contributions of Toledo's friends in the Mexican artistic elite, and influential intellectuals who supported COCEI for ideological reasons. Indeed, COCEI became a cause célèbre, which attracted anthropologists, journalists, and artists from around the world to Juchitán during the last months of the People's Government. Thus, Juchitán City Hall and the Casa de la Cultura became major stops for foreign artists, urban intellectuals, and social scientists passing through southern Mexico, along with more familiar sites on "the gringo trail" such as Palenque, San Cristóbal, and Puerto Escondido.

This was not the first time that Juchitán had appealed to such outsiders. In the 1920s and 1930s, Covarrubias, Diego Rivera, and Frida Kahlo came many times to the Isthmus to paint exotic scenes of Zapotec women, Isthmus flora and fauna, and local life. At about the same time, Eisenstein— impressed by "the fantastic structure of pre-logical, sensual thinking" he found in the Mexican tropics—filmed parts of a movie in Juchitán and San Blas (Richardson 1988:170). I have also noted the many intellectuals brought to the region by Henestrosa.[20]

What is important about these visits is their impact on local intellectual life. The Juchitecos' contact with Polish and French anthropologists, Australian and U.S. journalists, Japanese painters, and Chicano radicals publicized COCEI's activities and provided *Coceístas* with otherwise inaccessible forums for their ideas. The *Coceístas'* ties with famous Mexican intellectuals such as Elena Poniatowska, Carlos Monsiváis, and Arturo Warman shielded the Coalition, to a degree, from extreme government repression and gave it powerful spokespeople in the nation's capital. Moreover, Juchitán's connections to the national and international intellectual world and the left intelligentsia provided multiple outside influences on Zapotec intellectuals and artists, and helped Juchiteco painters gain access to more lucrative markets for their works.[21] In so doing, the COCEI intellectuals were able to bypass the bourgeois cultural establishment, which was hostile to their leftist political views and iconoclastic style. Because of Juchitán's political visibility and COCEI's ties to leftist power brokers in Mexico City, several Juchitecos even obtained scholarships to study in Eastern Europe. What distinguishes Juchitán from many other Mesoamerican rural communities is that these interactions with outsiders, rather than eroding indigenous culture, stimulated it and provided the raw material for new ethnic self-definitions and cultural productions on the Isthmus Zapotecs' own terms.[22]

Juchiteco Bohemians and Isthmus Cantinas

Isthmus cantinas are one of the key arenas for social interaction among Zapotec men (analogous to the women's social sphere in the Juchiteco market) and the main hangout of the Juchiteco bohemian intellectuals.

Although the word *cantina* may conjure up images of third-rate Western movies, COCEI intellectuals have cultivated them into a kind of provincial "cafe society." Thus, cantinas were a key site of cultural production during the *Ayuntamiento Popular*. Isthmus bohemian cantina life has a long history, which goes back at least to the days of the romantic musicians Jesús (Chu) Rasgado and Saúl Martínez (ca. 1900–1950s) and the *indigenista* poets of the *Neza* generation (1930s–1940s). The *Neza* literati, though, primarily frequented Juchitán cantinas while on vacations from their jobs in Mexico City or during the fiesta season.

Many of the current generation of Juchiteco intellectuals, likewise, first took part in cantina life when they came home to Juchitán during periods when their university classes were in recess. With the advent of COCEI, however, most young Juchitán intellectuals and activists returned permanently to their hometown. There, in addition to agitating for political change, they focused their energies on reviving and recreating Isthmus cultural traditions. One aspect of this process was active involvement in the cantina social world.

While the primary reason Isthmus men go to cantinas is simply to get drunk and have a good time, cantinas are also the setting for complex social interactions that may include making business deals, establishing political alliances, strengthening social ties, and exchanging gossip. In general, although worldly affairs are often transacted in Juchitán cantinas, the cantina experience mainly serves as a kind of time-out period or escape from the daily routine, in which Zapotec men can "let their hair down." Cantinas are thus an ideal spot for cultivation of the aesthetic or romantic side of life: engaging in philosophical discussions, telling jokes and lies, transmitting oral traditions and folklore, playing guitars, singing songs, and reciting poems. These are some of the main activities of the Zapotec bohemians.

In Juchitán bars open in the early afternoon and quickly fill up because the prime drinking hours in the Isthmus are during the day rather than at night as in the United States. Local peasants do most of their work during the cooler morning hours and are often free in the hot afternoons. The more popular cantinas attract an eclectic mix of peasants wearing red bandannas, huaraches, and rough work clothes; businessmen and professionals in *guayaberas* (an elegant type of shirt made in Yucatán), slacks, and dress shoes; workingmen; and poets, artists, and COCEI activists dressed like the peasants. At such cantinas, men of all strata of Zapotec society socialize freely in an atmosphere of alcohol-lubricated camaraderie, and engage in playful insults and double-entendre word play. Fights inevitably occur from time to time also.

An outsider entering La Flor de Cheguigo, a drab two-room, brick building, might not consider it a spot where much intellectual activity goes on. As he weaved past shouting drunks, small metal tables covered with beer bottles, plates of shrimp, and turtle eggs, and groups of men laughing and arguing—if he stayed for awhile—he might notice some interesting things happening. For example, some of the scruffy-looking types at one of the tables might have with them hand-written drafts of their own poetry, a copy of *Guchachi' Reza*, or a beat-up portfolio crammed with their recent watercolor paintings. If our proverbial outsider could forget about the garish posters of voluptuous blond gringas on the wall and the strong smell of urine wafting from a nearby cement trough, he might realize that in addition to the ritualized verbal jousting and endless joking, the bohemians would also be discussing their favorite poets, fine points of local history, and COCEI political strategy.

The atmosphere in the trendy Bar Jardín is more obviously arty, with large, bright paintings by the Juchiteco artists hanging from the walls and Zapotec songs blowing from a small stereo. Several other Juchitán bars are also frequented by the local art crowd, such as those around the old COCEI office on Adolfo C. Gurrión Street. Additionally, a COCEI leader created a combined cantina/restaurant (Ra Bache'za') which also serves as an art gallery. He has plans to create space in the building for a bookstore and a small school, where local kids with aptitudes in science and math will be able to study those subjects in the Zapotec language.

On any given day of the week, the bohemian drinking crowd at La Flor de Cheguigo, Los Tulipanes, the Bar Jardín, or similar establishments might include Israel Vicente, who has displayed his innovative paintings on stone slabs in an art show in San Francisco, California; Víctor Orozco, a talented wood sculptor and painter whose works are sold in a gallery in Mexico City's exclusive Pink Zone; or Miguel Angel Toledo, a student of Francisco Toledo, whose brightly colored, surrealistic canvases of Isthmus animals and erotica sell for hundreds of thousands of pesos. Other Juchiteco bohemians possibly on the scene could be Víctor de la Cruz, editor of *Guchachi' Reza*, author of numerous poems in Spanish and Zapotec, some of which have been published in the *Taos Review*, and author of many studies of Isthmus culture and history; or (prior to his death) Alejandro Cruz, a poet who captured Zapotec folk customs and the idiosyncrasies of everyday Isthmus life in his romantic and politically engaged verse. Until recently, the ringleader of this group of drunken aesthetes would have been Macario Matus, a consummate Isthmus joketeller, poet, chronicler of Juchiteco history, and director of the Casa de la Cultura, until he resigned and left Juchitán in 1989.

Excerpts from my fieldnotes from an afternoon I spent in February 1988 with a group of Coalition activists and intellectuals may help illustrate the cultural processes that take place in Juchiteco bohemian cantinas, as well as their distinctive atmosphere. On this occasion, we were in La Mixtequita, a small bar located next door to what was then the COCEI office. La Mixtequita is housed in an old-style Isthmus home, which has a high-peaked ceiling formed by large wooden beams and stuccoed brick walls painted a bright green color. The bar area consists of one large rectangular room. Against one wall is a small wooden counter, cases of beer stacked on top of each other, a metal cooler loaded with ice and beer bottles, and a small stove for preparing *botanas* (bar snacks). Against the opposite wall is a large jukebox, often turned up to full volume. The barroom contains about 10 small square tables surrounded by wooden chairs. This area is separated from the toilet and urinal troughs by a thin concrete partition.

I am quoting from fieldnotes dated 2/23/88 (the brackets contain clarifying statements derived from my fieldnotes):

> At about 3 PM we wandered over to the La Mixtequita bar and drank with Polo, Dionisio [Hernández], Vallejo, Che Toledo, and Deyo. . . . Obdulia [the anthropologist's spouse] was the only woman in the cantina besides the waitress, although no one seemed to care. There was a steady stream in and out of young girls selling turtle eggs [4,000 pesos/dozen], empanadas, and peanuts. The turtle eggs are brought in from the Huave area and sold hot in the bars. These ping pong ball-like objects are eaten with salt and lime juice and are delicious. People were drinking mostly *caguamas* [liter bottles] which rapidly accumulated on the tables. They were used as an accounting system of how much a person had drunk and hence remained on the table until there was little space, at which time a box was brought to collect a few bottles and make space for more . . .
>
> Guitarists strolled in and played tunes and sang in Zapotec. The cantina was also filled with the loud talking of the all-male clientele and the occasional banging on the metal tables to call for more beer. . . .
>
> Polo told a story of how when the 13th battalion [made up of Zapotec men led by Charis] went to a town in Michoacán during the Cristero Wars, the Juchiteco soldiers grabbed [and ate] every iguana in sight [these animals were abundant in the town] until it was bereft of iguanas. . . . Deyo drunkenly sang a song in Zapotec. . . . Che Toledo called Dionisio the *poeta sandiísta* because he grows

watermelons [while Dionisio recited lines of poetry, told jokes, and *mentiras*].

[While all of this was going on, Che Toledo discussed COCEI's political ideology, which he defined as "leftist" and "Marxist but not Communist," and noted that in earlier times the Zapotec had a kind of primitive communism of sharing and *tequios*, something which COCEI tries to revive, he said. Polo talked about how compelling Zapotec social ties are and how vitally important it is for Juchitecos to comply with the social obligations of the fiesta system. Dionisio spoke about the history of the Isthmus and told folktales. Other drinking companions described and lamented the death of COCEI poet Alejandro Cruz, while Che Toledo talked about the origins of the Isthmus cultural scene. He pointed out that in the Isthmus it is very common for the children of peasants to be given guitars, thus many youth learn to play music from a young age. The conversation subsided as "Pancho Tina" entered the cantina.]

While we were drinking and carrying on, "Pancho Tina," or "*Unión Latina*," appeared on the scene. This man from Unión Hidalgo plays an instrument he designed himself, which consists of an upside-down wash tub with a nylon cord running up through the center of it which is strummed like a bass fiddle and also has a deep throbbing sound like a bass. This sound is combined with the shaking of maracas, his mouth-harp playing, and his goofy singing. *Unión Latina* has a vast repertoire of local/traditional songs, which he sings in Zapotec and Spanish, as well as *cumbias, música tropical*, and the like, which he actually plays rather convincingly with a lot of funky body motion, musical nuances, and rhythm. His occasional comic interjections during the songs as well as his "*comerciales*" [jokes, literally commercials] in between songs, add to the overall effect of his performance.

We were told that *Unión Latina* had been on television and indeed he is a remarkable performer. Today he earned 12,000 pesos and 3 beers for about 1 hours work. *Unión Latina* is also the name of a [well-known] musical group, but Pancho [actually] takes this name from his residence in Unión Hidalgo coupled with his vocation of playing *la tina* [washtub]. The name *Unión Latina* is painted on his tub. He can also play tunes by blowing on the mouth of a beer bottle.

While it is difficult to recreate the complex goings-on of Isthmus cantinas, the above description provides insights into the cultural forums Juchitán cantinas have become. For COCEI intellectuals they are places to test their political ideas, read poems, give musical performances, learn about local history, and recite folklore. Not only is Juchiteco culture passed on and reproduced in cantinas, at times new songs, folklore, poems, and other artistic products are created there. Thus, along with the Casa de la Cultura and the workshops of local artists, cantinas have become key settings for the COCEI intellectuals, who created their own dynamic local cultural movement that flourished during the People's Government.[23]

XEAP: Radio Ayuntamiento Popular

Perhaps the most daring cultural project of COCEI's People's Government was the formation of a radio station, XEAP or *Radio Ayuntamiento Popular*, which (in January 1983) became the only station controlled by the left in Mexico, and the only one to broadcast full-time in both Spanish and an indigenous language (Alfaro Sánchez 1984; Bailón 1987:16). Although the Mexican Communications Ministry (SCT) denied XEAP permission to broadcast—despite the radio station's compliance with existing regulations—COCEI defied the ban and put its station on the air anyway (López Mateos 1988:18). On a clear day, the station could be heard in all major Isthmus towns.

XEAP's schedule consisted of 15 hours per day of programming, much of it in Zapotec and directed toward the poor and the peasantry (who also participated as announcers). Key programs included "*Igudxa*" (fertile land), also known as "the peasant hour," which gave technical advice about fertilizers and planting and discussed COCEI's agrarian struggles; "Minimum Wage," an hour devoted to matters of relevance to rural and urban workers; and an innovative children's program run by children (López Mateos 1988:18; Alfaro Sánchez 1984:171). The Casa de la Cultura also played a role in XEAP, with programming including Zapotec language classes, readings from *Guchachi' Reza*, poetry, news, and music. Whereas a local monopoly of radio stations run by Zapotec multimillionaire Humberto López Lena specialized in the denatured pop music of Menudo and the pro-government news of the Televisa network, XEAP featured indigenous culture and transmitted COCEI propaganda (Alfaro Sánchez 1984:214). The Coalition used its radio station to broadcast the political business of its neighborhood committees and allied nearby villages, and to call *Coceístas* to City Hall to protect it from assault by police and soldiers after the government impeached COCEI's administration.

Given high rates of illiteracy, the continuing importance of oral tradition, relatively few televisions, and poor circulation of newspapers, radio is presently the key mass medium in the Isthmus.[24] COCEI's shrewd use of radio communication paid dividends as it attracted many listeners and further legitimized the leftist government. However, XEAP programs teaching workers their rights, and the inflammatory Marxist rhetoric of several announcers, quickly annoyed powerful local and state-level interests, who lobbied for the closing of XEAP. Using the station's lack of federal permission to broadcast as justification, the SCT began jamming XEAP transmissions. COCEI responded by moving its transmitters from place to place to avoid interference and conducting sit-ins, marches, hunger strikes, and other protests in Mexico City and elsewhere (Alfaro Sánchez 1984:174–79). These actions were ultimately to no avail, as XEAP was totally drowned out by government static in November 1983 and the station's equipment confiscated in December (Alfaro Sánchez 1984:211).

Despite opposition from PRI and the Mexican government, the *Ayuntamiento Popular* transcended the narrowly political field and became a wide-ranging cultural movement. In addition to the cultural programs mentioned above, COCEI established a high school (*Prepa Popular*) and a teacher's college (*Escuela Normal Superior del Istmo*),[25] and conducted a two-year literacy campaign begun simultaneously with one run by the Sandinista regime in Nicaragua (Santana 1988:54). Perhaps more important than any specific program of the administration was the interest and pride in Isthmus Zapotec culture that COCEI and the Casa de la Cultura sparked among the general population. Consequently, large numbers of Juchitecos began to compose ballads and poems in honor of COCEI martyrs, revive disappearing arts and crafts, collect oral histories, write their memoirs, and improve their ability to speak Zapotec. Additionally, Juchitán became a town where 19-year-old indigenous youths discussed political philosophy and new trends in the art world as well as details of their own historical and cultural traditions.

Agrarian Struggles During the Ayuntamiento Popular: *The COCEI Peasantry*

Promoting Zapotec culture was not the *Ayuntamiento Popular's* only concern. However, making progress on the bread-and-butter issues of Juchitán life was a far more difficult task than publishing poetry books. Improving conditions for the peasantry—the majority of COCEI's constituency—was an especially problematic matter, although some advances were achieved during the *Ayuntamiento Popular*.

Peasant support for COCEI came from the landless and poorest landed

peasants (those with less than 5 ha) of Juchitán and several other communities such as Alvaro Obregón that were engaged in struggles over communal land (Martínez López 1985:69).[26] PRI peasants, a much smaller
group, were typically the "rich" peasants of Juchitán (i.e., those with more
than 5 ha) and the poor and middle peasants (those with around 5 ha) of
Juchitán's annexes (especially La Venta, La Ventosa, and Chicapa de Castro) with a tradition of private property ownership (Martínez López 1985).
Whereas PRI peasants tended to be less political because their major demands had been met, COCEI peasants were highly politicized from numerous clashes with the government and represented the "most explosive
sector of society" (Martínez López 1985:128).

Because of the agrarian bureaucracy's unwillingness to resolve long-
standing disputes, land invasions and mass mobilizations were COCEI's
principal recourse for regaining land. COCEI viewed invasions as legitimate attempts to recuperate communal territory. Large landowners saw
them as illegal encroachments on property rights that warranted harsh
responses. During the *Ayuntamiento Popular*, COCEI invaded agricultural
land in Comitancillo, Santo Domingo Ingenio, La Ventosa, San Francisco
del Mar, Ixhuatán, and Reforma de Pineda. COCEI also consolidated its
control over land in the Alvaro Obregón area (Santana 1988). In the most
well-known case, COCEI peasants occupied 280 ha near La Ventosa
owned by Pedro G. Roncaglia, a wealthy Spaniard (Toledo and de la Cruz
1983). The government sent state police to evict the squatters. When *Coceístas* arrived at the scene, gangs of *Priístas* assaulted them, resulting in
several injuries and destruction of a pick-up truck of the *Ayuntamiento Popular* (Bailón 1987:45). The police did nothing to prevent the attacks. In
another incident, 55 COCEI peasants occupying hectares in Santa Cruz
Montecillo (led by Elizabeth Orozco, a Zapotec woman) were attacked at
gunpoint by PRI ranchers and *pistoleros*, producing numerous injuries and
the recovery of land by the *Priístas* (*Hora Cero* 5/11/1983; interviews).

As the above examples illustrate, COCEI attempts to regain lost land
were frequently met by violence and eviction. In other cases, large landowners used legal injunctions to protect invaded lands, which resulted in
COCEI withdrawing to await drawn-out litigation (COCEI 1983). Meanwhile, the disputed lands remained idle. Overall, COCEI was able to recapture only a small portion of the land it claimed was stolen from poor
peasants by large landowners. COCEI was successful, however, in organizing peasants and pressuring for large amounts of agricultural credit or
healthy crop insurance settlements from the government. A portion of
these monies was used to fund the movement's operations.[27]

COCEI's efforts to formally organize the Isthmus peasantry during the 1981–1983 period began with sponsorship of the fourth national meeting of the *Coordinadora Nacional "Plan de Ayala"* (CNPA). Unfortunately for COCEI, the participants in this meeting were hesitant and divided, and little came of the event (Prieto 1986:86). Although the Coalition's 1981 meeting with national peasant organizations was inconclusive, in 1983 it held a regional encounter of Isthmus peasants which brought results. From this encounter emerged the *Unión Campesina Regional del Istmo* (UCRI), a COCEI affiliate composed of peasants from 20 towns and 32 solidary groups. The group has become a powerful force in local agrarian politics (Santana 1988:32). COCEI also participated in several statewide peasant organizations (MORCEO and CCOEZ).[28]

COCEI's other successes on the peasant front derived from numerous seizures of government buildings and protest marches to Oaxaca and Tehuantepec. In the most famous of these marches (February 13–21, 1983), 700 COCEI peasants hiked 270 km from Juchitán to Oaxaca despite harassment from state police (Bailón 1987:17). Although this grueling maneuver forced the government to negotiate COCEI peasant demands, its political impact transcended any material benefits that were obtained. Not only did COCEI demonstrate its ability to outmaneuver the state government, but it accomplished an even rarer feat in Mexican politics—it united the national left. In Mexico City COCEI's march was supported by academic, labor, political, and artistic organizations. Bailón (1987:18) notes that "the Juchiteco movement succeeded, as on few occasions in the capital, in putting in the same bag: radical anarchists, socialists, artists, and progressive intellectuals, in short, the entire formless gamut that still constitutes the left in Mexico."

Pictures of the COCEI march—of red-clad peasants, women wearing *huipiles*, children, and elderly Zapotecs marching up the Pan American Highway to Oaxaca—appeared in national newspapers, magazines, posters, and books. Even though COCEI peasants failed to regain most of Juchitán's communal lands, they had become a cause célèbre with powerful backing in Mexico City. Juchitán's growing fame as the only socialist municipality in Mexico, along with its "Indian" image, attracted numerous radical students, dissident intellectuals, bohemian artists, and just plain hangers-on to the town. Many of these individuals decided to stay and write their theses or an article about the town, while others just hung out at the Casa de la Cultura. Still others lent a hand with the daily tasks of maintaining COCEI's organization and administering local affairs. While the Coalition is ultimately responsible for any successes the People's Government may have had, it helped to have support from well-connected outsiders who defended COCEI's image against hostile propaganda from the pro-government Mexican news media.

COCEI and Labor During the Ayuntamiento Popular

According to Zermeño (1987:94–95), COCEI's links with the working class are completely irrelevant because "without the reference to the land, to the past, to the cultural heritage, there is no COCEI. . . . Its bases are the peasantry and urban poor in a city turned completely toward the countryside." This statement is only partially correct because most Juchiteco workers are also Zapotecs and feel an allegiance to the cultural and political ideas of COCEI. Moreover, Isthmus workers may also dabble in agriculture or come from peasant families, hence becoming a worker does not mean that one's connection to the land is severed forever. Secondly, COCEI's frequent successes in labor struggles—where its direct action, high-pressure tactics are most effective—has caused its labor sector, led by COCEI "maximum leader" (*jefe máximo*) Héctor Sánchez, to expand. Although COCEI's connections to non-Zapotec labor unions have little to do with its ethnic ideology, rather than signaling the end of COCEI, they represent its evolution in an era of proletarianization.

Since Juchitán has few heavy industries, COCEI's labor contingent is composed of a loosely connected front of low-paid, unskilled manual workers: porters, field laborers (*macheteros*), construction workers, horse cart drivers (*carretoneros*), taxi drivers, beer and soft drink delivery men, truck drivers, clerks, secretaries, and salt collectors. Most are native Juchitecos who speak the Zapotec language and identify strongly with the movement.[29] Because of the lack of large factories and the existence of tight-knit wards, COCEI's recruitment of workers occurs primarily in neighborhoods rather than in the work place. Family ties also play an important role in labor solidarity. COCEI workers belong to one of the movement's several labor organizations, which include the Isthmus Worker's Union, the Regional Worker's Coordinating Committee, and the Isthmus Worker's Central (CTI)—all founded during the *Ayuntamiento Popular* (Bailón 1987).

With COCEI firmly in control of City Hall in the spring of 1981, Juchitán labor unions took to the offensive in strikes that were quickly resolved in favor of workers. In October 1982 COCEI won a substantial settlement for Coca Cola company workers of Juchitán after the firing of 25 employees and a tense confrontation (Bailón 1987:28). In March 1983 members of the CTI struck two beer distributors, a lime factory, and an ice-making firm (Bailón 1987:40). In May workers at three other Juchitán companies took to the picket lines, and in June CTI bus and truck drivers from four different firms raised the red strike banner (*Hora Cero* 5/31/1983). However, the most significant labor action was a strike at the Barrilitos Okey soft drink plant in Juchitán which affected the interests of the president of the Oaxaca Chamber of Commerce (Martínez López 1985:141–42). In response, the Chamber of Commerce called for a temporary shutdown of businesses, and the government sent police to break the workers' strikes and guard the companies (Bailón 1987:41–43).[30] The normally divided Juchitán merchants had finally come together to combat COCEI and bring the Isthmus labor fiesta to a halt.

Juchitán Politics, 1981–1983: The Rise and Fall of the Ayuntamiento Popular

In 1981 COCEI had high hopes for its fledgling administration. According to one Coalition intellectual, the *Ayuntamiento Popular* would not have completed its mission if it had not revolutionized production in the countryside or at least produced enough surplus to pave Juchitán's main streets and build a bridge across the Perros River to connect an isolated pro-COCEI neighborhood (Cheguigo) to town (Zermeño 1987:75).[31] Although COCEI did not meet many of its objectives, the *Ayuntamiento Popular* was able to reconstruct the deteriorated City Hall, build and staff health clinics, extend water and sewer lines, build a small market, and make street improvements, in addition to the cultural projects previously discussed (Rubin 1987a:142).

One reason why COCEI did not reach its lofty development goals may have been its "lack of a minister of economic planning" (Zermeño 1987:75). This observation was valid. COCEI was more accomplished at grassroots mobilizing than at the technical side of running a town. However, COCEI's lack of administrative experience was greatly overshadowed by an even more important fact: the *Ayuntamiento Popular* had little money to work with because the state government withheld funding to the left-wing regime.

From the beginning of its rule, COCEI called on the state government to increase its public works budget which was too small to meet the demands of a medium-sized city deprived of all manner of urban services (TIS 1984:351). Lacking official funds, COCEI sought other means to finance its plans: radio marathons requesting donations (run by the Coalition's women's committee), solicitation of money door-to-door and from cars entering Juchitán, raising the rent of municipal buildings leased at low cost to wealthy *Priísta* businessmen, and demanding contributions from local merchants. The *Ayuntamiento Popular* took other measures that struck at the interests of the local elite, such as taking over urban land and parcels along the Perros River used by private parties, reclaiming sections of the cemetery monopolized by the families of ex-mayors, and placing a surcharge on lucrative beer sales by local beverage companies (Bailón 1987:26). COCEI's most successful move, however, was to plan a march (June 1981) on Oaxaca City to force the governor to negotiate the budget issue. Fearing a bloody confrontation, the governor caved in to COCEI's demands and upped the city's funding (Martínez López 1985:95). From that time forward, any possibility of an amicable coexistence between COCEI, the state government, and the local elite evaporated, and the combatants were locked into a prolonged trench war.

The Juchitán PRI's counterattack was led by an extraofficial, right-wing force known as the Central Committee for the Defense of the Rights of the People of Juchitán (CCDDPJ). For simplicity's sake, I will call this group the "Rojo gang," after the nickname of its leader, Teodoro Altamirano, a local *cacique*. Despite its lofty title, the Rojo gang was an anticommunist goon squad whose political weapons were violence and slander. Allegedly funded by high officials in the Interior Ministry, the gang conducted a red-baiting campaign of leaflets, graffiti, radio programs, and rallies, in which it depicted COCEI as a Cuban-supported revolutionary front bent on destroying local society through class warfare. At the same time the gang was accusing COCEI of "Central Americanizing" the Isthmus, it engaged in its own paramilitary tactics—breaking up COCEI meetings and shooting at its members (AI 1986). In October and November, one COCEI city councilman was killed, two *Coceístas* were wounded, and a right-wing gunman attempted to enter City Hall in search of the mayor (COCEI 1988:43; Monsiváis 1983; TIS 1984:351).

COCEI answered these attacks with a "Popular Tribunal"[32] condemning PRI/government violence, attended by prominent leftist leaders including Rosario Ibarra, leader of the National Front Against Repression (COCEI 1988:44). In the Tribunal, relatives of COCEI martyrs gave testimonies in Zapotec directly implicating the *azules*, judicial police, and PRI *pistoleros* in the killings of 17 *Coceístas*. Jesús Vicente, then COCEI's police chief, charged that the government was the intellectual author of many of these political crimes. Daniel López Nelio and Oscar Cruz also publicized the COCEI's cause on a speaking tour of southern California which attracted the support of a group of Chicano radicals who later visited Juchitán. Additionally, the well-known liberation theologian Arturo Lona, Bishop of Tehuantepec, condemned the violence and urged the government to call off the Rojo gang. Finally, the Coalition marched to Oaxaca and pressured the government into granting further budget concessions (*Hora Cero* 11/4/1981).

Unfortunately for the Coalition, Oaxaca politicians confined their concessions to written agreements, which were reneged upon after COCEI suspended its mobilizations. Consequently, the Coalition was forced to revive the *tequio*[33] (voluntary collective labor), described by Polín as "one of the best essences of social solidarity that our race has to rely on," in order to rebuild the crumbling, century-old City Hall building (*Hora Cero* 5/25/1981).

While COCEI struggled to carry out its administrative plan, the violence continued, resulting in one death and several injuries (Monsiváis 1983). Although most of the action took place in Juchitán, PRI and COCEI physically fought for control of numerous other Isthmus towns as well, such as Chicapa de Castro and La Ventosa, annexes of Juchitán allied with PRI,[34] and San Miguel Chimalapa, a Zoque town controlled by a COCEI affiliate. The casualties: 3 *Coceístas* dead, at least 13 wounded, and the loss of San Miguel Chimalapa to an armed PRI force (TIS 1984:360; Monsiváis 1983). COCEI got its licks in too; however, *Coceístas* were injured more often than *Priístas*. Moreover, the roster of *Coceístas* killed by police, *pistoleros*, soldiers, or *Priístas* now numbers approximately 30 individuals, whereas no more than three or four Juchitán *Priístas* have died in the COCEI-PRI conflict (AI 1986).

From the spring of 1982 to the summer of 1983, the two sides battled to a standoff, as COCEI's main weapons—political mobilizations and national publicity—confronted the PRI/government's control over funding and recourse to violence (Bailón 1987). In April 1982, when PRI presidential candidate Miguel de la Madrid visited Juchitán during his campaign, COCEI peasants blocked his entrance into town with 50 oxcarts (*Hora Cero* 5/2/1982). The same month, in a rally celebrating Polo's release from prison, the veteran leader proposed that the Isthmus secede from the state of Oaxaca if COCEI's budget demands were not met (*Hora Cero* 4/4/1982). The Coalition's ability to denounce state government policy increased with the election of Héctor Sánchez as federal deputy to the Mexican Congress. PRI responded to COCEI successes with calls for an audit of the *Ayuntamiento Popular*, which they accused of graft and patronage. Meanwhile, the Rojo gang continued its campaign of intimidation and brutality.

In the summer of 1983 political hostilities reached a crisis that PRI exploited to oust COCEI from City Hall. At the beginning of the year, however, COCEI's prospects seemed bright. The movement's regional presence was growing and the Coalition presented a distinct challenge to PRI victory in elections in eight Isthmus communities (Bailón 1987:20). In February a COCEI peasant march on Oaxaca signaled the zenith of the movement's negotiating capacity with government authorities. On May Day, *Coceístas* invaded a large section of state land adjacent to the pro-COCEI neighborhood of Cheguigo and established a squatter colony composed of several hundred houses. Although Oaxaca state police (*azules*) threw the squatters off the land six days later, COCEI returned en masse the following day, routing the *azules* and permanently controlling the territory, which they named the Rodrigo Carrasco Colony after a Coalition martyr (Bailón 1987:40). When things calmed down, COCEI negotiated directly with state and national officials, bypassing the local PRI power structure, as it had in the past (Rubin 1987a:143). After lengthy talks, the Rodrigo Carrasco Colony was legally recognized.

By summer 1983 PRI politicians openly called for military repression of COCEI, and the Rojo gang went on a rampage (Bailón 1987:46). In July *Priístas* attacked the entourage of Desiderio de Gyves, COCEI candidate for local deputy, in San Francisco del Mar, wounding several and burning a pick-up truck. The same month, the Rojo gang broke up a COCEI land invasion in La Ventosa and injured COCEI supporters (Monsiváis 1983). On July 31, 1983, COCEI–PRI tensions reached a climax as the election campaign came to a close.

COCEI celebrated its campaign with a march through Juchitán, led by approximately 100 oxcarts decorated with palm leaves, flowers, and COCEI colors, which culminated in a meeting in front of City Hall (Ruiz Cervantes 1983). Rojo and his partisans also chose the same time and a nearby location for their closing rally. When PRI and COCEI members crossed paths, they began an exchange of insults that escalated into a melee of rock throwing and gunfire that lasted for more than an hour (Ruiz Cervantes 1983). A sizable police contingent that observed the incident did nothing to end the fighting (AI 1986). In the end, two young men were dead and more than 20 people injured; each side said the other was at fault (AI 1986; TIS 1984:406–7).

A pro-government television channel filmed the incident and used the footage to blame COCEI for the violence. Thus began a national media blitzkrieg reproaching the *Ayuntamiento Popular* for the deaths and disorder in Juchitán, and calling for the ouster of COCEI. For a week following the incident, Juchitán and COCEI became the subject of numerous accounts, analyses, debates, and editorials on the pages of the national newspapers, as well as on national television. Despite conflicting versions of the events, the government accepted only PRI's interpretation and rapidly prepared for the impeachment of the COCEI government (Bailón 1987:47). Without offering COCEI an opportunity to challenge the legality of the action, the Oaxaca state legislature withdrew recognition of the *Ayuntamiento Popular* on August 3, 1983 (TIS 1984:412).[35]

COCEI defied the government decree by occupying City Hall and setting up a popular referendum in support of the impeached administration. The Coalition held an emotional rally in conjunction with the referendum, which was attended by an estimated 25,000 people including numerous journalists,[36] influential intellectuals, and leftist politicians (*Unomásuno* 8/7/1983; *Excélsior* 8/7/1983). The rally and referendum remain one of the high points of COCEI history. Moreover, the publicity generated by the rally brought COCEI recognition and support from the left throughout Mexico, and attracted a flock of reporters from many foreign countries.[37] Subsequently, stories about Juchitán appeared in the *Wall Street Journal*, *Time*, and syndicated newspapers across North America. Juchitán had become a media event!

Meanwhile, the government sent an interim PRI mayor to Juchitán, who was forced to set up his office in a heavily guarded school since COCEI occupied City Hall. Federal troops also arrived to patrol the streets and establish permanent barracks at four strategic points in town (AI 1986). Nonetheless, COCEI remained in control of City Hall, and *Coceístas* ridiculed the gay interim mayor with the nickname "Caramel Princess".[38]

In an effort to reestablish credibility for the November municipal election, PRI's interim government financed public works projects. These projects improved the Juchitán PRI's tarnished image and attracted followers through the patronage jobs they provided. Simultaneously, COCEI completed the renovation of City Hall, which was displayed in a gala celebration during which poor Juchitecos were allowed to parade through offices that had once been off-limits to all but the PRI elite (Bailón 1987). Despite this openness, dozens of COCEI peasants armed with clubs and the unarmed wives of COCEI leaders guarded the building against potential attack from the *azules* (Ruiz Cervantes 1983). The Coalition also set up an extensive network, composed primarily of women, to provision the occupants of City Hall, pass messages, and maintain the movement's activities during this time of crisis.

The November elections took place in a tense atmosphere of military vigilance and right-wing intimidation (Zermeño 1987:88–91). In order to ensure victory, PRI engaged in gerrymandering, multiple voting, and inflation of vote totals. In spite of these tactics, Daniel López Nelio, COCEI's mayoral candidate, was still able to obtain 46 percent of the vote, compared to 54 percent for PRI's man (Bailón 1987:49). Although COCEI staged a 15-day hunger strike in front of the National Palace in Mexico City to protest the fraudulent elections, the government refused to budge. Officials demanded that COCEI turn over City Hall to the newly "elected" PRI mayor.

PRI finally got what it wanted on December 13, 1983. In the middle of the night, a large group of police and *azules* broke past COCEI guards and recaptured City Hall, beating and jailing the approximately 90 *Coceístas* inside the building (*Excélsior* 12/14/1983; AI 1986). While police interrogated and tortured 86 COCEI captives in a Salina Cruz prison, soldiers cordoned off the area surrounding City Hall (AI 1986:18). Undaunted, about 3,000 *Coceístas*, with women in the lead, burst through the military blockade and penetrated the building, only to be turned back again by troops (*Hora Cero* 12/15/1983). Leftist Juchitecos viewed the soldiers' takeover of the town as a repeat of the repression of Che Gómez's movement. Hence, local passions were inflamed.

Street fighting continued for several days afterwards, as *Coceístas*, brandishing rocks and sticks, tried on five occasions to retake City Hall (*Excélsior* 12/15/1983). COCEI women participated fully in the resistance and helped organize activities in the absence of the movement's principal leaders, who were either jailed or in hiding (Bañuelos 1988:27–35).[39] Police responded to the assaults with cork bullets and tear gas, while *Coceístas* protected themselves from tear gas fumes with rags soaked in homemade vinegar and fought back (*Excélsior* 12/15/1983; interviews). During the action, soldiers detained hundreds of COCEI protesters, and numerous others were injured (Santana 1988:67). Eventually, the *azules* took control of the situation and established a virtual state of siege in Juchitán. Vehicles heavily laden with soldiers and police cruised the streets, forcing the populace to remain in their homes (Zermeño 1987:92). In the following months, COCEI members were frequently arrested and tortured, their houses raided, and demonstrations broken up (AI 1986:19–22).[40]

Aftermath of the Ayuntamiento Popular: *Repression, Reorganization, and Return to Office*

Once it regained control of Juchitán in 1984, PRI moved quickly to tear down the *Ayuntamiento Popular's* projects. The casualties included the Prepa Popular and teachers' college buildings, the COCEI bookstore, the

Víctor Pineda library, COCEI's radio station, and more than 500 market stalls of COCEI supporters that were destroyed with bulldozers (COCEI 1988:45; *Hora Cero* 1/11/1984). Likewise, the federal and state governments kept the Casa de la Cultura's subsidy down to pitiful levels, and Toledo's life was threatened and he was forced into exile in Europe. Although COCEI protested these actions and rallied around its *Ayuntamiento Libre* led by López Nelio, the PRI/government maintained its hard-line policy. On January 1, 1984, 15 *Coceístas* were wounded during protests against the inauguration of PRI's new mayor. Four *Coceístas* died as a result of skirmishes with *Priístas* and police or soldiers in the first two months of 1984 (*Excélsior* 1/2/1984; *Hora Cero* 3/17/1984). COCEI leaders later charged that the government had engaged in a "dirty war" of rape, torture, and murder against their members (AI 1986).

While PRI destroyed COCEI's projects and repressed the movement, it also invested enormous sums in public works designed to recapture public opinion. These included a bridge, sports fields, a hospital, and a market (Zermeño 1987:93). Ironically, many Juchitecos viewed the new facilities as an indication of the Coalition's ability to force the government into action, rather than as triumphs of PRI (Rubin 1987a:153). Likewise, the PRI/government's failure to address the poor's fundamental needs (e.g., improved educational and health care facilities, and water and sewage hookups) prevented them from co-opting COCEI's constituency. Moreover, "the very existence of state projects and goals provides the sort of environment in which the leaders of the COCEI have proven themselves most adept at fostering popular mobilizations and successful negotiations" (Rubin 1987a:153). Thus, despite an aggressive campaign of repression and premeditated government spending, COCEI had survived. In February 1984 the movement celebrated its 10-year anniversary with events in Juchitán and Mexico City (*Hora Cero* 3/7/1984).

Since COCEI political demonstrations and rallies in Juchitán were restricted by military force, the Coalition regrouped in weekly dances, fiestas, and neighborhood committee meetings (Zermeño 1987:95–96). Eventually, the movement was able to resume its grassroots political activities on a smallscale. In April 1984 COCEI obtained a large settlement for 400 Zapotec and Huave fishermen whose livelihoods were threatened by a PEMEX oil spill in the Isthmus lagoons (*Noticias* 4/6/1984).[41] It also had occasional successes in agrarian and labor conflicts. At the same time, pro-COCEI intellectuals created numerous essays, *corridos*, poems, paintings, and other works glorifying the *Ayuntamiento Popular*, local history, and Zapotec culture.

By 1985 COCEI could once again compete for public office. That year, Polín, the former Juchitán mayor, was elected federal deputy to the Mexican Congress, and Desiderio de Gyves became a state legislator. Long years of struggle within the dissident teacher's union (SNTE) also paid off, with the candidacy of Enedino Jiménez, a COCEI leader, for secretary general of the Oaxaca section of the union. At the base level, *Coceístas* of San Blas ousted the PRI mayor of town, beat up *azules* who came to his rescue, and took over City Hall until a less objectionable official was installed. On another front, repeated protests by COCEI women and international organizations led to the release of three Coalition leaders imprisoned since 1983 (*Noticias* 9/7/1984; AI 1986). Another sign of renewed COCEI strength was its rapprochement with the Mexican Socialist Party (PSUM) after years of petty squabbles with its predecessor (PCM). By 1986 COCEI had once again become a serious challenger to PRI control of the Isthmus.

The 1986 Election and Beyond:
COCEI Shares Power with PRI

The most noteworthy aspect of the 1986 Juchitán municipal election campaign was intense intra-PRI conflict. Relations became so strained that the moderate faction of PRI declined to support the party's candidate, who was linked to a right-wing *cacique*. Subsequently, the moderates formed a separate organization (MIPRI)[42] within the official party and called for annulment of the elections. PRI infighting at the local level occurred simultaneously with the rise of gubernatorial candidate Heladio Ramírez. Ramírez was a liberal *Priísta* who was more sympathetic to COCEI than previous governors had been.[43]

Official election results in Juchitán declared PRI the winner; however, the Coalition produced evidence of improper handling of voter identification cards and the list of registered voters. COCEI backed up its charges with highway blockages, demonstrations, and hunger strikes, which led to negotiations with the government. COCEI militancy, combined with bickering within the local PRI and the ascendancy of Ramírez, created a favorable context for resolution of the Coalition's demands. After extended discussions, Ramírez named another liberal *Priísta* as mayor of a coalition PRI–COCEI government composed of three officials from each group. COCEI also placed members on coalition governments in seven other Isthmus towns and controlled outright the town of Xadani.[44] On the day of the new Juchitán administration's inauguration, Héctor Sánchez declared, "Today ... December 15 [1986], the banners, *huipiles*, and red bandannas once again enter City Hall" (Zermeño 1987:96). COCEI had returned to power.

It came as no surprise to Juchitecos that tensions between COCEI and PRI quickly surfaced over the administration of City Hall. The new mayor, Felipe Martínez López (1985), had previously written a book about Juchitán politics in which he criticized COCEI. Likewise, Martínez and several COCEI leaders had participated in rival leftist student groups in Oaxaca in the 1970s. COCEI dissatisfaction over the direction of city government erupted in demonstrations, marches, and public declarations critical of the mayor. Yet, unlike in the past, these conflicts did not lead to violence in most cases. Although a talented COCEI poet and activist (Alejandro Cruz) was murdered by *Priístas* in 1987, this incident occurred in the heat of political conflict rather than being planned in advance, and the culprits were quickly jailed.

Even though the Coalition was not entirely happy with the bipartisan government, its advantages outweighed the disadvantages. For COCEI, participation in the government meant it could keep a watch on policy matters and finances, reduce police brutality and judicial improprieties (one judge was a *Coceísta*), and obtain equal access to city services. Disadvantages of the arrangement included COCEI's susceptibility to charges that the movement was at fault when municipal projects went awry, the disaffection of some *Coceístas* who viewed sharing power as a sellout, and PRI manipulation of the coalition government to imply that COCEI had been domesticated.

Ironically, from the 1986 elections to the present, internal PRI conflicts have generated as much heat as have COCEI–PRI conflicts. In the summer of 1987 the Rojo gang occupied City Hall for several days and accused Martínez of graft. In the spring of 1988 Rojo announced he was leaving the PRI after 33 years of service to join the presidential campaign of Cuauthémoc Cárdenas. Soon thereafter, the Rojo gang and the followers of a right-wing PRI lawyer engaged in a shootout after an argument. The major focus of PRI quarreling was the struggle between MIPRI and the *cacique* political machine for control of the local PRI municipal committee in preparation for the 1989 mayoral election.

While PRI weakened itself, COCEI stepped up its activities. A particularly successful maneuver was an invasion of a 15-ha tract of land (owned by a wealthy architect, now deceased) near the entrance to Juchitán in spring 1987. COCEI supporters quickly put up hundreds of shacks and earthen houses, which they painted with COCEI slogans and murals. The government eventually accepted the existence of this squatter settlement, named the Gustavo Pineda Colony after a COCEI martyr, in order to avoid a messy confrontation. Other COCEI accomplishments between the summer of 1987 and the summer of 1988 included winning strikes at two large Isthmus beer distributors and a major interstate bus company, and obtaining substantial credit and crop insurance settlements for peasants. COCEI also gained higher wages for salt collectors, secured payments for peasants and fishermen whose lands and lagoons were damaged by a PE-MEX pipeline and an oil spill, and held fiestas and bullfights that outshone those run by PRI.

Additionally, the Coalition expanded its influence to the Mixe, Chontal, and highland Zapotec areas, as well as to Salina Cruz and the southern Oaxaca coast. On the cultural front, employees of the Casa de la Cultura extracted higher wages and a larger subsidy from the state government after a brief strike in February 1988. Finally, throughout the 1987–1988 period, the COCEI leadership held festive rallies in front of Juchitán City Hall.

Although *Coceístas* also spent ample time in cantinas guzzling beer and engaging in what Zermeño (1987:96) considers "the great danger of the COCEI struggle" (viz., the "self-contemplation of its glorious past"), nostalgia did not prevent COCEI from continued mobilization. One ironic indication of COCEI's success was the frequent imitation of Coalition tactics by PRI, e.g., land invasions, highway blockades, building takeovers, and speaking Zapotec at rallies. Nonetheless, COCEI remained a step ahead of the divided local PRI, which began to claim that Governor Ramírez favored the Coalition over PRI in Juchitán.

COCEI returned to the national spotlight in 1987 when its leaders met with President de la Madrid and Ramírez, who described the *Coceístas* as "excellent Mexicans and distinguished social activists" (*Excélsior* 10/16/1987). The Coalition's presence in national politics continued during 1988, when the movement hosted rallies for Cuauthémoc Cárdenas and Heberto Castillo, leftist candidates for president, and ran a candidate in congressional elections.[45] Both rallies were heavily attended, with estimated crowds of between 10,000 and 20,000 attendees. Cárdenas' rally was especially large and represented the grandest display of COCEI militancy and enthusiasm since the 1983 referendum. [46]

COCEI's alliance with the PMS payed off in the election of Daniel López Nelio, COCEI peasant leader, to a federal deputy slot. According to COCEI, López Nelio's election occurred in spite of organized PRI fraud, which included multiple voting, inflated vote totals, and votes registered to fictitious names or deceased individuals. The Coalition backed up these allegations with a tape of citizen's band radio transmissions which documented PRI's collaboration with the military in vote fraud operations. Official election results stating that Carlos Salinas had defeated Cárdenas by a 3 to 2 margin in Juchitán, arguably the most anti-PRI town in Mexico, left townspeople incredulous (*El Sol del Istmo* 7/17/1988). No rational explanation other than fraud could explain Salinas' substantial victory.

COCEI protested the election outcome, but not as vigorously as they had in the past when a movement candidate was involved—a clear indication of the Coalition's regional orientation, which overshadows interest in national politics. Rapidly, the focus of COCEI politics returned to local concerns, such as the ambitious public works agenda promoted by the municipal government at the beginning of 1987. This included a wide range of projects concerned with street repair, housing construction, installation of water and sewer lines, and cleaning up the Perros River. Because of COCEI pressure, many of the public works were slated to improve living conditions in the poorer, peripheral neighborhoods of Juchitán. Unfortunately, by spring 1988 most of the projects had become bogged down by bureaucratic delays, bad weather, and corruption. Nonetheless, COCEI's presence in City Hall insured that its constituency would receive their share of city services.[47]

The 1989 Municipal Elections: The New Conditions in Which COCEI Returned to Power

COCEI's participation in a bipartisan municipal administration from 1986 to 1989 did little to diminish the movement's majority support in Juchitán. On the one hand, *Coceístas* blamed the PRI for the slow progress of public works projects, and complained that PRI mayor Martínez had rebuilt his family's Juchitán home and made other illegal acquisitions with municipal funds. On the other hand, many COCEI peasants and workers benefited during this period from the movement's successful negotiations with the agricultural bureaucracy, state government, and local bus and beer companies to obtain credit and crop insurance, higher wages, and severance pay. In the countryside, COCEI leader López Nelio represented thousands of peasants—who farmed between 30 percent (López Nelio's estimate) and 60 percent (a journalist's estimate) of the total area of Isthmus agricultural land insured by the government credit bank (*Proceso* 8/28/1989). In the city, Héctor Sánchez defended the interests of the majority of Juchiteco laborers.

As the 1989 election approached, the Juchitán PRI once again self-destructed in tactical errors and factionalism. The PRI's first mistake was to select an official of the previous municipal government as their mayoral candidate. Yet this individual was legally barred from serving in the next administration and had to quit the race. Subsequently, each of the three PRI runners-up demanded to replace the ousted candidate and the Juchitán PRI disintegrated in a flurry of name calling and infighting. At one point, the principal PRI peasant leader in Juchitán even accused Governor Ramírez of being a COCEI ally (*Proceso* 8/7/1989).

But PRI had only itself to blame for the final selection (actually an imposition from the Oaxaca state PRI headquarters) of an unpopular non-Zapotec businessman, Ramón Caraveo, as mayoral candidate. This violated the unwritten law in Juchitán politics that the mayor must be a native Juchiteco with strong ties to the community. Historically, Juchitecos have refused to be governed by outsiders, such as Caraveo, a wealthy store owner from northern Mexico who does not speak Zapotec.

The naming of Caraveo as PRI's official mayoral candidate "went over like a bomb" with Juchitecos, dissident *Priístas* and *Coceístas* alike. The supporters of a rival PRI candidate, who refused to withdraw his candidacy and support Caraveo, burned their voting credentials at a demonstration in front of Juchitán City Hall. Another group of *Priístas* vandalized Caraveo's office, and townspeople began derisively calling him "*Carafeo*" (ugly face). Several informants told me that middle-class and some upper-class Juchitecos, disgusted with Caraveo, decided to support COCEI. Other *Priístas* simply abstained.

Coalition leaders, who have appealed to Juchiteco ethnic pride since the movement's founding, could not have asked for a more auspicious turn of events. In his end-of-campaign rally, attended by 15,000 supporters, COCEI mayoral candidate Héctor Sánchez gave a vigorous speech in Zapotec condemning the *dxu'* (foreign) PRI candidate and calling for control of Juchitán by "true" Juchitecos like himself. Emotions ran high at this massive and colorful COCEI demonstration. Thus it came as no surprise when Sánchez easily defeated his discredited PRI opponent in the August 6, 1989, Juchitán mayoral election (7,277 COCEI votes to 5,609 PRI votes, according to COCEI's calculations).[48] COCEI also won the mayoral elections in Xadani, Mixtequilla, and Petapa.[49]

After the election, the big news was not that the national government accepted COCEI's victory (probably in order to prop up its "democratic" image). Rather, attention returned to Juchitán as a result of several scathing articles in the prominent Mexican weekly magazine, *Proceso* (8/14/1989, 8/

28/1989), alleging massive corruption in the COCEI leadership. What was unusual about these attacks was not their substance—many of the charges had been aired before—but the fact that they were published in a magazine that had formerly been a staunch defender of COCEI. It seemed that with a second COCEI municipal victory in Juchitán, *Coceístas* could no longer claim to be persecuted indigenous martyrs, and their cause célébre status in Mexico City was reduced.[50]

As the furor over the corruption charges subsided, the next controversial incident involving COCEI seemed to hearken back to earlier times of violent repression. On December 9, 1989, a group of *Priístas*, who were occupying the Santo Domingo Ingenio City Hall to protest the outcome of the 1989 elections, opened fire on a crowd of *Coceístas*, killing four of them. The local police blamed COCEI for the violence and imprisoned more than 20 *Coceístas*, including Polín (*Proceso* 12/18/1989). But political conditions had changed since the violent years of the mid-1970s and the 1983–1984 conjuncture, as was indicated by the rapid release of the *Coceístas* and the quick achievement of a settlement satisfactory to COCEI. The settlement was obtained when mayor-elect Sánchez spoke on the phone directly with President Salinas.

There were other indications that times had changed. Prior to the shooting in Santo Domingo, President Salinas had agreed to visit Juchitán to attend the town's 100-year anniversary celebration in December 1989 (*Proceso* 12/18/1989). Salinas' visit had to be postponed as a result of the violent incident, but on March 20, 1990, the President made an unprecedented appearance at a rally in Juchitán convoked by COCEI mayor Héctor Sánchez in front of a largely COCEI crowd. COCEI took considerable heat from the Cárdenas movement and other Mexican left groups for taking part in the event, even though the Salinas appearance was billed as a nonpartisan affair (COCEI 1990).

At the rally, Sánchez gave a lively speech in which he reiterated many of the ethnopolitical themes voiced by COCEI spokesmen over the previous 16 years:

> We are a people who over the generations have defended with pride, passion, and bravery our ethnic identity [and] our right as Juchitecos to democratically elect our communal and municipal authorities. We have a history and this makes us proud. . . . Our struggle, Mr. President, has always focussed on democracy and the right to land. . . . History defines us, the Juchitecos, as inflexible defenders of reason and justice and it is in this context that today we celebrate with you,

Mr. President, this ceremony . . . in a historical circumstance that requires that we treat each other as equals, with mutual ideological respect, toward a path of concord [*concertación*] and plural coexistence
[COCEI 1990:2].

Although Sánchez made the usual references to Meléndez, Che Gómez,
and the Juchiteco ethnic struggle, the tone in which he addressed the government had obviously changed. Dialogue, cooperation, and understanding were the watchwords of the day, rather than mobilization and struggle
as in the past. In turn, President Salinas promised to transform the Isthmus,
and especially Juchitán, with an expensive development program funded
by the federal government. Salinas offered potable water, sewage lines,
pavement, new schools, remodeled health clinics, and other improvements
(COCEI 1990).

In the simplest political terms, the Salinas appearance can be reduced to
a quid pro quo. COCEI gave up some of its independence, anti-government militancy, and radical image in exchange for future development projects and a degree of prestige and legitimacy for hosting the President. In
turn, Salinas sacrificed some budget funds and the government's previous
unwillingness to legitimize COCEI. In exchange, he obtained a chance to
use the Juchitán meeting to bolster his sagging democratic image, weaken
the Cárdenas alliance, and defuse the potentially delicate Isthmus political
situation. The pro-government Mexican media made a big deal of Salinas'
trip to Juchitán. Numerous articles claimed that the meeting between
COCEI and the President showed each party's "political maturity" and
was a sign that Salinas' strategy of seeking negotiated settlements with
selected opposition movements was working.

Nonetheless, the Juchitecos have dealt with federal government officials
many times in the past, only to watch in anger as politicians later reneged
on their agreements. Indeed, the jury is still out on whether the COCEI
leadership has sacrificed the movement's autonomy, or instead has pulled
off one of the great coups of the Coalition's history by bringing massive
investment to the Isthmus (for which COCEI can take credit).

The Salinas visit is one of the most controversial moves ever made by
members of the COCEI leadership. The controversy also stirred up tensions within the organization that had begun to surface after the *Proceso*
corruption stories, but which had been growing for several years. COCEI's
considerable unity and its long-term survival as an organized opposition
movement have been remarkable in light of the tendency towards division
and disintegration so often found among Mexican left organizations (Carr

1985). Thus, it should not be a surprise that COCEI eventually began to show fissures after such a long period of internal solidarity.

When I talked to Juchitecos in the spring of 1990, they told me stories about prominent COCEI figures sporting new vehicles or an expensive watch, sundry acts of graft by movement activists, and growing bureaucratism and authoritarianism among the leadership. Others complained that COCEI had become "institutionalized," that is, that the movement had become just another reformist party working within the system. Moreover, for the first time, major schisms had developed within the COCEI political commission itself. Unfortunately, the Juchiteco cultural movement was also riven by dissension, and the Casa de la Cultura was inactive and seemed to lack purpose since the resignation of the institution's long-time director, Macario Matus, in August 1989. Some local observers noted that winning the election was a mixed blessing for COCEI because it led to internal squabbling, and because the struggle to maintain power eventually takes its toll on the power holders themselves (*"el poder es desgastante"* was the way one informant put it).[51]

When I returned to Juchitán again in December 1991, I was impressed by the extensive public works projects in progress. It seemed as if every other street was either being paved or dug up in order to lay water or sewer pipes. So many streets were under construction that some Juchitecos even complained that change was occurring too rapidly. They told me they were bothered that trees were cut down in order to build the streets. Others lamented that oxcarts were being replaced by cars on the new concrete streets and that the brisk auto traffic made it impossible for townspeople to socialize on the curbs in front of their houses as they had in the past. Thus, even though the leftist administration has been able to bring more urban development money to Juchitán than any previous municipal government, COCEI is not immune from criticism. In general, though, I sensed satisfaction in the community with the COCEI-sponsored public works projects.

Individual COCEI leaders also drew criticism from several of my informants. Radical *Coceístas* griped that the leaders were working too closely with the Salinas regime and were, in effect, selling out. Another observer noted the development of a three-tiered hierarchy within COCEI, which separated the leaders (*"la cúpula"*) from middle-level activists (*"los cuadros medios"*) and the rank-and-file (*"el pueblo"*). He pointed out that COCEI members used to donate long hours of their time to the organization free of charge, but that today activists demand to be paid for supporting the movement. Clearly, the intense enthusiasm COCEI generated in the early

1980s was no longer evident. I was made painfully aware of this when I sat through COCEI mayor Héctor Sánchez's annual address to townspeople on December 27, 1991. Instead of his usual radical Zapotec speeches, Sánchez delivered a dry, formal talk in Spanish, which was devoted to self-congratulations for paving Juchitán's streets and thanking President Salinas for providing the necessary funds. Yet, if the fire and passion of previous Juchiteco mobilizations had temporarily died down, COCEI still retained enough support in Juchitán to win municipal elections in the fall of 1992. As of spring 1993, the Coalition, led by recently elected Juchitán mayor Oscar Cruz, remained a strong and successful grassroots organization in the Isthmus of Tehuantepec.

Summary and Conclusions

For *Coceístas*, the People's Government represents the movement's heyday, the glory years when Juchitán was front-page news in Mexico City, and Zapotec was spoken in the mayor's office and on the radio. From the beginning, COCEI leaders shrouded their *Ayuntamiento Popular* in ethnic symbolism and linked their current projects with the struggles of Zapotec heroes of the past. Yet COCEI's ethnic orientation was more than just rhetoric. Drawing on a rich history of Zapotec intellectual production, intense pride in local customs and language, and trends in radical art and literature, COCEI became a formidable regional political force and a wide-ranging cultural movement.

Notwithstanding COCEI's emphasis on ethnicity, the movement's political program did not originate from or exist in a provincial, indigenous vacuum. The Juchiteco cultural movement also has been fertilized by multiple outside influences. Additionally, COCEI strategies were heavily influenced by the experiences of other left movements in Mexico and abroad, and throughout the Coalition's history it has been affected profoundly by the policies of the Mexican government. For example, the Zapotec peasantry, who comprise the majority of COCEI's constituency, became radicalized by changes in land tenure, class structure, agricultural patterns, and living conditions wrought by the Benito Juárez Dam and irrigation project and government land decrees. Also, the rise of COCEI in the early to mid-1970s coincided with President Echeverría's support of grassroots movements in the countryside. Likewise, COCEI's opportunities to govern Juchitán were made possible by a 1977 national law that legalized leftist parties, and the government's willingness to recognize Coalition victories in the 1981 and 1989 elections. Moreover, the 1989–1992 COCEI administration in Juchitán depended almost entirely on the federal government for funding. Finally, the state has also demonstrated a capacity to repress COCEI by force, as it did in 1977 and, on a massive scale, in 1983 and 1984.

Ironically, expansion of the Mexican state apparatus into the Isthmus has, in some respects, strengthened COCEI. Indeed, the movement has benefited greatly from the growth of agricultural credit-granting institutions. Through building seizures, highway blockades, and other pressure tactics, COCEI has forced the farm bureaucracy to subsidize its peasant sector. Furthermore, the Coalition extracted sizable settlements from PE-MEX for peasants and fishermen affected by pipeline construction and oil spills. Finally, COCEI labor unions are very adept at coercing the state government into granting their members large indemnities and improved benefits in labor dispute arbitration. In all these arenas, the movement has demonstrated its ability to use the state for its own ends. Begrudgingly, the government has realized that it has few alternatives other than politically costly repression or negotiation when confronted with militant mobs of red-clad COCEI peasants camped out on the Pan American Highway.

COCEI's successes, flamboyant style, and "Indian" image have not gone unnoticed in Mexican intellectual and left political circles. During the *Ayuntamiento Popular* years, the Coalition attracted powerful supporters in Mexico City and spawned a mini-growth industry of academic and journalistic treatments of the movement. Juchitán became a key symbol of peasant resistance and indigenous cultural survival in contemporary Mexico. The support of the left, and Juchitán's increasing visibility and renown, helped legitimize COCEI.

Nevertheless, if Felipe Carrillo Puerto could not sustain his "first socialist government in the Americas" in the state of Yucatán in the 1920s (Joseph 1988:167), the chances of COCEI's *Ayuntamiento Popular* enduring within the confines of PRI-dominated Mexico were even more remote. Yet the fact that the Coalition was able to survive and grow, despite the full onslaught of Mexican political-military power, attests to the movement's resilience and deep roots in local society. Few contemporary Mexican grassroots movements—which have consistently fragmented, been co-opted, or been destroyed by the government—have had the staying power of COCEI. This has been possible because of the strength of Juchiteco ethnic identity and the binding power and inspirational appeal of Isthmus Zapotec culture—ethnic and cultural elements that many of the unsuccessful rural Mexican political movements have lacked (Zermeño 1987:73).

Only time will tell if COCEI can remain a strong, independent force on the Mexican left.

In Chapter 7 I examine the political and cultural alternative presented by COCEI in theory, as well as contradictions between COCEI ideology and Isthmus social reality, which obstruct fulfillment of the movement's plans.

■ ■ ■ ■ ■ ■ ■ ■ ■ ■ ■ ■ ■

CHAPTER SEVEN

Isthmus Intellectuals, Zapotec History and Culture, and COCEI's Ethnic Ideology

The idea that Indian people have history is now a scandal. It would seem that with this recognition ... [the Indian people's] past would leave the dark and mysterious regions of the fable through the intricate paths of mythology until it reached the illuminating light of scientific history. But does not this recognition also imply more risks and challenges for the poor indigenous peoples of America who can hardly get what they need to survive and now must appear naked or dressed in their rags before the gaze of the historians ... ?

But if the risks are real and great when the history of the Indian peoples is left in the hands and interests of the non-Indians, how will the indigenous intellectuals respond to the challenge of studying their own past?

VÍCTOR DE LA CRUZ (1984B) IN
"HISTORIA DE LOS PUEBLOS INDIOS (¿POR QUIEN Y PARA QUIEN?)"

Having examined the history of COCEI and the Isthmus Zapotecs from my own anthropological perspective, I will now discuss how that history and Zapotec culture are viewed by COCEI intellectuals and political leaders. In the above quotation, Víctor de la Cruz, a well-known Zapotec writer, raises some critical issues in relation to the "discovery" of native people's history, indigenous intellectual empowerment, and the study of the past by members of the society being studied. The problem that de la Cruz addresses is not confined to the Zapotecs or any other indigenous American group, but is one that is being confronted by native people's around the globe. In a paper concerned with these issues, Keesing

(1989:19) stated, "The process of recapturing the past, of reconstructing, of questioning Western scholarship—historical and anthropological—is important and essential."

In this chapter I will analyze the "recapturing of the past" and the creation of a discourse about Zapotec cultural authenticity by COCEI politicians and intellectuals. The most influential recent work on such matters is Hobsbawm and Ranger's *The Invention of Tradition* (1983). By debunking ersatz "traditions" and "artificially" created customs, their book has provided an important antidote to previously uncritical treatments of "ancestral" lifeways and "ancient" cultural heritages. If taken as an end in itself, however, the deconstruction of discourses about historical origins and cultural purity is itself sterile, since it reduces cultural practice to a kind of true-false test. Either a "tradition" is said to be truly rooted in the *longue durée* or it is not and, hence, it is considered a less legitimate recent creation.

It is important to move beyond the issue of whether particular customs or visions of the past are "real" or "mythical," and to examine historically and ethnographically the political processes within which such creations and recreations have significance (cf. Clifford 1988; Salomon 1987). This allows us to analyze not only the political consequences of particular "inventions" within existing political and economic conditions, but also their potential to inspire actions that transform these same conditions. Such an approach can further our understanding of the Juchiteco cultural movement and the COCEI political project to which it is linked.

Taking de la Cruz's provocative question as a cue, we may ask how did the COCEI intellectuals respond to the challenge of studying their own culture and history? What are the consequences of COCEI's ethnic ideology for political change in the Isthmus?

The Coalition's ethnic discourse grounds current COCEI politics in local history and Zapotec culture (Manuel Matus 1988). The movement's ideology is persuasive and effective because it defines contemporary *Coceístas* as the heirs of past Zapotec ethnic struggles and the current embodiments of the Juchiteco rebellious spirit. COCEI opponents, likewise, are framed as the present representatives of Oaxaca Valley and central government interests that have plagued Juchitán historically. COCEI, itself, is depicted in its own discourse as a natural, organic outgrowth of Isthmus Zapotec society. Juchiteco culture is presented as a morally superior way of life compared to the corruption and inequality of western capitalism and bourgeois Mexican society.

Yet COCEI ethnic ideology also illustrates many of the obstacles that stand in the way of an egalitarian society in the Isthmus. While COCEI discourse has proven potential to inspire large numbers of Juchitecos to mobilize against external enemies, the movement's cultural politics gloss over unresolved social contradictions within the Zapotec community, as well as the long-term, local ethnic conflicts that have prevented COCEI from expanding to other indigenous groups.

Isthmus History and COCEI Ideology

The Zapotec were the first to rebel against the arbitrary actions of colonialism. In 1660, a group of valiant women, tired of seeing their dignity and rights trampled on, led the struggle against the Spanish.

Our struggle, Mister President, has always focussed on democracy and the right to land. Che Gregorio Melendres, Che Gómez, Heliodoro Charis, Adolfo C. Gurrión, Roque Robles, and Valentín Carrasco, are examples of the dignity of the Istmeños who gave their lives for the defense of their lands, and for justice and democracy founded on reason and rights [COCEI 1990:1; Héctor Sánchez, COCEI mayor of Juchitán, addressing Mexican President Carlos Salinas de Gortari on March 20, 1990].

COCEI leaders, writers, and artists have created a cohesive framework of ideas in which selected aspects and visions of Isthmus Zapotec history are used to justify contemporary political practices. According to its spokesmen, COCEI is the continuation of Zapotec ethnic resistance historically, and COCEI politics are an Isthmus Zapotec cultural expression (López Mateos 1988:17; de la Cruz 1983c:55). These ideas began to crystallize during the *Ayuntamiento Popular* and are expressed in the abundant artistic productions and writings of the Zapotec intellectuals and artists.

In COCEI's millenarian interpretation of local history, Juchitán was founded by a band of the toughest Zapotec warriors, who later fended off Aztec and Mixtec incursions into the area. This account of Juchitán's origins may derive from a prose piece by Andrés Henestrosa in which Juchitán's patron saint, San Vicente rejected the oasis-like Tehuantepec River basin as a homeland in favor of the hot, dry Juchitán area. There, San Vicente's children (i.e., the Juchitecos) would grow up strong and brave instead of lazy and weak ([1929] 1987:59–60). *Coceístas* say this same indomitable spirit characterizes contemporary Juchitecos as well. According to COCEI's historical vision—which is frequently recited at rallies—the Isthmus Zapotec fought against colonialism from the very beginning and have continued to oppose foreign domination up to the present day. From this perspective, the Coalition is the contemporary link in an unbroken, historical chain of resistance and rebellion.

The Juchiteco writers argue that although the Spaniards exploited them, the Zapotec retained their language and many indigenous customs. According to Macario Matus (1981) and Víctor de la Cruz (1983c), persistent passive resistance characterized the colonial period, and large-scale ethnic rebellion erupted during the Tehuantepec Rebellion led by the *india Teresa* (1660). The Juchitecos' "primordial titles" (discussed in a widely distributed booklet published by the movement) play a key role in COCEI's view of colonial history, since these documents define the Zapotecs' ancient and legitimate claim to currently disputed lands in the irrigation district.

The nineteenth-century Zapotec leader Meléndez occupies a prominent place in COCEI historical ideology because he epitomizes Juchiteco resistance against Oaxaca Valley politicians (particularly Benito Juárez) and defense of communal natural resources (de la Cruz 1983e). Whereas Juárez is the most exalted hero in official Mexican history—a combined Washington and Lincoln-type figure with an inscrutable Indian mystique to boot—radical Juchitecos view him with scorn. In the many paintings, poems, books, and songs of the Juchiteco leftists, Mexican national symbols are turned upside down, and Isthmus symbols and historical figures are celebrated. For example, in one of Toledo's most successful art portfolios he demystifies and dethrones Juárez the nationalist hero (Toledo 1986).

One piece of this iconoclastic series of paintings, entitled "Project for a Monument to Juárez on the Outskirts of Juchitán," shows the famous statesman standing atop a two-headed turtle with a fishing pole in his hands. This is hardly the stately image of Juárez found in Mexican school books. In another painting, Juárez is sitting in a swing. Still another shows his head superimposed onto the body of a "typical" Oaxacan Indian peasant in an old postcard. In many of the 47 works that make up this series, Juárez's head is placed onto other bodies alongside or interacting with Oaxacan fauna in magical realist scenarios. In the few works involving relatively transparent symbolism, e.g., "Juárez and the McLane-Ocampo Treaty" (which would have granted the United States perpetual rights to transit across the Isthmus of Tehuantepec in the nineteenth century), "The Ghost of Juárez Patrolling Juchitán" (in which little lead soldiers symbolize Oaxaca government repression against COCEI's People's Government and against Juchitán historically), and "Although with Very Precise Words" (featuring a letter in which Juárez rationalized the burning of

Juchitán), the message is clear. Juárez may be a hero in official Mexican history, but in Juchitán he is a villain.[1]

COCEI intellectuals consider the Juchitecos' defeat of a French battalion in 1866 during the War of Intervention as not only another episode in their series of battles against outsiders, but as an ethnic victory over a European force. This demonstrates the town's toughness and favorable standing vis-à-vis other world civilizations. At demonstrations COCEI leaders often invoke the Zapotec heroine of this conflict, Tona Taati, as a symbol of Juchitecas' historical spirit of resistance. They say this spirit is incarnated in contemporary female *Coceístas*. Toledo (1986) treats the most important symbol of the battle, a French cannon captured by the Zapotec soldiers, in his sculpture "The Juchiteco's Cannon."

Another key event in COCEI's politicized chronology is the torture and killing of Félix Díaz (who, like Juárez, had attacked Juchitán) by Binu Gada and his gang of Juchiteco soldiers. Rather than concealing the gory details of the killing, contemporary Juchitecos justify it as a necessary reprisal against abusive authority. In general, Juchitecos enjoy describing the "barbarity" and "ferocity" of their forebears. Likewise, instead of trying to portray themselves as nonviolent altruists, *Coceístas* revel in their tough, roguish image and celebrate the ferocious reputation Juchitán has acquired from the Félix Díaz incident and other military and political events. Daniel López Nelio, COCEI peasant leader, epitomized these sentiments in his response to a Mexico City reporter who asked him to describe the character of the Juchitecos: "They are a bunch of bandits . . . and I am their leader" ("*Son una bola de bandidos . . . y yo soy el dirigente de ellos*").[2] Through such statements and attitudes, the Juchitecos undermine outside discourses critical of them by wallowing in and emphasizing those very characteristics and actions deemed objectionable by outsiders. They do this because they like to startle non-Juchitecos with their "barbarousness," and also because what is viewed negatively from outside has very different connotations when seen from within the Zapotec community.

The most important twentieth-century figure in COCEI's political pantheon is Che Gómez. Eulogized in poems, *corridos*, essays, paintings, and COCEI speeches, Gómez symbolizes Juchiteco militant defense of local land and political autonomy against the hegemony of *vallistos* and the national government (de la Cruz 1987b). The fact that Gómez was brutally murdered makes him even more attractive as a symbol. Thus, he is a martyr in a culture that attaches great importance to the cult of the dead. That Gómez was an upper-class Juchiteco with a mestizo lifestyle in no way diminishes his importance as a leader of Isthmus Zapotec rebellions in COCEI's history. What is more important for COCEI is that he was a valiant, uncompromising, and stylish opponent of Juchitán's enemies.

Not all Juchitecos who figured prominently in Mexican history have become a part of COCEI accounts of the past. Omitted from COCEI historical discourse are Juchitecos who fought on the "reactionary side of history," such as Juvencio Robles, a revolutionary general who decimated Morelos in pursuit of Zapata (Womack 1969), and Rosalino Martínez, another Juchiteco general who massacred workers at Río Blanco, Veracruz, in 1906 in one of the key incidents that led to the Revolution (López Gurrión 1976).[3] Such individuals do not fit COCEI's self-styled image of independence and rebelliousness.

The doctors Valentín Carrasco and Roque Robles, who initiated the last armed movement for Isthmus autonomy in 1931, are routinely invoked in COCEI speeches linking the present struggles to the past. General Heliodoro Charis Castro, however, represents a more problematical personage for COCEI intellectuals. On the one hand, Charis is a populist hero who demonstrated Juchiteco bravura during the Revolution and obtained land for his former soldiers in the Alvaro Obregón Colony. On the other hand, Charis maintained legal control of these lands, which were eventually taken from the families of the soldiers, and he ruled Juchitán as a *cacique* for more than 30 years. Furthermore, Rojo, his son-in-law, has become COCEI's archenemy and invokes Charis' name at every opportunity on behalf of conservative causes and his own political career (López Monjardin 1983).

Yet, COCEI is reluctant to distance itself too far from Charis' aura. One obvious reason is because of Javier Charis, who is a COCEI leader and the son of the general. The deeper reason, however, is that for the Isthmus peasantry—not just in Juchitán but in Xadani, San Blas, Unión Hidalgo, and elsewhere—Charis represents the quintessential Zapotec man. Hundreds of Zapotec peasants alive today dealt with Charis personally and remember him as one of their own in an unending repertoire of folktales and *mentiras*. Although he became a despot in his later years, Charis was nonetheless the ultimate Zapotec peasant (whom contemporary Zapotec farmers themselves describe as *"indio puro,"* pure Indian), and a colorful and often comical *macho* who spoke Spanish poorly, drank mescal, philandered, and rode a mule. Far more than Che Gómez or any other Zapotec figure of the past, Charis is the consummate folk hero/comic in Isthmus oral tradition.[4] Thus, COCEI's ideological treatment of Charis is, of necessity, ambivalent. In fact, COCEI literature has little to say about the

30-year period of Charis' rule when, from the movement's perspective, "nothing happened," i.e., there were no major uprisings and rebellions (López Monjardin 1983).

Recent history, from COCEI's standpoint, is more easily reduced to black-and-white categories. The good guys are the Zapotec peasantry; the bad guys, the state and national government and the regional bourgeoisie. In this scenario, urban politicians are responsible for the bungled and corrupt decrees that stripped Zapotec peasants of their land. Bureaucrats and politicians are also blamed for the inefficiencies and inequalities of the Benito Juárez Dam and irrigation project (COCEI 1983). COCEI spokesmen argue that large landholders and merchants benefited from greater insertion of the Isthmus into the national economy via the construction of the Pan American Highway, the Salina Cruz oil refinery, and the dam. Peasants and their way of life were threatened by these developments, they say. The last stage of this one-sided process, from COCEI's perspective, was the expansion of the government bureaucracy into the region to oversee economic development at the expense of the Zapotec poor. Therefore, according to COCEI ideology, the movement formed to defend the interests of the peasants, to restore indigenous cultural traditions, and to continue the lineal trajectory of Isthmus Zapotec resistance since pre-Hispanic times (COCEI 1990).

A particularly interesting aspect of COCEI's vision of the past is the way *Coceístas* link contemporary political events to "parallel" incidents in Isthmus history. For example, in 1983 COCEI peasants warned their leaders against sharing meals with their enemies, for fear that they would be poisoned like Meléndez in 1853 (López Monjardin 1983). The peasants also urged Polín not to travel alone during the *Ayuntamiento Popular* because he might be killed on the road the way Che Gómez was in 1911. Polo supposedly rang the San Vicente Church bells when soldiers threw COCEI out of the occupied Juchitán City Hall in 1983, just like Juchiteco fighters did in 1866 in the battle against the French. COCEI's current enemies, likewise, are viewed as likenesses of past opponents (López Monjardin 1983). COCEI ideologists see Oaxaca government repression of the movement as isometric with Juárez's burning of Juchitán (Toledo 1986), and the federal government's crackdown on the *Ayuntamiento Popular* as analogous to the state's suppression of the Che Gómez movement. Additionally, *Coceístas* saw the 1980s Alfa-Omega project for rapid transportation of cargo across the Isthmus as a revival of nineteenth-century gringo aspirations to take over the Isthmus. Finally, Macario Matus described the imposition of Caraveo as the Juchitán mayoral candidate in 1989 by the Oaxaca PRI establishment as a repeat of the imposition of Enrique León in 1911, which sparked the Che Gómez rebellion.

The use of history to justify political movements is very common in most, if not all, contemporary societies. It has been especially important in Mexico since the Revolution. Indeed, Chassen (personal communication 1992) describes the use of history as a political instrument in Mexico as "rampant in each political generation" and "far more important as [an] element of national unity than in [the] U.S." In official ideology, the legitimacy of the Mexican state (and the PRI) derives from its roots in the Mexican Revolution. By creating its own regional (and region-centered) version of history, COCEI has subverted bourgeois, nationalist interpretations of Mexican history and established its own bases of legitimacy.[5]

The best previous discussion of Juchiteco history making in the literature on COCEI is Aubague's clever essay (1985). Aubague argues that the COCEI political struggle is anchored ideologically in the Juchiteco collective memory of past conflicts and heroes. While I agree that COCEI mobilizes an ethnic past as a political weapon in the present, and affirms local history in the face of officialist national history, Aubague's phenomenological approach, rooted in psychoanalysis, can be criticized on a number of grounds. In particular, he overemphasizes the mythical/imaginary/ epic element of COCEI historiography at the expense of a grounded ethnographic analysis of Juchiteco ethnopolitics.[6] Although the Coalition's view of history is part of an ethnic discourse of political empowerment, to reduce this history to its supposedly mythical foundation and describe it as a dream or a utopia trivializes Juchitán's rich social history.

Meléndez, Che Gómez, and Charis exist in the minds of contemporary Juchitecos as more than just mythic heroes. Juchitecos' consciousness of their past is much more concrete. If you ask an older Juchiteco who Che Gómez was, he will not only tell you where his house was and who his descendants are, he will provide you with rich details about Gómez's personal and political life. This is why COCEI's references to the Juchiteco past are so effective: they touch on lived struggles, memories of which have been passed on from one generation to the next in minute and graphic detail. For example, when I interviewed Justo Pineda about Charis, Justo described the historical context (including the date, who was President at the time, and the major events of the period) of many of Charis' actions, and even mentioned the time of day, the street address or precise location at which the action took place, what clothing people were wearing, who was in the room or the area, who said what to whom, ad infinitum. While

Justo's memory was nothing less than phenomenal, there are large numbers of other Isthmus Zapotecs who can discuss the past with nearly as much clarity.

Furthermore, COCEI history making is more than just a textual creation. Several Juchiteco intellectuals associated with the Casa de la Cultura and COCEI (especially de la Cruz, Toledo, and Macario and Manuel Matus) have done extensive archival and oral history research on the Isthmus. This is serious research, not just myth-making. That the "facts" of such historical work become part of streams of political discourse does not mean that they are simply creations of the imagination (although Toledo's artwork could be described as such) or disembodied texts, as in parts of Aubague's analysis.

The weaknesses of such an approach have been amply demonstrated by Roseberry (1989:24), who notes that "To see culture as an ensemble of texts . . . is to remove culture from the process of its creation." This is why it is important to analyze cultural creations such as COCEI's view of history "not simply as socially constituted but also as socially constituting" (Roseberry 1989:28). The rest of this chapter is devoted to an examination of the ways Zapotec culture, ethnicity, and gender are constituted in COCEI ideology and the potential consequences (or lack thereof) of this ideology for political change in the Isthmus.

Zapotec Culture in COCEI Ideology: Kinship Relationships, the Zapotec Family, and "Juchiteco Democracy"

According to the movement's intellectuals, COCEI developed naturally out of Isthmus Zapotec culture and is simply the most recent incarnation of the Juchiteco rebellious spirit. Pro–COCEI writer Manuel Matus (1988:iii) summarizes these ideas as follows: "The consciousness of the COCEI movement derives from the cultural organization of the Zapotecs, of the concepts they have regarding property, unity, women, language, and solidarity." This view assumes that "traditional" Isthmus Zapotec society is inherently democratic and based on communal landholding and reciprocity, as exemplified by the term *guendalizaa* (cooperation among kinsmen), despite the class divisions discussed previously. Moreover, private property and capitalist values are said to be foreign concepts that have contaminated indigenous culture. In contrast to capitalist relations, *Coceístas* declare that they treat and address each other as *bichi* (a kin term implying all Zapotec men are brothers) or *hermanos* (brothers), as the Zapotecs used to do before outside ideas eroded these customs.

Daniel López Nelio, perhaps COCEI's key political ideologue, links the
Juchiteco ethos of resistance and Zapotec communal consciousness to early
childhood education. This, he says, has provided the "cultural antecedent"
to COCEI. At an early age, notes López Nelio, Zapotec children are taught
to love Juchitán and hate *dxu'*; and Zapotec child rearing inculcates toughness into children (*"te enseñaron a ser hombre"*[7]). As a youth his parents
constantly told him "be a man" (*"guca badu nguiiu"*). Male children are
given harsh training, López Nelio points out, in a kind of wrestling game
called *porrazo*. This, according to the Juchiteco peasant leader, is how one
learns to dominate his fear.

López Nelio described to me an incident that took place in his childhood, after he saw a rattlesnake. When he asked his father what to do, his
father replied "kill it," which he did, which gave him valor. On another
occasion, he returned home after being beaten up by a neighbor kid. Daniel's father told him to go back and beat up the kid this time or keep quiet
(*"Hay que madrear aquel o llegar quieto sin chillar a la casa"*). Juchitecos are
fearless, López Nelio said, because once you have played *porrazo* or killed
a rattlesnake you will never be scared again. Thus, the Zapotec family's
harsh discipline and training to confront the most difficult experiences are
described as the foundations for COCEI's militant politics. López Nelio
recalled that even as a child he used to organize his buddies to attack rival
gangs, which prepared him to be a political leader later in life. Finally, Lilí
Sánchez told me that the children of current COCEI leaders set up little
platforms, put red bandannas around their necks, and pretend to have their
own political rallies in imitation of their parents.

COCEI ideology also claims that Zapotec family life is democratic and
that every member is allowed to voice his or her opinions and is entitled
to sustenance under all circumstances (Santana 1988). If a son comes home
drunk, according to López Nelio, the parents may scold him, but he always
has a right to be fed. The Zapotec family may be the first source of education in "traditional democratic values" but, according to Santana
(1988:37), "the [Zapotec] people have developed the concept of democracy
in a particular way in all levels of social life." This is supposedly expressed
in the selection of leaders and in conflict resolution. For example, since
pre-Hispanic times the Zapotecs formed their own patterns for electing
their representatives, says Santana. Barrio headmen (*jefes de sección*), then,
could only be chosen if they were natives of the barrio and speakers of
Zapotec, with a tradition of struggle and the consent of the populace. Town
leaders were elected if they were "the most honest and capable of defending

Zapotec cultural identity; only then would [people] remain faithful to their leader to the very end" (Santana 1988:38).

In an obviously self-justifying comment, Polín once told me that COCEI leaders are traditional Zapotec leaders who are charismatic, energetic, good-humored, patient, and able to improvise long speeches or jokes. From this viewpoint, the relationship between COCEI leaders and their followers does not involve the imposition of ideas. Instead, the people closely identify with the leaders because they speak the Zapotec language and have the same customs and attitudes as the people. COCEI militants say that decisions are reached by consensus after discussions between the rank-and-file and the leadership. In fact, most political decisions are made first by the leadership and then revealed to *Coceístas* as a whole at political meetings. Likewise, conflicts within the movement are supposedly resolved with the participation and input of the individuals involved in the problem (Santana 1988:39). Consequently, during the *Ayuntamiento Popular*, some Coalition activists called Polín "*xaíque*" (chief, or literally, the "head of the group")[8] instead of *Presidente Municipal* to indicate the COCEI government's presumed grounding in Zapotec traditions.

When a marital spat divides a Zapotec couple, the wife normally returns to her parents' home, where she remains until the husband decides to reconcile. Before the wife returns, a meeting may be held between the couple, their relatives and godparents, and the barrio headman. All participants have a chance to express their views until a decision is reached. COCEI spokesmen claim the same type of democratic social organization is found in the political sphere, hence the Juchitecos' revulsion at outside imposition of local authorities (Santana 1988:40). Thus, for COCEI ideologists, the harmonious sociopolitical organization that results from Zapotec "democratic traditions" is exemplified in the term *yoo lahui* (the people's communal house), used to refer to City Hall (UNAM 1986:12–13).[9]

While Coalition spokesmen posit a unique Zapotec cultural basis for COCEI politics, it is important to bear in mind that kinship metaphors and notions of primal communalism have been common features of populist and *indigenista* discourses in Mexican politics since the Revolution (Padgett 1976:12–13). Such language and symbols have often been used to "naturalize" and legitimize social and political inequalities. Although within the Coalition there is considerable give-and-take between the leadership and the rank-and-file (in the neighborhood committees, cantinas, demonstrations, and *velas*), decision-making power is ultimately in the

hands of the COCEI political commission, which is composed of approximately 16 men. Furthermore, three leaders (Polín, López Nelio, and Héctor Sánchez) hold by far the largest share of power within the Coalition
inner circle.

In this respect, COCEI's metaphorical presentation of indigenous
household and kinship ethics "Zapotecizes," or culturally legitimizes, the
centralization of power by the COCEI leadership, and thus makes the
organization appear more democratic than it is in practice. Centralized
power is one of the main bones of contention in recent disputes and conflicts among COCEI members. Changing the concentration of power
within the Coalition may require concrete actions by COCEI leaders and
rank-and-file, and the development of new ways of thinking about power
and its relation to Juchiteco culture.[10]

The Zapotec Language and COCEI Politics

According to COCEI spokesmen, the Zapotec language is the glue that
binds members of the movement and one of the main reasons why Coalition politics have a distinctly ethnic character. As Manuel Matus
(1988:64–65) puts it: "It was [Zapotec] language that permitted COCEI to
consolidate itself as its own organization, because the language allows communication which is direct and attached to things. . . . It is an inexhaustible
source of unity and solidarity."

Juchiteco intellectuals are fascinated with their Zapotec language, which
they describe as naturally poetic and metaphorical. This is exemplified by
words such as *belegui'* (star), which they say translates literally into Spanish
as "ray of light", or *nisa guie* (rain) which becomes "water stone". Consequently, the Juchitecos say jokes are more enjoyable (*más sabroso*) in the
native tongue than in Spanish. Because of the great importance the Isthmus
Zapotec attach to their language, it is no surprise that COCEI emphasizes
the Zapotec language at all opportunities, e.g., in political graffiti, in signs
on buildings such as the Casa de la Cultura (*Lidxi Guendabiani*), and in a
sign over the entrance to town during the "People's Government" bidding
travelers a safe trip (*Sicarú Guyê*). The most strategic use of the language,
though, occurs in the COCEI rallies, which the movement describes as
simply an extension of the Isthmus fiesta tradition. Manuel Matus
(1988:66) notes that COCEI political speeches are given in Zapotec because "if it were otherwise the correct meaning of what is communicated
would not be transmitted." When Zapotec is used in the speeches, "un-

derstanding becomes more exact, and sentiments are converted into a human whirlwind in the political events" (Manuel Matus 1988:66).

The Local Economy, Indigenous Subsistence Practices, and COCEI Discourse

In interviews and essays, COCEI leaders describe the traditional Juchitán economy as one based on reciprocal exchanges among peasants, fishermen, and artisans. They also proclaim that communalism is integral to Zapotec land tenure, barrio organization, and economic practices. Isthmus land has been communal since time immemorial, according to COCEI, and the penetration of capitalism began to privatize it only in the last few decades (Toledo and de la Cruz 1983; COCEI 1983). From this perspective, the indigenous economy is based on subsistence-oriented peasant agriculture and the equal exchange of goods in the market. Surpluses are spent on *velas*, other ceremonial activities (birthdays, funerals, and so on), and the maintenance of ancestral customs. Therefore, capital accumulation is minimal (Santana 1988:14). In addition to distributing surplus wealth, the *velas* and other festivities supposedly reinforce community ties (but compare my earlier discussion of the *velas*). In COCEI discourse, *tequios* and *guendalizaa*, for instance, in the shared construction of the house of a young married couple, further strengthen kin and non-kin relationships in the indigenous community.

According to COCEI's anticapitalist rhetoric, the Zapotec engage in social labor, which promotes solidarity and collaboration between townspeople, unlike modern forms of production that produce only alienation. Moreover, in Toledo's stylish sculptures, paintings, and prints, animals and humans copulate freely, and the Isthmus appears as a pastoral environment in which humans and nature are in harmony and myth and reality are inseparable. Juchitán is the center of the Zapotec intellectuals' rural utopia, which they claim outsiders are destroying and COCEI is defending.

COCEI peasant leaders boast that native *zapalote* corn is better than new "synthetic" strains, and that peasant agriculture rather than the government's irrigation system is the only appropriate economic option for the Isthmus (Santana 1988). COCEI also supports fishing cooperatives, which reputedly use consensus decision making based on indigenous norms. Native craftsmanship is supposedly superior to industrialized, mass-produced products. Juchiteco intellectuals use the word *guixhe* (hammock or net) to exemplify the integrative role of artisanry in Isthmus life, since *guixhe* are used by fishermen to catch fish, by peasants to transport corn, and by everyone to sleep in—in addition to providing a livelihood for the hammock-maker (UNAM 1986:41).

According to COCEI activist Mariano Santana (1988:17), the sale or barter of fish, wild game, agricultural products, and craft goods in the traditional marketplace is a communal, reciprocal activity that provisions families and the community instead of producing profits. This leads into the notion that indigenous commercial activity reproduces native society and is separate from "big business," which is in the hands of outsiders (Santana 1988:18). This view does not jibe with my findings about the considerable wealth of a number of upper-class Zapotec families, especially the López Lenas.

Overall, COCEI's characterization of local subsistence patterns and economic practices reflects the crisis in Isthmus Zapotec society precipitated by recent capitalist developments. As indigenous forms of reciprocity, communal land tenure, and interdependence are challenged and transformed by capitalist relations, COCEI has chosen to defend an idealized model of a village economy and society in the political arena. This is the case for a number of reasons, not the least of which is the COCEI intellectuals' legitimate concern that government development projects have had a drastic effect on the physical environment, traditional agricultural and fishing methods, and community solidarity. Another primary reason for COCEI's defense of communal property, however, is its strong ideological and practical commitment to Zapotec peasants, who make up the majority of the movement's constituency, and whose hopes to regain or maintain their landholdings are dependent on a favorable resolution of long-standing conflicts over Juchitán's communal land. Finally, COCEI leaders' claims as to the superiority of Zapotec social and economic practices are also part of its general strategy of using local ethnicity and culture as an ideological weapon against the Mexican state. This strategy is also wielded against indigenous elites within Juchitán, whom the movement labels as sellouts who "have lost their democratic spirit" to capitalist, mestizo ways of life.

While the likelihood of COCEI rejuvenating the type of communal, subsistence economy it defends and advocates is relatively slim, the movement's strength among the Isthmus peasantry, fishermen, and artisans will probably continue until the state can devise more effective means for addressing their needs. In the meantime, the precarious survival of Juchiteco peasants, fishermen, and petty commodity producers will be closely linked to the concessions they can obtain with COCEI's help.

The Politics of Ethnicity in COCEI Ideology

COCEI leaders frequently state that the Coalition is not only a movement of the Zapotecs but of all the indigenous peoples of the Isthmus. Moreover, *Coceístas* also claim to struggle on behalf of all local peasants and workers, regardless of their ethnic identity. In fact, COCEI has had some ties to groups in Mixe, Huave, Chontal, Zoque, and Southern Zapotec communities. Mestizos and Istmeños of Middle Eastern descent (*Turcos*) participate in the movement, and COCEI has a large and powerful labor movement comprised of many mestizo Mexicans.

Nonetheless, the "ethnic question" remains COCEI's Achilles' heel, although it is simultaneously the movement's greatest strength. Here we find some of the most striking contradictions between COCEI ideology and Isthmus social life. Let us examine these contradictions in the case of Zapotec-Huave relations. In Chapter 2, I discussed the Zapotec's displacement of the Huave and Zoque from some of the best Isthmus land when they conquered the region in the fourteenth century. Since then, the much larger and more politically and economically powerful Zapotec group has dominated the Huave. Marginalized to some of the most desolate and harsh living environments in Mexico (barren sand dunes and beaches bordering the Isthmus lagoons), most Huaves must pass through Zapotec communities in order to sell their fish and obtain trade items, or gain access to social services, higher education, and other opportunities. Isthmus Zapotec merchants profit amply from their unequal trading relationship with the Huave, who have little choice but to accept the prices proffered by Zapotecs.

In the cultural realm, Zapotecs view Huaves as primitive inferiors and tell myriad derogatory jokes about them. Andrés Henestrosa (1969:17), in describing his own relatives, the Morales, notes that they were of a "defeated race [i.e., the Huave], subordinated by the Juchitecos, who cannot refer to them without first prefixing a denigratory adjective."[11] Zapotec men joke that Huave women's vaginas run sideways, and Zapotec people generally mistrust or are in awe of the Huave's talents as sorcerers. Huave women, in turn, complain that Zapotec women steal their fish, and they laugh at the "strange" behaviors of the "*Zapochuecos*" (Jesus María Pineda 1986:49). Both groups use words from their own languages, tinged with negative connotations, to refer to each other: Huave call the Zapotecs *colocho*, and the Zapotecs call the Huave *wabi* or *mareños* (sea-people).[12] Additionally, Huave, Mixe, and Zoque women have adopted the use of Isthmus Zapotec clothing.[13] The Huave and Zoque have also taken up the

Zapotec fiesta system (*velas*), and many Huaves speak the Zapotec language (of necessity), whereas few if any Zapotecs speak the languages of their indigenous neighbors (Hernández Díaz 1986:307). Zapotecs view these examples of cultural borrowing as evidence of their cultural superiority vis-à-vis other Isthmus indigenous groups.

Although Zapotec–Huave interactions may not take on the everyday viciousness of racial hatreds in South Africa or parts of urban North America, the potential for violence latent in the relationship occasionally comes to the surface. One of my housemates in the field (a Zapotec) once watched in horror as two Zapotec men literally crushed a Huave man to death with a boulder after a drunken argument. The witness assured me that the brutality of the crime was a result of racist attitudes. I also observed a fight between a Zapotec and a Huave man in San Blas. Thus, historically rooted undercurrents of hostility and mistrust are an obstacle to rapprochement between the mostly Zapotec COCEI and Huave people. Consequently, I have never seen a significant Huave presence at COCEI meetings.

Unfortunately for the Coalition, any chances it had of attracting much support in Huave communities was diminished by the killing of several Huaves and the expropriation of Huave-owned land by Zapotecs during COCEI's struggle for control of the ex-Charis haciendas around Alvaro Obregón in the late 1970s (Signorini 1979:24). In 1972, prior to the formation of COCEI, Huaves and Zapotecs also clashed over lands in the San Francisco del Mar area. COCEI leaders claim that it was really a fight between large landowners—some of whom just happened to be Zapotecs—and peasants who were both Huave and Zapotec (Santana 1988:2–3). I have no information that would prove or disprove this account. However, during 1987–1988 I did confirm that COCEI controlled the Huave community of San Francisco del Mar. Unfortunately, the pro-COCEI Huave mayor of town was murdered during this time under mysterious circumstances. COCEI supporters were also attacked there during the 1983 election campaign. Thus, COCEI's relations with Huave communities remain turbulent.

Zapotec–Mixe and Zapotec–Zoque interactions are also conflictive and hierarchical. Isthmus Zapotecs control Zoque economic production through the Niltepec and Matías Romero markets, and much of the Mixe coffee crop has been monopolized historically by Zapotecs of Ixtepec and Juchitán (Hernández Díaz 1986:306). In the political arena, the Juchitán PRI has counted on the nearly unanimous support of the Isthmus Mixe communities for decades and views their Mixe "supporters" as eminently docile and manipulable. *Coceístas*, likewise, see the Mixe, Southern Zapotec, and Chontals as meek and unrebellious, hence poor raw material for their radical movement (although many Chontals, motivated by dire poverty, have recently joined COCEI).

During elections the Juchitán PRI sometimes brings Mixe *acarreados* (voters hauled to the polls in cattle trucks) from San Juan Guichicovi to illegally pad PRI vote tallies. However, *Coceístas* claim the Mixes are instantly identifiable because they do not respond to verbal challenges, but instead cower in silence, something they say a Juchiteco would never do. In contrast, one COCEI leader told me that Isthmus Zapotec women are proud and strong and always look another person right in the eye instead of bowing. Another Zapotec man told me that Juchitecos are naturally egalitarian, unlike other Mexicans. Therefore, they always use the informal *"tu"* pronoun in Spanish when speaking to other people, rather than the formal *"usted"* form, which marks social distinctions and hierarchy.[14] *Coceístas* view these differences as examples of their superiority over other Mexican ethnic groups.

In sum, Zapotec ethnic militancy and COCEI's ethnopolitical ideology are a double-edged sword. By glorifying Isthmus Zapotec culture and history, COCEI leaders strengthen the movement internally, but limit possibilities for expansion to other Isthmus indigenous groups and mestizo Mexicans.

Gender and COCEI Ideology

According to COCEI leaders, women are the "shock troops" of the movement, and Isthmus gender relations confound feminist theories because women are equal to men in local society. Women do make up at least half of the Coalition's forces, and their participation has been crucial throughout the movement's history. In fact, one of the key incidents that sparked COCEI's expansion was the murder of Lorenza Santiago, a pregnant *Coceísta*, during a march protesting vote fraud after the 1974 elections. In election campaigns COCEI women march at the head of processions next to the political candidates (up to now, always male), and they place *guie'chaachi* wreathes around these men's necks in a gesture of honor and hospitality. Women's luxurious red *trajes* give sartorial flair to COCEI demonstrations, but women also take part in the "dirty work" of highway blockades, building takeovers, and land invasions. For instance, during my fieldwork I observed a COCEI blockade of the Pan American Highway in which Zapotec women cradled rocks in their *huipiles* and skirts, which they used to threaten truck drivers who attempted to break through the crowd of Coalition protestors.

Additionally, Isthmus women have a degree of freedom (that men do not have) to insult their political opponents or speak controversial "truths" in conflict situations without being immediately attacked. This is one reason they are often at the front of political marches. Thus, when PRI presidential candidate Carlos Salinas stopped at Ixtepec, but avoided Juchitán, during his 1988 campaign, a Zapotec woman scolded him, "Only those with balls go to Juchitán" (*Nada más los que tienen huevos llegan a Juchitán*), implying the politician was lacking them (*Excélsior* 3/18/1988). In 1983 a large group of *Coceístas* (men and women) were imprisoned for occupying the Guatemalan and Indian embassies in Mexico City in protest of vote fraud. When the jailers brought a Zapotec-speaking man to interrogate the Juchitecos in their native language, the Zapotec women prisoners let loose a verbal torrent against the "traitor," which so embarrassed him that he failed to carry out his mission.[15]

The gendered character of Isthmus Zapotec social organization is reproduced within the Coalition political movement. Hence women's involvement in COCEI is linked to their roles in the marketplace, small businesses, neighborhoods, and the family. (Men's roles as peasant agriculturalists and laborers are the primary basis from which they participate in the movement.) For example, two influential female *Coceístas*, Idalia Linares and Lilia Ortega, have gained prominence for their work as *juez de plaza* (a kind of administrator of market affairs) and representative of women who run market stalls, respectively. Likewise, Rosa Velásquez, a feisty *cantinera*, has been a staunch COCEI supporter and defender of the interests of Juchitán tavern owners. In addition, Dolores Pineda, who runs a small snack bar in Juchitán's Revolution Park, is also a prominent activist in her COCEI neighborhood committee of the second ward. Finally, the female family members of many COCEI activists and politicians are influential Coalition figures, such as Hermila Guerra (widow of a COCEI martyr), Luisa de la Cruz (mother of Polín and spouse of Polo), and Lilí Sánchez (wife of the mayor and director of a government-funded social services office from 1989 to 1992).

Isthmus Zapotec women's separate social spaces and roles are also reproduced in some COCEI political activities and mobilizations. In marches and demonstrations, for example, women often group together apart from men. On other occasions, female *Coceístas* hold all-women protest marches, and women have their own separate political committee within the movement, which sometimes organizes special actions such as fundraisers and protest vigils. When COCEI occupied Juchitán City Hall after being impeached from office in August 1983, female relatives of the COCEI leadership gathered in front of City Hall to guard against attack by soldiers. Additionally, Juchitecas acted as messengers and suppliers of food (which they smuggled in their blouses and skirts) for the men barricaded inside the City Hall building during this period. Finally, women's roles as protectors of the family, the sacred, and the dead are reproduced in hunger strikes held in the main Mexico City cathedral, demonstrations in the Oaxaca City cathedral, and other protest actions carried out by female relatives of COCEI martyrs and political prisoners.

Women's symbolic role in COCEI's public image is almost as important as their concrete contributions to the movement. Perhaps the most well-known and attractive images of the Coalition are posters and book covers of powerful, proud, Zapotec women marching through the Juchitán streets with raised fists, or holding COCEI flags with their long hair, rebozos, and flowing skirts blowing in the wind. Cándida Santiago and Hermila Guerra, widows of two famous COCEI martyrs, are frequently depicted in such poses, often wearing dark mourning clothes. Such imagery is not accidental. According to national and local folklore, Isthmus Zapotec society is matriarchal, and this is said to be the most distinctive feature of the ethnic group.

Thus, Isthmus women become key symbols of power, conservation of tradition, and indigenous ethnic identity in COCEI ideology. Depicted as heroines and the wives and mothers of martyrs (analogous to the mothers of the Plaza de Mayo in Argentina), they are also repositories of moral righteousness and militancy. In photographs portraying their market role—carrying baskets of *totopos*, fish, hammocks, or iguanas on their heads—women represent industry and nurturing of the community. Finally, as mothers and midwives they are viewed as "the mothers of all the people on earth" (UNAM 1986:49).[16]

With these images and ideas of Isthmus Zapotec women's power, COCEI tapped into the rich folklore about "matriarchal Tehuanas"— which goes back to at least the mid-nineteenth century and has been embellished repeatedly in traveler's reports, tourist guides, the writings of male Zapotec intellectuals, and an extensive local oral tradition concerned with women's actions. For COCEI ideologues, contemporary Zapotec women continue in the tradition of *la india Teresa*, the Indian woman who supposedly killed a Spaniard during the Tehuantepec Rebellion (Matus 1981). They also carry on the heritage of Tona Taati (the Juchiteca lover

and aid to Porfirio Díaz), who was said to have goaded on Juchiteco men
in battle against the French Interventionists by crying, "If you men won't
fight them, we women will do it ourselves" (Macario Matus 1988:61).

As in other contexts, COCEI views current political struggles in terms
of "parallel" events in the past. Thus, I was told that Víctor de la Cruz's
spouse collected rocks in her *enaguas* to throw at *Priístas* during armed
struggle in San Francisco del Mar in 1983, and Juchitecas passed information to their besieged *compañeros* in the COCEI-occupied City Hall in
1983, just as the *soldaderas* had hidden weapons, *totopos*, and messages in
their *huipiles* and *faldas* during the Revolution. Another recurrent theme in
oral history and mythology about Isthmus women's involvement in conflict
is the image of men hiding inside the petticoats of matriarchal women, as
Porfirio Díaz supposedly did in the skirts of Juana C. Romero (Macario
Matus 1988:61; Krauze 1987:18). During the rock-throwing brawl in which
Coceístas threw the PRI mayor of San Blas out of office in 1984, *Priístas*
reputedly hid underneath women's *enaguas* until they could escape.

As noted in relation to history, ethnicity, and Isthmus culture, COCEI
ideology regarding women simplifies a more complex social dynamic. Although the Coalition claims to defend the interests of Isthmus women, the
movement really has no plan or program to address women's needs. Moreover, women's supposed equality in the movement is belied by the realities
of political decision making and social opportunities in Juchitán. There are
no women members of the Coalition's political commission (although
there were two females on the COCEI city council from 1981–1983) and
no Zapotec women play major roles in the cultural revival movement. Unfortunately, Gudelia Pineda, a talented COCEI politician destined for
prominence, died in a freak accident in the mid-1980s. The few women
who do have leadership positions in COCEI are either the spouses, wives,
mothers, or other relatives of male leaders, the widows of martyrs, or leaders of typically female occupational groups such as tavern owners, market
women, and nurses. Thus, women's power at the highest level of the movement is either mediated through men or restricted to stereotypically female
domains. Women are vitally involved in all grassroots activities of the
movement, from participation at COCEI neighborhood meetings and distributing leaflets to hunger strikes and street fighting against the police and
Priístas. Yet, the myth of matriarchy obscures the reality of women's sec-
ond-class status in political decision making.

The gendered terminology of COCEI discourse reveals other facets of
Juchitán political culture and the subordination of women in Isthmus politics. For instance, I noted above how López Nelio linked COCEI mili-

tancy to Zapotec child rearing practices, in which boys are told to "be a man." Likewise, COCEI ideologists use the words *bichi*[17] and *hermano*, which mean "brother" in Zapotec and Spanish, respectively, to symbolize the supposed communal unity of the movement. Through such male-centered concepts and language, COCEI leaders "naturalize" (i.e., make appear as natural or ethnically primordial) the reputedly democratic, courageous, and collective character of the movement. Additionally, COCEI political insults often have a gendered quality, such as when a male Coalition leader ridiculed the divided Juchiteco *Priístas* by comparing them to the allegedly sparse pubic hair of Mixe women (note also the ethnic element in this political taunt), or when *Coceístas* call the PRI "*Prihuela*" (*huela* means "old woman" in Zapotec). These examples indicate that although COCEI ideologists may talk of gender equality, in other instances they equate maleness with power and femaleness with weakness. Thus, gendered concepts are both a vehicle for the "naturalization" of COCEI's ideal self-image, and at the same time reflect male-dominant attitudes within the Coalition hierarchy.

COCEI ideology is not the only source of politicized discourses about Isthmus women. As Juchitán and COCEI's notoriety grew, dozens of writers and social scientists descended on the Isthmus in search of primitive communism and matriarchal women. Overwhelmed by women's seeming dominance of economic and ceremonial life, some outside observers came to the conclusion that Juchitán is a kind of pre-patriarchal, feminist paradise. Thus, for Poniatowska (1989:13), Juchitecas are Amazons for whom men are merely cats wandering between their legs or restless cubs that need to be scolded. In Juchitán, gender roles are reversed:

[Women] grab men who watch them from behind the fence, pulling at them, fondling them as they curse the government and, sometimes, men themselves. They are the ones who participate in the demonstrations and beat policemen. . . . You should see them arrive like walking towers, their windows open, their heart like a window, their nocturnal girth visited by the moon. You should see them arrive; they are already the government, they, the people, guardians of men, distributors of food, their children astride their hips or lying in the hammocks of their breasts, the wind in their skirts, flowered vessels, the honeycomb of their sex overflowing with men. Here they come shaking their wombs, pulling the *machos* toward them, the *machos* who, in contrast with them, wear light-colored pants, shirts, leather sandals, and palm hats which they lift high in the air as they shout: "Long live Juchitec women" [Poniatowska 1989:13–14].

While this makes for amusing reading and excellent literature, it does little to advance our ethnographic understanding of Juchitán life.[18] Nor does Bennholdt–Thomsen's Orientalist comment (1989:4) about all Juchitecas being lesbians. This is a misreading of the fact that Zapotec women dance together at fiestas and are very affectionate and intimate physically in a nonsexual way in everyday interactions, unlike the "hands–off" behavior of Westerners.[19] In criticizing these romanticized views of Juchitecas, I have no intention of simply reducing Juchitán to just another standardized example of a male-dominated society. Indeed, there are many idiosyncrasies of Isthmus life that are liberating for women and that give them high social status in the community.

One of these characteristics is their freedom from the oppressiveness of an imposed "slim-is-better" body aesthetic. Isthmus Zapotec women are very proud of their ample breasts, wide hips, and broad biceps. For Juchitecas, fat is not a feminist issue (to invert a once trendy phrase). Skinniness is viewed as a sign of ill health, not a virtue. Unlike many North American women, Zapotec women have considerable control over their own standards of physical beauty and feel comfortable with their body forms.

Women also play a key role in household affairs in terms of child raising, kinship networking, and money management. Women's control of the household purse strings in Juchitán is symbolized by the evocative Zapotec expression *xhquie ni* ("his penis"), which refers to the small portion of money that a man retains for his personal use for drinking or other recreational pursuits after he delivers to his wife the proceeds of the harvest or of his other economic endeavors.

Another aspect of Isthmus life that has many positive consequences for women is the "women-only space" of the marketplace and the degree of economic independence they derive from market activities. Zapotec women have been key participants in Isthmus markets since colonial times, if not before, as Torres de Laguna ([1580] 1983) and many subsequent observers have noted. Gadow (1908:150), for example, stated that "the whole of the trade is in their [Zapotec women's] hands; so much so, indeed, that all commercial transactions are done by them, or at least require their sanction." However, although many external observers have celebrated Zapotec women's marketing role, vending is, in fact, hard work, which involves carrying heavy baskets, standing or squatting in the fiery Isthmus sun, traveling on rickety buses for hours, and dealing with abusive tax collectors. Moreover, competition in the marketplace is intense and volatile. Some women are even excluded from participating, and others must squat in uncomfortable positions in the grimy streets amidst heavy foot and automobile traffic. As in Isthmus society generally, some vendors do much better than others, whereas the average market woman just struggles to make a living. Isthmus Zapotec women are segmented by social class, something that Poniatowska-style glamorization ignores.

An additional positive feature of Isthmus lifeways for women is the separate women's social sphere, and the prestige they enjoy in fiestas and other ceremonial domains. Chiñas notes that "Isthmus Zapotec women are the primary actors in the vigorous fiesta system for which the region is famous. Women not only occupy central roles in all ceremonies, they frequently are principal sponsors (*mayordomas*), build chapels dedicated to saints, and are owners of the essential costumes and gold jewelry worn in rites" (quoted from the abstracts of the 86th Annual Meeting of the American Anthropological Association held in 1987).[20]

Other aspects of Zapotec culture that are beneficial to women include their great pride in Zapotec ethnic attire, the considerable degree of solidarity among women, and the sexual freedom of widows and some other single women. Zapotec women's strong character, personal dignity, and social self-confidence, and their important roles in family, economic, festive, and religious life are other features of Isthmus life that are positive for women (Chiñas 1983). Such circumstances have led some local observers to suggest that Juchitán women have developed a kind of "natural feminism." Yet the culturally specific components of Isthmus life that elevate women's status should not blind us to undesirable things that Zapotec women share with many women cross-culturally. These include the sexual double standard, the "double day," fewer educational and occupational opportunities, domestic violence, and restricted access to positions of juridical and political power.[21]

Although Chiñas (1983:117) states that Isthmus Zapotec gender relations are "emphatically egalitarian," I have concluded that the balance of power and privilege in Isthmus Zapotec society is actually tipped towards the side of men. Historically, Isthmus Zapotec women have had few other occupational options besides market trading, various other forms of commerce, and low-paid jobs like clothes washing. Because educating the young beyond secondary school requires great sacrifices for the predominantly low-income population of the Isthmus, most families can afford to send only one child at most to high school or college. In most cases, Zapotec families have given male children this privilege and, consequently, men dominate the white-collar professions in the Isthmus. Although a few especially talented Isthmus women such as Juana C. Romero, Aurea Procel, Gudelia Pineda, Guadalupe López Lena, and Neli Toledo have made names for themselves as doctors, merchants, judges, or civic leaders, the Isthmus public sphere is generally controlled by men.[22]

Conversely, although Zapotec women's market role is as demanding as the occupations of men, women are wholly responsible for the care of children. This is a difficult task in an area of deeply-rooted poverty, large families, and high infant mortality. Women are also expected to do most domestic chores such as cooking and cleaning. These activities are made more difficult by Isthmus men's high rate of alcoholism, which is often associated with physical abuse of women and children, abandonment of the family, or squandering of scarce family funds.

Whereas the beauty, gregariousness, and supposed sexual availability of Isthmus Zapotec women have attracted the fancy of male observers such as Brasseur, Charnay, Gadow, Vasconcelos, and Covarrubias, in fact, men have far more freedom than Zapotec women to engage in premarital and extramarital liaisons or sexual relationships generally. Moreover, the "*casa chica*" is common in the Isthmus, as in other parts of Mexico. Young Zapotec women's sexuality is tightly controlled through the cult of virginity. Traditionally, a bride must be able to demonstrate her virginity through the presentation of a white sheet with bloodstains on it during her wedding night. Women have also been subject to *rapto* (abduction), often against their will.

Finally, the courts, police force, and political offices in the Isthmus are directed almost exclusively by men. Despite these circumstances, Chiñas (1983:93) argues that Isthmus Zapotec women's nonformalized roles "lead to a fine balance of equality between the sexes." However, one might question what kind of equality can prevail when one sex is systematically deprived of full rights to educational and occupational options, has an unequal burden of domestic responsibilities, is subject to rape, spousal abuse, and recurrent infidelity, and is controlled by a political and legal system run, almost exclusively, by members of the other sex!

Nonetheless, COCEI women themselves do not view feminism—which they consider a foreign, urban ideal—as the answer to their problems. Earlier I pointed out that there is a COCEI women's committee and that female *Coceístas* frequently engage in all-women marches, building takeovers, and other protest actions. But these actions are not conducted within the context of a feminist ideology, although they do build on the female solidarity and preexistent tradition of separate women's activities in Zapotec culture. Cándida Santiago says that the Juchitecas do not need women's liberation or independence, but simply want to struggle alongside their COCEI *compañeros* (Volkow et al. 1983:62).[23]

Female *Coceístas*, likewise, were not impressed by *Priísta* Carlos Salinas' appeal to Zapotec women, whom he described as "the vanguard of progress in the Isthmus," during his whirlwind 1988 presidential campaign tour through the area. Salinas' visit ended with a televised meeting with Isthmus women, which was described by the PRI as the "national synthesis" of his campaign interactions with Mexican females. Maura Matus of COCEI was angered that no peasant women were allowed to speak at the meeting, even though their problems were discussed by a female (PRI) Oaxaca senatorial candidate, television personalities (Lourdes Guerrero and "*la China*" Mendoza), and wealthy Zapotec women dressed in *traje*. Nor were COCEI women pleased when the urbane, senatorial candidate, fearing contamination, refused to eat traditional Isthmus cuisine, but insisted on only boiled chicken and well-washed, disinfected fruits.

The Juchitecas' disdain for PRI manipulation of Isthmus women was made clearer to me when I saw the empty PRI buses marked "*Mujer*" (Woman), which were scheduled to take Juchitecas to meet candidate Salinas. Apparently, few Juchitecas were willing to participate in PRI's event. Finally, COCEI women were deeply offended when two blond, white, television personalities, "*la Chiquitibum*" and "*la rubia de categoria*" (the high-class blond) were brought to Juchitán to promote Superior beer during the May 1987 *velas*. The "*Chiquitibum*" became famous as a result of a popular television commercial promoting Superior beer during the 1986 World Cup soccer competition held in Mexico. In the advertisement, she was shown dancing and cheering on the Mexican team in her trademark ultra-short, bra-less t-shirt with her big breasts bouncing to the beat of the tune "chiquitibum-a-la-bim-bom-bam. . . ." During and shortly after the World Cup, this advertisement and several spinoffs rocketed in popularity.

The advertisement did not gain popularity among Juchitecas, however, who resent the imposition of commercialized North American standards of beauty, sexuality, and behavior. Most Juchitecas continue to prefer wearing *huipiles* and *enaguas* to T-shirts and jeans, value dark skin, eyes, and hair, and do not flaunt their sexuality in a brazen fashion for the voyeuristic pleasure of men. Maura Matus, for example, was disgusted by the crass commercialism and vulgar sexuality of *La Chiquitibum*, who dressed in her cutoff T-shirt displaying her ample bosom while participating in the traditional *tirada de frutas*.

Thus, for now, COCEI women are content to continue their political

activity through the movement (despite the contradictions between
COCEI ideology and Isthmus gender reality) and within local cultural
forms, instead of accepting either urban feminism, commercialized standards of female decorum, or PRI's top-down approach to "the women
question." COCEI women view their political activity as a normal aspect
of their social lives which women have always engaged in, rather than as a
"women's issue."

Isthmus Zapotec Muxe' and Juchitán Politics

Another aspect of the gender "dialectic" in Isthmus Zapotec society addressed by COCEI ideology is the issue of male homosexuality. According
to COCEI ideologues, gays are not discriminated against by the movement
or by Zapotec people in general (de la Cruz 1983a). Two North American
anthropologists (Chiñas 1985; Cook 1986) have also concluded that effem-
inate males (muxe'), who occupy a "third gender role" similar to the berdache among American Indians, are freely accepted and tolerated in
Isthmus Zapotec society.

In contrast to the findings of these female anthropologists, I found considerable disdain among many "straight" Zapotec men toward muxe'. The
male group that I hung out with at night after my daily fieldwork constantly
mocked muxe', even though they also had muxe' friends and possibly had
had sexual relations with muxe' at some time during their lives. My im-
pression is that Zapotec women are very tolerant and accepting of muxe',
partially because they do not feel threatened by them. Straight men, however, often have very ambivalent, or even hostile, feelings about muxe',
whom they may view as a threat to their masculinity. Several of the gay
males I spoke with complained of discrimination and did not view Isthmus
Zapotec society as especially tolerant of muxe'. In a variation on the theme
of "the gender of the fieldworker affects the type of information received,"
I think that the fact I was male talking with more men than women meant
that I was more likely to be exposed to anti-muxe' opinions than had I been
female interviewing mostly women (who, I suggest, are more tolerant of
muxe').

Whether respected or discriminated against, muxe' play vital roles in the
Juchitán economy as embroiderers, tailors, bakers, prostitutes, tavern owners, and hairdressers. Blaseños sometimes jokingly and derisively refer to
Juchitán as "Muxe'tán" because of the supposedly large numbers of muxe'
residing there. Whatever their relative numbers compared to other Isthmus communities, muxe' are certainly active in Juchitán political life, where

they tend to favor PRI over COCEI. In fact, the most well-known Juchitán *muxe'* organization, *"Las Intrépidas,"* which sponsors its own annual *vela* during which they crown a queen *"Miss Intrépida,"* is openly supportive of PRI.

Muxe' solidarity with PRI apparently began during the period immediately following COCEI's ouster from office, when the PRI mayor was a prominent gay man. At that time, a local musical group composed a humorous *cumbia* depicting PRI-controlled City Hall as run entirely by gays from the mayor to the street sweepers (whereas COCEI attacked and ridiculed the gay mayor). One informant told me that the *muxe's* support of PRI is actually nonideological and is simply a result of the fact that PRI openly courts the *muxe'* vote with fiestas overflowing with beer. On at least two occasions PRI politicians have crowned *"Miss Intrépida"* in front of a *muxe'* crowd dressed in drag. Another reason for *muxe'* support for PRI is the popularity, organizational ability, and influence of a wealthy *muxe' Priísta* who has attracted many other *muxe'* to the party.

Despite its egalitarian rhetoric, COCEI is not particularly supportive of *muxe'* and historically has made little attempt to attract their vote.[24] The Coalition protects certain influential homosexual party members out of self-interest, but they generally treat gays with a degree of joking and social marginalization. For example, a famous, gay Mexican intellectual who has been a vital defender of COCEI in the national media is formally treated with respect while in Juchitán, but laughed at when he is not around. Moreover, a key member of the Isthmus Zapotec cultural movement was frequently mocked by COCEI members because of his supposed bisexuality. Additionally, one informant angrily lamented to me: "Neither the PRI or COCEI knows what to do with the non-effeminate gay male" (i.e., male homosexuals who do not take on the *muxe'* role).[25]

Unfortunately, in the case of gays, as also with women, COCEI's ideology of equality remains at the level of discourse, with little done at the practical level to actually achieve egalitarian relations. In this sense, COCEI's self-cultivated image as tough, indomitable fighters and the macho bravura that goes along with it may be obstacles to more enlightened ideas and practice in regard to gender and sexuality.[26]

Summary and Conclusions

COCEI leaders and intellectuals have developed a rich ethnic discourse whose central elements are a politicized view of Isthmus history and the grounding of current Coalition politics in their supposed Zapotec cultural roots. The *Coceísta* intelligentsia recast Juchiteco history as a lineal trajectory culminating in COCEI, and framed contemporary political events in terms of "parallel" events in Juchitán's past. While the Coalition's emphasis on historical continuity and parallelism has some basis in local political chronology, its discourse about Zapotec culture, gender, and ethnic relations obscures social tensions and contradictions within the movement and Isthmus society in general. Transcending these contradictions may be the key to COCEI remaining a united, militant organization in the Isthmus of Tehuantepec.

CHAPTER EIGHT

■■■■■■■■■■■■■

Conclusions

At the beginning of this book I noted that anthropologists no longer trust in the authenticity of the cultures and traditions they study. Instead, discourses about historical origins and cultural purity, whether by other anthropologists or the members of the studied society, are open to criticisms from many different angles. It has become fashionable to say that traditions are invented, communities imagined, and customs constructed.

While I have no intention of reinstating outmoded, essentialist definitions of culture, it seems to me that if taken to extremes the deconstruction of cultures and the emphasis on invented traditions may lead to theoretical dead ends. One dead end would be to make deconstruction an end in itself. This is a nihilistic practice in which debunking "traditions" has no other aim but to undermine ersatz discourses of cultural authenticity, without presenting an alternative explanation beyond the idea that "x" or "y" custom is a recent invention. Another limited approach would be to overemphasize the spectrum of creative possibilities at the expense of a thorough understanding of the political and economic contexts that constrain or facilitate particular cultural constructions.

For example, James Clifford, in a very influential recent book (1988:338, 11), notes that elements of identity are "replaceable" and "conjunctural," and talks of cultural complexes in terms of invention, mobility, and pastiche, as if changing cultural traits were as easy as changing clothes. However, when whole cultural orders and their physical bearers are destroyed—as is happening with the Lacandón people of southern Mexico—they can never be replaced.[1] Likewise, Clifford's glib comments about cultural rootlessness, invention, and translation may overestimate the malleability of culture while paying insufficient attention to the arduous political struggles that shape the process of cultural change (cf. Roseberry 1989). For these reasons, I suggest that greater attention needs to be focused on the historical and contemporary political processes in which cultural inventions and recreations of the past are embedded.

Thus, in order to understand the contemporary COCEI ethnic political movement and cultural revival project, I have argued that it is necessary to look closely at Isthmus Zapotec history from pre-Spanish times through the colonial period and nineteenth century to the present. History provides the keys to understanding the emergence of COCEI in the long-term ethnic and class conflicts of the Isthmus region. The first significant moment in local history is the Zapotecs' conquest of the Isthmus, which allowed them to take control of the prime habitation sites, agricultural areas, and natural resources from Huave and other indigenous groups who lived in this ecologically diverse region. Since this time, Isthmus Zapotecs have dominated these groups, strengthening their economic standing but preventing the multiethnic alliance called for in COCEI ideology. Likewise, the Isthmus' geographical separation from Highland Oaxaca has contributed to the Istmeños' sense of cultural distinctiveness from other Oaxacans.

Ethnic conflict between the Zapotecs and other Isthmus indigenous peoples, Aztecs, Mixtecs, and especially the Spaniards shaped a culture of ethnic political resistance. In the early colonial period, Zapotec resistance occurred in Tehuantepec, the center of the pre-Hispanic Isthmus Zapotec polity. The Zapotec community was not united in resisting colonialism, however, since the nobility often collaborated with the colonialists in opposition to rebellious commoners. As the colonial period unfolded in cycles of economic boom and bust, Juchitán—a smaller community with greater internal unity—emerged as a new site of ethnic resistance rooted in illicit commerce, defense of communal lands and salt flats, an adversary relationship to the Marquesado hacienda, and opposition to colonial and mestizo Tehuantepec.

Historically, Juchitán has occupied a peripheral position vis-à-vis regional and national power centers. The Isthmus is a peripheral part of a state (Oaxaca) which is itself peripheral to national power in the Valley of Mexico. This somewhat autonomous geographical, political, and economic location was a key factor in Juchitecos' preservation of a distinct ethnic identity and their equation of this sense of ethnic distinctiveness with political independence.

Juchiteco ethnic resistance solidified during frequent nineteenth- and early-twentieth-century conflicts that hardened animosities between residents of Juchitán and authorities of Tehuantepec, Oaxaca City, and Mexico City. These conflicts instilled in Juchitecos an intense, politicized ethnic identity, a chauvinistic localism, and a love for the Zapotec language and customs. While some other Mexican communities may have equally rich histories of rebellion and resistance (Katz 1988), Juchitán stands out among rural towns for its maintenance of a positive, indigenous ethnic identity (Royce 1982:169). This identity is linked to the Juchitecos' collective memory of local political struggles and to a cultivated self-image of rebelliousness.

After a period of relative social stability during the Charis *cacicazgo*, large-scale capitalist developments transformed the Isthmus landscape, economy, and social relations, fostering new conflicts for land and political power in Juchitán. COCEI emerged to defend the interests of peasants, workers, and lower-middle-class Juchitecos against outsiders and bitter class enemies within the Zapotec community. The Coalition, thus, took on a more marked *agrarista* character than the Juchiteco movements of the past, and intra-ethnic class struggle became more acute than before. Yet, COCEI leaders and intellectuals also viewed their struggle in ethnic terms and sought to revive and strengthen Zapotec culture against the onslaughts of capitalist development, encroaching national culture, and PRI hegemony.

Until the 1970s Juchiteco politicians used Zapotec ethnicity and claims to cultural authenticity primarily as weapons against political opponents in Tehuantepec, Oaxaca City, and Mexico City. As class differentiation divided the Juchiteco community, "peripheral" (i.e., poorer, politically marginalized) elements within Juchitán also began to use ethnicity as a weapon against members of the old Juchiteco elite.[2] Thus, ethnicity has been a key element of the political projects of Isthmus Zapotec people in their struggles with outsiders as well as among themselves.

With the advent of COCEI, a group of Juchiteco writers, activists, and artists—whose ethnic identity was heightened and politicized by education in Mexico City and Oaxaca City—took up the challenge of promoting Zapotec culture and Coalition politics in an ethnic vision rooted in local history and social practices. Although the COCEI intellectuals are heirs to a rich corpus of local intellectual production and self-commentary, they differ from their elite predecessors in their social backgrounds and radical political agenda. Indeed, since the advent of COCEI, the reevaluation of collective memories and the terms of Juchiteco self-image themselves have become contested ground.

Now, the celebration of and embellishment on Zapotec ethnic style and custom are no longer the sole province of the Juchiteco bourgeoisie. Instead, lower- and lower-middle-class Zapotecs have taken the lead in redefining local culture. This redefinition of customs, practices, and symbols is very much a political process, not just because it occurs within the context of political struggle, but because the very forms of the newly defined cultural elements take on distinct political meanings. Thus, COCEI public events, their hallmark large political rallies and marches, are modelled on aspects of Isthmus *velas* and processions with the express purpose of using Zapotec culture to bolster COCEI's political project.

The Zapotec language, formerly viewed by Zapotec elites as a stigma unless spoken in "pure" form by them, has been appropriated by COCEI and made the "official" political language of Juchitán and a symbol of the ethnic pride of poor Zapotecs, the backbone of the movement. Likewise, COCEI has revived the *tequio* and endowed it with the connotation of ethnic reciprocity at the same time that it is used to promote overtly political programs. COCEI has also seized on the matriarchal image of Zapotec women as a symbol of ethnic pride and political resistance to the PRI and the government. Finally, the Casa de la Cultura has become a center for Zapotec cultural promotion and the creation of a leftist, ethnic ideology.

In the Juchiteco bohemian art scene, the creation of new cultural forms is even clearer, since the Isthmus Zapotec communities have no significant indigenous painting tradition. Hence, the Juchiteco artists have used an "outside" medium to elaborate on ideas and concepts from Zapotec mythology and folklore and to defend COCEI. The Juchiteco poets also have begun for the first time to write poems in Zapotec or translate famous poems into the native language. COCEI's radio station manifested the movement's penchant for appropriating "foreign" media to promote its political program, the Zapotec language, and local customs, while simultaneously syncretizing local cultural forms with ideas and elements from Mexican national culture and the international art scene. Through contact with foreign journalists, anthropologists, painters, and activists, COCEI intellectuals gained access to new forums for their political ideas and cultural creations outside the Zapotec community and broadened their own intellectual horizons. In all these areas, COCEI intellectuals view Juchiteco cultural localism as not in conflict with international trends, but as intrinsically worthy of respect as European traditions. At the same time, they critique and appropriate elements from those traditions.

A politicized view of Isthmus history is the main element of the ethnic ideology created by Zapotec intellectuals and politicians. According to this ideology, which is expressed in COCEI speeches, writings, and artistic creations, the movement is the lineal continuation of Juchiteco resistance since colonial times, and COCEI's current actions parallel those of the heroes of the great Zapotec past. COCEI ideologues consider Zapotec culture and social organization to be the very foundations of the political movement. While the ideology selectively emphasizes key moments of Isthmus history and suppresses others, COCEI's view of local history is not so distant from the diachronic findings of this book. It would be misleading to simply reduce COCEI historiography to "the invention of tradition." In fact, in an important survey of recent Mexican social movements, Knight (1990:80) found that "the 'new' social movements display more continuity than often imagined, and are not necessarily that new." In this sense, COCEI may indeed manifest "continuity-within-change" (Knight 1990:100) with respect to previous Juchitán political movements, and some aspects of the Zapotec intellectuals' view of history are corroborated by academic research.

Perhaps a more important matter than whether COCEI intellectuals wrote "real" history or invented tradition, however, is the capacity of an Isthmus Zapotec intelligentsia to challenge foreign representations, to replace them with their own representations in several mass media, and to do so with considerable acumen. This is significant because self-determination (COCEI's ultimate objective) is more than just struggles over material resources and electoral politics; it is also a battle of ideas. While Clifford and other writers in the postmodern genre view such processes largely in terms of cultural mobility and the creation of collages of identity, this approach does not do justice to the intensely political context and complex historical processes that have shaped the Zapotecs' self-representations and cultural creations.

Indeed, the sophistication of the recent Juchiteco cultural movement—which is perhaps unique in its scope in rural Mesoamerica—would not have been possible without the relative political autonomy achieved by COCEI in Juchitán and the economic resources the Coalition and its well-endowed supporter, Francisco Toledo, could channel into the local intellectual scene. For this reason, it is important to stress that the opportunity for creation of new self-representations and cultural forms is enmeshed in political processes and may be, to some degree, a product of successes in political struggle. Members of many other Mexican indigenous groups may be inclined to create a dynamic local cultural movement similar to that of the Juchitecos, but they simply do not have the political power or economic resources to do so.

If political strength made possible many aspects of the recent Juchiteco intellectual movement, the Coalition's ideology calls for further transformations of Isthmus society that remain unrealized. In the economic sphere, COCEI has been unable to reorient Isthmus agriculture away from large-scale, mechanized, and irrigated agriculture and toward small-scale, peasant corn farming. It also calls for support of local craftsmen, artisans, and workers instead of the massive PEMEX oil refinery, but has made limited progress in this area. In the political arena, the Juchiteco goal of local sovereignty and freedom from arbitrary Oaxaca and Mexico City authorities has not been achieved, despite COCEI electoral victories, because the Mexican government can cut off funding to COCEI administrations or send in the troops at any moment. Likewise, COCEI's "Juchiteco democracy" has not given equal rights to Zapotec women or *muxe'*, despite ideological pronouncements to the contrary. Additionally, Zapotec conflicts with other Isthmus ethnic groups continue to be an obstacle to COCEI expansion.

Although *Coceístas* have not achieved all of their ambitious goals, they have offered Isthmus Zapotec people a provocative alternative to PRI politics, laissez-faire economics, and Mexican national culture. If the movement can overcome its internal problems and the seductions of power, it may continue to offer this alternative to Isthmus people for many years to come. If not, COCEI has already established itself as one of the most successful and long-lived popular movements in recent Mexican history.

Notes

PREFACE

1. COCEI stands for the *Coalición Obrera Campesina Estudiantil del Istmo*, the Worker-Peasant-Student Coalition of the Isthmus of Tehuantepec. Throughout the book, the terms "COCEI" and "the Coalition" ("*la Coalición*") will be used interchangeably, as they are in Juchitán.

2. This book is concerned with the Oaxacan portion of the Isthmus of Tehuantepec inhabited by Isthmus Zapotec people. Following local usage, I will refer to this area as simply "the Isthmus" ("*el Istmo*"). The reader may assume that when I refer to "the Isthmus" or "the Isthmus of Tehuantepec" I am writing exclusively about the Oaxacan part of the region and not the Veracruz section.

INTRODUCTION

1. The corpus of ethnographies of Mexican rural people could fill a small library. Some of the classic works include Redfield (1941), Aguirre Beltrán (1958), Wolf (1959), Lewis (1963), Foster (1967), Bartra (1974), and Friedrich (1986). Here, I am not referring to any specific study but to the fact that anthropological research on Mexican indigenous peoples, in spite of the sympathies of its practitioners, has tended to assume that Indians are by definition victims, poor, or socially marginalized.

2. Anthropological and historical research on peasant resistance has expanded exponentially in recent years, especially after the publication of James Scott's *Weapons of the Weak: Everyday Forms of Peasant Resistance* (1985). My work has been heavily influenced by this trend, especially through reading fine volumes like those edited by Stern (1987) and Katz (1988). My point, though, is that even the resis-

tance literature offers few cases of Indian political victories, other than those which occurred during relatively short periods of time.

3. Whether or not Isthmus women and gays indeed enjoy social equality will be examined in some detail in Chapter 7.

4. Some of the best previous work on COCEI is that of Zermeño (1987), Rubin (1987a, 1987b, 1990, 1991), and López Monjardin (1983). Similarities and differences between my work and theirs will be discussed briefly in Chapter 5. My comments on the studies of Juchitán politics by Prévot–Schapira and Riviere d' Arc (1984), Royce (1975, 1982), Martínez López (1985), and Aubague (1985) will appear at various points throughout Chapters 3–7. Important sources of ethnographic information about Juchitán include Covarrubias (1946), Royce (1975), and Campbell et al. (1993).

5. Conservative, red-baiting articles attacking COCEI were frequently published in Mexican newspapers and magazines such as *El Heraldo de México*, *Noticias*, *Impacto*, and *Siempre* in the early 1980s. Martínez López (1985) treats COCEI as merely a momentary phenomenon, disconnected from Isthmus history. Prévot–Schapira and Riviere d'Arc (1984:14–16) view COCEI as a class-oriented organization and question the significance of ethnicity to the movement. Royce (1982:3, 169–81) sees Juchitán politics as an ethnic struggle between Zapotec insiders and non-Zapotec outsiders that cannot be understood through class analysis.

6. Ethnic populism refers to a kind of anthropological practice that emphasizes in-depth, empirical studies of village society. Often such community studies treat indigenous cultures as isolated, self-contained entities with unique religions, economic systems, and social structures. This divides Oaxaca into separate, autonomous ethnic regions whose cultures and histories can only be understood in terms of endogenous factors.

7. Much of Cook's extensive, and high-quality, Oaxacan field research has been carried out in and around the Oaxaca Valley in areas where Zapotec ethnicity is indeed losing its importance as a factor in villagers' lives and as a concept in anthropological analysis. I argue, however, that Zapotec ethnic identity continues to be very strong in the Oaxacan Isthmus of Tehuantepec, and must be taken seriously by anthropologists who work there.

It is also important to bear in mind that 600 years of geographical and cultural separations have distanced Valley and Isthmus Zapotec peoples. Today, they represent, to a considerable extent, distinct ethnic groups, although with many common features. Hence, referring to both groups as Zapotec may imply a pan-Oaxacan Zapotec unity that does not exist.

8. My approach also differs from another key trend in anthropology. The literary, reflexive, postmodern trend stresses the role of the anthropologist in the construction of knowledge (or contingent fictions) about "others." While not denying the central role of the anthropologist as writer and part of the social drama from which anthropological information is produced, I argue that the history of people like the Zapotecs is far more interesting and significant than the adventures

and misadventures of anthropologist hero/clowns. The literary obsession with the role of the anthropologist, in fact, grossly overemphasizes the impact of a lone, usually Western, foreigner in the presence of "native others." In the history of Juchitán, Oaxaca, the occasional visits of Howard Campbell can be no more than a blip. Far more significant is the story of the rebel leader Che Gómez, of General Charis, and COCEI. That my experiences in Juchitán affect how I interpret, create or "invent" that history is true, but a very obvious point. Thus, I prefer to keep the focus on the Zapotecs and their history. That my lens has been influenced at every turn by interaction with Zapotec people should be clear to the reader, who may decide for him or herself the significance of this encounter, although when most relevant, I will explicitly discuss my own personal experiences.

CHAPTER ONE

1. All Zapotec words in the text (excluding words quoted from other authors) will be spelled according to Pickett (1983). Zapotec words not appearing in Pickett will be spelled as they appear in the sources cited. Translations from Spanish are my own, unless otherwise specified.

2. *Nahuals* are animal spirits—said to be associated with each individual—which are part of the autochthonous belief systems of most Mesoamerican indigenous groups.

3. Víctor de la Cruz (1981:3) even claims that the Zapotecs were the original inhabitants of the Isthmus although this is disproved by Zeitlin (1978, 1989).

4. The nature of the relationship between the Highland Zapotec state, centered in Monte Albán, and peoples living in Zaachila and the Isthmus, as well as the chronology of this process, remain an incompletely understood subject. According to Robert Zeitlin (1990:259), who has done the most thorough and recent research on the subject: "From what is known today, the southern Isthmus seems best interpreted as a region profoundly influenced by and consistently interacting with surrounding societies, yet one which retained its political autonomy until almost the end of its lengthy prehistory when, in the course of less than two centuries, it succumbed in short order to the rule of Zapotec, Aztec, and finally Spanish conquerors."

The exact connection between Tehuantepec and Zaachila, prominent centers of Zapotec power in precolonial times, also remains unclear. The king of Zaachila in late pre-Hispanic and early precolonial times was Cosijoeza, whose son Cosijopi later ruled Tehuantepec. Marcus (1983b:308) notes that the two cities shared power. According to Tutino (1993), however, Tehuantepec became the maximum center of Zapotec culture in the fifteenth century after Zaachila was defeated by Mixtecs. Whitecotton (1984) states that Tehuantepec was settled by Zapotecs from Zaachila and the Valley of Oaxaca.

5. The Zapotecs apparently were very capable negotiators and strategists (Paddock 1983:351–53). Flannery (1983:319) notes that the Zapotecs' main strategy

during their wars with the Aztecs was to have the Mixtecs do the fighting for them and in the process debilitate both the Aztecs and Mixtecs.

6. The Guiengola site is also revered as a mysterious place of power by modern Zapotec, as Brasseur ([1861] 1981:161–99) discovered in the nineteenth century (his Zapotec guide prevented him from going there), and as I did in the early 1980s, when my own excursion to the area became a source of much commentary by Blaseños (residents of San Blas Atempa).

7. Varese (1982:3) notes that Mesoamerican societies in general evolved from autonomous and semi-autonomous agricultural villages into politico-religious theocracies, and, finally centralized militaristic formations, as exemplified by the Aztec state. Zapotec civilization, he argues, followed a different development trajectory: centralization first appeared in the militaristic Monte Albán II stage, followed by a relatively decentralized theocracy, and then a fragmentation into a series of head towns and tributary villages.

8. It is not clear in the *Relación* whether this statement is based on direct observation by Spaniards or testimony elicited from the male nobility or other members of the Zapotec community.

9. Whitecotton (1984:132) attributes the fragility of intra-Zapotec social relations to colonization and competition by a growing population for scarce resources, factors which led to divisions between the various Zapotec city-states.

10. The self-classificatory term *binni za* is used by Isthmus Zapotec; other Zapotec groups of Oaxaca use similar terms.

11. My thanks to Frank Salomon for his suggestions on this point.

12. Zeitlin and Thomas (1992) studied 2 criminal complaints lodged against Don Juan Cortés in 1553 by indigenous residents of Tehuantepec. The complaints illustrate the growing separations between native elites and commoners in colonial times, as well as differences between Spanish and Zapotec notions of justice.

13. An example of the enormous tribute burden endured by Tehuantepec Zapotecs, can be obtained from the mid-sixteenth-century census of Baltasar de San Miguel. According to his count, the local peasants delivered the following amounts of goods every 80 days: 310 pesos and 1 *tomin* of gold dust, 835 mantles, and 124 chickens (Paso y Troncoso 1905:312).

14. However, Judith Zeitlin, in a paper presented at the 1989 meetings of the American Anthropological Association (AAA) in Washington, D.C., argued that depopulation was not much worse in lowland areas of Mesoamerica than in highland areas. Whatever the outcome of this issue may be, the immediate impact of European diseases on the Isthmus Zapotec was a drastic reduction of the population, although population levels began to rise again during the mid-seventeenth century.

15. According to Zeitlin (1989:44), 1,100 Indians participated in the construction of a Spanish galleon in Tehuantepec in 1556.

16. Brockington's work (1989) seems to indicate that the Marquesado hacienda on the Isthmus does not meet the pattern of relatively minor Spanish landholdings

that Taylor found in the Oaxaca Valley (1972). Instead, the Isthmus Marquesado hacienda—in size at least—may have more closely resembled the big northern Mexican haciendas.

17. In 1547 when Cortés died, he owned more than 10,000 head of cattle in the Tehuantepec area alone (Brockington 1982:26).

18. In 1618 Tehuantepec was renamed the Villa de Guadalcazar by colonial authorities. However, this name never caught on in New Spain, and most writers continued to refer to the town by its (Aztec) pre-Hispanic name.

19. The 50,000 figure may be an exaggeration; however, the large size of Spanish livestock herds by the 1600s has been well documented by Brockington (1982; cf. Zeitlin 1989:36).

20. Gay ([1881] 1986:149–55), however, the principal source for this information, never explicitly mentions the involvement of Isthmus Zapotecs in these events.

21. The treatment of Isthmus native people by the Dominicans probably falls somewhere between the extreme cruelty practiced by Bishop de Landa against the Maya of Yucatán (Clendinnen 1987) and the more benign behavior of the Jesuit friars in the Yaqui region (Hu–DeHart 1981).

22. From 1540 to 1610 the Isthmus outpaced all other regions of Oaxaca in total number (150) of land grants to Spaniards for livestock-raising (Romero 1988:131). Additionally, Zeitlin (1989:38) counted 209 requests for land or actual colonial land grants to Spaniards (other than members of the Cortés family) in the Tehuantepec area between 1550 and 1639.

23. Zeitlin (1989:47) recorded 66 requests by Indians for land grants for sheep and goat herds between 1580 and 1620.

24. In a particularly detailed case, Jalapa residents charged a Spanish Lieutenant with the following offenses:

> . . . raping a woman who nearly died as a result; drafting 240 Indians to plant crops without any pay; transporting goods by pack teams long distances paying only the freight costs and not the Indians in charge, whose absence (from their community) caused suffering; forcing almost the entire village to weave cotton for him, without adequate payment . . . [Brockington 1982:274].

Other Zapotec complainants protested the following abuses: Indigenous women were forced to grind the Spaniards' corn or wheat, Ixtepec *principales* were obliged to perform personal services; Indian lands were illegally occupied in Jalapa; and European residents of Tehuantepec and travelers damaged Indian property (AGN Mercedes, vol. 6, fa. 416 vta.; AGN Indios, vol. 2, exp. 30, vol. 21, exp. 311, vol. 5, exp. 202). Isthmus Zapotecs registered both collective and individual charges, many of which (e.g., the Jalapa case cited above) were judged favorably by New Spanish officials, in part because of the Crown's ongoing power struggle with the Cortés family for control of the Marquesado del Valle.

25. Indians from non-Marquesado towns also complained of mistreatment by Marquesado bosses who forced them to work as human cargo bearers (*tamemes*) or

messengers. Indian protests were so prolific that, in one case, colonial authorities ordered Tequisistlán residents to stop complaining (AGN Indios, vol. 13, exp. 42).

26. This occurred even during the administration of a popular estate manager, as a Marquesado slave testified: "The Indians slaughter cattle daily, even though Espinosa continually lodges complaints with the authorities. Try as he may, he cannot control the Indians" (Brockington 1982:129).

27. Tehuantepec Indians later testified that they had been forced to provide the Spanish *alcalde mayor* with more than 20,000 pesos in gold and 18,000 cotton mantles annually (Manso de Contreras [1661] 1987:22).

28. Tensions between Spanish administrators and Zapotecs had already risen as early as 1657, when Tehuantepec Indians complained that the Marquesado manager had refused payment to Indian shepherds. After this manager was fired for corruption and mismanagement, his replacement raised graft and incompetence to new heights, offending local people who later testified against him to colonial authorities (Brockington 1982:139–42).

29. Manso de Contreras' report ([1661] 1987) is ambiguous on the subject of the victims of the rebellion. At one point (p. 18), he claims that an Indian *cacique* from Quiechapa was killed in addition to the *alcalde*, a Spanish servant, and an African servant. However, he also included in his report (p. 20) a letter from Spanish witnesses to the event, who note that two Spanish servants died along with the *alcalde* and the African.

30. Catholic priests also took advantage of their powerful positions to sexually exploit indigenous women, as a friar who had worked in Juchitán confessed to the Inquisition in 1812 (Ynquisición [1812] 1985:13).

31. The Chontal also may have followed a messianic figure known as Fane Kantsini or Tres Colibrí. Such symbolic figureheads were probably local manifestations of a larger "mythical-religious substrate" shared by numerous indigenous groups of ancient Oaxaca (Barabas 1986:240–41).

32. The Tehuantepec rebellion apparently occurred simultaneously with uprisings in Tlaxcala, Otumba, and several other communities; however, I am unaware of any relation between these events (Rojas 1964:34–35).

33. Numerous other prisoners received equally brutal punishments. The native *gobernador* was killed and his body broken into four pieces, which were placed at the entrances to town (Manso de Contreras [1661] 1987:45). At least four other rebels were also executed (Covarrubias 1946:211).

34. The exact meaning of *Golaba* is unclear. *Ngola* is a Zapotec word for great, large, or old. De la Cruz (1983c:62) suggests that *Golaba* was a priest in what remained of the Zapotec religion. Carmagnani (1982:116), however, noted the existence of a political office in colonial Cuestlaguaca known as the *golaven tequitlato*, which was concerned with economic affairs. Whitecotton (1984:140) found that representatives of Zapotec rulers in smaller communities were called *colaabachiña*, or *tequitlato* in Nahuatl. Zeitlin (1989:45) also states that [*collabachinja*] were Indian

nobles who oversaw labor *repartimientos.* In any case, *Golaba* referred to a Zapotec leader of some sort.

35. For an alternative analysis that appeared as I finished this book, see Carmagnani (1992:81–101). Carmagnani prefers to call the "Tehuantepec Rebellion" a "political movement" because the Zapotec protestors' intentions were to reconstruct colonial society rather than overthrow it. See Díaz-Polanco and Manzo (1992) for other alternative treatments of this period in Oaxaca history as well as newly published documents concerned with events surrounding the "Rebellion."

36. Florencia Mallon (personal communication summer 1990) hypothesizes that women may have played a unifying role in Isthmus rebellions by spreading news about a revolt to members of other Zapotec communities through their commercial connections and travels related to marketing.

37. Brockington (1982:64), for example, notes that "Not everyone could afford the luxury of cotton. . . . Excepting the traders and village leaders, few natives could afford more than one cotton outfit."

38. Aspects of the indigenous political structure, such as the Zapotec nobles' role as administrators of native irrigation systems, persisted at least in the early colonial period, however (Zeitlin 1989:51–53). This was illustrated in an incident in 1553 in which the Zapotec *cacique,* Don Juan Cortés, had three central-Mexican Indians soundly beaten for not working on a canal construction project (Zeitlin 1989:52). The incident also demonstrated the continuing ethnic tensions between the Isthmus Zapotecs and other Mesoamerican Indian groups.

CHAPTER TWO

1. Excerpts from Juárez's speech are reproduced in *Guchachi' Reza* 8, pp. 7–8, 1981.

2. It may have been the sheer numerical superiority of the Zapotecs that allowed them to dominate the Huave and Zoque, rather than inherent characteristics of their state-level social organization, which (supposedly) made it more "adaptive" than the non-state sociopolitical organization of the other two groups (cf. Zeitlin 1989:57–60).

3. While elites in many agrarian societies, most notably in the Aztec case, have presented human sacrifice as a means for protecting the population against natural or supernatural dangers, this ideology may not have been shared equally by all members of such societies. In particular, one might question whether lower strata groups, from which sacrificial victims were taken, fully accepted this belief system.

4. I am not suggesting that the Tehuantepec elite's actions were unilaterally detrimental to commoners. Undoubtedly, the Zapotec nobility at times sheltered (Zeitlin 1989:52–53) as well as exploited their collectivities. I am arguing, however, that in order to understand the history of Isthmus Zapotec resistance over time it is important to examine the differential social (and spatial) interests within the

ethnic group and not assume that what was good for one strata or community within the population was always good for all stratas or communities.

5. An interesting illustration of the different class interests within Isthmus society in the late colonial period is provided by Widmer (1988–1989). He notes that a smallpox epidemic in 1795 and 1796 was manipulated by crown officials, local authorities, and businessmen in order to protect the economic interests of the Tehuantepec merchant elite at the expense of the poor indigenous people of the region. Tehuantepec shopkeepers were able to overcome a decree prohibiting travel and the transportation of merchandise affected by the smallpox epidemic. Thus, a quarantine that might have slowed the spread of disease was abandoned so that merchants could maintain their profit margins. Likewise, indigenous people who came down with smallpox were fed only *pozole*, rather than a more nutritious and complete diet, in a policy of triage. Moreover, the inoculation of Indian people, which was conducted ostensibly to prevent the spread of disease, actually killed a high percentage of the inoculated. Concludes Widmer (1988–1989:85): "The sanitary policy carried out by the crown in Tehuantepec in 1795 had as its exclusive end 'to contribute to an adequate economic dynamic' in the region, in a clear defense of the public treasury and the interests of the hegemonic bloc."

6. Of Tehuantepec's approximately 15 barrios, only Santa María, Santa Cruz, Guichivere, and Bixana have large numbers of residents who frequently speak Zapotec today.

7. In 1811 Von Humboldt wrote that mule trains transporting cochineal from Tehuantepec took 3 months to reach the port of Veracruz (Tutino 1978:203).

8. Hamnett (1986:12) states that by 1740 the indigenous population of Oaxaca had, for the most part, recovered from the demographic catastrophes of the sixteenth century.

9. Lockhart (1985:475) notes that the "primordial" land titles had a strongly indigenous character, which set them apart from documents more heavily influenced by Spanish traditions. He explains that the main component of the "primordial titles" was frequently "the statement of the town's principal representative that 'this is my land, my property.' " This was important because in pre-Hispanic times "a strong statement of fact or recommendation under solemn circumstances, made before a non-demurring audience, had something like binding legal force, and . . . this view continued to prevail among indigenous people in postconquest times."

10. The only land document that survived the fire concerned a 1682 dispute in which the Juchitán community regained control of a hacienda from a mulatto who had taken it from them.

11. These sentiments were summed up in the original Spanish as follows: "*las an gozado de ynmemorial tiempo acá sin contradicción ni pleyto alguno más que el presente*" (TPJ [1736–1737] 1987:9).

12. The descendant of Cosijoeza claimed to need the *salinas* because of his dire poverty. The depressed condition of offspring of the former Zapotec king had

already been demonstrated in 1672, when a direct descendant had to be fed at the Cuilapan convent (Covarrubias 1946:205, fn. 27). Of course, it is also easy to imagine that impostors might claim noble heritage in order to obtain advantages from the colonial bureaucracy.

13. Strangely, Reina (1986:231), who provides only a brief sketch of this incident, states that the leaders of the uprising were a Spanish priest and a military commandant. It is not clear how these officials became the leaders of what she describes as an "indigenous uprising."

14. Hart (1989:34) found that similar uprisings occurred throughout southwestern Mexico in the mid-1840s. He considers these events to be a "peasant war" comparable to the 1910 Revolution. Further research will be needed to identify the particular relationship between the Meléndez rebellions and similar movements in Guerrero, the Costa Chica, and elsewhere.

15. This action may have been what finally forced the Cortés family to sell the Marquesado ranch lands in 1839 to Maqueo and a Frenchman named Guergue (Brockington 1989:184). The uprising also hurt the state government, which complained of the economic hardship of having to arm a company of civilians and supply the troop's commissary. As a consequence, the government was two months behind in the payment of salaries to state employees (MA 1835).

16. The state had difficulty enforcing privatizing laws at this time because of the U.S.–Mexican War, which consumed its attention and weakened government control over the provinces (Tutino 1978:207).

17. Although this now seems like a terrible mistake on Juárez's part, one of his motivations was that he felt that Meléndez would be the most capable military leader of Istmeños in the event of an invasion of the area (via Coatzacoalcos) by North Americans (MA 1848). As it turned out, Meléndez was indeed a competent military strategist; however, he used those talents in pursuit of Isthmus independence.

18. From this period to the present day, dissident Zapotecs of San Blas (then a barrio of Tehuantepec) and Juchitán have been firm allies in numerous political movements, military encounters, and miscellaneous *tumultos*—often in opposition to mestizo Tehuantepec.

19. Juchiteco rebels referred to themselves as *el común entero de este pueblo or la masa general de este pueblo* in protest documents (de la Cruz 1983e).

20. The term *vallistocracia* was coined by the Juchiteco intellectual Víctor de la Cruz. It has also been used and discussed in some detail by leftist Oaxaca City intellectual Víctor Raúl Martínez Vásquez (1986).

21. In 1861 Brasseur ([1861] 1981:145) described the relationship between Juchitán and Tehuantepec as follows:

Juchitán almost entirely populated by Zapotec and Mixe Indians endured with impatience the yoke of Tehuantepec, where mestizos and creoles, the sole repositories of governmental authority, were previously in the majority.

22.   Año 50, el día 14 de Abril
                        empezó la guerra civil
                        en La Venta; que tenía
                        la culpa Echeverría;
                        y les quitamos el Mapa,
                        les jugamos bonita treta
                        al rigor de varas de carreta [Orozco 1946:29–30].

In the year of 1850, on April 14th the civil war began in La Venta [near Juchitán]; Echeverría was to blame; and we took the map back, we played a good trick on them, and beat them with the staves of our oxcarts.

23. Mallon (1988:3) observes that after independence, the Spaniards were still "deeply implicated" in nineteenth-century political conflicts in Mexico. There was considerable anti-Spanish sentiment in rural Mexico at this time, and attacks on Spaniards were symbolic of the concrete struggles of popular classes to assert their rights and defend their interests within the context of the nascent Mexican nation-state.

24. According to Juchiteco folklore, the night prior to Meléndez's death, a large flock of owls hooting loudly presaged the tragic event (Orozco 1946:29).

25. However, according to a Oaxacan newspaper (La Cucarda, Feb. 21, 1851, cited in Guchachi' Reza 10:12, 1982), at least one Spaniard participated in Meléndez's movement.

26. That Isthmus Zapotec people had good reason to be wary of Garay is evidenced by the fact that at the end of his survey the Mexican government granted him control of approximately 5 million acres of land along both sides of the proposed route for a ship canal through the Isthmus (Meier 1954:14).

27. Brasseur, for example, was sent by Napoleon's government to study Mexico and Guatemala shortly prior to the French Intervention. His observations were undoubtedly useful to French military authorities as they prepared to take control of Mexico. In this regard, his amusing broadsides at the North American politicians and businessmen meddling in the Isthmus must be viewed as more than simply casual commentaries on his travels. Instead, they should be examined within the context of superpower rivalries for control of Mexico.

28. I translated the first sentence of this quotation from Brasseur ([1861] 1981); the rest of the translation appears in Covarrubias (1946:226).

29. An element of sexual desire permeates some of these descriptions, such as that of a Catholic friar who commented on the "immorality and lewdness" of the women of Juchitán and then proceeded to confess having had sexual contact with one of them (Ynquisición [1812] 1985:13).

30. Rival Juchiteco political factions continued to differentiate themselves through the use of green or red colors during the struggles of the revolutionary period. Today, the same colors—displayed in Isthmus huipiles, bandannas, banners, etc.—are used by the two main political organizations in Juchitán (PRI and

COCEI), but with one main difference from past usage. Red is now the color of the Juchiteco leftist opposition (COCEI) and green has become the identifying color of the pro-establishment PRI.

31. One reason for the Juchitecos' opposition to the civil registration law—which they viewed as an attack on local religion—may have been their support of the liberal cleric Mauricio López. Brasseur ([1861] 1981:148) stated that López, on one occasion, led the sacking of Tehuantepec. After his death, the liberals placed a portrait of López in the Juchitán church and venerated him along with the saints.

32. Díaz (1947) was both impressed by the military prowess of the Juchitecos, whom he described as "eminently warlike" (p.85), and horrified by their lack of discipline. As he put it (Díaz 1947:93): "The Juchitecos constitute a great danger to the chief who tries to lead them, if he does not know them, because before each battle or before leaving their town, if they have to go fight far away, they get so exaggeratedly drunk that they commit all kinds of disorder, they hurt and kill each other in large numbers and consume a lot of ammunition."

33. Though it was the largest barrio of Tehuantepec, San Blas was (and continues to be) physically divided from the rest of town by a large hill (*Cerro Cruz Padre López*), and its Zapotec residents were looked down upon by the more affluent, Europeanized Tehuano families who lived in the central barrios. Tehuanas did their shopping in San Blas because, they said, things were cheaper there, whereas a Tehuana known as "*Macha Neva*" whipped any Blaseñas she caught entering the Tehuantepec market (Molina 1911:18, 9). Additionally, at siesta time Tehuanos arrogantly strung their hammocks across the narrow passage that connects San Blas and Tehuantepec and forced all non-Tehuanos who wanted to enter Tehuantepec to stoop as they made their way unceremoniously below the filled hammocks (Molina 1911:18). Finally, Remigio Toledo, the captain of the Tehuantepec national guard, refused to let Blaseños join his army, and he and other Tehuanos referred to Blaseños derisively as big-eared ones (*Blaseños orejudos*, or *diaga laga* in Zapotec) (Molina 1911:8).

34. Juchiteco hostility toward its neighbor community was increased by the fact that Maximilian had suppressed Juchitán's status as an independent district, consolidating it and Tehuantepec—the center of imperial power on the Isthmus—into one entity (López Gurrión 1976:97). If the French had not been overthrown, Juchitán, once again, would have been subjected to domination by Tehuantepec.

35. "*Yanna padre Vicente, lúu guiácabe, o láacabe o láanu pero rarí qui zadídicabe*" is the original phrasing in Zapotec, according to Aurelio Martínez López (1966:72). In Martínez López's text, the first word of the old Juchiteco's exclamation in Zapotec is given as "*ella*," which he translates as *ahora* (now) in Spanish. This appears to be an error; hence, I have replaced "*ella*" with "*yanna*," the usual Zapotec word for "now."

36. "*Pa quizanda cuée tu láacabe ndaani shquizhinu, lagui ní, ne gudítu co guíbaca láadu guhnáa, ti gul tu pa sabée du láacabe o cóo*" (A. Martínez López 1966:82).

37. *Nalgas* means derriere in Spanish.

38. This is how the granddaughter of a Juchiteca combatant, described the battle as it was recounted to her by her grandmother:

> ... When the French entered Juchitán, they climbed to the top of the church and saw that they were under siege on all sides. The French were scared by the situation. Munaratu's mother and another woman, possibly Tona Tati, egged on our people to attack the French. They defeated them over there by the lagoon. These women were the ones who rang the church bells and cried out that the Juchitecos should attack the French, who were in retreat. There they killed them. They also defeated the Tehuanos who united with the French ... (Anastasia Martínez 1985:21).

39. In the aftermath of the triumph, the Juchiteco–Blaseño soldiers ransacked and burned Tehuantepec, especially the stores and cantinas of town, until General Porfirio Díaz arrived and brought the soldiers under control (Molina 1911:44).

40. Chassen (1986:272) noted: "Pineda ... was a person who was greatly trusted by Porfirio Díaz. ... [As a key] member of the Chamber of Deputies, he was a political counselor of the President, besides being on occasion his political troubleshooter. Pineda ... was the real man behind the 'good' *científicos* in opposition to the rich *científicos* like Limantour, Macedo, and Casasús."

41. As in other parts of postcolonial Mesoamerica, in Juchitán Zapotec people created a rich system of religious beliefs that incorporated indigenous American conceptions with imposed Catholic ideas and symbols. While such belief systems are often generically labelled "folk Catholicism," it is important to bear in mind that for their rural believers (in this case, the Juchitecos) the rituals, concepts, symbols, etc. of which they are comprised are viewed as their own distinctive local religion. Such beliefs and practices are often referred to by Istmeños as "*nuestras costumbres.*"

42. Falcone (1990:508) discovered that Juchitán peasants engaged in the contraband trading of indigo and brasilwood (used for making dyes). De la Cruz (1983c:67) points out that the Juchitecos wanted to retain the taxes they would otherwise pay to the Oaxaca government and use them for public works projects.

43. According to Juchiteco folklore (see the folklore piece entitled "Historia de San Vicente y la Virgen Generala" in *Guchachi' Reza* 10:8, 1982), San Vicente supported poor oppressed Indians, unlike the *Virgen Generala* saint of San Cristóbal, who sided with the Chiapas creoles who mistreated Indians.

44. In an essay glorifying the actions of then *jefe político*, Francisco (Pancho) León, López Trujillo (1984) states that Mexu Chele was paid by a French company to damage the Tehuantepec railroad in order to further the company's interests vis-à-vis construction of the Panama Canal. I was unable to corroborate this assertion.

45. On the relationship between railroad construction and popular protest, see Coatsworth (1981).

46. This statistic refers to land in both the Oaxaca and Veracruz sections of the

Isthmus of Tehuantepec. Esparza (1992:52) discovered that 26 percent of the land in the Juchitán district was privatized during the Porfiriato.

47. Also important during this period was the extraction of dyes from brasilwood.

48. Tehuantepec also went into a decline as a result of several severe earthquakes that struck the community around the turn of the century (Starr 1908:161).

49. Although these criteria for inclusion in the ethnic group seem very clear-cut and unproblematical, definitions of who is "legitimately" a Juchiteco are open to challenge and strategic manipulation for political purposes, as Royce (1975) has aptly discussed in relation to a recent Juchiteco political figure (Tarú) (see Chapter 5).

50. One reason for this identification of mixed-race Juchitecos with the Zapotec community may have to do with the fact that there were only a few European families in Juchitán, and most of them arrived during the nineteenth century; hence, Zapotec culture predominated. In Tehuantepec, conversely, Europeans had formed a substantial community whose customs and culture had become the standards for prestige and status early in the colonial period.

51. As previously discussed, Zeitlin (1989), in an analysis primarily concerned with Tehuantepec in the colonial period, has argued that Zapotec society survived historically because of elite mediation of conflicts with outsiders and the Zapotecs' complex social hierarchy. My argument (here concerned with nineteenth-century society) differs from hers in that I emphasize the relative lack of a developed social hierarchy in Juchitán as a key factor in the defense of Zapotec people against outside encroachments. Thus, I suggest that shared social interests of Juchitán's popular classes—rather than social stratification—made that community such a formidable adversary for Oaxacan soldiers, Tehuantepec merchants, and government politicians. Furthermore, rather than emphasizing the special powers of elites to defend popular classes, as Zeitlin does, I argue that the absence of a powerful, entrenched elite in Juchitán lessened the differences between peasants and leaders, and that this relative egalitarianism was an effective weapon against outside attack. Thus, it was not the social distance between elites and peasants which made nineteenth-century Juchitán resilient in the face of incursion, but the existence of a considerable degree of cross-class solidarity.

52. Despite Knight's description, I have found no evidence to indicate that Gómez was a mestizo. Nuñez Ríos (1969:9) notes that Gómez's parents were both natives of Juchitán, and a niece of Gómez recalled that Gómez's father was initially a poor fireworks maker (Matus 1985:105), a trade that is practiced exclusively by Zapotec people in Juchitán, before he became wealthy (by local standards) through the sale of brasilwood, from which a red dye is extracted. Hence, it seems likely that both Gómez and his father were Zapotec rather than mestizos. In any case, Gómez is viewed by contemporary Juchitecos as a member of the Zapotec community.

53. The evocative Zapotec term for placenta, doo yoo (literally, "house rope"),

indicates the primordial importance Juchitecos attach to birthplace in drawing ethnic boundaries (see Royce 1975:194).

54. Much more research needs to be done to provide a fuller picture of who Gómez was and precisely what his movement represented. For example, Francie Chassen (personal communication spring 1993) discovered that Gómez used the informal "*tu*" form when corresponding with Porfirio Díaz, "which was very rare among Porfirian politicians." Thus, interpretations of Gómez that emphasize his radicalism may have to contend with the fact that Gómez was also well-connected with national elites.

55. "*Los del gobierno querían que ocupara el puesto un extraño y 'Ché Gómez' pedía que lo fuera una gente de nuestro pueblo, porque son de nuestra sangre*" (Matus 1985:85). The interview from which this quote was excerpted was conducted in Zapotec by Macario Matus, who translated it into Spanish.

56. While de la Cruz (1987b) says that Gómez was elected mayor, Knight (1986:374) states that he was installed "by means of the then fashionable political riot."

57. Although the *Chegomista* forces outnumbered their government adversaries, the soldiers' cannons and other weaponry eventually overpowered the poorly armed Juchitecos. The cannons, in particular, took a tremendous toll on the Che Gómez forces, as well as the houses and other buildings of Juchitán.

CHAPTER THREE

1. More specific variations in community subsistence patterns can be found in Binford (1983) and Dorsett (1975).

2. The largest haciendas in the Isthmus were located in the Juchitán district. In addition to the Santo Domingo estate, they included La Providencia hacienda near El Barrio (48,000 ha), La Venta of Ixtaltepec (41,000 ha), and El Modelo in San Juan Guichicovi (45,000 ha) (Chassen and Martínez 1990:66). None of these haciendas was actually within the areas cultivated by Juchiteco peasants, except possibly La Venta (Chassen and Martínez 1990:66). Among the crops grown on these properties were cotton, indigo, cane, beans, corn, and tobacco.

Chassen and Martínez (1990:66) also note the existence in 1904 of the Tehuantepec Mutual Planters Co. in the Juchitán district, which exported sugar cane, oranges, tomatoes, and bananas. Oranges do not grow well near the town of Juchitán. It appears that this plantation was located at some distance from town. Additionally, Chassen and Martínez (1990:67) found that there were 12,818 agricultural workers in the Juchitán district in 1907. But it is not clear to what extent these workers were a landless proletariat or merely peasant farmers who occasionally did work on the haciendas.

The extent of U.S. involvement in Isthmus agriculture is also unclear. Hart (1989:8) states that rebels on the Isthmus of Tehuantepec expelled hundreds of North American companies and individuals who owned land in the region, but he provides little description of the Americans or the process through which they were expelled (see also Hart 1989:103, 256). An Isthmus *corrido* also refers to an incident in which Zapotec peasants confiscated 1,200 ha of land from an American woman at Ixhuatán, possibly during the 1930s *agrarista* period (de la Cruz 1983b:51). Ruiz Cervantes (1992:14) briefly discusses claims filed by two Americans against the Mexican government for Isthmus properties they lost during the Revolution. See Ruiz Cervantes et al. (1986:48) for information about 24 foreign individuals or companies who claimed to have lost property or have been injured in the Isthmus during the Revolution. Also see Segura (1988:279) for a list of American landowners in the Isthmus whose lands were expropriated by the government. All of this information points to the need for historical research on American control of Isthmus land prior to the Revolution and the impact of the Revolution on these holdings.

3. This section is concerned primarily with the Isthmus coastal plain where the Zapotec community is concentrated. It is not necessarily applicable to the highland areas around Chimalapas and Matías Romero, or the Chahuites area where the Zapotec peasant population is smaller and more open range land was available for plantations or cattle ranches.

4. Among the most prominent Middle Eastern merchants with businesses in Juchitán in 1919 were Mitre Nazara y Hattar, Miguel Musalem, and Salomón Nacif (Sánchez Silva 1985:22). Some of my information about the Middle Eastern families in Juchitán comes from an interview with linguist Velma Pickett.

5. Of course, there were also Zapotecs from Juchitán who left the community and completely assimilated into Mexican national society. But these individuals were probably a minority at this time.

6. Unfortunately, the history of the Juchiteco Green and Red Parties prior to the Che Gómez rebellion remains a poorly documented and little understood subject.

7. Velma Pickett (personal communication 1992) observed that in the 1940s the middle- and upper-class people of Juchitán referred to the residents of the poorer neighborhoods of Cheguigo and the seventh section as "*binni riri*" (uncivilized, primitive people).

8. For a discussion of the 1910–1920 period in the state of Oaxaca, see Garner (1990), and for various other regions of Mexico, see Benjamin and Wasserman (1990:1–14, 319–57).

9. For a partially fictionalized account of the life of an Isthmus soldadera, see Poniatowska (1969).

10. See *Guchachi' Reza* 23:19–29 (1985) for the oral histories of various Juchiteca *soldaderas*.

11. This is a translated excerpt from an interview I conducted with Juventino Jiménez in the Alvaro Obregón Colony near Juchitán. The transcript of this interview has been published in a book called *Relatos sobre el General Charis* (de la Cruz, ed. 1989:65–72).

12. For further discussions of postrevolutionary *caciques*, see Benjamin and Wasserman (1990), Kern (1973), and Friedrich (1986).

13. According to Justo Pineda (personal communication 1988)—a contemporary of Charis with a prodigious memory of Juchiteco historical events—the independent Yaquis stated they did not want to fight Charis because he was an *indio* just like them. But such quasi-ethnic sentiments did not deter the general.

14. According to Justo Pineda (1986), Charis bought the lands that eventually became the Alvaro Obregón Colony from the Santibañez family of Tehuantepec.

15. Justo Pineda (1986:22) recalls that Charis also required the peasants residing on "his" lands to pay him a tax on an annual basis. Additionally, President Obregón had promised to give plots of land to the "*Juanas*," as he called the Juchiteca *soldaderas* who had accompanied Charis. But these women never received any land, nor did they ever forgive Charis for his ungratefulness (Matus 1985).

16. In a January 1931 (AGN, Pascual Ortíz Rubio, exp. 7, reg. 1073) letter to Mexican President Ortíz Rubio, opponents of Charis expressed their dissatisfaction with his actions:

The community of Xadani . . . solicited *ejidos* which inevitably should be taken from the *latifundio* belonging to General Heliodoro Charis, who protecting his patrimony, created a utopian congregation of peasants, baptizing it with the pompous name of Military Agricultural Colony . . .

The letter criticizes Charis' maneuvers for benefitting him personally, while depriving Xadani peasants of their rights under agrarian law. It also attacks Charis for forming militias to prevent peasants from obtaining the *ejido* lands, which it says are "a debt the Revolution has pending with the miserable Xadani residents."

17. Rubin (1991:65–82) argues that the extent of Charis' power in Juchitán has been overrated, and the degree to which reformers were able to influence local political events has not been adequately addressed. I agree, in general, with this analysis, but I have chosen to focus on the history of Charis because of the major role he plays in Isthmus Zapotec oral history (and COCEI's version of that history, which will be discussed in detail). For Isthmus peasants, Charis is probably the most significant local figure of the twentieth century.

18. Because of Charis' controversial past—he simultaneously represents Juchiteco opposition to outside domination and exploitation of the peasantry—he does not figure in COCEI's pantheon of folk heroes. Instead, Che Gómez, Binu Gada, and other less problematical Zapotec leaders are emphasized (for further discussion of the Charis legacy, see López Monjardin 1983).

19. Charis was not merely a Zapotec leader, however, because at different times during his army career he also commanded the loyalty of many Huave—who fought with him against the Cristeros—and mestizo soldiers as well.

20. One of my informants, Mario López, stated that there were always groups opposed to Charis. He said that "always 2, 3, or 4 candidates have competed to be mayor" in Juchitán. An initial challenge to Charis' control over the Juchitán may-

or's office took place in the early 1940s, when a local federal deputy, Alberto Ramos Sesma, backed by President Avila Camacho, succeeded in imposing Pedro López Llaco as the local mayor. Charis first opposed this arrangement, but eventually agreed, reluctantly, to accept it (Rubin 1991:71; de la Cruz 1992a:66).

21. By the end of the 1950s, Charis' power had begun to decline.

22. The following people were my principal sources for oral information about General Charis: Javier Charis, Justo Pineda, Margarita Genico, Manuela López Lena, and numerous *campesinos* from San Blas and the Colonia Alvaro Obregón.

23. Rubin (1991:82) argues that a main reason for the success of COCEI was the previous "absence of mass organizations in Juchitán." In Rubin's analysis (1991:9), "the PRI hardly existed at all in the Isthmus between 1930 and 1960" and there was a "relative absence of . . . national peasant and worker confederations" (p. 49). Thus, in his treatment of the 1930–1960 period, Rubin focuses on the professional and business groups which opposed Charis.

While I agree with Rubin that PRI's relative weakness in Juchitán was an important factor in COCEI's success, more research needs to be done on grassroots activism during the Charis era. Arellanes (1988:63) found that 12 Isthmus organizations with a total of 2,353 members belonged to the Confederation of Socialist Leagues of Oaxaca in 1934. Additionally, he discovered that there were 25 peasant organizations with 219 members in the Juchitán district in the same year (Arellanes 1988:67). Binford (1992) has also uncovered information on workers' organizations in the Isthmus.

Of course, some of these organizations may have existed only on paper. Furthermore, if they were indeed viable movements, we need to know more about their ideologies and relationships to the national party or other parties and organizations. But until we know this information, it may be premature to conclude that there was little political activity in Juchitán during the 1930–1960 period, other than that associated with Charis and the business and professional groups which opposed him.

24. Weetman Pearson, the British engineer who built the Tehuantepec railroad, was also responsible for the construction of the Salina Cruz dry dock facilities and the infrastructure (streets, potable water, solid housing, etc.) for the modern city of Salina Cruz (Young 1966). These construction projects provided employment for many Istmeños and stimulated the economy of the region.

25. One of my informants remembered that only a few Juchitán buildings had electricity in 1944 and none had piped water or a sewage system. According to Robles (1946:27), there were no paved streets in the town in the mid-1940s. Additionally, Velma Pickett recalled that there was only one car in Juchitán in the early 1940s (which was owned by a man from Espinal). She said there were few street names and no street numbers. Houses were located by their proximity to large trees or other physical landmarks. Juchitán "was just a village," noted Pickett. Poor Juchitecos lived in one-room, wattle-and-daub houses and even the wealthier local people did not have cement homes as they do today, according to Pickett.

When Pickett first came to Juchitán, she "could almost count the number of people who did not speak Zapotec."

26. In 1919 there were but 36 storefront merchants in the Juchitán district as a whole (Sánchez Silva 1985:13).

27. According to Bradomín (1984:58), the Benito Juárez Dam and reservoir cover a 7,000-ha area and have a capacity of 1 million cu m of water. The dam, which became one of the largest in southern Mexico, was designed to irrigate approximately 55,000 ha.

28. The introduction of antibiotics, improved public health care, and economic growth were among the key factors in Mexico's population boom from the 1950s onward. A Ministry of Urban Development and Ecology report (SEDUE 1988) states that Juchitán's population grew at a rate of 4.6 percent per year from 1950, when it totalled 13,814, to 30,218 in 1970. From 1970 to 1987, Juchitán's population grew by 5.77 percent per year (SEDUE 1988). As of 1970, about 50 percent of the Isthmus population was urban (Comisión 1976), and by 1980 that figure had increased to 60 percent (Gobierno del Estado de Oaxaca 1980:96). The population of the Isthmus region increased by more than 100 percent between 1950 when it was 165,789 (Ortíz 1971:42–43), to 342,438 in 1980 (Gobierno del Estado de Oaxaca 1980:96).

Preliminary results from the 1990 INEGI (1990:162) census of Mexico lists Juchitán's population as 66,525, a figure that I feel is far too low. Eighty thousand is my own estimate.

29. Precise data on Isthmus land tenure are very hard to come by, and a wide range of figures appear in different sources (e.g., Rueda Jiménez 1976:42; Instituto de Geografía–UNAM 1984:47). Perhaps the most reasonable estimates for contemporary land distribution in the irrigation district are those used by Binford (1989:13), who notes that average landholdings run from 2 to 10 ha with variation between municipalities. This is consistent with the 4.5 ha/landholder figure I was given by an upper-level SARH official. Binford also states that there are holdings ranging from 100 to 500+ ha, especially in the vicinity of Juchitán.

30. Bustillo (1968:10) made the same observation in relation to Tehuantepec in the years before the Revolution (ca. 1910). Ruiz Cervantes (1988:392–94) found that the Isthmus produced fewer requests for land redistribution between 1915 and 1920 than did most other regions of Oaxaca, although this may have simply been a result of a lack of government offices in the region to appeal to rather than the absence of agrarian demands. In any case, little land had been redistributed in the Isthmus as of 1930 (Ruiz Cervantes 1988:394, fn. 169). Between 1920 and 1923, Istmeños produced only nine requests for land (only 7 percent of the state total), of which seven came from the Juchitán district (Ruiz Cervantes 1988:409). In 1932 only 10 percent of petitions for land in the state of Oaxaca came from the Isthmus, 28 of which were from the Juchitán district (Arellanes 1988:119).

31. The Isthmus still has far more communal land than most areas of Mexico.

32. Mexico has three forms of land tenure: *pequeña propiedad, ejido,* and com-

munal. *Pequeña propiedad*, literally "small property," varies in size, but in all cases is private property, bought and sold at the whim of the owner. *Ejidos* are collective landholdings that were expropriated from large haciendas and granted to village residents by the Mexican government (which retains ultimate ownership) after the Revolution. *Ejido* lands are legally exempt from sale or rental and are governed by locally elected authorities. Unlike *ejidos*, communal lands were not granted to Indian groups by the postrevolutionary government. Communal tenure pertains to lands controlled by indigenous communities since the pre-Hispanic era. A council of community members controls distribution of communal lands, which are legally exempt from sale. In practice, all three types of land tenure function like private property, since Isthmus land is rented, bought, and sold regardless of its legal status.

According to the Oaxaca state development plan (Gobierno del Estado de Oaxaca 1980) for the 1980–1986 period, Isthmus land tenure is divided as follows: 78 percent communal, 21.5 percent *ejido*, 0.5 percent *pequeña propiedad*.

33. Large landholders opposed the *ejido* decree because they thought it would lead to redistribution of their lands to peasants, or to reduction of their right to control land privately. Peasants feared that the establishment of *ejidos* might entail movement from their existing lands to plots located elsewhere, or simply to loss of lands without recompense. Although theoretically the *ejido* system would have granted peasants 10 ha each, one peasant summed up his concerns as follows: "If I have always been the owner of these four hectares . . . Why are you going to give me 10? You [i.e., the government] are doing something bad" (*Neza Cubi* 6:17, 1969).

34. Warman (1972:18) noted in 1972 that two thirds of Isthmus peasants within the irrigation district had less than 3 ha each, whereas 200 people had more than 20 ha, 10 had more than 50 ha, and 4 had more than 100 ha. Ministry of Agrarian Reform (SRA 1971) files in Juchitán contain a local peasant leader's claim that 94 individuals controlled more than 30 ha each. In 1968 a Juchitán agricultural association complained that most peasants in the irrigation district had insufficient landholdings. However, COCEI leaders, SARH officials, and agricultural engineers agree that in the Juchitán area there are few, if any, *latifundios* such as those found in northern Mexico.

35. These rumors may have contained a degree of veracity, since politicians had previously obtained Isthmus land through shady transactions during the building of the railroad and highways (Warman 1983:2).

36. One result of the land titles morass was the creation of a new property designation, *propiedad privada de origen comunal* (private property of communal origin); the Isthmus is the only place in Mexico where such a category exists (Bailón 1987:12). Alas, this new category has only increased confusion.

37. Binford (1989) explains that control of major aspects of Isthmus agricultural production are decided by a committee composed of government agricultural bureaucrats and chaired by the SARH district manager, a political appointee. Peasant organizations have token representation but no clout.

38. Mayors of Juchitán and other city administrators were especially adept at amassing huge parcels of land through illicit maneuvers. This was possible because City Hall, in lieu of formal agricultural associations, authorized the opening of new lands for peasants (López, n.d.). Juchitán politicians took advantage of this situation and seized chunks of land formally belonging to the community as a whole.

Another means by which land found its way into the hands of the elite was through the practice of private usury—a common source of short-term cash for peasant cultivators of sesame. When peasants were unable to pay back their loans (because of crop failure, family illness, etc.), their lands were transferred to the merchants and others who had lent them money.

The COCEI also complains that the *Ley de Tierras Ociosas* (Idle Lands Law) was manipulated by bureaucrats, in collusion with large landholders, to expropriate land belonging to the peasantry. Local newspaper articles, public opinion, and COCEI political statements implicate numerous public officials (of SARH, SRA, BAN-CRISA, etc.) in miscellaneous other acts of corruption. The buoyant financial status of former and current administrators of government agricultural organizations can be confirmed by observing the expensive life styles, lavish houses, and well-stocked private businesses of these individuals in Tehuantepec, Juchitán, and elsewhere.

39. For a list of large landowners in the Isthmus as of the late 1950s and early 1960s, see Segura (1988:280–81).

40. Private property in the irrigation district, however, rose from just 6 percent of the total land area in 1962 to 76 percent in 1980 (de la Cerda 1980:43).

Likewise, control of land became more concentrated in the hands of a small group of individuals. Whereas about 50 percent of the irrigation district area was composed of small holdings of under 3 ha controlled by 4,060 peasants, a small group of 234 large landholders controlled approximately 20 percent of the land (de la Cerda 1980:72).

41. Segura (1988:259) found that the initial intention for building the Isthmus dam was to support the cultivation of basic food crops such as corn, beans, wheat, etc. This changed during the Alemán era, when more emphasis was placed on the growing of commercial crops, an emphasis that is maintained today.

42. Ortíz Wadgymar (1971:67) stated that there were only 20 tractors in the Isthmus at the time of his research. Soon thereafter, the government established bureaucracies in the Isthmus to promote and proffer new cultivation techniques, modern agricultural equipment, credit, and crop insurance.

One reason why peasants initially avoided accepting credit was that they feared that unpaid debts could lead to forfeiture of land. Another reason was peasant insecurity about the land titles they were required to use to document their tenure standing.

Credit contracts also gave government inspectors the right to make important decisions governing the use of fertilizer, machinery, irrigation, and the scheduling of activities—something peasants were not anxious to relinquish. Additionally, these new arrangements distributed capital-intensive tasks to tractor and other machine operators. Labor-intensive work, such as cleaning irrigation canals, became the responsibility of peasants. Notes Binford (1989:11), "This was something wholly different from the relatively simple routinized cultivation of corn and sesame of the pre-irrigation epoch, where farm manager, practical agronomist, and day laborer had been concentrated in the body and mind of the direct producer."

43. The indigenous *zapalote* corn is well adapted to arid Isthmus conditions.

44. Warman (1972:15–27) points out that in 1968 only 20,000 of the approximately 50,000 ha scheduled for irrigation were actually being irrigated. Moreover, of these 20,000 ha, 15,000 had been irrigated using simpler methods prior to the dam. Thus, the Benito Juárez Dam and canal project irrigated only 5,000 new hectares. Additionally, of the 20,000 ha, 16,000 were planted in corn and grown essentially as rain-fed crops. The irrigation canals were used only for an occasional last-ditch watering when the rains came late.

45. A SARH-Tehuantepec pamphlet (n.d.), entitled "General Plan of Irrigation District #19," indicates the depth of the local agricultural bureaucracy's contempt for Zapotec culture, and desire to replace it with higher technology farming methods, consumer products, and "modern" attitudes. This pamphlet is illustrated with childish drawings designed, condescendingly, to convince illiterate peasants to give up their "primitive" ways and accept the "benefits" of the dam and irrigation project. Consider the following excerpts:

> We need to abolish ancient agricultural systems. . . . The agriculturalist should exert himself, helped by the official and private bank, to eliminate the agricultural system shown in picture 1 [which depicts a peasant plowing with oxen and planting seed by hand]. . . . Currently with the antiquated agricultural systems and incorrect irrigation, these are the yields obtained in the harvest of maize [picture of skimpy corn plant] . . .

The pamphlet criticizes Indian thatch and adobe houses for being uncomfortable, unsafe, unsightly, and "depressing to the spirit," and for giving the occupants an inferiority complex. The alternative dwelling promoted by SARH is made of concrete (in reality, such houses are much hotter than indigenous ones) and is described as safe, comfortable, attractive, and "uplifting to the spirit." The manual states that the slow and monotonous oxen should be replaced with cars, tractors, and trucks, which are faster and more comfortable. Ironically, the only way 95 percent of Isthmus peasants could afford such items would be by robbing the credit banks or committing other crimes.

46. According to a local newspaper (*La Voz del Istmo* 8/15/1963), one reason why cotton was promoted in the Isthmus was that a powerful SARH official owned a cotton gin with which he hoped to reap large profits.

In precolonial and colonial times, cotton fibers were collected from native silk–cotton trees and made into clothing for sale and personal use. The cotton plant introduced by the government, however, was unsuitable for Isthmus conditions.

47. CADIR 19 and PRONAGRA were two governmental programs used to

"modernize" Isthmus agriculture during the 1970s. ANAGSA is the acronym of the federal bureaucracy concerned with insuring crops.

48. One clear sign of corruption in the allocation of Isthmus agricultural credit during the 1980s was the granting of credit to *muxe'*, who by definition do not engage in agriculture. I was told of numerous other credit scams by peasants, employees of the agricultural bureaucracy, and many other people. This was one of the few subjects that my informants agreed on, regardless of political affiliation or social status; clearly, corruption permeates government subsidization of Isthmus agriculture.

49. See Binford (1992), Arellanes (1988:88–90), and Piñon Jiménez (1988:329–31) for information about the recent history of sugar cane production in the Isthmus.

50. According to Chassen (personal communication 1993), the failure of sugar cane in the Isthmus has historical antecedents. During the Porfiriato, Isthmus sugar cane fields dried up due to a lack of irrigation and irregular rainfall.

After I had completed most of the work on this book, I also learned that the large sugar mill located between Juchitán and Espinal had been closed by the Mexican government. Clearly, sugar cane production is not the answer to Isthmus economic problems.

51. Ronfeldt (1973:218), in relation to a similar case, noted "the politicizing effects of ejidal organization and cane agriculture." . . . "Certainly throughout history few other types of agriculture have been so closely associated with peasant unrest."

52. CNC stands for *Confederación Nacional de Cañeros* (National Confederation of Cane Growers), which has branches affiliated with the *Confederación Nacional Campesina* (National Peasant Confederation), abbreviated CNC–CNC, and the *Confederación Nacional de la Pequeña Propiedad* (National Confederation of Small Property Owners), abbreviated CNC–CNPP.

53. Binford (1983:188–284) points out that there have been success stories and failures among both large and small cane growers, with neither group having a monopoly on agricultural prosperity. However, he notes, in the long run the interests of small and large growers, who view the former as obstacles to their own expansion, will probably diverge.

Churchill (1987:115) observed a process of increasing social differentiation in Espinal, spawned by the expansion of commercialized cane agriculture. Socioeconomic divisions in Espinal roughly correspond with political polarities, which pit a peasant–oriented faction against a group led by professionals and including others who treat farming primarily as a capital investment (although some peasants are also members of the latter group). Both groups are officially affiliated with PRI. In Juchitán, the political split between small producers and large landowners is more clearly defined, the former usually supporting COCEI and the latter siding with PRI.

54. Binford (1989) cites statistics indicating a decline of corn production from

60 to 75 percent of total land in the irrigation district in 1969 to 28 percent in 1984.

55. Manuel Caso, president of the National Agricultural Council, stated that in fall 1988, the average cost to produce corn in Mexico was 540,000 pesos/ton and the guaranteed price for its purchase was just 370,000 pesos/ton (*The News* 10/12/ 1988).

56. My information about the politics of Isthmus sugar cane comes primarily from cane growers of Juchitán and San Blas, BANCRISA and SARH officials, and Juchiteco peasant leaders. Because of the risks of disclosing such information in the violent world of Isthmus agrarian politics, these informants will have to remain anonymous.

57. Rubin (1991:84, fn. 1) argues that the Juchiteco peasantry was not threatened with physical extinction by the changes wrought by economic development of the Isthmus. While this is probably true, it does not pay sufficient attention to the harm done to many Isthmus peasants by the dam and irrigation project and oil refinery. Although displaced peasants could find jobs in the urban economy, as Rubin points out, the emotional consequences for peasants of losing their land and traditional livelihood should not be downplayed.

In an effort to discredit the views of COCEI leaders and researchers who have studied the Isthmus economy, Rubin argues that COCEI supporters were often satisfied with the their economic standing and not seriously endangered by recent economic transformations. He observes that "Juchitecos expressed satisfaction with prices and incomes" (1991:417–18), and "Juchitecos expressed some satisfaction in the 1980s with the agricultural institutions that COCEI harshly and uniformly condemned" (p. 418). These statements are quite surprising in light of the severity of the recent Mexican economic crisis and the degree of contempt held by most Istmeños towards the government agricultural bureaucracy. Indeed, in the 13 years I have been visiting the Isthmus, I cannot recall a single instance in which a person "expressed satisfaction with prices." Moreover, the only individuals I met who showed any comfort with their incomes were white-collar professionals and/ or members of the local bourgeoisie. With regard to agricultural institutions, I have seldom met a Zapotec peasant who was not highly critical of SARH, SRA, or the other branches of the government agricultural bureaucracy in the Isthmus. In fact, these organizations were held in such low regard that even their employees and administrators discussed them in very negative language and with a degree of self-loathing. Furthermore, most of the Zapotec people I know, even PEMEX employees, view the Salina Cruz oil refinery as an ecological disaster that has seriously damaged local agriculture and ecosystems. This is a far cry from "satisfaction."

58. The second-in-command at the SARH regional office in Tehuantepec told me that only about 50 percent of agricultural loans are paid back by Isthmus peasants. BANCRISA field inspectors suggested that the percentage is closer to 40 percent.

The SARH official viewed agricultural credit as a form of public assistance to the peasantry. As he phrased it: "Credit is the peasant's modus vivendi."

59. From the 1960s until January 1989, Joaquín Hernández Galícia ("La Quina") single-handedly controlled the national PEMEX worker's union; hence, most workers at the Salina Cruz plant came from La Quina's home state of Tamaulipas or other nearby areas (as well as Mexico City). Fauverge (1982:260) indicates that only 25 percent of the PEMEX labor force (and the companies that do contract work for it) in Salina Cruz are from the Isthmus. La Quina's replacement, Sebastian Guzmán Cabrera, was an Isthmus Zapotec from a town near Juchitán. However, immediately following La Quina's ouster, the Salina Cruz facility was in disarray and many of its operations were, at least temporarily, curtailed.

60. Salina Cruz's role in the national economy and significance as an industrial growth pole in the Isthmus would have increased considerably if the notorious Alfa–Omega project had prospered. This much-discussed, and heavily financed, plan was designed to establish Coatzacoalcos, Veracruz, and Salina Cruz as terminals for transcontinental shipping of containerized freight along the Tehuantepec railroad (*Proceso* 4/23/1984). As a consequence of many factors, including bureaucratic bungling, poor planning, corruption, and the downturn in the Mexican economy, Alfa–Omega had to be shelved and its expensive machinery (cranes, special loading vehicles, train cars, etc.) left to deteriorate. Once again the dream of bypassing the Panama canal along the Isthmus landbridge had gone bust.

61. Monsiváis (1983:12) suggests that the constant labor migration of Juchitán men to distant oil fields, and their resultant absence from community life, has strengthened women's position in local society and increased their political participation.

62. Spokesmen for Isthmus businessmen claim that only 2 percent of materials used at the plant are sold to them by local merchants. This is probably an exaggeration, but the preeminence of outside suppliers, especially from Mexico City and Veracruz, is unquestionable.

63. That some fortunes were made during the 1970s boom period is indisputable. To cite only one example, an Australian man teamed with a British emigré earned $40,000 in only eight months by plowing fields with their two tractors. The Juchitán gringo partnership filled an economic niche—few tractors were available at this time and government money was flowing into the area—which they exploited handsomely. Upper-class Zapotec and mestizo outsiders took advantage of other business opportunities and established hardware, clothing, and automotive stores, hotels, restaurants, and various other enterprises.

64. Brito de Martí (1982) cites the following statistics on Juchitán living conditions: 34.7 percent of homes had dirt floors, 37.2 percent were hooked up to sewer systems, and 57.7 percent had running water. In San Blas, only 18 percent of homes were connected to sewer lines.

65. Another illness that currently plagues the Isthmus is diabetes which is probably linked to high levels of fat and alcohol consumption, village endogamy, and obesity.

66. A Juchitán couple expressed cynical pleasure about a magazine report stating that London yuppies pay astronomical sums ($23 per kilo) to consume "exotic" iguana meat imported from Florida. They were also proud, however, that their gusto for iguana, consumption of which is a badge of identity for Isthmus Zapotecs, was shared by stylish Europeans.

67. My discussion of Isthmus alcohol consumption has no moralistic intent; rather, it is aimed at describing the impact that recent economic developments have had on the region. Like many visitors to the area, I have been fortunate to attend and participate in dozens of hedonistic *velas* and afternoons in Isthmus cantinas. The profound social significance of such occasions and settings is undeniable. However, I think it is also important to note the pathological consequences that excessive drinking has had on many Isthmus families. In this regard, I particularly want to emphasize the pernicious activities of beer and liquor companies in the Isthmus, which have designed innumerable strategies for expanding their sales, including engaging in many types of promotions, subsidizing radio programs, providing bands, ice, and metal frame "*stands*" to house the *velas*, and so on. The enormous warehouses of the beer firms, which line the Pan American Highway between Salina Cruz and Juchitán, attest to their extraordinary sales volume.

68. Isthmus Zapotec philosophy is expressed in poetry and folk songs such as *La Martiniana* and *Guendanabani* (de la Cruz 1983b).

69. A judge in Tehuantepec, who had previously worked in several other districts of Oaxaca, told me that crime rates were higher in the Isthmus than in most other parts of the state, although Greenberg's book (1989) indicates that violence may be even more prevalent in the Chatino area than in the Isthmus.

Some homicide statistics from a small Midwestern U.S. city with approximately the same population (ca. 50,000) as Tehuantepec may help put this matter into perspective. A Moline, Illinois, newspaper article entitled "Crime rate takes leap in Moline," which describes a dramatic jump in criminal offenses in this economically depressed community, notes that two murders were committed in the city during 1988 (*Quad–City Times* 5/6/1989); Tehuantepec, by comparison, had 16 recorded homicides in 1986. While this comparison is only of impressionistic value, it does provide insight into the level of insecurity in Isthmus communities.

70. By comparison, Chiñas (1968:143) reported three homicides during her 1966–1967 fieldwork in San Blas.

71. See Amnesty International's report on human rights abuses in southern Mexico (1986) for a brief discussion of violent acts committed against members of COCEI by *pistoleros* (described in the report as "armed civilians"). My own information on Isthmus *pistoleros* comes from local judges, politicians, relatives of a *pistolero*, and many other informants who must remain anonymous. Binford (personal communication 1989) also uncovered a startling history of murders and *pistolero* activity in the small Isthmus town of Laollaga.

72. One of my informants, while working on the 1988 excavation of a PEMEX gas pipeline in the countryside outside Juchitán, repeatedly encountered cadavers buried in shallow graves. He concluded that the bodies were victims of vigilante

violence. Whether or not these particular skeletons resulted from the bullets of *pistoleros,* few Istmeños would deny that *pistoleros* have been responsible for numerous uninvestigated killings.

During my fieldwork, I had the misfortune of seeing the consequences (i.e., dead bodies) of *pistolero* shootings on two occasions.

73. Dorsett (1975:357) observed that Isthmus economic development has led to greater individualism and a decline of kinship relations.

74. Although during the twentieth century the elements and trait list which make up Juchiteco "indigenous" culture changed significantly through the substitution of mass-manufactured goods for local craft products, the spread of Spanish words into the Zapotec language, the adoption of Mexican national customs, miscellaneous processes of cultural syncretism, etc., Juchitecos continue to feel strongly that they possess a distinct culture. As Royce (1982:176–77) noted: "The Zapotec experience no feelings of inconsistency when they adopt elements of national culture. . . . The symbols of what is considered to be Zapotec are constantly being revised as Juchitecos move with the times."

CHAPTER FOUR

1. The extent of Zapotec monolingualism in most Isthmus towns (other than Tehuantepec) was considerable at this time. Molina (1911:48–50) noted that in 1869 only 9 Blaseños could read, write, and speak Spanish. By 1911, a mere 30 of the approximately 4,000 residents of San Blas spoke Spanish.

2. The word "infested" here reflects de la Cruz's own perspective as a militant Zapotec nationalist.

3. According to Kowalewski and Saindon (1992), the social and ideological movement of the Mexican Revolution promoted greater schooling and literacy among rural people of Oaxaca.

4. My information on Henestrosa comes from several of his writings (1929 [1987], 1969, 1987), as well as an interview I conducted with him in Mexico City on January 9, 1988.

5. When the publication began it was known as *Nesha,* but became *Neza* as of October 1935.

6. For an interesting discussion of Mexican cultural nationalism in the 1920s, see Vaughan (1982:239–66).

7. Unruh (1989:47) notes that throughout Latin America during the 1920s and 1930s an aesthetic vanguard concerned with indigenous cultural traditions and experimental art forms produced a flurry of "little magazines, manifestoes, or manifesto-style creative texts, and occasionally serious interdisciplinary investigations into language, history, folklore, and politics." *Neza* was clearly part of this pan-Latin American artistic movement which Unruh links to major social and economic changes that occurred after World War I.

8. Daniel López Nelio, formerly COCEI's federal deputy in the Mexican Con-

gress, in an interview with me described his own love for Zapotec culture as narcissistic, like someone looking at themselves in a mirror.

9. For a novelistic description of the photographers Edward Weston and Tina Modotti in Juchitán, see Poniatowska (1992).

10. For the original poem in Spanish, see Covarrubias (1946:318). The translation is also from Covarrubias.

11. See de la Cruz (1983b:68–69) for the original poem in Spanish. Here I have reproduced only the last stanza of the English translation by Nathaniel Tarn (the entire translated poem is contained in Campbell et al. 1993).

12. The main oral sources for my information about the older generation of Juchiteco intellectuals were Henestrosa, Macario Matus, Víctor de la Cruz, and Dr. Gaudencio Salud of San Blas, who met many of the expatriate Isthmus intellectuals while he was a medical student in Mexico City.

13. That the Juchiteco writers themselves were very aware of their growing assimilation into Mexican national culture is evident in (somewhat defensive) statements like this from Henestrosa (*Neza* 1:3, 1935): ". . . and as I conserve the indigenous sensibility, despite my readings in Occidental culture."

14. Some of the information in this section came from interviews I conducted with three talented contemporary Juchiteco musicians: Mario López, Heber Rasgado, and Israel Vicente.

15. The object of *mentiras* (lies) is not to trick the listener, who knows not to take these "lies" literally, but to impress him or her with the audacity and humor of the teller's poetic exaggerations (de la Cruz 1983b:23).

16. The term *vela* is less-often used in Tehuantepec and San Blas.

17. This description of the *velas* is based on my observations in the 1980s but is equally applicable, as far as I can determine, to the mid-twentieth century period discussed in this section of the chapter.

18. For example, in the first issue of *Neza* (1:1, 1935), Gabriel López Chiñas proclaimed, "Politics . . . will be untouchable for us."

19. The primary sources for this discussion of the *Neza Cubi* generation are numbers 1–14 of the magazine (1968–1970) and extensive interviews with Matus, de la Cruz, and other Isthmus intellectuals including López Nelio and César Pineda.

20. In fact, López became a prominent member of PRI. He is thus one of the few of the younger Zapotec intellectuals who did not participate in COCEI.

CHAPTER FIVE

1. My point is not that indigenous resistance is rare, but that, as Scott (1985) has noted, "everyday forms of peasant resistance" occur more commonly than do successful, long-lived opposition movements, such as COCEI.

2. Rubin (1990:247–48) argues that contemporary Mexican social movements such as COCEI should not be viewed as "new forms of political activity" because

they balance "similar sets of concerns in somewhat similar contexts" like popular movements of the past. While I find his article persuasive for Mexico as a whole, it is less convincing regarding Juchitán because of his apparent inclusion of both the reformist FRD (comprised of business people and professionals) and the radical COCEI (made up predominantly of peasants and laborers) in the single category "popular movements." Although the Coalition repeated many of the calls for democracy and administrative reforms made by the FRD, I suggest that COCEI represented a significant departure from the FRD in its (i.e., COCEI's) strong emphasis on land invasions and land redistribution, traditional agricultural practices and communal land tenure, strikes and other labor protests, and Zapotec ethnic self-determination versus the FRD's support of "economic investment" and "urbanization," and opposition to "traditional agriculture" and "indigenous isolation" (Rubin 1990:252). I also argue that Juchitán should be viewed in terms of political continuity, inasmuch as COCEI carries on Juchiteco struggles for local autonomy and ethnic self-determination that date to the mid-nineteenth century.

3. Friedrich (1986:241) found a similar phenomenon in Naranja, Michoacán, although he suggests that "Naranja is not all that different from many other communities with a developed or even exacerbated political (self-)awareness often the result of specific, historical causes."

4. Interestingly, both male and female Zapotecs of Juchitán view themselves as courageous and audacious. In this aspect of ethnicity/self-image, there is little variation by gender.

5. Génico's medical talent (he gave papers at international conferences and made innovations in local medical techniques), and the fact that he was an "Indian" from San Blas working in the rival, mestizo-dominated town of Tehuantepec, aroused envy and hostility from upper-class Tehuanos. Génico's intense and feisty demeanor also irked the Tehuantepec elite, who were accustomed to lording it over San Blas' mostly Zapotec peasant community.

My information about Génico comes from his ex-wife, a cousin, and numerous residents of San Blas, Tehuantepec, and Juchitán (especially Leopoldo de Gyves Pineda and Gaudencio Salud).

6. My data on Isthmus religion comes from participant-observation and discussions with my Blaseña spouse.

7. For a more extensive examination of Juchitán politics from 1960 to 1973, see Rubin (1991:162–272).

8. Information about Polo comes from Polo himself, as well as from Oscar Cruz, Macario Matus, and an interview published in *Hora Cero* (3/21/1982).

9. Royce uses the term "Zapotec style" to refer to a flexible complex of Isthmus Zapotec ethnic characteristics (women's clothing, gold jewelry, Zapotec language, indigenous poetry and music, *velas*, etc.) that are mobilized against opponents in the Juchitán political arena.

10. Guadalupe Musalem, Macario Matus, and Leopoldo de Gyves Pineda provided useful background information on the Musalem family.

11. Current COCEI leaders to whom the description also applies include Daniel López Nelio, Héctor Sánchez, Polín, Desiderio de Gyves, Javier Charis, Oscar Cruz, Alberto Reyna, Mariano Santana, and Feliciano Marín—all of whom I interviewed, except de Gyves and Reyna.

12. For an amusing discussion of COCEI's origins in student activism, see Zermeño (1987:69–70). My information about López Nelio comes from several interviews I conducted with him in the spring of 1988.

13. When I interviewed him, López Nelio jokingly noted that when PRI agents offered him a condominium in Acapulco in order to get him to quit organizing the peasants, he was compelled to turn it down because there are no pigs in the streets of Acapulco like there are in Juchitán, so he would not feel at home there.

14. When the 1964 *ejido* decree was first announced, peasants—influenced by large landowners who violently opposed *ejidos*—were against it. However, by the 1970s COCEI peasants considered *ejido* status preferable to the 1966 decree which had made the land around Juchitán subject to private ownership. COCEI's position is that Isthmus land should be owned and exploited collectively. The legal status of land around Juchitán remains ambiguous and a source of considerable discontent even today.

15. COCEI defended workers at the following types of businesses or institutions between 1973 and 1976: a lumber company, rice plant, shoe store, a chain of corn mills, a tile manufacturer, a welder's union, an agricultural research station, agricultural enterprises, and others (COCEI 1988).

Student support for the Coalition came from the local vocational school/high school (ITRI), several Isthmus secondary schools, and Juchitecos attending high schools and universities in Oaxaca and Mexico City (Santibañez 1980). In 1977 COCEI students formed the Student Council for Popular Support and called for educational and land reform (Gutiérrez 1981:259).

16. The following discussion of the Casa de la Cultura and the Juchiteco cultural scene is based on interviews and participant-observation with the following individuals: Macario Matus, Víctor de la Cruz, Oscar Martínez, Miguel Angel Toledo, Manuel Matus, Sabino López, Miguel Angel Salinas, Enedino Jiménez, Guillermo Archila, Jorge Magariño, Israel Vicente, Omar Luis, Víctor Orozco, Dionisio Hernández, Julio Bustillo, Manuel López Mateos, Maura Matus, and "Puga."

17. Macario Matus noted that the idea of creating a Casa de la Cultura was born when Francisco Toledo was painting murals in the home of then-Oaxaca governor Víctor Bravo Ahuja around 1971. In lieu of his regular fee, Toledo asked the governor to construct a Casa de la Cultura in his pueblo. A decaying but majestic nineteenth-century building, which formerly housed a secondary school, was renovated for this purpose. Today the Casa is a very attractive facility with beautiful flowering trees in its open courtyard.

18. Information on Charis and the Alvaro Obregón Colony can be found in Martínez López (1985), López Monjardin (1983), and Calvo Zapata (1981). During my fieldwork, I conducted numerous interviews with residents of the Colony in-

cluding Ricardo Martínez, Antonio López Luis, and Juventino Jiménez (all of whom have been powerful figures in the area at various times), several contemporaries of Charis, and one of his sons. These interviews are the source for much of the information contained in this section.

19. Originally, the government planned to expropriate and redistribute 2,300 ha, but Rasgado claimed to have already redistributed 1,300 ha to 80 peasants, so the total was reduced to 1,000 ha (Martínez López 1985). The 1,000 ha were converted into the stridently pro–COCEI Ejido Zapata in 1977. In 1981 the PRI counterattacked, creating the Ejido Charis with land granted by Charis' daughter to 100 peasants in the Alvaro Obregón area. However, many of the peasants of the Ejido Charis later also became COCEI partisans.

20. The initial residents of Colonia Alvaro Obregón included peasant families from Juchitán, San Blas, Xadani, and the Huave area, although the Juchiteco settlers were the most numerous. Many of the second generation of Alvaro Obregón peasants continue to identify with the hometowns of their parents, even though the Colonia is now a large village in its own right.

21. One of the main reasons Javier Charis distanced himself from his father's *cacique* political legacy was undoubtedly the harsh personal treatment he received from his father. General Charis never formally recognized Javier (whose mother was not married to the general) as his son, nor did he bequeath him any of his fortune in land, livestock, and properties. Another reason for Javier's affiliation with COCEI was the convergence of his own progressive political philosophy with that of the movement.

22. Santana (1988:41) points out that land invasions occurred all over the Isthmus in 1975 and 1976, despite threats and provocation from regional *caciques*. As justification, COCEI claims that 25,000 ha of land in the Isthmus irrigation district have been illegally privatized and monopolized by large landowners who they derisively refer to as *acaparadores* (Ornelas Esquinca 1983:27).

23. The Juchitán elite responded to COCEI control of the communal land board with legal maneuvers designed to annul the election that had brought COCEI to power. After COCEI won the 1978 elections for communal lands officers, the elite obtained writs preventing the communal lands organization from functioning or holding new assemblies to elect officers. Consequently, Juchitán currently has no communal land board (*Comisariado de Bienes Comunales*), which presents logistical problems for peasants who could otherwise use such a board to obtain credit and resolve land disputes.

The struggle for control of the land board has been a central focus of COCEI's efforts to regain lost land within the irrigation district and secure benefits for the Juchitán peasantry.

24. ON–FDU, FCI, COCEM, COCEO, and CNPA are the acronyms of the main organizations in which COCEI participated. ON–FDU stands for the Netzahualcoyotl Cultural Organization (ON) of the Benito Juárez University of Oaxaca, an affiliate of the Democratic University Front (FDU). The FCI is the

Independent Peasant Front of Tuxtepec, Oaxaca. COCEM is the acronym for the Peasant Student Coalition of Mexico. COCEO is the Worker-Peasant-Student Coalition of Oaxaca. CNPA is the National Plan de Ayala Coordinating Body, which held its 1981 meeting in Juchitán. COCEI's relations with CNPA began in 1979, some years after it developed ties to the three other organizations in the mid-1970s. I included CNPA with the others because in all five cases COCEI maintained considerable distance between itself and the other movements. COCEI has also had a stormy relationship with the Partido Obrero Socialista (POS), a tiny Trotskyite sect that developed in Juchitán prior to COCEI, but has never had more than a handful of members.

Martínez López (1985:37–42) discusses COCEI's difficult relationships with other grassroots organizations. He notes that COCEI's intense localism and emphasis on autonomy limits its capacity for alliances with other groups, because COCEI leaders want to either dominate them or maintain absolute independence.

For more discussion of COCEI's place in Oaxaca state politics and the relationship between COCEI and other Oaxacan political movements, see Rubin (1991:340–51).

25. Unfortunately, I was never able to obtain a copy of this booklet of poems by Alejandro Cruz who, ironically, was also killed by the PRI. However, I would like to thank Oscar Cruz for reading some of the poems to me, as well as the line from Roque Dalton used as an epigram by Alejandro in his booklet.

26. During the Charis era, Juchiteco peasants were not well organized (politically) and the level of agrarian conflict was less severe; hence, violence against individual peasants did not provoke the same unified and radical response it would during the COCEI period. By then, intense land tenure conflicts and local political struggles had caused a broad segment of the Isthmus peasantry to band together in COCEI. Thereafter, attacks by soldiers, police, and *pistoleros* on Zapotec peasants were viewed within a polarized political context, rather than as isolated incidents, as they may have appeared to be during Charis' time.

27. In 1975 COCEI took over the Agrarian Reform Ministry (then known as the Department of Agrarian Affairs and Colonization) offices in Mexico City. Subsequent negotiations led to a deal between COCEI and the ministry, calling for annulment of the 1966 private property decree, recognition of the *ejidal* status (converted from originally communal terrain) of Juchitán land, and elimination of monopolies over land in the irrigation district (Santana 1988:8). A brigade of technicians was sent to Juchitán to study the situation and carry out reforms (COCEI claims these studies corroborate their view, i.e., that Juchitán land is communal land converted to *ejido* status rather than private property). Hence, large landowners' private titles were legally challenged, and bank credits to "monopolists" were cancelled. The landed bourgeoisie responded by shooting up a meeting between COCEI leaders with Agrarian Reform authorities in a well-known incident (Santana 1988:10). They also took political and legal measures to protect their land. After its principal leaders were exiled from Juchitán as a result of a violent clash

with a rival agrarian leader, COCEI's efforts to reverse the 1966 decree and expedite land reform were stalled, and the government canceled fledgling efforts to execute the 1975 agreement. This hardening of government policy toward the Juchitán peasant movement was probably at least partially a result of the more conservative agrarian policies of President López Portillo, who replaced the populist Echeverría in 1976.

28. According to informants, COCEI section leaders "emerge from the community" and consist of people who have presence, courage, some education, popular support, and fluency in Zapotec.

29. Víctor's mother, *Na* China Henestrosa, engaged in numerous long, dangerous hunger strikes in Mexico City and elsewhere, despite her advanced age and fragile health. This fearlessly devoted and dedicated woman became an inspiration to *Coceístas* and other left-wing activists in Mexico. *Na* China is beautifully depicted in a photograph by Garciela Iturbide (see Iturbide and Poniatowska 1989), and was interviewed on several occasions by leftist journalists (see, e.g., *El Buscón* no. 6, 1983).

30. Rubin characterizes COCEI as "disorganized" because "the movement was not well organized enough to act on all fronts effectively" (Rubin 1991:423). I feel that such a characterization is unfair, given that it could be made about almost any grassroots political movement anywhere. In fact, I would argue that COCEI is very well organized given its relative lack of funds and resources, and the severe repression the movement has had to confront at various times in its history. COCEI has demonstrated an ability to mobilize hundreds and thousands of people on very short notice for rallies, protests, and communal work parties. Much of this is possible because of the dense network of personal and family relationships in Isthmus Zapotec communities, and the ethic of reciprocity and shared activity that underlies local social interactions. The lack of committees, strict adherence to time schedules, and notions of gringo-style efficiency should not be taken as a sign of "disorganization" but as a different cultural approach to organization.

31. For a more detailed treatment of Juchitán politics in the 1970s, see Rubin (1991:273–360).

32. *Ley de Organizaciones Políticas y Procesos Electorales.*

33. This point became very clear to me during my fieldwork when I would ask *Coceístas* if the movement would not be better off downplaying ethnicity and regionalism in order to forge larger political alliances. The reply was always very negative. Typically, the *Coceístas* would praise their local accomplishments and ask why they should change an obviously successful strategy in order to attain a broader political unity whose consequences and benefits for Juchitecos were unproven and illusory. Instead, they would ask, "Why shouldn't the national left conform to our way of doing things?"

34. Rubin (1987a:136) notes that COCEI's success among the peasantry can be attributed, in part, to the weakness of official peasant organizations (particularly the *Confederación Nacional Campesina*, or CNC) in Juchitán. Unlike other regions

of Mexico where the CNC became the political organ of government-created *ejidos* between 1930 and 1960, the Isthmus' relative isolation and subsistence agricultural economy prevented the establishment of an *ejido* and CNC branch until 1964. Formation of mass political organizations in Juchitán, such as the CNC, were also blocked by Charis and other members of the political elite in order to maintain their dominance.

35. Although these figures are especially low, Martínez López (1985) says that abstentionism rather than high voter turnouts are the norm in Juchitán. Martínez Assad (1985:238) cites the following figures on abstentionism in Oaxaca from the Mexican federal election commission: 1976, 40.5 percent; 1979, 54.08 percent; 1982, 39.77 percent.

36. The government responded to COCEI's embassy occupations by sending police and soldiers to evacuate the *Coceístas*. Subsequently, the participants (male and female Juchitecos) were jailed and tortured. After a week of punishment and questioning, all but six *Coceístas*, the leaders of the action, were released. The remaining six suffered through six months of incarceration in the infamous Eastern Penitentiary of Mexico City before COCEI mobilizations forced their release.

37. Bailón (1987:55) argues that PRI's willingness to accede to COCEI demands was strongly influenced by a power vacuum in the state government at this time. The November 1980 elections and subsequent COCEI protests occurred during a changing of the guard, as Governor Jiménez Ruiz was replaced by Pedro Vázquez Colmenares. Both the lame-duck governor and his successor wanted the transition to take place in an atmosphere of tranquility and therefore avoided confronting COCEI, which had already "gotten the goat" of one Oaxaca governor.

38. Martínez López (1985:71) points out that PRI's generic 1981 campaign rhetoric lacked the immediate impact of the concrete demands voiced by COCEI (e.g., "restitution of communal lands to poor Juchitán peasants"). He also notes that unlike the divided and disorganized local PRI, COCEI had a militant following united around specific issues and organized for mobilizations at a moment's notice.

39. Martínez López (1985:90) states that COCEI celebrated a grand Isthmus *vela* after their election victory. He notes that once again the secular customs of Juchitán were used to "informally formalize" municipal power.

40. "People's Government" is Rubin's (1987a) apposite translation of *Ayuntamiento Popular*, the term *Coceístas* used to refer to their municipal administration. This name reflects the vanguard, radical style of COCEI at this time in its history.

CHAPTER SIX

1. The following text is the segment of Polín's speech discussed above:

"naquiiñe' chu'nu vigilante, naquiiñe' chu'nu unidu. . . . laanu racalá'dxinu gápanu tratu ne gobiernu de estadu . . . Purti' laacabe nga naazecabe stale fuerza ne stale recursu ni naquí'ñenu para gusiró'banu xquidxinu. . . . Gobiernu ri' nuu para guni defender patrimonio sti' binni pobre de Juchitán" [de Gyves de la Cruz 1981:11].

It is necessary to be vigilant, it is necessary to be united. . . . We want to have dealings with the state government because they are the ones who hold in their hands much power and many resources which we need in order to improve our town. . . . This government is here to defend the patrimony of the poor people of Juchitán.

2. My description of the atmosphere of the *Ayuntamiento Popular* is based, in part, on several visits I made to Juchitán between 1981 and 1983.

3. Many Isthmus Zapotec informants who grew up in the 1960s (or afterwards) told me that they were punished for using Zapotec at school and that their parents discouraged them from speaking the language because they felt it would impede their children's ability to learn Spanish.

4. Another irony here is the fact that the Zapotec spoken by the peasants was deemed inferior precisely because it contained Spanish words, while the upper-class Juchitecos claimed to speak an "unadulterated" version of the language (Royce 1975:78).

5. Royce (1975:100) observed that very few lower-class Zapotecs were members of *vela* societies and "any feature of [Zapotec style] exhibited by the lower class is above all, an economic problem" (p. 78). Thus, e.g., if lower-class Zapotec women wore *huipiles*, it was because they could not afford to wear Western garb. If they spoke the Zapotec language, it was because they had been unable to go to school to learn Spanish (1975:78).

6. COCEI leaders also acquired a penchant for naming their offspring after leftist heroes such as Lenin, Sandino, etc.

7. *PRIhuela* is a "Zapotecized" COCEI slur on the name of Mexico's dominant party (PRI). *Huela* is a Zapotec word that means "old woman"; here, it has the derogatory connotation of something worn out, old, or used up.

8. In the expressions *binni laanu* and *binni xquidxinu*, both the speaker and the people spoken to form part of a collective "we," or "us," as opposed to when the pronoun *laadu* is used. When the *laadu* form is employed, only the speaker and his/her companions are part of the "we," and the people spoken to are excluded.

9. My thanks to Leigh Binford for giving me a cassette tape of COCEI's first *informe* (i.e., the COCEI administration's first formal report to the populace about its activities).

Jiménez's original statement in Zapotec was "*¡Casi ca bisee'tenu dxi bizulúnu bicálunu para ganda qui'banu ra yoo lahui sti' guidxi Xabizende ri', ne rarí' nuuca nu!*" The following is a rough translation: "Just as we hoped—the day we began to struggle to try to take over the Juchitán City Hall building— here we are!"

10. The original joke in Zapotec: "*Ca Priísta ca nuucabe divididu casi xhquie guná' Mixe, ti guicha rarí', ti guicha raca'.*" As this joke reflects, the Isthmus Zapotec tend to look down their noses at the other (generally poorer and more humble) indigenous groups of the Isthmus, such as the Mixe, Huave, Zoque, and Chontals. The machismo of the COCEI leadership is also evident in this joke.

11. *"Pa yoo lahui ca nuxhiaxi' la, irá' Priísta ca niree ñe' para gabiá."*

12. In this case, the Zapotec word *gueu'*, meaning, literally, "coyote," but idiomatically, "coward," or "homosexual," was transposed onto the last name of Mexico's current president. The Isthmus Zapotec people cultivate their skills at verbal banter and double entendre. No one is immune from playful attacks, and even the native language is laughingly referred to as *"Zapochueco."* *Chueco* in Mexican Spanish refers to "something which is crooked, illegal, or tainted."

13. There are quite a few variations on the basic COCEI demonstration discussed here. Often they begin at the COCEI office and then, following a long march through the Juchitán streets, continue in front of City Hall before disbanding. My description of COCEI demonstrations is based on attendance at dozens of such events between 1986 and 1989. Based on hundreds of photographs I have seen of COCEI meetings and rallies that occurred between 1981 and 1983, audio tapes of COCEI speeches given during that time, journalistic and academic accounts of the period, and my field interviews, it is clear to me that their basic style during the *Ayuntamiento Popular* was much as I have described it.

14. Prior to recent quarrels between Toledo and COCEI leaders, as well as between the famous painter and the prime movers behind the Casa de la Cultura, Toledo regularly supplied a subsidy for COCEI activities. Toledo has also established a small publishing firm (Ediciones Toledo) in Mexico City, which produces high-quality books about Isthmus Zapotec history and culture.

Toledo's support of Juchiteco cultural activities has been multifaceted. In addition to donating dozens of valuable paintings and prints from his personal art collection, Toledo gave the Casa de la Cultura boxes of expensive painting materials and a large number of costly art books.

15. Salvador Musalem, one of Juchitán's wealthiest businessmen and a relative of the deposed director, then wrote a letter to the editor of the popular magazine *Siempre* attacking Toledo's erotic art as obscene (*El Satélite* 2/16/1975).

16. My information about the political history of the Casa came primarily from numerous interviews with Macario Matus, as well as a number of articles in the Juchitán newspaper *El Satélite* between 1975 and 1980.

17. This is how de la Cruz (1980:2) describes Toledo's work in relation to Zapotec culture:

> In the presence of the work of Francisco Toledo I discover my incapacity to think in any other language which is not Zapotec (*didxaza*); that is: upon seeing it [Toledo's work] I can only spell it and read it based on the code of this language . . . because it deals to a great extent with the writing and version of these concepts and the images of *didxaza* in forms that derive from a system of painting-writing common to all of Mesoamerica in the pre-Hispanic era which was based on glyphs, signs charged with meaning not only ideographic or magico-religious but at times also phonetic. . . . To affirm that Francisco Toledo is a Zapotec painter is to situate him in his natural context, without

negating what he has seen and learned from the West to improve his vision and knowledge of the characteristic outlines of his culture, as all his work shows us, without folklorisms; to be Zapotec without falling into indigenism. . . . Above all, we reclaim Toledo as our painter, a Zapotec.

18. Several older, more-established Juchitán writers (e.g., Henestrosa and the now deceased Gabriel López Chiñas), however, have sided with the PRI. Although Henestrosa's writing is revered by the current generation of Juchitán intellectuals, his conservative political career within the PRI is the object of much scorn and has earned him the derisive nickname Andrés *"nos destroza,"* a distortion of the author's last name.

19. Ditmars (1936:27–28) notes that "a large, spiny-tailed iguana is a really dangerous creature. . . . If cornered, it flashes into a state of viciousness that might stand off a well-trained dog. The tail is lashed from side to side and the powerful jaws are open and ready to seize the enemy in a strong grip."

A Juchiteco intellectual told me that once an iguana bites into another animal or human to defend itself, it will never let go. Juchitecos' fascination with iguanas is not surprising since they revel in their own feisty, ferocious reputation. Iguanas, then, are an apt symbol for characteristics Juchitecos value in their own self-image. The Juchitecos also use the fact that they eat iguanas to distinguish themselves from other groups of people who do not. For example, Leopoldo de Gyves Pineda loves to tell his story about how when a band of Juchiteco soldiers were stationed in Michoacán, they quickly ate up all the iguanas in the surrounding area to the astonishment of the local population.

20. My thesis advisor, Frank Salomon, observed in relation to outside intellectuals' romantic attachment to the Isthmus, that, "It's as if one of the terms of Zapotecs' negotiated otherness vis-à-vis the nation is to function (Orientalistically) as the Kingdom of Feeling." Indeed there is an impressive lineage of romantic treatises on the Isthmus by outsiders, e.g., Brasseur, Charnay, Starr, Gadow, von Tempsky, and Covarrubias. What is also interesting, though, is a self-cultivated image of exoticism and "primitiveness" by Juchiteco writers themselves, beginning with Henestrosa and continuing through the current generation of Isthmus Zapotec intellectuals.

21. This is not to say that the only way new ideas have entered Juchitán is through the arrival of outsiders. After the Revolution, an increasing number of Juchitecos were aware of, or involved in, national events or public issues far away from their hometown. For example, a Juchiteco, Tito Marín, died while fighting against the Fascists in the Spanish Civil War. Another Juchiteco designed the Mexican embassy in Tokyo. Enrique Liekens, who became a Mexican diplomat, traveled widely outside the country. These individuals, and other Juchitecos who pursued opportunities outside the community, frequently returned and passed on their knowledge and experiences to local people.

22. I admit that I may make an overly optimistic interpretation of the interaction

between outside intellectuals and the Juchitecos. Naturally, I have a vested interest in such an interpretation. To be fair, I should note that *Coceístas* have repeatedly complained about social scientists who do studies of the area—hassling them with questions, interviews, etc., and extracting rich information—but return nothing (not even a copy of their book, article or thesis) to the community. Overall, however, I think that Juchitán and COCEI have also benefited much from these contacts. This was especially noticeable during crisis times in 1983 and afterwards, when urban intellectuals defended COCEI against a media slander campaign and Amnesty International pushed for release of Juchiteco political prisoners.

In relation to the contacts between *Coceístas* and outside intellectuals, Frank Salomon suggests that this may have involved a degree of "packaging and exporting ethnicity, cut to fit ideals of cultural plurality which appeal in various nonlocal markets" by Coalition intellectuals themselves. There is no doubt that some of this has gone on. For example, when COCEI leaders are interviewed by foreign journalists and social scientists, they may accentuate those aspects of local society and the movement which appear most exotic or "Indian" to outside observers. Likewise, Toledo's art exploits to the hilt his "indigenous" background. Nonetheless, this point should not be taken too far because, ultimately, the Juchitecos' discourse about their "Zapotecness" is primarily for their own internal consumption (with the exception of Toledo's art and some of the writings and paintings of the cultural movement).

23. My information about Juchitán cantinas is based on dozens of long afternoons and some evenings spent drinking and socializing with the Zapotec intellectuals between 1987 and 1989. I have no reason to believe that the Juchiteco bohemian cantina scene was significantly different during the *Ayuntamiento Popular* from how I describe it here, with the one exception being that Julio Bustillo's trendy *Bar Jardín* and several other bars mentioned above were not then in existence.

I have changed some of the grammar and verb tenses of my original footnotes to make them more legible, and I slightly altered the order of several sentences, but otherwise the notes are a replica of my original descriptions of an afternoon in La Mixtequita.

24. Local fiestas, weddings, birthday parties, political rallies, etc.—that is, the major social events in the Isthmus—are frequently broadcast on the radio. However, the number of televisions is rapidly increasing in the region.

25. Both the COCEI high school and the teacher's college continued to function for some time despite destruction of school buildings by the PRI regime that replaced the *Ayuntamiento Popular* (Santana 1988:54). Today, the COCEI teacher's college has disappeared, although the Prepa Popular continues.

26. According to one source, as of 1978 there were 9,000 peasants associated with the 58,000 ha of the Juchitán *ejido* (*Punto Crítico* 7/16/1978). If we apply Rubin's estimate for COCEI support in Juchitán (i.e., 60–70 percent) to this figure, we obtain a sum of between 5,400 and 6,300 pro-COCEI peasants in the Juchitán vicinity alone. Additionally, Daniel López Nelio, leader of the COCEI peasant

sector, told me he represents between 5,000 and 10,000 Isthmus peasants and counsels many other groups of peasants as well. Although these figures can only be considered rough approximations, they correspond with other field observations, previous studies, and the opinion expressed nearly unanimously by PRI and COCEI leaders that COCEI attracts the support of the majority of Juchitán peasants.

Similarly, in San Blas, the COCEI activist Octavio Morales represents most local peasants as well as agriculturalists from Tierra Blanca and Santa Rosa. COCEI affiliates dominate the peasant sectors of many other Isthmus towns, including Huilotepec, Comitancillo, Xadani, Alvaro Obregón, and Santo Domingo Ingenio.

27. Extracting agricultural credit, crop insurance settlements, fertilizer, etc., from the government has been a primary tactic used by COCEI throughout the 1980s and early 1990s to support its peasant constituency and raise funds to keep the movement going.

28. MORCEO stands for *Movimiento de Organizaciones Revolucionarias y Campesinas del Estado de Oaxaca*. The CCOEZ is the *Coordinadora Campesina Oaxaqueña Emiliano Zapata*, founded in 1985.

29. Other labor groups COCEI has defended include female beer-sellers (*taberneras*), employees of Juchitán's few industries (a lime factory, sugar cane mill, tile factory, etc.), salt mill workers, water utility employees, bottling company workers, cement company employees of Lagunas, Oaxaca, tractor drivers, and a Salina Cruz welder's union. Recently, COCEI has made alliances with construction workers along the southern Oaxaca coast, especially Huatulco, the site of a massive new tourist development similar to Cancún. During my fieldwork, a COCEI-backed union won a 200-million-peso settlement (for severance pay) from the Cristóbal Colón bus company after a two-month strike that paralyzed passenger travel from Oaxaca City to Tuxtla Gutiérrez, Chiapas. In this case, COCEI labor leaders advised the bus company employee's union, rather than directly controlling it, as it does many others (mainly in Juchitán). COCEI's reputation for militancy, willingness to engage in prolonged conflict, and capacity for violent action (if provoked) are powerful negotiating tools.

30. Bailón (1987:41) states that confrontations between workers and bosses are more violent in Oaxaca and similar regions, where commerce and small industrial enterprises are the main sources of capital accumulation, than in more industrialized parts of Mexico. Consequently, in these areas (including Juchitán), strikes provoke tense reactions from owners, who fear the loss of narrow profit margins if they provide workers with conditions that are common elsewhere in Mexico. Likewise, in Juchitán labor struggles may take on a very hostile character due to the close proximity of worker and employer residences and the highly personal nature of local life.

31. The section that follows is based on many interviews in addition to the sources cited. Almost every resident of Juchitán has an opinion on or vivid memories of the events discussed here, hence my sources of information are too numerous to list. Many of my key informants are acknowledged in other footnotes

throughout this book. Additionally, I would especially like to thank Geoff and Edith Hartney, Elí Bartolo, and Peter Hisscock, who provided me with many new perspectives on life in Juchitán.

32. My thanks to Oscar Cruz for supplying me with audio tapes of the Tribunal.

33. *Tequio* is a Nahuatl term that has replaced to some extent the Zapotec word *guendalizaa* in everyday usage in the Isthmus. *Guendalizaa* refers to cooperative labor among relatives in, e.g., the raising of a roof, or the building of an *enramada* for a fiesta or wedding celebration. In a more general sense, *guendalizaa* refers to sharing and cooperative activity among members of the Zapotec community. The word *tequio*, historically, has referred to community work parties organized by municipal authorities, for example, to build a road or some other public facility. But this custom had fallen into disuse in Juchitán prior to the *Ayuntamiento Popular*. In recent years, COCEI has used this word to encourage contributions of time and labor to the movement from the rank-and-file.

34. PRI's dominant presence in La Venta, La Ventosa, and Chicapa de Castro results from the post-Revolution regime's grants of land to peasants in those areas. These peasants and their descendants have, for the most part, remained loyal to the "official" party (Martínez López 1985:53–54).

35. According to Bailón (1987:48), the Oaxaca constitution does not permit state authorities to impeach municipal administrations, and therefore the legislature violated its own laws in taking away COCEI's power to govern Juchitán. COCEI charges that Rojo and company provoked the July 31, 1983, incident in order to provide an excuse for impeaching COCEI. Such a scenario is plausible because of the intense hatred the *Ayuntamiento Popular* had inspired in the Juchitán elite and the strategic importance of removing COCEI from City Hall prior to the 1983 elections. A leading Juchitán PRI intellectual has even admitted that had COCEI not been booted out of office, it would have won the elections, thus granting the movement three more years in power, an unacceptable situation for state and local elites (Martínez López 1985:143).

36. During this time, some Mexican journalists began to compare the government's reaction to the Juchitán conflict with Reagan's treatment of Nicaragua. (For a discussion of Juchitán's significance within Mexican politics and how the COCEI-vs.-government showdown was treated in the news media, see Manuel Buendía's column in *Excélsior* 8/18/1983.) COCEI leaders and an influential leftist social scientist took this analysis a step further, suggesting that if events in Central America and Juchitán continued to heat up, the Reagan administration could use this (and the specter of revolution moving northward) as an excuse to intervene in the Isthmus of Tehuantepec (Zermeño 1987:91).

37. Geoff Hartney, an Australian man married to a Juchiteca who ran a clothing store in Juchitán during this period, was astounded by the number of foreign observers who arrived on the scene. Since Geoff was one of the few foreigners residing in Juchitán at the time, he frequently entertained these visitors until he eventually tired of being a tourist guide for intellectuals.

38. A *muxe'* social/political group known as *Las Intrépidas* also backed the interim mayor and PRI, as they continue to do today. Additionally, Rojo was reputed to have a gang of gay thugs who intimidated COCEI voters during elections. The support of PRI by Juchitán gays is a result, in part, of their personal ties with the gay interim mayor and a prominent gay businessman allied with PRI.

Two other members of the interim city council were gay, which prompted composition of a popular local salsa tune depicting the interim PRI government as entirely gay, from the mayor on down to streetsweepers.

39. Historically, Mexican indigenous women have often been in the vanguard of popular political protest (Taylor 1978:190; 1979).

40. Amnesty International (1986) later named four COCEI activists (who were imprisoned without trial) prisoners of conscience, including Polo.

41. Rubin (1991) repeatedly argues that the livelihoods of Zapotec people were not threatened by capitalist development of the Isthmus. Fishermen of Juchitán, Xadani, and Alvaro Obregón who had to quit fishing because their lagoons were polluted by the Salina Cruz oil refinery would not agree with this analysis. Nor would the Zapotec peasants who were thrown off land in Salina Cruz so that PE-MEX could build the refinery. The same could be said of the residents of Jalapa del Marqués, whose original town was inundated by the Benito Juárez Dam. Peasants, whose lands were damaged by pipeline oil spills and excessive salinity due to the government's failed rice cultivation program and improper irrigation, are other examples. And there are many more. Finally, government-directed economic development is directly responsible for serious environmental damage in the Isthmus. Thus, I feel that it is legitimate to consider these developments a threat to the livelihoods of Isthmus indigenous people.

42. MIPRI stands for *Movimiento Integrador Priísta*.

43. My information on the 1986 elections comes from interviews I conducted during my fieldwork in 1987, as well as a short trip to the Isthmus in the summer of 1986. For further discussion of the context of the elections, see Rubin (1987a).

44. In addition to Juchitán and Xadani, COCEI obtained representation in the governments of the following Isthmus towns: Ixtepec, Ixtaltepec, Santo Domingo Ingenio, Ixhuatán, Unión Hidalgo, Comitancillo, and Huilotepec. COCEI also claims to have followers in 60 towns.

The establishment of coalition governments in many Isthmus municipalities are a result of recent changes in Mexican electoral laws regarding proportional representation (Rubin 1987b:4).

45. Castillo was, initially, the presidential candidate of the Mexican Socialist Party (PMS). When the PMS formed an electoral alliance with the Cardenist Front (FDN), Castillo declined his candidacy in favor of that of Cárdenas, son of a popular former president. COCEI backed Castillo, then Cárdenas, who made two campaign trips to Juchitán. COCEI's successful rallies with the two influential leaders reflected the movement's temporarily improved relations with national leftist parties. COCEI did not support the candidacy of Rosario Ibarra of the Trotskyist PRT,

even though Ibarra had been an influential advocate for COCEI and the rights of political prisoners. The winning candidate, Carlos Salinas of PRI, did not visit Juchitán during his campaign, perhaps because he feared being repudiated by the Juchitecos.

46. Cárdenas' populist coalition during the 1988 election included an unusual amalgam of small parties, including the traditionally conservative PARM. After quarreling with rival Juchiteco *Priístas*, who prevented him from becoming a legislative candidate through the local PRI, Rojo jumped ship and joined the PARM, which made him a candidate for federal deputy, a position he ultimately obtained. This presented an ironic situation in which both Rojo and COCEI, mortal enemies, were allies of Cárdenas during the 1988 campaign. When Cárdenas came to Juchitán, however, COCEI completely dominated the political march and rally held to support his candidacy. *Coceístas* physically prevented Rojo and his supporters from taking part in the pro-Cárdenas rally.

47. My discussion of Juchitán political events from 1987 to 1989 is based on participant-observation and interviews with the leadership of COCEI, rank-and-file *Coceístas*, Juchiteco intellectuals associated with the Casa de la Cultura, and several prominent members of the Juchitán PRI.

48. An employee of the Oaxaca government's regional office in Tehuantepec told me that the national and state government allowed COCEI's electoral victory in exchange for the Coalition agreeing to cease defending workers and displaced residents at the expensive new tourist zone of Huatulco, Oaxaca, which is just a short drive from the Isthmus. COCEI's grassroots organizing talents were becoming a thorn in the side of Huatulco developers, who have invested massive sums in the area, hoping to turn it into a mini-Cancún, but prior to the election, the movement apparently ended its involvement there. Only the COCEI leadership and high government officials know for sure whether or not a deal was struck, and they refuse to discuss this issue.

49. The sources for my discussion of the 1989 Juchitán municipal election are interviews with COCEI leaders and rank-and-file members, members of the Juchiteco cultural movement, *Proceso* 8/7/1989, an interview with Isidoro Yescas, an influential Oaxaca journalist, articles in the Oaxaca papers *Noticias* (8/8/1989) and *El Imparcial* (8/5/1989), and articles in the Mexico City papers *Unomásuno* (7/31/1989) and *La Jornada* (8/8/1989).

50. The exact political motivations behind the *Proceso* articles attacking COCEI remain a bit of a mystery. The simplest explanation is that the articles were designed to discredit COCEI in order to encourage the government to annul the movement's electoral victory. However, one well-placed informant suggested to me that the articles were also designed to weaken Governor Ramírez by stirring up trouble in the Isthmus and criticizing Ramírez's supposed support for COCEI. This would strengthen the hand of one of the governor's rivals within the PRI, who supposedly is connected by marriage to the publisher of *Proceso* and is the person who persuaded *Proceso* to publish the articles. I cannot confirm this hypothesis, however.

51. For obvious reasons, I cannot divulge the sources of my information about alleged corruption and tensions within COCEI and infighting amongst members of the Isthmus Zapotec cultural movement.

CHAPTER SEVEN

1. See Toledo (1986) for reproductions and the original Spanish titles of these paintings.

2. This comment and other verbatim statements from COCEI members presented in this chapter come from interviews I conducted during my 1987–1988 fieldwork, unless otherwise specified.

3. I am grateful to Justo Pineda for providing information about Robles and Martínez.

4. The principal written sources for COCEI's view of Isthmus Zapotec history are COCEI (1983, 1988, 1990), de la Cruz (1983b), Macario Matus (1981), Manuel Matus (1988), Santana (1988), and miscellaneous writings by other Zapotec intellectuals. This section of the chapter is also based on extensive interviews with many of the major COCEI leaders and ideologues. López Monjardin's (1983) observations on Isthmus history, as seen through the eyes of *Coceístas*, have also been helpful.

5. In relation to COCEI's interpretation of Isthmus history, Chassen (personal communication 1992) has observed that "history [is] reinvented with each generation."

6. The basis of Aubague's essay is an analysis of a newspaper article ("Momentos Políticos de Juchitán") by Macario Matus (1981), published under the pseudonym "Fernando Contreras."

7. "They taught you to be a man."

8. *Ique* is the Zapotec word for head.

9. Interviews with Manuel López Mateos, Oscar Cruz, Enedino Jiménez, Polín, López Nelio, Mariano Santana, and Héctor Sánchez provided substantial data for this section and the following two sections of the chapter.

10. Strangely, Rubin (1991:361–450) asserts that COCEI's lack of internal democracy is a strength of the movement rather than a weakness. In my experience, each time I have returned to Juchitán since 1987 the number of complaints about the authoritarianism of COCEI leaders has increased. In recent years, many COCEI sympathizers and followers have told me that the concentration of power in the hands of a few leaders is the most divisive issue confronting the movement and the one most likely to cause internal fragmentation.

11. *"Como los Morales eran huabes, es decir de raza vencida, pospuesta por los juchitecos, quienes no pueden referirse a ellos sin anticiparles un adjectivo denigrante . . ."* (Henestrosa, 1969:17). Moreover, Henestrosa makes the interesting and accurate point that the Huave were conquered twice, first by the Zapotecs and then by the Spaniards.

12. Frank Salomon (personal communication 1988) notes that the Zapotec–

Huave relationship is quite similar to that of the Aymara and Uru of Bolivia, in which one native South American group views the other as primitive, archaic, and "water people." Salomon suggests that this pattern of ethnic stereotyping of one indigenous group by another "may touch on some very ancient American concepts."

13. Many mestiza Istmeñas also wear Zapotec clothing, especially at fiesta time.

14. As my informant put it: "*Los Juchitecos facilmente te tutean, te hablan de tu.*"

15. My thanks to Oscar Cruz—one of the *Coceístas* jailed for taking part in the embassy takeovers—for telling me about this incident.

16. The original phrase in Zapotec is "*gunaa nga ñaa guirá' binni nuu guidxilayú.*" Ironically, Sokoloff (1993) observed that the most famous Juchiteca midwife, Joaquina, who was celebrated by both the COCEI and the PRI as "the mother of all" (*la madre de todos*), was actually not a Zapotec woman. Additionally, many of the midwives Sokoloff studied have formal medical training rather than simply being practitioners of ancient community traditions. As in many aspects of Juchitán life, what appears or is said to be a purely indigenous custom or tradition turns out, under closer scrutiny, to be a hybrid of local and imported ideas and practices.

17. Although equivalent Zapotec words exist for referring to female siblings (*benda* when a woman is speaking, or *biza'na'* when a man is speaking), this is not mentioned in COCEI ideological statements, whereas much emphasis is placed on the use of the word *bichi*.

18. In fact, such idealized treatments of Isthmus Zapotec women seem to be more oriented towards advancing an urban feminist agenda than trying to understand the complexities of everyday life as it is lived by Juchitecas. Although Poniatowska is a brilliant writer who has produced a beautiful, lyrical evocation of Zapotec women's power, her feminist vanguard approach may actually reproduce many of the matriarchal stereotypes that have colored many previous descriptions of the Isthmus by male writers such as Brasseur and Covarrubias. While Poniatowska has a long acquaintance with Isthmus peoples and is very familiar with local culture and history, she has chosen to present only one side of Zapotec women's experience. I argue, however, that in order to obtain a more realistic sense of Isthmus women's lives, we need to look at them in their entirety. This includes examining such things as poverty, spousal abuse, class inequalities, and the sexual double standard, as well as exploring images of women's beauty and grandeur.

Less-sophisticated interpretations of Isthmus life than that of Poniatowska, such as those found in tourist guides and journalistic accounts of Juchitán, are often based on very short trips to the Isthmus spent primarily at fiestas where the more successful and affluent Zapotec women are seen drinking and partying dressed up in their finery. In the meantime, the average Zapotec woman of *la séptima*, Cheguigo, San Blas, or any other Isthmus village or poor barrio is hustling to provide enough food for her many children, keep her often-inebriated husband under control, clean the house, look after her elderly relatives, pay the bills, and keep her one worn-out *huipil* from falling apart.

19. Another problem frequently found in descriptions emphasizing Isthmus Za-

potec women's power and splendor is that such descriptions homogenize women with statements like "Juchitecas drink more than their men do," "Zapotec women dominate Zapotec men," and so forth. While, in some cases, these statements might have some validity, there is obviously a great deal of variability among the large Isthmus Zapotec population. Furthermore, human relations are volatile and subject to change over time.

The indeterminacy of power relations and the variability of social practice of any given couple or family was made clear to me in interviews with many Zapotec women. For example, I asked one Blaseña (herself a heavy drinker) if it was true that in the Isthmus women sometimes drank more than men, and she replied "*Si hay dinero, si hay garganta, y si su religión le permite, sí*" ("If the woman has the money, the throat to handle it, and her religion allows her to do it, yes"). Likewise, a common response I received to the question "Do Zapotec women dominate their men?" was "*Si el hombre se deja*" ("If the man allows it to happen"). In other words, some Zapotec women may drink more than Zapotec men or have more power than men in the family, but the situation could just as easily be reversed.

20. Rubin (1991:440) asserts that women have a greater role than men in the reproduction of Isthmus Zapotec culture: "It was primarily women who perpetuated the vibrant daily Zapotec culture." I feel that this analysis is incorrect. While Isthmus Zapotec women certainly contribute their share to the maintenance of Zapotec customs and traditions, so do men. The one area in which women's role is clearly greater is in terms of clothing. Zapotec women are the wearers of the *huipiles*, *enaguas*, and *trajes* that are a key symbol of indigenous identity, whereas Zapotec men wear nondistinctive western garb, for the most part. But most other aspects of Zapotec ethnic practices are shared relatively equally by men and women, or each sex has its own distinctive sphere within the practice, or engages in a parallel activity. Perhaps the single most important element of Zapotec identity, the native language, is spoken by approximately equal numbers of men and women.

One might argue that women's market activity is one area in which women alone promote local customs with little contribution from Zapotec men. Yet, by the same token, men carry on Isthmus indigenous agricultural practices with little participation by women. Likewise, it could be suggested that women's role in fiestas is greater because they are the ones who dress elegantly for them and dance in the middle of the crowd. But men also take part in fiesta customs and preparations for the fiesta.

Furthermore, there are also aspects of Zapotec culture that are sustained mostly by men, such as musical traditions, certain verbal performances (e.g., the pre-wedding sermon of the *chagoola'*), and various arts and crafts.

Overall, the perpetuation of Zapotec culture is clearly a joint enterprise, with neither gender having a predominant role.

21. Chiñas (1983:4) asserts that "the essence of Isthmus Zapotec culture [is] sexual egalitarianism." She argues that behind the "patriarchal overlay" of the "ideal culture" lies the "real culture" of the Isthmus Zapotec, which is matrifocal.

According to this perspective, women's nonformalized roles compensate for women's lower status in the formal social realm, leading to a "fine balance of equality between the sexes" (1983:93).

My fieldwork experience gave me a very different view of Isthmus gender relations. Although both local people and outsiders frequently spoke to me of Zapotec matriarchy and gender equality, this seemed to be the ideal rather than the everyday reality for Zapotec women (the reverse of Chiñas' findings). Indeed, high rates of male alcoholism (and the social pathologies associated with it), wife-beating, the *casa chica*, sexual abuse, irresponsible fatherhood, and the cult of female virginity are all too familiar realities for Isthmus women. To give just one anecdotal example: one of my major female informants had to leave the community as a teenager to avoid a marriage arranged by her father to an older man she despised; two of her uncles died of alcoholism; her father and brother each maintained a *casa chica*; and her sister's sex life at the age of 30 was still controlled by her father. The women affected by these circumstances complained bitterly to me about them.

Thus, I cannot honestly categorize Isthmus Zapotec society as sexually egalitarian, even though there are areas of Isthmus social life in which women enjoy high status (so ably described by Chiñas). Binford, who worked in the Zapotec community of Espinal, also denies the sexual egalitarian thesis. Binford's views on the subject were heavily influenced by an incident in which he had to subdue a drunken Espinaleño who was brutalizing his (i.e., the Espinaleño's) wife.

22. The occupations of these talented Zapotec women are (or were) as follows: Juana C. Romero (merchant and civic leader), Aurea Procel (doctor and professor), Gudelia Pineda (teacher and politician), Guadalupe López Lena (judge), and Neli Toledo (judge). Of these five, only López Lena and Toledo are alive today.

23. In this respect, female *Coceístas* seem to be concerned with what Molyneux defines as "women's practical gender interests" (i.e., women's immediate needs), rather than their "strategic gender interests" (i.e., the questioning and transforming of the sexual division of labor) (Safa 1989:12). Thus, Isthmus Zapotec women's thinking about their political roles may more closely resemble what Kaplan (1982:545) calls "female consciousness" ("a sense of rights and obligations that provide motive force for actions" which derive from a "recognition of what a particular class, culture, and historical period expect from women"), rather than mainstream feminist ideologies.

24. Anthropologist Sal Ortega informed me in 1993 that COCEI has recently begun to make a concerted effort to attract *muxe'* support and is having some success.

25. Nonetheless *muxe'* have contributed to COCEI's success, as in the case of "*Malocha*," a resourceful individual who devised a remedy made of homemade vinegar (*curado*) for tear-gas intoxication during streetfighting between *Coceístas* and soldiers after the COCEI's ouster from City Hall in 1983.

26. Unfortunately, I have very little information about Zapotec lesbians to contribute to this discussion of homosexuality, politics, and culture in the Isthmus.

CHAPTER EIGHT

1. In fairness to Clifford, he briefly mentions (1988:16) that languages, traditions, and cosmologies are sometimes "literally murdered," but he quickly qualifies this by noting that cultures considered extinct have been revived or continued as in the cases of the Tasmanians of Australia and California tribal groups. My point is not to dwell on the morbid, but to take more seriously the politics of cultural invention and tradition, which may be neglected by Clifford's overemphasis of cultural creativity, borrowing, and self-fashioning. His discussion (1988:277–346) of Mashpee "Indian" identity comes closer to the type of politicized analysis of cultural invention I am advocating, although he concludes with a wishy-washy relativism which undermines the sharper political analysis that informs earlier segments of the essay.

2. In contemporary Juchitán, the periphery-versus-center dynamic has an interesting political/spatial dimension, since the poorer, largely pro-COCEI segments of town (*la séptima*, Cheguigo, and the second and fifth wards) and the pro-COCEI villages of Xadani and Alvaro Obregón encircle the downtown area of Juchitán, where the predominantly pro-PRI Zapotec elite dwells.

Principal Acronyms and Abbreviations Used in the Text and Bibliography

AEJ	Asociación de Estudiantes Juchitecos
AGEO	Archivo General del Estado de Oaxaca
AGN	Archivo General de la Nación
AI	Amnesty International
CCDDPJ	Comité Central de Defensa de los Derechos del Pueblo Juchiteco
CCJ	Comité Cívico Juchiteco
CNC–CNC	Confederación Nacional de Cañeros–Confederación Nacional Campesina
CNC–CNPP	Confederación Nacional de Cañeros–Confederación Nacional de la Pequeña Propiedad
CNPA	Coordinadora Nacional Plan de Ayala
COCEI	Coalición Obrera Campesina Estudiantil del Istmo
CTI	Central de Trabajadores del Istmo
ESF	Escuela Secundaria Federal de Juchitán, Oaxaca
FRD	Frente para Renovación Democrática
FUDJ	Frente Único Democrático Juchiteco
IAPO	Instituto de Administración Pública de Oaxaca
INAH	Instituto Nacional de Antropología e Historia
INBA	Instituto Nacional de Belles Artes
INEGI	Instituto Nacional de Estadística Geografía e Informática
INI	Instituto Nacional Indigenista
MA	Memorias Administrativas
MIPRI	Movimiento Integrador Priísta
PCM	Partido Comunista Mexicano

PEMEX	Petróleos Mexicanos
PLM	Partido Liberal Mexicano
PMS	Partido Mexicano Socialista
PPS	Partido Popular Socialista
PRD	Partido de la Revolución Democrática
PRI	Partido Revolucionario Institucional
PSUM	Partido Socialista Unificado de México
SARH	Secretaría de Agricultura y Recursos Hidráulicos
SEDUE	Secretaría de Desarrollo Urbano y Ecología
SRA	Secretaría de la Reforma Agraria
TIS	Taller de Investigación Sociológica
TPJ	Títulos Primordiales de Juchitán
UNAM	Universidad Nacional Autónoma de México

ABBREVIATIONS

exp.	expediente
fa., fas.	foja, fojas
vta.	vuelta

Bibliography

ARCHIVAL SOURCES

Archivo General de la Nación (cited in text as AGN), Mexico City

BRANCHES
Abelardo L. Rodríguez
Indios
Mercedes
Pascual Ortíz Rubio
Tierras

Archivo General del Estado de Oaxaca, Oaxaca, Oaxaca

SOURCES
Memorias Administrativas (cited in text as MA)
Exposición

The National Archives of the United States, Washington, D.C.

SOURCE
Dispatches from United States Consuls in Tehuantepec 1850–1867, National
archives Microcopy No. 305 (cited in text as Consul)

PERIODICALS

El Buscón, Mexico City
El Imparcial, Oaxaca, Oaxaca
El Satélite, Juchitán, Oaxaca

El Sol del Istmo, Salina Cruz, Oaxaca
El Universal, Mexico City
Excélsior, Mexico City
Guchachi' Reza, Juchitán, Oaxaca
Guiengola, Tehuantepec, Oaxaca
Hora Cero, Oaxaca, Oaxaca
La Jornada, Mexico City
La Voz del Istmo, Salina Cruz, Oaxaca
Neza, Mexico City
Neza Cubi, Mexico City
Noticias, Oaxaca, Oaxaca
Ovaciones, Mexico City
Proceso, Mexico City
Punto Crítico, Mexico City
Quad-City Times, Davenport, Iowa
The News, Mexico City
Unomásuno, Mexico City

BOOKS, ARTICLES, THESES, AND MANUSCRIPTS

Aguirre Beltrán, Gonzalo
  1958   *Cuijla: Esbozo etnográfico de un pueblo negro*. Mexico: Fondo de Cultura
          Económica.
Alfaro Sánchez, Carlos Javier
  1984   *El Contexto Económico, Político, y Cultural de los Medios de Comunicación:*
          El Caso de XEAP, Radio Ayuntamiento Popular de Juchitán, Oaxaca.
          Licenciatura thesis, UNAM, Mexico City.
Altamirano Conde, Guillermo
  1985   *Anécdotas. El Famoso General Charis*. Mexico City: Editorial Libros de
          México.
Amnesty International (cited in text as AI)
  1986   *Mexico: Human Rights Violations in Rural Areas*. London: Amnesty
          International.
Anderson, Benedict
  1983   *Imagined Communities: Reflections on the Origin and Spread of Nation-*
          alism. London: Verso/New Left Books.
Arrellanes, Anselmo
  1982   Juchitán: Ley de amnistía, historia vigente. *Guchachi' Reza 12:12–13*.
  1988   Del Camarazo al Cardenismo (1925–1938). In *Historia de la Cuestión*
          Agraria Mexicana, Estado de Oaxaca, vol. 2, 1925–1986, ed. by Leticia
          Reina, pp. 23–125. Mexico: Juan Pablos Editor.

Arrellanes, Anselmo, V. R. Martínez Vásquez, and F. J. Ruiz Cervantes, eds.
1988   *Oaxaca en el Siglo XX: Testimonios de historia oral.* Oaxaca, Oaxaca: Ediciones Meridiano 100.

Aubague, Laurent
1985   *Discurso Político, Utopía y Memoria Popular en Juchitán.* Oaxaca: UABJO:IIS.

Bailón, Moisés J.
1987   Coyote Atrapa a Conejo: Poder regional y lucha popular— el desconocimiento del ayuntamiento de Juchitán en 1983. In *Juchitán: Límites de una Experiencia Democrática*, pp. 7–64. Cuadernos de Investigación Social 15. Mexico City: UNAM.

Balsalobre, Goncalo de
1988
[1656]   Relación avtentica de las idolatrías, svpersticiones, vanas observaciones de los indios del Obispado de Oaxaca. In *Idolatría y Superstición entre los Indios de Oaxaca*, pp. 91–135. Mexico City: Ediciones Toledo.

Baltazar, Toribio
1982   Che Gorio Melendre. In *Guchachi' Reza* 10:14.

Bañuelos, Marta
1988   Ellas no son diferentes, protesta, exige, la mujer de Juchitán. In *Juchitán, Lucha y Poesía*, ed. by Marta Bañuelos, pp. 27–35. Mexico City: Editorial Extemporáneos.

Barabas, Alicia
1986   Rebeliones e insurrecciones indígenas en Oaxaca: La trayectoria histórica de la resistencia étnica. In *Etnicidad y pluralismo cultural: La dinámica étnica*, ed. by Alicia Barabas and Miguel Bartolomé, pp. 213–56. Mexico: INAH.

Barrios, Roberto, and Constantino López
1987   *El Istmo de Tehuantepec en la Encrucijada de la Historia de México.* Mexico City.

Bartolomé, Miguel, and Alicia Barabas
1986   La pluralidad desigual en Oaxaca. In *Etnicidad y pluralismo cultural: La dinámica étnica en Oaxaca*, ed. by Alicia Barabas and Miguel Bartolomé, pp. 13–95. Mexico: INAH.

Bartra, Roger
1974   *Estructura agraria y clases sociales en México.* Mexico: Ediciones Era.

Basauri, Carlos
1940   *La población indígena de México*, Etnografía tomo II. Mexico: SEP.

Benjamin, Thomas, and Marcial Ocasio–Meléndez
1984   Organizing the Memory of Modern Mexico: Porfirian Historiography in Perspective, 1880s–1980s. *Hispanic American Historical Review* 64(2):323–64.

Benjamin, Thomas, and Mark Wasserman, eds.
   1990   *Provinces of the Revolution: Essays on Regional Mexican History, 1910–1929.* Albuquerque: University of New Mexico Press.
Bennholdt-Thomsen, Veronika
   1989   Women's Dignity is the Wealth of Juchitán (Oaxaca, Mexico). *Anthropology of Work Review* 10(1):3–10.
Berry, Charles
   1981   *The Reform in Oaxaca, 1856–76: A Microhistory of the Liberal Revolution.* Lincoln: University of Nebraska Press.
Berthe, Jean–Pierre
   1958   Las Minas de Oro del Marqués del Valle en Tehuantepec, 1540–1547. *Historia Mexicana* 8(1):122–31.
Binford, Leigh
   1983   *Agricultural Crises, State Intervention and the Development of Classes in the Isthmus of Tehuantepec, Oaxaca, Mexico.* Ph.D. diss., University of Connecticut.
   1985   Political Conflict and Land Tenure in the Mexican Isthmus of Tehuantepec. *Journal of Latin American Studies* 17:179–200.
   1989   Development, Migration and Occupational Structure in an Irrigation District of Southern Oaxaca. Manuscript in possession of author.
   1990   The Political Economy of the Velas in the Isthmus of Tehuantepec. In *Class, Politics, and Popular Religion in Mexico and Central America*, ed. by Lynn Stephen and James Dow, pp. 77–92. Washington, D.C.: AAA.
   1992   Peasants and Petty Capitalists in Southern Oaxacan Sugar Cane Production and Processing, 1930–1980. *Journal of Latin American Studies* 24:33–55.
Blanton, Richard, Stephen Kowalewski, Gary Feinman, and Jill Appel
   1981   *Ancient Mesoamerica: A Comparison of Change in Three Regions.* Cambridge: Cambridge University Press.
Borah, Woodrow
   1943   *Silk Raising in Colonial Mexico.* Ibero-Americana 20. Berkeley: University of California Press.
Bradomín, José María
   1984   *Monografía del Estado de Oaxaca.* Mexico City.
Brasseur, Charles
   1981   *Viaje por el istmo de Tehuantepec 1859–1860.* Mexico City: SEP.
   [1861]
Bravo Izquierda, Donato
   1948   *Lealtad Militar (Campaña en el Estado de Chiapas e Istmo de Tehuantepec 1923–1924).* Mexico City.
Brioso y Candiani, Manuel
   1941   *La evolución del pueblo Oajaqueño.* Mexico City.

Brito de Martí, Esperanza
1982 *Almanaque de Oaxaca*. Oaxaca: Gobierno del Estado de Oaxaca.
Brockington, Lolita Gutiérrez
1982 *The Haciendas Marquesanas in Tehuantepec: African, Indian, and European Labor and Race Relations: 1588–1683*. Ph.D. diss., University of North Carolina.
1989 *The Leverage of Labor: Managing the Cortés Haciendas in Tehuantepec, 1588–1688*. Durham: Duke University Press.
Bucuvalas, Tina
1986 *Continuity and Change in a Traditional Craft: Hammockmaking Among the Zapotec in Juchitán, Oaxaca, Mexico*. Ph.D. diss., Indiana University.
Burgoa, Fray Francisco de
1934 *Geográfica Descripción*. 2d ed., 2 vols. Mexico City: Talleres Gráficos
[1674] de la Nación.
Bustillo Bernal, Angel
1968 *La Revolución Mexicana en el Istmo de Tehuantepec*. Mexico City.
Cadenhead, Ivie
1960 Some Mining Operations of Cortés in Tehuantepec, 1538–1547. *The Americas* 16(3):283–87.
Cajígas Langner, Alberto
1954 *Monografía de Tehuantepec*. Mexico City: Imprenta Manuel León.
Calvo Zapata, Paquita
1981 En Prisión el Mayor Leopoldo de Gyves Habla a Por Esto! *Por Esto* 1(3):49–50 (7/16/81).
Campbell, Federico
1988 A 140 años, los tratados de Guadalupe Hidalgo, vigentes; preservaron la existencia de México como nación: Angela Moyano. *Proceso* no. 589 (2/15/88).
Campbell, Howard
1993 Tradition and the New Social Movements: The Politics of Isthmus Zapotec Culture. *Latin American Perspectives* 20(3), issue 76:1:82–96.
Campbell, Howard, Leigh Binford, Miguel Bartolomé, and Alicia Barabas, eds.
1993 *Zapotec Struggles: Histories, Politics, and Representations from Juchitán, Oaxaca*. Washington: Smithsonian Institution Press.
Campbell, Obdulia
1993 Representations of Isthmus Women: A Zapotec Woman's Point of View. In *Zapotec Struggles: Histories, Politics and Representations from Juchitán, Oaxaca*, ed. by Howard Campbell et al., pp. 137–41. Washington: Smithsonian Institution Press.
Cancian, Frank
1965 *Economics and Prestige in a Maya Community*. Stanford: Stanford University Press.

Carlock, Armando
  1990   Down with Carranza! Part I. *The News.* 4/6/1990.
Carmagnani, Marcello
  1982   Local Governments and Ethnic Governments in Oaxaca. In *Essays in the Political, Economic and Social History of Colonial Latin America,* ed. by Karen Spalding, pp. 107–24. Latin American Studies Program Occasional Papers and Monographs, No. 3. Newark, Delaware: University of Delaware.
  1988   *El regreso de los dioses: El proceso de reconstitución de la identidad. Siglos XVII y XVIII.* Mexico City: Fondo de Cultura Económica.
  1992   Un movimiento político indio: La "rebelión" de Tehuantepec, 1660–1661. In *El fuego de la inobediencia: Autonomía y rebelión India en el Obispado de Oaxaca,* ed. by Héctor Díaz–Polanco and Carlos Manzo, pp. 81–102. Mexico City: CIESAS.
Carr, Barry
  1985   *Mexican Communism, 1968–1983. Eurocommunism in the Americas?* San Diego: Center for U.S.–Mexican Studies.
Chance, John
  1978   *Race and Class in Colonial Oaxaca.* Stanford: Stanford University Press.
  1986   La dinámica étnica en Oaxaca colonial. In *Etnicidad y pluralismo cultural: La dinámica étnica en Oaxaca,* ed. by Miguel Bartolomé and Alicia Barabas, pp. 143–72. Mexico City: INAH.
  1989   *Conquest of the Sierra: Spaniards and Indians in Colonial Oaxaca.* Norman: University of Oklahoma Press.
Charnay, Desiré
  1982   Ciudades y Ruinas. *Guchachi' Reza* 12:6–9 (excerpts from Charnay's
  [1863] book *Cites et Ruines Americaines,* Paris, 1863).
Chassen, Francie
  1985   Los precursores de la Revolución en Oaxaca. In *La Revolución en Oaxaca, 1900–1930,* ed. by Víctor Raúl Martínez Vásquez, pp. 35–87. Oaxaca: IAPO.
  1986   *Oaxaca: Del Porfiriato a la Revolución, 1902–1911.* Ph.D. diss., UNAM.
Chassen, Francie and Héctor Martínez
  1990   El desarrollo económico de Oaxaca a finales del Porfiriato. In *Lecturas históricas del estado de Oaxaca,* vol. 4, *1877–1930,* ed. by Ma. de los Angeles Romero, pp. 47–72. Mexico: INAH
Chiñas, Beverly
  1968   *Women of San Blas Atempa: An Analysis of the Economic Role of Isthmus Zapotec Women in Relation to Family and Community.* Ph.D. diss. UCLA. (the diss. is filed under the name Beverly Newbold Litzler).
  1983   *The Isthmus Zapotecs: Women's Roles in Cultural Context.* Prospect Heights, Illinois: Waveland Press.

1985   Isthmus Zapotec 'Berdaches.' *Newsletter of the Anthropological Research Group on Homosexuality* 7(2):1–4 (May).

n.d.   Matrifocality: The Essence of Isthmus Zapotec Culture. Manuscript in possession of author.

Chiñas Flores, Alberto

1955   *La Propiedad Comunal Entre los Zapoteca en el Istmo de Tehuantepec.* Licenciatura thesis, UNAM, Mexico City.

Chopitea, José María de

1961   *Guieshuba: Jazmín del Istmo.* Mexico.

Churchill, Nancy

1987   *Knock on any Door: Social Differentiation and Political Process in a Community of Southern Oaxaca, Mexico.* M.A. thesis, University of Connecticut.

Ciudad Real, Antonio de

1980   Paso por el Istmo de Tehuantepec del padre Fray Alonso Ponce en
[1586] su viaje de México a Guatemala. *Guchachi' Reza* 4 (excerpts from *Tratado curioso y docto de las grandezas de la Nueva España*, [1586] 1976, Mexico: UNAM.)

Clendinnen, Inga

1987   *Ambivalent Conquests: Maya and Spaniard in Yucatán, 1517–1570.* Cambridge: Cambridge University Press.

Clifford, James

1988   *The Predicament of Culture: Twentieth-Century Ethnography, Literature, and Art.* Cambridge: Harvard University Press.

Coatsworth, John

1981   *Growth Against Development: The Economic Impact of Railroads in Porfirian Mexico.* Dekalb: Northern Illinois University Press.

1988   Patterns of Rural Rebellion: Mexico in Comparative Perspective. In *Riot, Rebellion, and Revolution: Rural Social Conflicts in Mexico,* ed. by Friedrich Katz, pp. 21–64. Princeton: Princeton University Press.

COCEI

1983   COCEI: alternativa de organización y lucha para los pueblos del istmo. *Revista COCEI: Organo Informativo de la COCEI.* Juchitán, Oaxaca.

1988   Cronología de lucha de la Coalición Obrero-Campesino-Estudiantil del Istmo. In *Juchitán, Lucha y Poesía,* ed. by Marta Bañuelos, pp. 36–48. Mexico City: Editorial Extemporáneos.

1990   *Discurso Pronunciado por Héctor Sánchez,* 3/20/90.

Cohn, Bernard

1981   Anthropology and History in the 1980s. *Journal of Interdisciplinary History* 12(2):227–52.

Comisión para el Desarrollo del Istmo de Tehuantepec (cited in text as Comisión)
    1976   *Plan para el Desarrollo integral del Istmo de Tehuantepec.* Mexico City: Comisión para el Desarrollo del Istmo de Tehuantepec.
Cook, Della Collins
    1986   Isthmus Zapotec Muxe': Social and Biological Dimensions of a Third Gender Role. Paper presented at the AAA meeting in Philadelphia.
Cook, Scott
    1982   *Zapotec Stoneworkers: The Dynamics of Rural Simple Commodity Production in Modern Mexican Capitalism.* Washington: University Press of America.
    1990   Preface. In *Obliging Need: Rural Petty Industry in Mexican Capitalism,* ed. by Scott Cook and Leigh Binford, pp. xi–xv. Austin: University of Texas Press.
Córdova, Juan de
    1987   *Arte del Idioma Zapoteco.* Mexico City: Ediciones Toledo.
    [1578]
Cosío Villegas, Daniel
    1980   Félix Díaz en el Istmo. *Guchachi' Reza* 4:25–28. (Excerpts from *Historía Moderna de México, "La Republica" Restaurada,* pp. 262–66, 1965, Mexico City: Editorial Hermes).
Covarrubias, Miguel
    1946   *Mexico South: The Isthmus of Tehuantepec.* New York: Alfred A. Knopf.
de Gyves de la Cruz, Leopoldo
    1981   Discurso Pronunciado por Leopoldo de Gyves de la Cruz en la toma de posesión el 10 de marzo de 1981. *Guchachi' Reza* 9:10–11.
de la Cerda, Clemente
    1980   *Sociedad, Cambios y Problemas Políticos en el Distrito de Riego de Tehuantepec, Oaxaca.* Mexico: Centro Nacional de Investigaciones Agrarias.
de la Cruz, Víctor
    1980   Toledo, Binigula'sa' (La obra de Francisco Toledo desde la perspectiva de la cultura Zapoteca). Cultural Supplement of *Siempre* magazine, 4/9/80.
    1981   *Las Guerras entre Aztecas y Zapotecas.* Juchitán: H. Ayuntamiento Popular.
    1982   *Diidxa' Sti Pancho Nácar.* Juchitán, Oaxaca.
    1983a   Las mil caras culturales de la política. *El Buscón* 6:63–67.
    1983b   *La flor de la palabra.* Mexico: Premia Editora.
    1983c   Rebeliones indígenas en el Istmo de Tehuantepec. *Cuadernos Políticos* 38:55–71.
    1983d   Un descendiente de Cosijoeza reclama propiedad de las salinas de Tehuantepec. *Guchachi' Reza* 14:2.

1983e   *La rebelión de Che Gorio Melendre.* Juchitán: H. Ayuntamiento Popular de Juchitán.

1984a   Hermanos o ciudadanos: dos lenguas, dos proyectos políticos en el Istmo. *Guchachi' Reza* 21:18–24.

1984b   Historia de los Pueblos Indios (¿Por quien y para quien?). *Guchachi' Reza* 20:3–7.

1987a   *La rebelión de Tehuantepec.* Mexico City: Ediciones Toledo.

1987b   La rebelión de los juchitecos y uno de sus líderes: Che Gómez. *Historias* 17:57–71.

1992a   El General Charis y la Educación. *Cuadernos del Sur* 1:61–70 (May/August).

1992b   Identidad y Caciquismo: El Caso del General Charis. *Guchachi' Reza* 36:23–29.

de la Cruz, Víctor, ed.

1989   *Relatos sobre el General Charis.* Mexico City: Ediciones Toledo.

del Conde, Octavio, and José Piedra

n.d.   Problemática del Distrito de Riego, No. 19. Tehuantepec, Oaxaca. Manuscript in possession of author.

Díaz, Ignacio Félix

1984   El Area Urbano–Regional del Estado de Oaxaca en el Istmo de Tehuantepec. In *El Puerto Industrial de Salina Cruz*, pp. 8–33. Mexico City: Instituto de Geografía—UNAM.

Díaz, Porfirio

1947   Archivo del General Porfirio Díaz. Mexico City: Editorial "Elede" (pp. 86–88 reprinted in *Guchachi' Reza* 2:15–16, n.d.).

Díaz–Polanco, Héctor, and Carlos Manzo, eds.

1992   *Documentos sobre las rebeliones indias de Tehuantepec y Nexapa.* Mexico City: CIESAS.

Diskin, Martin

1986   La economía de la comunidad étnica en Oaxaca. In *Etnicidad y pluralismo cultural: La dinámica étnica en Oaxaca*, ed. by Alicia Barabas and Miguel Bartolomé, pp. 257–97. Mexico: INAH.

Ditmars, Raymond

1936   *The Reptiles of North America.* Garden City, New York: Doubleday, Doran & Co.

Doniz, Rafael

1983   *H. Ayuntamiento Popular de Juchitán: Fotografías de Rafael Doniz.* Juchitán: H. Ayuntamiento Popular.

Dorsett, James

1975   *Variations in Isthmus Zapotec Kinship and Ecology at Juchitán and Tehuantepec, Oaxaca.* Ph.D. diss., Tulane University.

Eckstein, Susan, ed.
   1989   *Power and Popular Protest: Latin American Social Movements.* Berkeley:
           University of California Press.
Escobar, Arturo, and Sonia Alvarez, eds.
   1992   *The Making of Social Movements in Latin America: Identity, Strategy,
           and Democracy.* Boulder: Westview Press.
Escuela Secundaria Federal de Juchitán, Oaxaca (cited in text as ESF)
   1976   *Homenaje al General Heliodoro Charis Castro.* Juchitán, Oaxaca: ESF.
Esparza, Manuel
   1988   Los Proyectos de los Liberales en Oaxaca. In *Historia de la Cuestión
           Agraria Mexicana, Estado de Oaxaca, Vol. 1: Prehispánico–1924,* ed. by
           Leticia Reina, pp. 269–330. Mexico City: Juan Pablos Editor.
   1990   Las Tierras de los Hijos de los Pueblos: El Distrito de Juchitán en
           el Siglo XIX. In *Lecturas históricas del estado de Oaxaca, Vol. 3: Siglo
           19,* ed. by Ma. de los Angeles Romero, pp. 387–434. Mexico: INAH.
   1992   Penetración Capitalista en Oaxaca 1890–1920. *Cuadernos del Sur*
           1:51–59 (May/August).
Everson Museum of Art (cited in text as Everson)
   1978   *Toledo, Recent Work 1977–78.* Syracuse, New York: Everson Museum
           of Art.
Everts, Dana
   1990   *Women are Flowers: The Expression of a Dominant Metaphor in Isthmus
           Zapotec Expressive Culture.* Ph.D diss., Indiana University.
Falcone, Frank
   1990   Benito Juárez contra los hermanos Díaz: La política en Oaxaca,
           1867–1871. In *Lecturas históricas del estado de Oaxaca,* vol. 3, ed. by
           Ma. de los Angeles Romero, pp. 493–514. Mexico: INAH.
Farriss, Nancy
   1984   *Maya Society Under Colonial Rule: The Collective Enterprise of Survival.*
           Princeton: Princeton University Press.
Fauverge, Sylvie
   1982   Cambios en el Istmo de Tehuantepec: El ejemplo de Salina Cruz,
           Oaxaca. In *Impactos regionales de la política petrolera en México,* ed. by
           Leopoldo Allub and Marco Michel, pp. 241–75. Mexico City.
Fernández MacGregor, Genaro
   1954   *El Istmo de Tehuantepec y Los Estados Unidos.* Mexico City: Editorial
           "Elede."
Flannery, Kent
   1983   Zapotec Warfare: Archaeological Evidence for the Battles of Huitzo
           and Guiengola. In *The Cloud People: Divergent Evolution of the Zapotec
           and Mixtec Civilizations,* ed. by Kent Flannery and Joyce Marcus, pp.
           318–22. New York: Academic Press.

Flannery, Kent, and Joyce Marcus
  1983   *The Cloud People: Divergent Evolution of the Zapotec and Mixtec Civilizations.* New York: Academic Press.
Fossey, Mathieu
  1983   Viage a Mejico. *Guchachi' Reza* 15:18–32.
  [1844]
Foster, George
  1967   *Tzintzuntzan: Mexican Peasants in a Changing World.* Boston: Little, Brown & Co.
Friedrich, Paul
  1970   *Agrarian Revolt in a Mexican Village.* Englewood Cliffs, New Jersey: Prentice-Hall.
  1986   *The Princes of Naranja: An Essay in Anthrohistorical Method.* Austin: University of Texas Press.
Gadow, Hans
  1908   *Through Southern Mexico: Being an Account of the Travels of a Naturalist.* New York: Charles Scribner's Sons.
Gage, Thomas
  1958   *Travels in the New World.* Ed. by J. Eric Thompson. Norman: University of Oklahoma Press.
  [1648]
Gailey, Christine
  1985   The State of the State in Anthropology. *Dialectical Anthropology* 9:65–89.
Gardiner, Harvey
  1955   Tempest in Tehuantepec, 1529: Local Events in Imperial Perspective. *Hispanic American Historical Review* 35(1):1–13.
Garner, Paul
  1990   Oaxaca: The Rise and Fall of Sovereignty. In *Provinces of the Revolution: Essays on Regional Mexican History, 1910–1929,* ed. by Thomas Benjamin and Mark Wasserman, pp. 163–83. Albuquerque: University of New Mexico Press.
Gay, José A.
  1986   *Historia de Oaxaca.* Mexico City: Editorial Porrúa.
  [1881]
Gillow, Eulogio
  1978   *Apuntes históricos sobre la idolatría y la introducción del cristianismo en la*
  [1889] *diócesis de Oaxaca.* Graz, Austria: Akademische Druck u. Verlagsanstalt.
Gobierno del Estado de Oaxaca
  1980   Plan Estatal de Desarrollo, 1980–1986. Oaxaca: Gobierno del Estado de Oaxaca.

González Obregón, Luis
    1907   *Las Sublevaciones de Indios en el Siglo 17*. Mexico City: Imprenta del
    Museo Nacional.

Greenberg, James
    1989   *Blood Ties: Life and Violence in Rural Mexico*. Tucson: University of
    Arizona Press.

Gurrión, Evaristo C.
    1983   *Biografía de Adolfo C. Gurrión*. Juchitán: H. Ayuntamiento de Juchi-
    [1935] tán.

Gutiérrez, Roberto J.
    1981   Juchitán, Municipio Comunista. *A: Análisis Histórico y Sociedad Mex-
    icana* 2(4):251–80.

Hamnett, Brian
    1971   *Politics and Trade in Southern Mexico, 1750–1821*. London: Cam-
    bridge University Press.
    1986   *Roots of Insurgency: Mexican Regions, 1750–1824*. Cambridge: Cam-
    bridge University Press.

Hanson, Allan
    1991   Reply to Langdon, Levine and Linnekin. *American Anthropologist*
    93(2):449–450.

Hart, John
    1988   The 1840s Southwestern Mexico Peasants' War: Conflict in a Tran-
    sitional Society. In *Riot, Rebellion, and Revolution: Rural Social Conflict
    in Mexico*, ed. by Friedrich Katz, pp. 249–68. Princeton: Princeton
    University Press.
    1989   *Revolutionary Mexico: The Coming and Process of the Mexican Revolution*.
    Berkeley: University of California Press.

Hassig, Ross
    1985   *Trade, Tribute, and Transportation: the Sixteenth-Century Political Econ-
    omy of the Valley of Mexico*. Norman: University of Oklahoma Press.
    1988   *Aztec Warfare: Imperial Expansion and Political Control*. Norman: Uni-
    versity of Oklahoma Press.

Henderson, Peter
    1983   Un gobernador maderista: Benito Juárez Maza y la Revolución en
    Oaxaca. *Guchachi' Reza* 16:3–9.

Henestrosa, Andrés
    1987   *Los hombres que dispersó la danza*. Mexico City: SEP.
    [1929]
    1969   *Andrés Henestrosa*. Mexico City: Editorial Novaro.
    1987   Presentación. In *Neza* (facsimile edition). Mexico City: Ediciones
    Toledo.
    1989   *Divagario*. Mexico: Publicaciones Mexicanas.

Henestrosa de Webster, Cibeles
1985   *Juchitán: un pueblo singular.* Mexico: Editorial Alcaravan.
Hernández Díaz, Jorge
1986   Relaciones interétnicas contemporáneas en Oaxaca. In *Etnicidad y pluralismo cultural: La dinámica étnica en Oaxaca,* ed. by Alicia Barabas and Miguel Bartolomé, pp. 299–329. Mexico City: INAH.
Hill, Jonathan
1988   *Rethinking History and Myth: Indigenous South American Perspectives on the Past.* Urbana: University of Illinois Press.
Hobsbawm, Eric
1983   Introduction: Inventing Traditions. In *The Invention of Tradition,* ed. by Eric Hobsbawm and Terence Ranger, pp. 1–14. Cambridge: Cambridge University Press.
Hobsbawm, Eric, and Terence Ranger
1983   *The Invention of Tradition.* Cambridge: Cambridge University Press.
Hu-DeHart, Evelyn
1981   *Missionaries, Miners and Indians.* Tucson: University of Arizona Press.
INEGI
1990   *Resultados Preliminares: XI Censo General de Población y Vivienda, 1990.* Mexico: INEGI.
Instituto de Geografía–UNAM
1984   *El Puerto Industrial de Salina Cruz, Oaxaca.* Mexico City: Editorial Libros de México.
Iturbide, Graciela, and Elena Poniatowska
1989   *Juchitán de las mujeres.* Mexico City: Ediciones Toledo.
Iturribarría, Jorge Fernando
1939   *Historia de Oaxaca. Vol. 2.* Oaxaca, Oaxaca.
Jackson, Jean
1989   Is There a Way to Talk about Making Culture without Making Enemies? *Dialectical Anthropology* 14:127–43.
Jiménez, Juventino
1989   Testimonio de Juventino Jiménez (transcript of an interview conducted by Howard Campbell). In *Relatos sobre el General Charis,* ed. by Víctor de la Cruz, pp. 65–72. Mexico City: Ediciones Toledo.
Joseph, Gilbert
1988   The United States, Feuding Elites, and Rural Revolt in Yucatán, 1836–1915. In *Rural Revolt in Mexico and U.S. Intervention,* ed. by Daniel Nugent, pp. 167–97. San Diego: Center for U.S.–Mexican Studies.
Júarez, Benito
1981   Discourse given by Juárez as Governor of Oaxaca at the inauguration
[1850] of the ninth period of ordinary sessions of the Oaxaca State Congress (July 2, 1850). Reprinted in *Guchachi' Reza* 8:7–9.

Kaplan, Temma
  1982   Female Consciousness and Collective Action: The Case of Barce-
          lona, 1910–1918. *Signs* 7(3):545–66.
Katz, Friedrich
  1981   *The Secret War in Mexico: Europe, the United States and the Mexican
          Revolution.* Chicago: University of Chicago Press.
  1988   Rural Uprisings in Preconquest and Colonial Mexico. In *Riot, Re-
          bellion, and Revolution: Rural Social Conflict in Mexico,* ed. by Friedrich
          Katz, pp. 65–94. Princeton: Princeton University Press.
Katz, Friedrich, ed.
  1988   *Riot, Rebellion, and Revolution: Rural Social Conflict in Mexico.* Prince-
          ton: Princeton University Press.
Keesing, Roger
  1989   Creating the Past: Custom and Identity in the Contemporary Pacific.
          The Contemporary Pacific 1(1&2):19–42.
Kern, Robert, ed.
  1973   *The Caciques: Oligarchical Politics and the System of Caciquismo in the
          Luso–Hispanic World.* Albuquerque: University of New Mexico Press.
Knight, Alan
  1986   *The Mexican Revolution. Vol. 1: Porfirians, Liberals and Peasants.* Cam-
          bridge: Cambridge University Press.
  1990   Historical Continuities in Social Movements. In *Popular Movements
          and Political Change in Mexico,* ed. by Joe Foweraker and Ann Craig,
          pp. 78–102. Boulder: Lynn Rienner.
Kowalewski, Stephen, and Jacqueline Saindon
  1992   The Spread of Literacy in a Latin American Peasant Society: Oaxaca,
          Mexico, 1890 to 1980. *Comparative Studies in Society and History*
          34(1):110–40.
Krauze, Enrique
  1987   *Porfirio Díaz: Místico de la autoridad.* Mexico City: Fondo de Cultura
          Económica.
Laclau, Ernesto, and Chantal Mouffe
  1985   *Hegemony and Socialist Strategy: Toward a Radical Democratic Politics.*
          London: Verso.
Levine, H. B.
  1991   Comment on Hanson's "The Making of the Maori." *American An-
          thropologist* 93(2):444–45.
Lewis, Oscar
  1963   *Life in a Mexican Village: Tepoztlán Restudied.* Urbana: University of
          Illinois Press.
Liekens, Enrique
  1952   *Los zapotecos no son zapotecos sino zaes: Ensayo etimológico de la voz zá.*
          Villahermosa, Tabasco.

Linnekin, Jocelyn
  1991   Cultural Invention and the Dilemma of Authenticity. *American An-thropologist* 93(2):446–48.
Lockhart, James
  1985   Some Nahua Concepts in Postconquest Guise. *History of European Ideas* 6(4):465–82.
López, Alejandro
  n.d.   La situación agraria en la comunidad de Juchitán de Zaragoza. Paper presented at the Escuela Agropecuaria de Comitancillo, Oaxaca. Manuscript in possession of author.
López Chiñas, Gabriel
  1971   *Juchitán. Segundo Canto.* Mexico.
  1974   *Vinnigulasa: Cuentos de Juchitán.* Mexico City: UNAM.
  1975   *Guendaxheela El Casamiento.* Mexico City.
  1982   *El Zapoteco y la Literatura Zapoteca del Istmo de Tehuantepec.* Mexico City: Talleres Gráficos.
López de Gómara, Francisco
  1964   *Cortés: The Life of the Conqueror by his Secretary.* Translated and edited
  [1552] by Lesley Byrd Simpson. Berkeley: University of California Press.
López Gurrión, Ricardo
  1976   *Efemerides Istmeñas.* San Luis Potosí, Mexico.
López Marín, Galdino
  1985   *Vida y hazaña del General de División Heliodoro Charis Castro.* Mexico City.
López Mateos, Manuel
  1988   Una experiencia: Cuando la voz de la radio es la voz del pueblo. In *Juchitán, Lucha y Poesía,* ed. by Marta Bañuelos, pp. 17–26. Mexico City: Editorial Extemporáneos.
López Monjardin, Adriana
  1983   Juchitán, las histórias de la discordia. *Cuadernos Políticos* 38:72–80.
López Nelio, Ruperto
  1981   Sobre Valentín Carrasco y Roque Robles. *Guchachi' Reza* 6:7–12.
López Trujillo, Germán
  1984   *Biografía de Dn. Francisco León: Artífice de Juchitán Contemporáneo.* Juchitán, Oaxaca.
MacLeod, Murdo
  1973   *Spanish Central America: A Socioeconomic History, 1520–1720.* Berkeley: University of California Press.
Mallon, Florencia
  1988   Peasants and State Formation in Nineteenth-Century Mexico: Morelos, 1848–1858. *Political Power and Social Theory* 7:1–54.

Manso de Contreras, Christobal
    1987   *La rebelión de Tehuantepec.* Mexico: Ediciones Toledo.
    [1661]
Marcus, Joyce
    1983a   The Genetic Model and the Linguistic Divergence of the Otoman-
             gueans. In *The Cloud People: Divergent Evolution of the Zapotec and
             Mixtec Civilizations,* ed. by Joyce Marcus and Kent Flannery, pp. 4–
             9. New York: Academic Press.
    1983b   Zapotec Religion. In *The Cloud People: Divergent Evolution of the Za-
             potec and Mixtec Civilizations,* ed. by Joyce Marcus and Kent Flannery,
             pp. 345–51. New York: Academic Press.
Marcus, Joyce, and Kent Flannery
    1983   An Introduction to the Late Postclassic. In *The Cloud People: Diver-
            gent Evolution of the Zapotec and Mixtec Civilizations,* ed. by Joyce Mar-
            cus and Kent Flannery, pp. 217–26. New York: Academic Press.
Martínez, Anastasia
    1985   Recuerdos de Anastasia Martínez (recording and translation by Ma-
            cario Matus). *Guchachi' Reza* 23:19–21.
Martínez Assad, Carlos
    1985   Las elecciones legislativas y la ilusión democrática. In *Las elecciones
            en México: Evolución y perspectivas,* ed. by Pablo González Casanova,
            pp. 231–57. Mexico City: Siglo XXI.
Martínez Gracida, Manuel
    1883   *Colección de cuadros sinópticos de los pueblos, haciendas y ranchos del Estado
            de Oaxaca.* Oaxaca: Imprenta del Estado.
Martínez López, Aurelio
    1966   *Historia de la Intervención Francesa en el Estado de Oaxaca.* Mexico City.
Martínez López, Felipe
    1985   *El crepúsculo del poder: Juchitán, Oaxaca, 1980–1982.* Oaxaca:
            UABJO:IIS.
Martínez Vásquez, Víctor Raúl
    1986   *Movimiento Popular, Vallistocracia, y Política en Oaxaca (1968–1986).*
            Ph.D. diss., UNAM, Mexico City.
Matus, Macario
    1981   Momentos Políticos de Juchitán. *Hora Cero* (5/25/81).
    1985   La Revolución en Juchitán, Oaxaca. In *Mi Pueblo durante la Revolu-
            ción, Vol.* 2, pp. 75–167. Mexico City: INAH.
    1987   *Juchitán tiene algo que ver con la fotografía.* Mexico: Consejo Mexicano
            de Fotografía.
    1988   Mujeres de Tehuantepec. *México Indígena* 21(4):60–62.
Matus, Manuel
    1988   *Política y Cultura en el Municipio de Juchitán 1981–1983.* Licenciatura
            thesis, UNAM, Mexico City.

Meier, Matthias
　1954　*History of the Tehuantepec Railroad.* Ph.D. diss., University of California-Berkeley.

Molina, Arcadio G.
　1894　*La rosa del amor.* San Blas, Oaxaca.
　1899　*El jazmín del Istmo.* Oaxaca, Oaxaca.
　1911　*Historia de Tehuantepec, San Blas, Shihui y Juchitán en la intervención Francesa en 1864.* Oaxaca, Oaxaca.

Monsiváis, Carlos
　1983　Ya se va a levantar todo el pueblo de la tierra. Prologue to *H. Ayuntamiento Popular de Juchitán: Fotografías de Rafael Doniz,* pp. 7–20. Juchitán: H. Ayuntamiento Popular de Juchitán.

Moro, Cayetano
　1844　*Survey of the Isthmus of Tehuantepec.* London: Ackermann and Co.

Munch, Güido
　1985　*Zaa Guidxi, Las Fiestas del Pueblo Zapoteco en Gui Si o Tehuantepec.* UNAM: Anales de Antropología.

Nuñez Ríos, Heron
　1969　*Datos biográficos sobre la vida del famoso guerrillero Gregorio Melendrez.* Juchitán, Oaxaca.

O'Gorman, Edmundo
　1973　*Historia de las divisiones territoriales de México.* Mexico City.

Olsson-Seffer, Helen
　1910　The Isthmus of Tehuantepec: "The Bridge of the World's Commerce." *National Geographic* 21(12):991–1002.

Ornelas Esquinca, Marco Antonio
　1983　*Juchitán, Ayuntamiento Popular.* Licenciatura thesis, ITAM, Mexico City.

Orozco, Gilberto
　1946　*Tradiciones y Leyendas del Istmo de Tehuantepec.* Mexico City: Editorial Revista Musical Mexicana.

Ortíz Wadgymar, Arturo
　1971　*Aspectos de la Economía de Tehuantepec.* Mexico City: UNAM.

Paddock, John
　1983　Mixtec and Zapotec National Character: Some Early Views (A.D. 1580–1880). In *The Cloud People: Divergent Evolution of the Zapotec and Mixtec Civilizations,* ed. by Kent Flannery and Joyce Marcus, pp. 351–53. New York: Academic Press.

Padgett, L. Vincent
　1976　*The Mexican Political System.* Boston: Houghton Mifflin Company.

Parmenter, Ross
　1984　*Lawrence in Oaxaca: A Quest for the Novelist in Mexico.* Salt Lake City: Gibbs M. Smith.

Parrish, Timothy

1982   Class Structure and Social Reproduction in New Spain/Mexico. *Dialectical Anthropology* 7:115–36.

Paso y Troncoso, Francisco

1905   *Relación de la visita que hizo Baltasar de San Miguel del pueblo de Tecoantepec y su probincia.* Papeles de Nueva España. 2a. Serie. Geografía y Estadística. Madrid.

Pastor, Rodolfo

1987   *Campesinos y reformas: La Mixteca, 1700–1856.* Mexico City: El Colegio de México.

Peterson, David

1990   Guiengola: Fortaleza zapoteca en el Istmo de Tehuantepec. In *Lecturas históricas del estado de Oaxaca. Vol. 1: Epoca prehispánica,* ed. by Marcus Winter, pp. 455–88. Mexico: INAH.

Pickett, Velma

1983   *Vocabulario Zapoteco del Istmo.* Mexico City: Instituto Lingüístico de Verano.

Pineda, Jesús María

1986   Comerciantes y tejedoras de San Mateo del Mar. *México Indígena* 12:48–51 (September–October).

Pineda, Justo

1986   Recuerdo de líderes. (Compilation and transcription by Víctor de la Cruz). *Guchachi' Reza* 26:21–23.

Piñon Jiménez, Gonzalo

1988   Crisis Agraria y Movimiento Campesino (1956–1986). In *Historia de la Cuestión Agraria Mexicana: Estado de Oaxaca, vol. II 1925–1986,* ed. by Leticia Reina, pp. 291–374. Mexico: Juan Pablos Editor.

Poniatowska, Elena

1969   *Hasta no verte Jesús mío.* Mexico: Ediciones Era.

1989   El Hombre del Pito Dulce. In *Juchitán de las Mujeres* (photographs by Graciela Iturbide and text by Elena Poniatowska), pp. 11–26. Mexico City: Ediciones Toledo.

1992   Tina Modotti en Juchitán (I). *Guchachi' Reza* 31:2–9.

Prévot-Schapira, Marie–France, and Hélene Riviere d'Arc

1984   Los Zapotecas, el PRI y la COCEI, enfrentamientos alrededor del Estado en el Istmo de Tehuantepec. *Guchachi' Reza* 19:11–26.

Prieto, Ana María

1986   Mexico's National Coordinadoras in a Context of Economic Crisis. In *The Mexican Left, the Popular Movements, and the Politics of Austerity,* ed. by Barry Carr and Ricardo Anzaldúa M., pp. 75–94. Monograph No. 18. San Diego: Center for U.S.–Mexican Studies.

Ramírez, Alfonso Francisco
   1970   *Historia de la Revolución Mexicana en Oaxaca.* Mexico: Instituto Nacional de Estudios Históricos de la Revolución Mexicana.

Ratzel, Friedrich
   1981   *Apuntes Mexicanos: Impresiones de viajes de los años 1874 y 1875* (ex-
   [1878]   cerpts published in *Guchachi' Reza* 9:4–9).

Redfield, Robert
   1941   *The Folk Culture of Yucatán.* Chicago: University of Chicago Press.

Reina, Leticia
   1986   *Las rebeliones campesinas en México (1819–1906),* 3d ed. Mexico City: Siglo Veintiuno.
   1988   De las Reformas Borbónicas a las Leyes de Reforma. In *Historia de la Cuestión Agraria Mexicana: Estado de Oaxaca. Vol. 1: Prehispánico— 1924,* pp. 181–268. Mexico: Juan Pablos Editor.

Reina, Leticia, and Francisco Abardía
   1990   Cien Años de Rebelión. In *Lecturas históricas del estado de Oaxaca. Vol. 3: Siglo XIX,* ed. by María de los Angeles Romero, pp. 435–92. Mexico: INAH.

Ricard, Robert
   1986   La conquista espiritual. In *Lecturas históricas del estado de Oaxaca. Vol. 2: Epoca colonial,* ed. by María de los Angeles Romero, pp. 79–92. Mexico City: INAH.

Richardson, W. H.
   1988   *Mexico Through Russian Eyes, 1806–1940.* Pittsburgh: University of Pittsburgh.

Riding, Alan
   1985   *Distant Neighbors: A Portrait of the Mexicans.* New York: Alfred A. Knopf.

Robles, Alberto
   1946   *Informe Sanitario del Municipio de Juchitán, Oaxaca.* Licenciatura thesis, UNAM, Mexico City.

Rojas, Basilio
   1964   *La Rebelión de Tehuantepec.* Mexico City: Sociedad Mexicana de Geografía y Estadística.

Romero, Ma. de los Angeles, ed.
   1986   Oaxaca y su historia: De 1519 a 1821. In *Lecturas históricas de Oaxaca. Vol. 2: Epoca colonial,* ed. by Ma. de los Angeles Romero, pp. 19–64. Mexico City: INAH.
   1988   Epoca Colonial (1519–1785). In *Historia de la Cuestión Agraria Mexicana: Estado de Oaxaca. Vol. 1. Prehispánico–1924,* ed. by Leticia Reina, pp. 107–79. Mexico: Juan Pablos Editor.

Ronfeldt, David

1973   *Atencingo: The Politics of Agrarian Struggle in a Mexican Ejido.* Stanford: Stanford University Press.

Roseberry, William

1989   *Anthropologies and Histories: Essays in Culture, History, and Political Economy.* New Brunswick: Rutgers University Press.

Royce, Anya Peterson

1975   *Prestigio y Afiliación en una Comunidad Urbana: Juchitán, Oaxaca.* Mexico: INI.

1981   Isthmus Zapotec Households: Economic Responses to Scarcity and Abundance. *Urban Anthropology* 10(3):269–86.

1982   *Ethnic Identity: Strategies of Diversity.* Bloomington: University of Indiana Press.

Rubin, Jeffrey

1987a   State Policies, Leftist Oppositions, and Municipal Elections: The Case of the COCEI of Juchitán. In *Electoral Patterns and Perspectives in Mexico,* ed. by Arturo Alvarado, pp. 127–60. Monograph 22. San Diego: Center for U.S.–Mexican Studies.

1987b   Elections, Repression, and Limited Reform: Update on Southern Mexico. *LASA Forum* 18(2).

1990   Popular Mobilization and the Myth of State Corporatism. In *Popular Movements and Political Change in Mexico,* ed. by Joe Foweraker and Ann Craig, pp. 247–67. Boulder: Lynne Rienner Publishers.

1991   Rethinking Post-Revolutionary Mexico: Regional History, Cultural Identity, and Radical Politics in Juchitán, Oaxaca. Ph.D. diss., Harvard University.

Rueda Jiménez, Ma. Magdalena

1976   *Estudio Geográfico-Económico del Municipio de Juchitán, Oaxaca.* Licenciatura thesis, UNAM, Mexico City.

Rueda Sáynez, Ursulino

1990   *Personajes Revolucionarios Juchitecos.* Mexico.

Rueda Sáynez, Ursulino, and Ma. Magdalena Rueda Jiménez

1981   *Juchitán: Un pueblo típico zapoteca.* Mexico.

Ruiz Cervantes, Francisco José

1983   Los siete días y siete noches de Juchitán. *El Buscón* 6:81–89.

1985   El movimiento de la Soberanía en Oaxaca (1915–1920). In *La Revolución en Oaxaca 1900–1930,* ed. by Víctor Raúl Martínez Vásquez, pp. 225–308. Oaxaca: IAPO.

1988   De la Bola a los Primeros Repartos. In *Historia de la Cuestión Agraria Mexicana: Estado de Oaxaca. Vol. 1. Prehispánico–1924,* ed. by Leticia Reina, pp. 331–423. Mexico: Juan Pablos Editor.

1992   Notas Sobre el Istmo Oaxaqueño y el Comité de Reclamaciones Mexico-Estados Unidos. *Guchachi' Reza* 33:12–14.

Ruiz Cervantes, Francisco José, and Anselmo Arellanes
   1986   *Aspectos del Movimiento Obrero en Oaxaca: Fuentes.* Oaxaca: Casa de la Cultura Oaxaqueña.

Ruiz Santos, Marcos
   1991   La Curtiduría: Una remembranza nostálgica. *Guiengola* 3:28–29 (March–April).

Safa, Helen
   1989   Towards a Theory of Women's Collective Action in Latin America. Manuscript in possession of author.

Salas, Elizabeth
   1990   *Soldaderas in the Mexican Military: Myth and History.* Austin: University of Texas.

Salomon, Frank
   1987   Ancestors, Grave Robbers, and the Possible Antecedents of Cañari "Inca-ism." *Etnologiska Studier* 38:207–32.

Sánchez Silva, Carlos
   1985   *La Revolución en Oaxaca 1900–1930: Empresarios y comerciantes en Oaxaca.* Oaxaca: IAPO.

Santana, Mariano
   1988   Untitled Licenciatura thesis, Universidad Autónoma—Iztapalapa, Mexico City.

Santibañez Orozco, Porfirio
   1982   Oaxaca: La crisis de 1977. In *Sociedad y Política en Oaxaca, 1980: 15 estudios de caso,* ed. by Raúl Benítez Z., pp. 309–29. Oaxaca: Instituto de Investigaciónes Sociológicas, UABJO.

SARH
   n.d.   *Plan general de distrito de riego, no. 19.* Tehuantepec, Oaxaca.
   1985   *Resumen del Proyecto de Mejoramiento del Distrito de Riego, No. 19 Tehuantepec.* Tehuantepec, Oaxaca.

Scott, James
   1976   *The Moral Economy of the Peasant: Rebellion and Subsistence in Southeast Asia.* New Haven: Yale University Press.
   1985   *Weapons of the Weak: Everyday Forms of Peasant Resistance.* New Haven: Yale University Press.
   1986   Everyday Forms of Peasant Resistance. *Journal of Peasant Studies* 13:5–35.

SEDUE
   1988   *Plan de desarrollo urbano de centro de población de Juchitán de Zaragoza, Oaxaca.* Mexico: SEDUE.

Segura, Jaime
   1988   Los Indígenas y Los Programas de Desarrollo Agrario (1940–1964). In *Historia de la Cuestión Agraria Mexicana: Estado de Oaxaca. Vol. 2. 1925–86,* ed. by Leticia Reina, pp. 189–290. Mexico City: Juan Pablos Editor.

Signorini, Italo
 1979   *Los Huaves de San Mateo del Mar, Oaxaca.* Mexico City: INI.
Smith, Anthony
 1984   Ethnic myths and Ethnic revivals. *European Journal of Sociology* 25:283–305.
Smith, Waldemar
 1977   *The Fiesta System and Economic Change.* New York: Columbia University Press.
Sokoloff, Shoshana
 1993   The Proud Midwives of Juchitán. In *Zapotec Struggles: Histories, Politics and Representations from Juchitán, Oaxaca,* ed. by Howard Campbell, Leigh Binford, Miguel Bartolomé, and Alicia Barabas, pp. 267–77. Washington: Smithsonian Institution Press.
Soto, Consuelo
 1984   Tipología de los espacios rurales en el Istmo de Tehuantepec. In *El puerto industrial de Salina Cruz, Oaxaca,* pp. 34–52. Mexico City: UNAM—Instituto de Geografía.
Sparks, Amy
 1989   A Glimpse of the Art of Francisco Toledo. Paper presented at the December 1989 Latin American Studies Association meeting, Miami, Florida.
Spores, Ronald
 1984   Multi-Level Government in Nineteenth-Century Oaxaca. In *Five Centuries of Law and Politics in Central Mexico,* ed. by Ronald Spores and Ross Hassig, pp. 145–72. Publications in Anthropology, No. 30. Nashville: Vanderbilt University Press.
SPP–INEGI
 1984   *X Censo General de Población y Vivienda–1980, Estado de Oaxaca,* vol. 2, Tomo 20. Mexico: SPP–INEGI.
SRA
 1971   Expediente no. 375 de Dotación Perteneciente al Poblado de Juchitán de Zaragoza. Vol. 2. Juchitán, Oaxaca. SRA.
Starr, Frederick
 1908   *In Indian Mexico: A Narrative of Travel and Labor.* Chicago: Forbes & Co.
Stern, Steve
 1987   The Struggle for Solidarity: Class, Culture and Community in Highland Indian America. In *Sociology of "Developing Societies": Latin America,* ed. by Eduardo Archetti, Paul Cammack, and Bryan Roberts, pp. 33–48. New York: Monthly Review Press.
Stern, Steve, ed.
 1987   *Resistance, Rebellion, and Consciousness in the Andean Peasant World: 18th to 20th Centuries.* Madison: University of Wisconsin Press.

Stirling, Matthew
    1941   Expedition Unearths Buried Masterpieces of Carved Jade. *National Geographic* 80(3):278–321.

Taller de Investigación Sociológica (cited in text as TIS)
    1984   Juchitán: El Fin de la Illusión. In *Oaxaca, una lucha reciente: 1960–83*, ed. by René Bustamente, pp. 306–452. Mexico: Ediciones Nueva Sociología.

Taylor, William
    1972   *Landlord and Peasant in Colonial Oaxaca.* Stanford: Stanford University Press.
    1978   *La Indiada: Peasant Uprisings in Central Mexico and Oaxaca, 1700–1810*, vol. 3, pp. 189–96. Proceedings of the 42nd International Congress of Americanists, Paris.
    1979   *Drinking, Homicide, and Rebellion in Colonial Mexican Villages.* Stanford: Stanford University Press.

Terrones López, Ma. Eugenia
    1990   Istmeños y subversión en el Porfiriato: 1879–1881. In *Lecturas históricas del estado de Oaxaca. Vol. 4: 1877–1930*, ed. by Ma. de los Angeles Romero, pp. 135–70. Mexico: INAH.

Titulos Primordiales de Juchitán (cited in text as TPJ)
    1987   Documents contained in volume 578, expediente 6, fojas 1 to 53.
    [1736–   Ramo de Tierras of the AGN, Mexico City.
    1737]

Toledo, Francisco
    1986   *Toledo: Lo que el viento a Juárez.* Mexico City: Ediciones Era.

Toledo, Francisco, and Víctor de la Cruz
    1983   Entrevista a Daniel López Nelio. *Guchachi' Reza* 17:19–25.

Torres de Laguna, Juan
    1983   *Descripción de Tehuantepec.* Juchitán, Oaxaca: H. Ayuntamiento Popular.
    [1580]

Torres Medina, Violeta
    n.d.   *Canciones de Vida y Muerte en el Istmo Oaxaqueño* (essay accompanying a record of the same name). Record No. 25. Mexico City: INAH.

Tutino, John
    1978   Indian Rebellion at the Isthmus of Tehuantepec: A Socio-Historical Perspective. *Proceedings of the 42nd International Congress of Americanists* 7(3):197–214. Paris.
    1993   Ethnic Resistance: Juchitán in Mexican History. In *Zapotec Struggles: Histories, Politics and Representations from Juchitán, Oaxaca*, ed. by Howard Campbell, Leigh Binford, Miguel Bartolomé, and Alicia Barabas, pp. 41–61. Washington: Smithsonian Institution Press.

UNAM
    1986   Modelo Pedagógico de Díalogo Cultural y Alfabetización: Para la
            Población de Juchitán y el Istmo de Tehuantepec. Mexico: UNAM:
            IIA Casa de la Cultura-Juchitán, Oaxaca.
Unruh, Vicky
    1989   Mariátegui's Aesthetic Thought: A Critical Reading of the Avant-
            Gardes. *Latin American Research Review* 24(3):45–70.
Varese, Stefano
    1982   Apuntes para una historia de la étnia zapoteca. *Guchachi' Reza* 11:2–
            6.
Vasconcelos, José
    1963   *A Mexican Ulysses: An Autobiography.* Translation and abridgment of
    [1935] *Ulises Criollo.* Bloomington: University of Indiana Press (excerpts re-
            printed in *Guchachi' Reza* 2:10–11, n.d.).
Vaughan, Mary Kay
    1982   *The State, Education, and Social Class in Mexico, 1880–1928.* Dekalb:
            Northern Illinois University Press.
Volkow, Verónica, Christopher Domínguez, and Ilán Semo
    1983   Mujeres del alba: Conversación con Cándida Santiago de Pineda. *El
            Buscón* no. 6.
von Tempsky, G. F.
    1858   *Mitla: A Narrative of Incidents and Personal Adventures on a Journey in
            Mexico, Guatemala and Salvador in the Years 1853 to 1855 with Obser-
            vations on the Modes of Life in Those Countries.* Ed. by J. S. Bell. Lon-
            don: Longman, Brown, Green, Longmans & Roberts.
Wachtel, Nathan
    1977   *The Vision of the Vanquished: The Spanish Conquest of Peru through
            Indian Eyes, 1530–1570.* New York: Barnes and Noble.
Warman, Arturo
    1972   *Los Campesinos, Hijos Predilectos del Régimen.* Mexico City.
    1983   El futuro del istmo y la presa Juárez. *Guchachi' Reza* 15:2–4.
Warren, Kay
    1992   Transforming Memories and Histories: The Resurgence of Indian
            Identity. Manuscript in possession of author.
Waterbury, Ronald
    1975   Non-Revolutionary Peasants: Oaxaca Compared to Morelos in the
            Mexican Revolution. *Comparative Studies in Society and History*
            17(4):410–42.
Whitecotton, Joseph
    1984   *The Zapotecs: Princes, Priests, and Peasants.* Norman: University of
            Oklahoma Press.

Widmer, Rolf
    1988–   Política sanitaria y lucha social en Tehuantepec, 1795–1796. *Historias*
    1989   21:71–89 (October 1988–March 1989).
Williams, J. J.
    1852   *The Isthmus of Tehuantepec.* New York: D. Appleton & Co.
Winter, Marcus
    1989   *Oaxaca: The Archaeological Record.* Mexico: Editorial Minutiae Mexicana.
Wolf, Eric
    1959   *Sons of the Shaking Earth.* Chicago: University of Chicago Press.
    1969   *Peasant Wars of the Twentieth Century.* New York: Harper and Row.
Wolf, Eric, and Edward Hansen
    1972   *The Human Condition in Latin America.* London: Oxford University Press.
Womack, John
    1969   *Zapata and the Mexican Revolution.* New York: Alfred A. Knopf.
Ybarra, Roxana A.
    1949   *Los transportes en el Istmo de Tehuantepec.* Licenciatura thesis, UNAM, Mexico City.
Ynquisición
    1985   Ynquisición de México y Abril 16 de 1812. *Guchachi' Reza* 22:13.
    [1812]
Young, Desmond
    1966   *Member for Mexico: A Biography of Weetman Pearson, First Viscount Cowdray.* London: Cassel.
Yurchenco, Henrietta
    1976   Liner notes for the recording *Mexico South: Traditional Songs and Dances from the Isthmus of Tehuantepec.* New York: Folkways Records.
Zarauz, Héctor
    1988   *Archivo de Adolfo C. Gurrión.* Mexico City: Ediciones Toledo.
Zeitlin, Judith
    1978   *Community Distribution and Local Economy on the Southern Isthmus of Tehuantepec: An Archaeological and Ethnohistorical Investigation.* Ph.D. diss., Yale University.
    1984   Colonialism and the Political Transformation of Isthmus Zapotec Society. In *Five Centuries of Law and Politics in Central Mexico,* ed. by Ronald Spores and Ross Hassig, pp. 65–85. Vanderbilt University Publications in Anthropology, No. 30. Nashville: Vanderbilt University Press.
    1989   Ranchers and Indians on the Southern Isthmus of Tehuantepec: Economic Change and Indigenous Survival in Colonial Mexico. *Hispanic American Historical Review* 69(1):23–60.

Zeitlin, Robert
  1990   The Isthmus Zapotec and the Valley of Oaxaca: Questions about
           Zapotec Imperialism in Formative Period Mesoamerica. *American
           Antiquity* 55(2):250–61.
Zeitlin, Judith, and Lillian Thomas
  1992   Spanish Justice and the Indian Cacique: Disjunctive Political Systems
           in Sixteenth Century Tehuantepec. *Ethnohistory* 39:3:285–315 (Sum-
           mer 1992).
Zermeño, Sergio
  1987   Juchitán: La cólera del régimen (crónica y análisis de una lucha so-
           cial). In *Juchitán: Límites de una experiencia democrática*, pp. 65–97.
           Cuadernos de Investigación Social 15. Mexico City: UNAM.

Index

Monte Albán, 8, 249n.4
Morales, Bernabe, 126
Moro, Cayetano, 44
Musalem, Amira, 180
Musalem, Manuel. *See* Tarú

Nácar, Pancho, 124
Neza, 123–24, 125–27, 134
Neza Cubi, 134–35
Nicolás, Ignacio (Mexu Chele), 56

Obregón, Alvaro, 76, 77
Orozco, Gilberto, 128
Orozco, Víctor, 186
Ortega, Lilia, 230
Ortíz, Tadeo, 57

Partido Revolucionario Institucional.
  See PRI
Party of the Democratic Revolution,
  165
Pearson, Weetman, 57, 59, 263n.24
PEMEX oil refinery, 92–94, 95, 96,
  270n.59
Pickett, Velma, 82, 122, 133
Pineda, César, 157, 158
Pineda, Dolores, 230
Pineda, Gudelia, 232, 236
Pineda, Justo, 220
Pineda, Rosenado, 52, 61, 120–21,
  258n.40
Pineda Henestrosa (Yodo), Víctor,
  161
Polín, 219; as COCEI leader, 158,
  166; as federal deputy, 201; as
  mayor, 174; photo, 110; speech by,
  279–80n.1; as traditional leader,
  223
Polo, 187; as COCEI leader, 156,
  158, 196, 219; imprisonment of,
  159; as mayoral candidate, 145;
  photo, 110

Poniatowska, Elena, 184, 233–34,
  289n.18
Popular Socialist Party, 154
PRI: attacks on radical intellectuals,
  181–82; attempts to gain control of
  Casa de la Cultura, 180–81; control of sugar cane industry, 90–92;
  courting of homosexuals (*muxe*'),
  239; destruction of COCEI projects, 199–200; internal conflict,
  165–66, 201, 202, 205; mishandling of campaigns, 167–68; peasant support, 191, 228–29; power-
  sharing with COCEI, 201–2; use
  of COCEI tactics, 203; violence
  against COCEI, 153–54, 195–97,
  206; Zapotec women and, 237
Procel, Aurea, 236

Quetzalcoatl, 16

Ramírez, Heladio, 201, 203
Rasgado, Federico, 154, 155
Rasgado, Jesús (Chú), 130, 185
Red Party, 74–75, 80
Rice, 89
Rivera, Diego, 184
Robles, Juvencio, 52, 218
Robles, Roque, 218
Rodrigo Carrasco Colony, 197
Rojo, 195, 202, 218, 287n.46
Romero, Juana C., 47, 51, 236
Roncaglia, Pedro G., 191
Roseberry, William, xviii, 221
Royce, Anya Peterson, 72, 73–74
Rubin, Jeffrey, 269n.57, 273–74n.2

Salina Cruz, 59, 94–95, 96, 99–100
Salinas, Carlos, 206, 207, 230, 237
Salinas, Miguel Angel, 109
Salt, 33–34, 38–39, 40
San Blas: burning of, 50; COCEI in,
  201; discrimination against,